Beer in The Netherlands

· TIM SKELTON ·

· THE ·
HOMEWOOD
· PRESS ·

First published in 2014 by
The Homewood Press Limited
2 Chene Mews
St Albans
Hertfordshire AL3 5QF

Publisher: Joanna Copestick
Series Editor: Tim Webb
Book design/typography: Dale Tomlinson
Maps: John Macklin

ISBN 978-0-9572787-1-4

A catalogue record for this book is available from
the British Library.

10 9 8 7 6 5 4 3 2 1

Printed and bound in the United Kingdom by
Berforts Information Press

Symbols used in the book

  Main railway station (NS)

  Metro

🚲 ABT member (see page 216)

Picture credits:
Front Cover photograph: Tim Skelton
Back cover Tim Skelton portrait: Amanda Skelton

All photographs are by Tim Skelton
apart from the following:

Page 17: Eurostar
Page 30: Adrian Tierney-Jones
Page 31: Dreamstime
Page 32: La Rulles brewery
Pages 35, 54: Jopen brewery
Pages 47, 166 (top, lamp detail): Peter Sherwood
Page 99 (bottom): Joe Stange
*Pages 110, 111, 112, 113, 123, 127, 147, 145, 153, 155 (top),
   156 (top & bottom); 163, 169, 190, 191 (top), 201,
   202*: Rob Gras
Page 212 (bottom): Rebke Klokke*

Order this book and other related titles from
www.booksaboutbeer.com

Contents

Welkom

To say this book is overdue is an understatement. The last English language guidebook about beer in the Netherlands was CAMRA's *Good Beer Guide to Belgium & Holland*, published in 2002. At that time the country had only 40 breweries and 150 places in which to drink decent beer. There are now officially 200+ brewers, the number of specialist beer cafés has doubled and interesting beers appear commonly in shops the length and breadth of the land. Not bad growth for a single decade.

With the words 'Dutch beer' and 'scene' now happily reunited in the same phrase and its beer culture gaining momentum rapidly, word is getting out that the Netherlands is making a bid to join the big league of craft brewing nations.

This does not make every beer delicious though. There are still some shockers out there, as the first wave of enthusiasts makes way for a new breed of hi-tech beer artist. But the ratio of good eggs to rotten ones is now far more encouraging, as the consistency and infection problems that once plagued beers from Dutch micros have become rarer.

The future is bright for smaller brewers yet despite this, industrial-scale pilsener remains the *bier* of choice for a majority of drinkers, with half a dozen names enjoying the lion's share of an easily pleased market. Such conservatism means that some smaller producers have trouble even breaking into the café sector, with most relying on sales through specialised shops and appearances at festivals to get themselves known.

So why throw this book into the mix now? Because we want the world at large (and the smaller world of Dutch café and restaurant owners) to realise that new Dutch beer is worth checking out and deserves respect. With the dominance of Pils being drawn into question, there is a growing sense that this is a country that needs to start shouting about its beers.

Around the world the craft beer revival is rolling and shows no sign of slowing. Why would it? While we celebrate this, it makes our work in keeping up with developments both a nightmare and a thrill ride.

On these pages we have listed all existing breweries and their regular beers, as well as recommending the best places to drink, and the best shops for taking away. There is also a calendar containing the beer festivals where you'll find the lesser known brewers and their one-off creations. And some history and practical advice to make it all simple.

We hope we can tell you why to come; how to get here; what to drink once you arrive; and where to find it. In short, everything you will need for a voyage of discovery through the world of Dutch beer.

Proost!

TIM SKELTON
Eindhoven
March 2014

The Dutch beer revival since 1975

Beer after Heineken

Any beer lover travelling back in time to the Netherlands in 1970 would be horrified. A land that a few centuries earlier had boasted hundreds of ale breweries had fallen lock, stock and advertising slogan for a skinny froth-topped blond called 'pilsener'. Even the monks had succumbed.

The popularity of pilsener brewed for its looks rather than its taste, in brew runs the size of Olympic swimming pools, was one of several factors that led to the closure of almost all of the Netherlands' smaller breweries. In 1970 the Netherlands had just 22 breweries and many of these were operated by conglomerates. Few, if any, cafés showed an interest in more unusual beers. Back then, *Beer in the Netherlands* would have been a pamphlet, not a book.

Then a few brave publicans, spotting how much more interesting beer was south of the border in Belgium, and sensing that they were not alone in thinking this, began opening bars that encouraged customers to try something a bit more daring. Among the first were the Beyerd in Breda (page 144), which took a beery turn in the early 1970s; the Mug in Middelburg (page 206) looking ancient as soon as it opened in 1973, and the original Gollem in Amsterdam (page 165), which ventured out in 1974.

Despite their enthusiasm, these remained oases in a national beer Sahara, their crusade seeming futile as the industrial mantra of brewery acquisitions and closures continued to be followed. By 1980, the total number of operating breweries had dipped below 20, producing between them fewer than 100 beer brands, the best selling of which tasted virtually identical to one another.

Then something unexpected but pivotal occurred. A small band of Dutch members of a UK beer consumer group called CAMRA (the CAMpaign for Real Ale), inspired by its early successes in reviving the UK's pub and brewery scene, put out a rallying cry in the organisation's magazine What's Brewing, calling on Dutch readers to join forces and establish a Dutch branch.

This request was promptly dismissed by the parent organisation, which in the manner of all revolutionary groups set on becoming a bureaucracy, said the Netherlands was not part of its remit. Undeterred the pioneers set up their own association and in October 1980, PINT came into being, campaigning to get Dutch cafés to sell, Dutch brewers to make and Dutch drinkers to ask for, decent beer.

A few years later a second group joined the fight from the other side of the trade. The handful of publicans serving great beer realised they were getting nowhere acting alone. So at a PINT meeting in 1983, the landlords of the Locus Publicus in Rotterdam (page 196), Vanouds Jan Primus in Utrecht (now Jan Primus, page 202), and Breda's Beyerd agreed to band together. They were soon joined by the Gollem in Amsterdam, and by the time they launched ABT – the 'Alliance of Beer Tappers' – in 1986, had been joined by a dozen others.

Three of the initial founders, the Beyerd, the Vlaamsche Reus in Wageningen (page 129), and Amsterdam's In De Wildeman (page 168) have remained members throughout, some 42 bars are currently involved and of the 70 or so that have dipped in and out, most continue their beery interests.

To begin with, the Dutch beer revival was heavily dependent on promoting imported beers. With Belgium to the south, Germany to the east and the UK just across the water, the Netherlands was surrounded by three of the four traditional brewing nations that had retained a semblance of their brewing culture's heritage. Reviving Dutch brewing was to take a little longer.

Among the first of the new wave of small ale breweries were De Hemel in Nijmegen (page 52), founded in 1983, 't IJ in Amsterdam (page 54) and Friese in Friesland (page 49) in 1985, St Christoffel in Limburg (page 84) in 1986, and 't Kuipertje in Gelderland (page 59) in 1987. Others followed, albeit slowly, and by the turn of the millennium their number was up to around 40.

With the revival of the breweries came a renaissance of older beer styles. Dark Dutch autumnal *bokbier* was among the first to be embraced as a new-old institution, said to be inspired by the bocks from Einbeck in Germany but in truth more akin to Norwegian *bokøl*, a near black lagered beer brewed to see off the previous year's grain. By the 1980s most breweries had given up on it - hard to believe when most modern Dutch breweries today see it as their national duty to make at least one.

Other older styles would eventually follow, starting with other seasonal boks, kuit and most notably stout, which had been a popular Dutch drink before all was drowned when the pilsener tsunami flooded over the dykes. In the interim, the Dutch beer revival leant heavily on Belgian styles, new breweries distinguishing themselves by making imitations of spiced wheat beer, and 'abbey-style' dubbels and tripels, only not as well.

Many brewers seemed not to care if each batch turned out different from the last, or if some bottles effervesced with infected failure. Dutch beer was still better then it had been even if it wasn't great. For things to become really interesting, the industry would need a hefty kick up the backside. And this it got, in 2004.

To infinity and beyond – the De Molen effect

By the dawn of the new millennium the Dutch beer scene was climbing back from its low point of the early 1980s. Proof came in 2000 with the opening of the Arendsnest in Amsterdam (page 162) – the country's first beer café focusing exclusively on domestic rather than imported beers. Things were beginning to head in the right direction, even if you needed a stop-motion camera to spot changes that were glacially slow at times.

A devoted core of enthusiasts enjoyed drinking great beers in a growing number of good bars, where they were mostly content with Belgian imports. Few were noticing the winds of change blowing through the wider beer world, or expected the much-needed shot in the arm that Dutch brewing required.

Although much lauded as the industry's white knight, De Molen's brewmaster Menno Olivier did not appear completely out of the blue. He already had 12 years' experience of making beer before his now globally famous brewery opened for business in 2004. Beginning as a hobby brewer, he had worked his way through the ranks at Texel (page 74) and De Prael (page 69) before becoming brewmaster at De Pelgrim in Delfshaven (page 68).

It was when Menno and his team of upstarts installed a small brewery at the Arkduif windmill, in the prim and proper South Holland town of Bodegraven that things started to move. Unlike most of their peers, they took little notice of what had gone before, in either Belgium or the Netherlands. Nor did they look towards Germany. Instead, they went further afield for inspiration, to the newest breed of craft brewers who were starting to make waves in the US and elsewhere.

De Molen embraced the hop, aroma and all, and the instinct that bold flavours should be relished, not feared. Before long they were brewing IPAs and imperial stouts that would go on to be fêted as the equal of anything on the planet.

From a quiet start, people began sitting up and taking notice. A growing reputation

spread by word of mouth caused output to rise by 40% a year. The tiny 500-litre capacity plant located in a windmill could not keep up, so the brewery expanded into an ambitiously large site down the road, which is itself now starting to creak.

But one brewery alone does not a beer revolution make. Rather it was down to the effect that de Molen's success had on the rest of the Dutch brewing scene that mattered and this cannot be overstated.

Other newly established breweries such as Emelisse (see page 47) got inspired to up their game. They too began looking beyond Belgium, with varieties of IPAs and stouts becoming their mainstays. A new generation of hobby brewers, many of whom had been on the edge of commercialising for years, saw there was a market beyond their living rooms for the expressive, bold beers they loved to make. Dozens then took the plunge and turned professional.

This has led to an unprecedented growth in the number of commercial Dutch breweries. Thirty new companies appeared in 2013 alone, albeit not all with their own kit, but that's an argument for elsewhere. They broke through the magic 200 barrier in early 2014.

As more Dutch brewers create more craft beers, their availability also widens, with more café owners are willing to stock them alongside their more familiar Belgian and German brands. That too, we celebrate.

But let's not get carried away. Just as smaller brewers who fail to master basic technique produce bad beers that can blight the reputations of all small brewers, so also the technical perfectionists who run large breweries threaten the standing of beer more generally through their complaisance with making obsessively perfect beers that are dull beyond redemption.

Big players and bland beer continue to dominate. Just four firms – global Heineken, AB InBev and SAB Miller (appearing as Grolsch), plus independent Bavaria – produce more than 90% of the beer brewed in Netherlands. Industrial Pilsener still accounts for around 85% of all the beer drunk. Heineken alone accounts for 50% of that.

Bizarrely, this dominance may be convenient, for now. If every Dutch beer drinker awoke one morning and determined to try an IPA in the next few days, let alone decided that they preferred it to pils, Dutch craft brewing would likely sink without trace, or at least be spotted running hot-tail into the North Sea, clutching its head and screaming, "Enough! Enough!". Even if they could ramp up production sufficiently quickly, recent traditions dictate that corners would be cut and standards deflate.

Not that the Dutch café system could allow such a luxurious problem. The system of loan ties that has barred the entry of better Dutch beers into many local cafés may be approaching its death rattle but it is still breathing as we write.

A bigger problem is the government's imposition of disproportionate duties on beer compared to other alcoholic beverages, a curious habit that is shared by governments in Scandinavia. It contrasts, or perhaps not, with the interesting EU policy of subsidising wine-making far more than beer-making through the Common Agricultural Policy, to the tune of many billions of Euros. The theory goes that political types tend to prefer wine.

Some smaller brewers and many café owners fear that it is tax, not trade restrictions that may yet drive them out of business.

So where is Dutch beer right now, seven decades on from Freddy Heineken's discovery of the power of advertising?

Let us say that for a Dutch craft brewer the world is an ever-deepening bed of roses that is starting to feel wonderful. Were it not for the thorns.

Brewing in the Netherlands 1865–1975

Getting ready for the big time

It might come as a surprise to those familiar with the big names of Dutch brewing such as Heineken, Amstel and Oranjeboom that not too long ago the Netherlands was a relatively insignificant brewing nation, producing far less beer than its smaller southern neighbour, Belgium.

Dutch brewing also lagged far behind Britain and Germany. In the 1870s and 1880s for exam ple, beer production was a feeble 1.3 to 1.5 million hectolitres per annum (hl pa), significantly less than the 2.0 million hl pa that had been brewed in the province of Holland alone in the early 1600s. To put this in proportion, the figures for Britain and Germany (which was yet to absorb Bavaria) were over 40 million hl pa at that time, and for Belgium between 9 and 10 million hl pa.

The advent of lager brewing

The development of the Netherlands into a major player in world brewing began in the 1860s and 1870s with the establishment of a new type of brewery inspired by new developments in central Europe, called a bottom-fermenting or lager brewery.

The first of these was the Royal Netherlands Bavarian Beer Brewery, founded in 1866. In 1870, the Heineken family began brewing lager at their new brewery in Amsterdam, where the Bavarian Brewery de Amstel was founded in 1871. Taking advantage of experimentation and innovation elsewhere in Europe, they were soon among the most modern on the continent.

A range of lager styles was produced in a variety of strengths and colours and pilsener-like beers had yet to take pole

Heineken Rotterdam beers in 1911					
Bier	OG Balling	FG Balling	app. degree attenuation	% ABV	Colc
Pils	13.2	4.15	68.56%	4.8	
Lager	9.8	3.3	66.33%	3.4	
Gerste	12	5	58.33%	3.7	1
Beiersch	13.1	5.3	59.54%	4.2	
Bok	16.7	7.5	55.09%	5	

Source: Heineken brewing records held at the Amsterdam Stadsarchief

position. Indeed the first bottom-fermented beer produced by Heineken was Beiersch, a Munich-style dark lager.

While these new concerns were more in tune with their times and were undoubtedly successful, they did not lead to an overall increase in Dutch beer production, which remained stagnant at around 1.5 million hl pa in the years before the First World War.

Dutch breweries by province					
	1890	1900	1910	1920	1930
North Brabant	241	214	191	72	65
Gelderland	42	31	27	13	10
South Holland	35	25	24	14	–
North Holland	22	19	17	12	10
Zeeland	36	33	31	25	25
Utrecht	12	7	7	4	3
Overijssel	10	9	7	3	3
Friesland	2	2	2	2	2
Groningen	20	16	14	1	1
Drenthe	1	1	1	0	0
Limburg	236	216	201	77	66
Total:	**657**	**574**	**522**	**223**	**198**

Source: Nederlands Etiketten Logboek, 1998

The First World War and its aftermath

The outbreak of war had a devastating impact on the country, despite the Netherlands' neutrality. The German U-Boat campaign that began in 1917 wreaked havoc with international trade. Being mostly dependent on imported barley, Dutch brewers began to run out of raw materials and despite drastic reductions in beer strength, by 1918 production had fallen to 720,000 hl pa – or half the pre-war level.

After the war ended, commercial brewing revived somewhat and by the end of the 1920s output was up to 1.7 million hl pa, finally exceeding the 1914 figure, though the number of breweries had fallen from 522 in 1910 to 223 by 1920. The biggest fall was in the provinces of North Brabant and Limburg, traditionally the home of large numbers of village and small town breweries.

Heineken Rotterdam beers in 1930

	OG Balling	FG Balling	app. degree attenuation	% ABV	Colour
	12.2	3.8	68.85%	4.7	4
t	9.2	3	67.39%	3.5	3
ker	9	3.2	64.44%	3.5	11
erisch	13	5.45	58.08%	5	14
	17.6	8.45	51.99%	7.1	15

rce: Heineken brewing records held at the Amsterdam Stadsarchief

Brewing suffered again in the Great Depression, when beer production plummeted for a second time. It was only clawed back in the latter half of the 1930s and by 1939 was spookily close to what it had been in 1914.

It was during these inter-war years that pilsener had gradually gained ground at the expense of other styles, though breweries continued to brew mainly low-strength *licht* (pale) and *donker* (dark) lagers, plus the stronger *Beiersch*.

The Second World War and the new Europe

The Second World War had an even greater impact on Dutch brewing. The disruption to world trade once more crippled an industry dependent on imported raw materials. Output figures for this time are deceptive as there were successive cuts in the strength of beer as the war progressed, starting as early as January 1941.

Initially, pils was reduced from 12° to 10° Balling (roughly 5% to 4% ABV) in strength, and *licht* from 9° to 7° Balling (or 3.6% to 3% ABV). By October 1942, the equivalent strengths were down to 7.7° (3.2%) and 3.9° (1.5%) respectively. By the last year of the war, barely 1.0 million hl of even this puny beer was produced.

It was the post-war years that saw a transformation in Dutch brewing. Exports and production soared after 1955 as Heineken grew increasingly successful in the American market. By 1970, output had more than quadrupled. Pils now dominated the domestic market, with older styles like *licht* and *donker* all but disappearing, the latter to be replaced by *Oud Bruin*.

Heineken's leading position in the market was cemented with the takeover of their main rivals Amstel in 1968 as the number of breweries continued to fall. Of the 85 that had survived the Second World War to exist in 1945, just 19 remained by 1979, with no new breweries to bolster their numbers. As the industry became concentrated on four large companies – Heineken, Skol, Grolsch and Bavaria – each making almost exclusively blond lagers, an economically bouyant nadir of the Dutch beer culture had been reached.

RON PATTINSON
www.europeanbeerguide.net

The growth of Dutch brewing after the Second World War

year	output (hl)	year	output (hl)	year	output (hl)	year	output (hl)	year	output (hl)
1946	1,873,000	1951	1,603,000	1956	2,485,000	1961	3,802,000	1966	5,695,000
1947	1,852,000	1952	1,611,000	1957	2,733,000	1962	3,965,000	1967	6,571,000
1948	1,514,000	1953	1,832,000	1958	2,941,000	1963	4,408,000	1968	6,849,000
1949	1,336,000	1954	1,978,000	1959	3,398,000	1964	4,965,000	1969	7,841,000
1950	1,413,000	1955	2,321,000	1960	3,552,000	1965	5,402,000	1970	8,772,000

Source: European Statistics 1750–1970 by B.R.Mitchell, 1978.

The Netherlands
A brief history of the nation of traders

BEFORE cheap airfares made criss-crossing the globe routine, the world had the Dutch.

Always the great merchant traders of Europe, Dutch influence began to rise as the domination of the Spanish and Portuguese waned with the emergence of the growing British and French empires. Yet to this day, their small nation punches well above its weight.

Much of the story of the Dutch nation is linked inextricably to water – no surprise when half the country lies below sea level.

It is known there were tribes here in the Bronze Age, though much of the land remained too boggy to be cultivated.

By the time that the region lay on the northern fringes of the Roman Empire, it was occupied largely by three Germanic peoples – the Frisians, the Low Saxons and the Franks. But it was another tribe, the Batavians, that set the regional identity rolling.

The Romans revered the Batavians as fine soldiers and cleverly employed them to defend the borders of their Empire. However, when the Romans enslaved others of their number this provoked an entire tribal revolt in AD 69. Although this failed, the revolt was conjured centuries later by writers comparing it with the uprising against Spanish rule in the 16th century. The original capital of the Dutch East Indies (now Indonesia) was named Batavia in their honour, as were several ships.

Despite the early glimmer of nationalism, throughout the Dark Ages the western half of the Netherlands remained barely inhabited until the 11th century, when local farmers began the ambitious project of draining the swamps, which went on to become the millennium-long obsession with reclaiming land from the sea.

The name Holland first appeared in 1083, referring to a region now comprised of the province of South Holland and the southern part of North Holland. The area's power grew and the Counts of Holland added neighbouring Zeeland and West Frisia to their portfolio.

Guilds were established, with trade flourishing as new markets were discovered and developed. New towns sprang up and merchants grew in wealth and power, buying privileges as Holland expanded. Some cities became semi-independent and joined the powerful trading bloc called the Hanseatic League, an ancient forebear of the EU.

Eventually Duke Philip the Good of Burgundy gained control of the region through a skillful mix of natty trade deals, lucky inheritance and old-fashioned violence. Numerous Dutch noblemen

INDE·OVDE·SCHANS

welcomed him, taking advantage of the chance to integrate with Flanders and as a result, the Burgundian Netherlands first appeared in 1433.

Consolidation paid off. The unified state managed to break the trade restraints of the Hanseatic League in key sea battles, and the region's economy rocketed once more, Amsterdam becoming the leading port of Northern Europe.

Things were going swimmingly. Holy Roman Emperor Charles V (1500–58), at the time the most powerful man who had ever lived, introduced religious tolerance of sorts and declared the Netherlands independent of German and French rule. However, as he grew older and tired of power he handed over its jurisdiction to his staunchly pro-Catholic Spanish heir, the Duke of Alva, who was not a nice man.

During the 16th century, Reformation fever had swept the northern Netherlands. The moralistic Protestants – mostly Calvinists – were initially tolerated by the authorities but they did that thing that religious groups seem to keep doing over the centuries, and claimed their piety and humility was morally superior to the "excess" of the Catholics, who they also condemned as Spanish, i.e. foreign.

When the Inquisition arrived, the Calvinists cried foul.

In 1566, William the Silent – better known as Willem van Oranje, father of the nation – led an uprising that became known as the Eighty Years' War. Under his leadership, the northern provinces formed the Republic of the Seven United Netherlands, or the United Provinces, which declared independence in 1581. The south became the Spanish Netherlands, covering an area that would encompass much of modern Belgium, Luxembourg and the Dutch provinces of North Brabant and Limburg.

As its name implies, this was a war that dragged on and it was not until 1648 that independence was finally recognised. The new country became known as Holland, and thus began its Golden Age.

Trade, industry, the arts and sciences all flourished, and for a time Holland was the most economically powerful nation in Europe, helped by having a massive fleet of ships used primarily for trading but also for bullying its rivals. It had to import barley for its own brewing needs but records survive of massive importation and onward export of beers from all its barley-growing neighbours.

One name rose above all others – the Verenigde Oostindische Compagnie (VOC),

or Dutch East India Company. Founded in 1602, it was in effect the world's first multinational and, for much of the 17th century, the world's largest business. Financed by share issues that created the first modern stock exchange, it got rich from what became known as the spice trade, dealing mostly in India and Indonesia. A lucrative trade monopoly with the tightly self-sufficient empire of Japan did not hurt either.

The Dutch dominated northern European trade through being handily positioned on the continent's northern coast and at the mouth of two large rivers – the Rijn (Rhine) and the Maas (Meuse). Elsewhere, the more adventurous were founding colonies, not only in the East Indies (Indonesia) but in North America at Nieuw Amsterdam (New York), in South Africa and the West Indies.

At home, a climate of humanism and tolerance, begun a century earlier with Erasmus, was attracting religious refugees. Jewish merchants from Portugal and French Huguenot shopkeepers arrived, adding to the melting pot and propelling the economy forward. Scientists and free thinkers came

from across Europe. The arts flourished, nurturing artists such as Rembrandt and Vermeer.

Meanwhile, big-thinking civil engineers were fighting and winning another battle, expanding the land mass by use of hydraulics. Lakes were converted into polders, using windmills to pump out water. Canals were dug in and around cities, merchants building grand waterside houses to show off both their wealth and confidence.

All this prosperity made the neighbours, most notably England, deeply envious, resulting in three Anglo-Dutch wars. The second, in 1667, famously ended when the Dutch fleet raided Kent by sailing up the Medway, a victory that marked the peak of Dutch power.

Five years later, 1672 would become known as the *Rampjaar*, or Disaster Year. First England declared war, then France, and then the city states of Münster and Cologne. An Anglo-French sea invasion failed but only just. To thwart a French land attack, the Dutch had to breach dykes and flood their own land. Defeating Cologne and Münster required the equally dodgy manoeuvre of buying the support of other German states with chunks of Dutch territory. Peace was restored, but the dazzling performance of the Dutch economy was not.

Then in 1688, ironically perhaps, the country's leader, Stadtholder William III, was invited to take the throne of England by Protestant nobles opposed to its Catholic king, James II. Hence England got its William III, of Orange, and the Dutch gained a crucial ally in wars against the French.

Despite all this, the Golden Age was over. Northern European trading shifted focus from Amsterdam to London and Dutch power continued to wane throughout the 18th century. In 1795 Holland became briefly the Batavian Republic, initially a satellite of Napoléon's French empire, but later a full imperial province.

When Napoléon went into retreat, the Dutch seized their moment, and the United Kingdom of the Netherlands was declared in 1813, with the House of Orange returning as its monarchy. Initially this included most of modern Benelux, but in 1830 an eruption of local tensions in Brussels, expertly stoked by the British, led to the creation of a breakaway state called Belgium.

The Dutch finally agreed its borders in 1839, and in 1848 the Netherlands became a parliamentary democracy with a constitutional monarch.

The early 20th century saw the Dutch remain neutral during the First World War (1914–18) – the German Schlieffen Plan entailing invading Belgium only en route to Paris. The deal may have enabled the Dutch to avoid trench warfare but its isolation from the trade routes affected the economy badly and imposed massive deprivations.

The Great Depression of the 1930s saw a time of ambitious public building works – pre-empting US President Franklin Roosevelt's New Deal as a creative approach to tackling high unemployment. Most prominent was the Afsluitdijk, the sea dyke that closed off the Zuiderzee inlet and created the freshwater IJsselmeer lake in 1933.

The rise of Nazism in Germany was a cause for concern but most Dutch people assumed Hitler would, like the previous generation of German leaders, respect their neutrality. He did not, and on 10 May 1940 invaded, drawing the Netherlands into the Second World War. When the Dutch showed signs of holding out, the Luftwaffe bombed and destroyed Rotterdam, killing 900 and leaving 78,000 homeless. A threat to repeat the exercise on Utrecht persuaded the Dutch government to surrender.

The occupation was harsh, prompting many to join the resistance, though worse befell the country's 140,000 Jews. Some 40,000 went into hiding, like the family of Anne Frank in Amsterdam, or fled. Of the 100,000 who stayed, only 1,000 survived.

In 1944, following D-Day, much of the Netherlands was liberated, though parts of the nation remained occupied into 1945. Upset by Dutch defiance, the Nazis cut off food supplies, resulting in mass starvation during the *Hongerwinter* of 1944–45. Many died, with others kept alive mainly by being 'bombed with bread' by the Allies.

After the Second World War the Netherlands once more focussed on rebuilding itself, a plan that pushed steadily forth, even in the face of massive flooding in 1953, when a huge storm caused dykes to collapse in Zeeland, inundating the land. Around 1,800 people drowned, prompting the government to commission the building of the Delta Works flood barrier, yet another wonder of the modern world, which eventually became operational in 1986.

The modern Netherlands is again prosperous thanks to its trading prowess, though as elsewhere it is prone to economic downturns, with unemployment rising.

Its liberal values have led to it being famed as a land where prostitution and soft drugs are accepted. Yet joblessness brings out the worst intolerance in some, putting discontent about immigration on the political agenda.

There are blips, but I have lived here long enough to know that while not everything is perfect, there are far worse places to be.

As you would expect
from a country that has
for centuries sat at the
centre of world trading,
there are almost
infinite ways to get here.

Getting

end up being considerably higher. You may also incur charges if you bring more than hand luggage, cannot check in on-line, or want to choose your seat.

Some budget airlines like to herd their customers like cattle; some make them scrum at the gate before fighting for a seat; and others spend the whole flight trying to sell you stuff. It is all part of the price paid for saving.

Full-price airlines can sometimes end up remarkably similar on price, give you more legroom and an allocated seat, though in-flight catering on short-haul routes has been cut back, typically to a free drink and a "delicious snack" – currently biscuits in the case of the national carrier.

Cheap ticket websites may offer a good way of comparing fares, but seldom offer better value than buying directly from airlines. Try several before settling on the best deal.

Airports

Amsterdam Schiphol (www.schiphol.nl), known in the Netherlands as Schiphol, is by far the largest Dutch airport, accounting for 92% of all air arrivals, with over 50 million passengers passing through each year. It has direct flights to/from no fewer than 24 UK airports at the last count. Flights take roughly an hour from England, 90 minutes from Scotland, most connecting several times per week and some several times daily.

Be warned that budget airlines from the UK often dock at the distant 'H' gates, located in a neighbouring parish and a bracing walk away.

Connections to the centre of Amsterdam are easiest via one of up to 8 direct trains every hour – they even run hourly throughout the night. Other trains head directly to most major Dutch cities, plus Antwerp and Brussels. The airport station is also on the high-speed network.

The second largest Dutch airport is **Eindhoven**, which takes 4% of the flow including the Ryanair flights from London Stansted and Dublin. Regular buses (lines 400 & 401) link the airport with Eindhoven train station.

there

By AIR

The continued success of low-cost airlines means that from the UK – and most other parts of Europe besides Belgium and Germany – the fastest and cheapest way to get here is to fly, whatever the environmental impact. For those arriving from beyond Europe, who have no other option, the good news is that Amsterdam's Schiphol airport – the only airport constructed on the site of a major sea battle – is one of Europe's largest international hubs.

The range of options for getting by air from the UK has gone, er, skywards but study the prices carefully as few companies are entirely transparent about how much you pay. Up-front fares are designed to look tempting but may not include airport charges, credit card fees, fuel surcharges and tax, which can

The magnificent Afsluitsdijk

Ryanair also flies from Stansted to **Maastricht–Aachen**, which links to Maastricht via bus 59.

The business-orientated **Rotterdam– The Hague** airport gets CityJet (KLM-Air France) flights from London City and British Airways from Gatwick, though neither is cheap. The airport is linked to central Rotterdam by bus 33.

Up north, Groningen has a commercial airport but this is currently only used for holiday charter flights to the Mediterranean.

Airlines

Air France-KLM – www.klm.com – may have acquired a semi-Gallic moniker but is still considered by the Dutch to be Royal Dutch Airlines, the national flag carrier. It operates its many short-haul routes (to regional UK airports for example) as KLM Cityhopper. Tickets can be pricey.

British Airways – www.ba.com – leaves the regional services to the others and only flies to Schiphol from London's Gatwick, Heathrow and City airports (the latter as BA CityFlyer). Prices as for KLM.

CityJet – www.cityjet.com – targets the business market and tends to be the highest priced of all, operating out of London City, offering convenience from central London but little else.

EasyJet – www.easyjet.com – was the low-cost pioneer that first shrunk North Sea prices and still offers some of the most convenient and cheapest services from several UK regional airports. You even get a designated seat these days.

Jet2.com – www.jet2.com – flies to Amsterdam Schiphol from Leeds–Bradford airport.

FlyBe – www.flybe.com – or 'Fly mayBe' as it is known by regulars, flies to Schiphol from half a dozen UK airports.

Ryanair – www.ryanair.com – operates no-frills operations, its only UK options currently being from Stansted to Eindhoven and Maastricht–Aachen, so the only way is Essex.

By SEA

The alternative mode of travel from the UK to the Netherlands is one of the ferry routes, though the length of the crossings means you have to see the crossing as part of the holiday.

Drivers coming from southern England find it faster and more convenient to travel from Dover to Calais or Dunkerque, though foot passengers and cyclists will find the absence of onward public transport connections to the Netherlands from the French seaports frustrating. For drivers the fastest motorway connection is usually via Ghent and Antwerp.

Individual ferry company websites are listed below, but www.aferry.com is a handy one-stop shop for comparing fares. For short visits, 5-day excursion fares booked at least a week in advance can be significantly cheaper than last-minute bookings.

Direct routes:
UK–the Netherlands

Newcastle–Ijmuiden: operated by DFDS Seaways (www.dfdsseaways.com) takes 16 hours. Cabin reservations are compulsory. Once a day crossings travel overnight in each direction, leaving at 17.00 and arriving the following morning at 09.00.

Hull–Rotterdam Europoort: operated by P&O North Sea Ferries (www.poferries. com) takes 11 hours. Cabin reservations are compulsory. Once a day crossings travel overnight in each direction, leaving at 21.00 and arriving the following morning at 09.00.

Harwich–Hoek van Holland: operated by Stena Line (www.stenaline.co.uk). There are two crossings in each direction each day. The day service takes around 6½ hours, with the overnight service taking an extra hour but allowing three more hours on board. Cabin bookings are essential on the night service.

Other routes:
UK–France or Belgium

Dover–Calais: operated by P&O, DFDS and My Ferry Link (www.myferrylink.com). Still the most frequent, popular and fastest route from Britain to mainland Europe, with up to 40 sailings a day between the three services in high season, taking around 90 minutes from quay to quay. Calais is a 2½-hour drive from the nearest Dutch city, via the unpredictable Antwerp Ring.

Dover–Dunkerque: operated by DFDS Seaways with 2-hour sailings every two hours, no coach parties and no foot passengers. Often the cheapest, 20 km closer and a slick operation.

Hull–Zeebrugge: operated by P&O North Sea Ferries, with a similar service to the Rotterdam route (above), departing a bit earlier. No obvious advantage for travel to the Netherlands, except that the food is better.

By TUNNEL

Le Shuttle: operated by Eurotunnel (www.eurotunnel.com), is the fastest road-to-road connection from southern England. Drive to junction 11A of the M20 motorway and onto a transporter train through the Channel Tunnel to junction 42 of the E15 French coastal autoroute. Up to four an hour. Fast, efficient and as entertaining as watching paint dry.

Eurostar: is the UK's token fast train service (www.eurostar.com) from London or Ebbsfleet to Brussels (2 hours), where you can catch an onward connection to its cheaper equivalent Thalys, to Rotterdam (total 4 hours) or Amsterdam (4 hours 45 mins). Advance seat reservations are obligatory. A cheaper express connection from Brussels, the much-vaunted Fyra 'Hispeed' train (www.nshispeed.nl) has had major teething problems, to the extent that the unreliable rolling stock was banned from Belgian tracks at one point. Services linking Brussels and Antwerp to Rotterdam, The Hague and Amsterdam are intended to be hourly.

By TRAIN FROM ELSEWHERE

Intercity Express (ICE) runs direct trains to Amsterdam and Utrecht from a large number of German cities without many problems, as you would expect being operated by Deutsche Bahn (DB). Seat reservations are required.

Six local train services connect border towns with Germany: Groningen–Leer; Hengelo–Bad Bentheim; Enschede–Münster; Enschede–Dortmund; Venlo–Hamm (via Düsseldorf); and Heerlen–Aachen.

To/from Belgium there are slow trains running Maastricht–Liège; and Roosendaal–Antwerp.

Both Eurostar and Deutsche Bahn/ICE intend to be operating a direct high speed train service between London and Amsterdam by 2016 at the latest, taking just four hours.

By BUS

You can make the trip from London and other cities in Europe to Amsterdam on a Eurolines bus (www.eurolines.com), if you have more time than shekels, though it is a buttock-numbing experience. Likewise Megabus (www.megabus.com) operates between London and Amsterdam.

Novice travellers need not fear. English is spoken everywhere, prices are generally as displayed and those locals who are not friendly are usually incredibly efficient, unless they have sunken eyes and a crack pipe sticking out of their pocket.

Being

SLEEPING

The Netherlands has all the various sleeping options you would expect in a First World country, from campsites, hostels and B&Bs, via small family-run guesthouses, to chain franchise or international standard five-star hotels.

The ease of finding a room depends on when and where you go, though Amsterdam is always a special case. Many hotels there appear to be permanently full so book as far ahead as possible, as last-minute deals tend to favour daylight robbery over basement clearance rates.

Elsewhere, except during special events, finding somewhere to stay is generally not a problem. And while cute country inns may fill at weekends, business hotels that are full on weekdays may offer substantial discounts.

If you arrive somewhere without a reservation, the best place to head is the local tourist office (VVV), though most ask a small booking fee to cover costs.

Hotels

Dutch hotel star ratings fall more or less in line with other international systems. Three stars and up should mean a comfortable room with bathroom en suite. Like anywhere,

ratings only measure facilities, while real quality will vary depending on intangibles like design, how recently it was renovated, and how charming the staff are feeling.

Like-for-like, room rates tend to be higher than in neighbouring Germany and a bit above Belgium too. Prices in Amsterdam head skywards in high summer. On the other hand, a room in a backwater town out of season can be a steal. Most cheaper hotels include breakfast; the top international chains often charge extra for the pleasure.

Small hotels are not required to have lifts and older Dutch staircases can be notorously steep, tight and narrow. Do your research beforehand if this is a consideration. Be aware too that some older city centre places are not always properly soundproofed against nearby bars that stay open with loud music into the early hours.

Pensions and B&Bs

There are B&B options throughout the country, priced cheaper than hotels, though quality can vary from superb to not. To book try Bed & Breakfast Holland (www.bbholland.com) or Bed & Breakfast Service Nederland (www.bedandbreakfast.nl).

there

Youth Hostels

If you don't mind sharing with strangers, hostels offer cheap, basic accommodation. Most hostel beds are in shared dorms, though some have a few 'twin-bed' rooms with en-suite bathrooms, though the twins might be bunks and you might pay extra for bedding. Most hostels include breakfast, and can provide other meals with advance booking.

The national hostel chain Stayokay (www.stayokay.com), runs 27 places up and down the country. There are a fair number of independent places in Amsterdam but few in other cities.

MOVING ABOUT

Public transport

For train information use www.ns.nl. For the broader public transport network try 9292.nl. As a last resort try the premium rate phone-line 0900 9292, a truly fleecing experience.

Trains

The train is generally the most efficient way to travel round the Netherlands. Lines are plentiful, services on most routes run at least twice and sometimes up to six times an hour, while delays do occur they tend to be short and most trains run to time. Fares are generally lower than in the UK.

There are broadly two types of service. Intercity trains stop only at major stations, while Sprinters defy their name by stopping everywhere. Seat reservations are not possible on either, so if you need to be seated, travel outside peak hours or get good at pleading with busy commuters.

Smoking is no longer permitted on trains or outside designated zones at stations.

Metro

Only Amsterdam and Rotterdam have suburban metro networks, though one of Rotterdam's lines goes all the way to Den Haag. In Amsterdam, most visitors find the tram and bus system more convenient as there are few metro stops in the centre, though this may change when the seemingly interminable work to open the North-South line is completed.

Buses & trams

City and regional buses, and in some places trams, are excellent and frequent. Buses are clean, and sometimes benefit from having dedicated lanes. Routes are clearly marked on maps in bus stations, and at many stops. A recorded voice, LED and/or TV screen informs passengers about each stop. Most bus and tram routes start or end at a railway station, making connections both logical and simple.

The longer bus routes essentially substi-tute for trains in areas where the lines never spread. We have no hesitation in recommend-ing them to inexperienced travellers who normally drive but want to bevvy.

Ticketing

Few countries have more advanced ticketing systems for public transport than the Netherlands. The OV-chipkaart is a nationally valid electronic payment card that covers the whole domestic public transport network of buses, trams and metro. It works similarly to London's Oyster Card. Hold it against detectors whenever you enter and leave buses, trams or metro stations and it will be debited for the actual distance travelled. You have to check off one vehicle and onto the next, each time.

For short visits, pre-loaded cards can be bought from metro, train and bus stations, magazine kiosks, or from bus and tram drivers. If staying longer, buy one online at www.ov-chipkaart.nl at a discounted rate. All cards can be topped up at machines in metro and train stations.

A few cities also offer unlimited travel tickets, valid on their local networks for 1, 2 or more days.

The OV-chipkaart system also works on domestic trains, checking in and out using pillars within the station. However, you need a minimum balance of €20.00 to check in on an anonymous card (€10.00 with a personalised card). You do not need to check out and in when changing train unless switching to a different train operator.

It is intended that regular train tickets will be phased out altogether eventually and replaced by direct electronic payments.

For now you can buy a ticket online, or from machines found on all stations, or from a human being sat behind a ticket counter – though the latter has a €0.50 surcharge. You cannot buy tickets on board a train.

You can break your journey at will before midnight. First-class travel costs 50% more than second. Return (*retour*) tickets are largely useless, costing the same as two single fares (*enkele reis*) and only being valid until 04.00 the following morning.

Non-folding bicycles (€6.00) and any animal not carried in a bag (€3.00) need their own day ticket. The former are banned from trains on Mo-Fr 06.30–09.00 & 16.30–18.00.

Three Dutch chain stores – Blokker, Kruidvat, and Albert Heijn – regularly offer heavily discounted train tickets. Instead of the normal price (€49 in 2013) for an unlimited 2nd Class day ticket (*dagkaart*), they offer the same for around €17.

At Blokker and Kruidvat you buy actual tickets that must be validated in the normal way in yellow machines on station platforms (or checked in and out if they contain a chip, as some do) on the day of travel.

In the case of Albert Heijn you get a code that when entered online generates a PDF ticket that you must print off and carry with you on all journeys.

If you have long journeys planned, it can save a fortune. Look for 'NS Aktie' posters in shop windows, or check their respective websites.

Taxis

Convenient they may be, cheap they are not. You cannot hail a taxi in the street – phone or else pick one up at a designated rank. Licensed cabs have blue number plates. Most drivers are helpful and courteous. They do not expect a tip as the fare is already damaging enough.

Private transport

Cycling

The Dutch are enthusiastic cyclists and make considerable provision for cycles in towns, across the countryside and both at stations and on trains. That said, pedal power demands concentration in busy cities and especially after a few beers, we do not recommend it.

You can rent a bicycle from most railway stations for a reasonable daily rate but the be warned that standard models use a disconcerting braking system that relies on back-pedalling gently. This can throw the uninitiated, sometimes off the bike altogether. Machines with handlebar brakes are not always available and cost extra.

Driving

A dense network of well-maintained motorways and other roads traverses the country, though traffic can be heavy, especially in the Randstad. Tolls are mostly reserved for tunnels and river ferries.

Fuel prices fluctuate around the higher end of the European norm, though diesel is significantly cheaper than in the UK. Fuel is available 24/7 on motorways, elsewhere from 06.00 to 22.00 without difficulty, though rural areas can be awkward on Sunday.

Parking Street parking is a problem in many towns, especially Amsterdam, where the risks of taking your car often outweigh the benefits.

Many urban centres are pedestrianised, town centres metered and other areas reserved exclusively for resident permit-holders (*vergunninghouders*). In Blue Zones you need to display a blue timer disc on the dashboard, which you can buy from ANWB motoring shops, some newsagents and police stations. Illegally parked cars may get clamped or towed.

All towns have multi-storey car parks, which are usually the most convenient option but rarely cheap. Parking may be free in suburban areas, smaller towns and villages, at Park & Ride centres, and almost anywhere besides city centres and tourist spots on Sundays.

Tips and rules The Dutch authorities are about as keen on drunk driving as the rest of us.

On motorways the speed limit is 130 kilo-metres (80 miles) per hour unless otherwise stated; on rural highways it is 80 kph (50 mph) unless clearly marked as 100 kph (60 mph) ; in built-up areas it is 50 kph (30 mph), dropping to 30 kph (20mph) sometimes, for example around schools.

In towns or on minor roads, English-speaking drivers can be alarmed by traffic merging from the right that acts like it owns the road. In fact it probably does – unless a yellow diamond sign indicates you are on a road with priority. Local drivers often pull out without looking, if they have right of way.

The Dutch veer towards aggressive driving in other ways too, for example pulling out into implausibly small gaps between cars travelling at speed in the outside lane of a busy motorway. Many take the view that using their indicator when doing so might cause it to wear out.

Other national driving games include beeping the driver in front if they fail to react within a millisecond of a traffic signal turning green, and ploughing through amber signals.

Be wary of cyclists. Most seek self-preservation by observing the rules of the road but many do not, preferring to ignore red lights and swerve in front of you in the hope you will feel sorry for them and give way. They know that in any legal tussle the law will favour their cycle over your car, no matter whose fault the accident may have been. They will also claim priority from the right (as above), to the occasional horror of all concerned.

Although map makers and the transport planners of the European Union have applied the Europe-wide E-numbering system to Dutch motorways, sign makers in the Netherlands have not. Motorways (*snelwegen*) are designated 'A' roads, while other main roads are called *nationaal* or 'N' roads.

Seatbelts are compulsory, front and back. Using a handheld mobile phone while driving is illegal as well as dim. Fog lights must be used in fog. Winter tyres are not compulsory as in Germany, but are advisable in colder winters. All cars must by law carry a first aid kit, plus a warning triangle for breakdowns. The French requirement to carry two breathalyser kits does not apply, yet.

For breakdowns, contact the ANWB on **T** 088 269 2222 (or **T** 088 269 2888 in an emergency), or via **www.anwb.nl**.

The legal alcohol limit is 0.5 mg/ml, which is lower than in the UK and USA (0.8mg/ml). The Netherlands also has a campaign to encourage drivers not to drink at all and be 'Bob' – the designated driver. Punishments for exceeding the limit include imprisonment.

Oh, and drive on the right.

Island hopping

The Frisian Island chain dribbles like a string of massive bulwarks protecting the northern coast of the Netherlands and German Lower Saxony from being ravaged by the North Sea. The Western Frisian or Wadden Islands have a windswept, solitary beauty.

Listed below is the ferry information for islands with a beery draw. The Vlieland boats are operated by the same company as for Terschelling, and those for Schiermonnikoog by the Ameland crew.

Texel

Car ferries between Den Helder, at the northern tip of North Holland, and Texel are operated by TESO (**www.teso.nl**). Tickets can be bought at the port or on line. Boats leave the mainland on the hour and Texel on the half hour, from 06.00 to 21.30 each day (starting later on Sun). The crossing takes 20 minutes and it is neither necessary nor possible to book a specific sailing. There is no check-in on the return leg – just turn up and board. Den Helder port is a 20-minute walk from its station, or you can take bus 33.

Terschelling

Ferries between the Friesland port of Harlingen and West-Terschelling are operated year-round by Rederij Doeksen (**www. rederij-doeksen.nl**), between 5 and 10 times daily, with even more in summer. The car ferry takes 2 hours, while the 45-minute boat takes foot passengers only. Buy tickets on line, or at the port, which is next to Harlingen Haven train station. For short stays it is cheaper to leave your car in Harlingen's long-stay car park.

Ameland

Ferries between the Friesland coastal village of Holwerd and the quay at Nes on Ameland, are operated by Wagenborg (**www.wpd.nl**) typically six times a day, with fewer on Sunday and more in summer. Crossings take 45 minutes each way and tickets can be bought on line or at the port. There is also a water taxi (www.wadtaxi.nl). As for Terschelling, for short stays it is cheaper to leave cars on the mainland. Bus 66 from Leeuwarden station takes 48 minutes to reach Holwerd.

EATING

In years gone by, before the likes of Delia Smith, Jamie Oliver and Hugh Fearnley-Whittingstall up-ended our meagre culinary traditions, when French, Belgian and Italian friends poked gentle jibes at British cooking, one easy defence was, "Have you tried Dutch?"

Traditional Dutch cooking tends towards simple, filling, and frankly unexciting. The emphasis at the national HoReCa (hotel-restaurant-catering) cookery course was always on competence and cleanliness, rather than imagination and pzazz. Thus there were few shockers in cafés and restaurants, but not much to make a song and dance about either. Flair is a word that has only recently entered the average Dutch chef's lexicon.

In the 25 years we have been observing things, restaurants and bistros have made huge strides. Pub grub on the other hand is only grudgingly inching away from the familiar and comforting.

Meals & mealtimes

A typical breakfast (*ontbijt*) in a mid-range hotel means sliced bread or rolls with thin-sliced cheese and ham, yoghurt, jams, fruit and a hard-boiled egg – the last of these being the only warm item. Fancier hotels will offer greater variety, leaning on other countries' traditions to present a cooked breakfast. The other distinctly Dutch addition is sprinkled chocolate 'hailstones' (*hagelslag*), which generations of Nederlanders have sprinked on their bread and butter of a morning since early childhood.

Lunch is typically sandwiches, rolls or soup, with cheese and ham featuring once more. Most cafés will start serving at 12.00,

and while many stop at 14.30 or 15.00, some will continue until 17.00, making a seamless transition to an early supper.

Dinner is generally a heartier meal, and may be advertised as fixed-price three-course menu (*3-gangenmenu*). Most places start at 17.00 or 17.30, with closing times varying but most stopped by 22.30. To err on the safe side, arrive by 21.00 and note that the Dutch eat out early on Sundays, when restaurants may be packed at 17.30 and empty by 20.00.

Portions can be huge and as elsewhere, the more expensive the dish the smaller the plate. Café food is often more generous than restaurant fare.

Etiquette dictates that once your food is served, your waiter will say '*eet smakkelijk*', literally 'eat tastily'. Smile warmly and benignly at this point. Halfway through eating, or when they come to take away your plate, they will ask if you are enjoying/have enjoyed your food. At this point you say '*lekker*', an untranslatable word that transmits positive regard and means roughly 'tasty' in this context, regardless of whether it was.

Beer snacks

The national bar snack is *bitterballen* – made from meat mechanically recovered from the bones of a cow, ground to a mush, rolled into balls, deep-fried in breadcrumbs and served searingly hot. Dipping them into bland yellow mustard cools them a little and disguises the flavour, helpfully.

Bitterballen

Other drinking snacks (*borrelhapjes*) include cubes of semi-hard cheese (*kaas*) and/or salami, served with the same dull mustard. Ossenworst is raw or lightly cured beef sausage, like a tubular variant of steak tartare. Nuts (*noten*) in various formats are normally dispensed free – peanuts in shell being popular in wooden-floored bars where the shells should be thrown on the floor and trodden in to provide wood-preserving oils, allegedly. Hard-boiled eggs in the shell may appear in traditional brown cafés.

Other snacks

The national staple is *frietjes*, the local incarnation of chips/frites/fries, served from street stalls in cardboard cones, smothered in a great gob of some high calorie dollop and then eaten with a wooden fork. Most pub main courses come with frietjes.

Another streetside favourite is a *Hollandse nieuwe* or *matjes haring* – a beheaded, scrubbed and largely filleted raw herring that is offered with chopped raw onion and pickled gourd of some sort. Eat in squares or

Matjes haring, the Dutch sushi

else tip your head back, lower the fish into your waiting mouth and devour, like a performing dolphin bobbing for rewards.

Other fish snacks found at altogether grander stalls include pickled herring, marinaded cooked herring, breadcrumbed or battered fish bits, and variations on smoked, cured and sauced sea and freshwater fish.

At the other end of the dietary health scale, you may also encounter an odd snack format seen in stations and elsewhere – hole-in-the-wall, coin-operated vending machines that dispense alleged food items through a bank of small doors. We urge you to leave these to the experts – drunks, students and those who have lost all sense of taste and smell following an unfortunate injury. High-end contents include dry burger patties, descending via all manner of deep-fried objects such as *kroketten* (big *bitterballen*) to *frikandellen* (skinless tributes to the science of meat rendering).

Soup

Soup (*soep*) is considered an essential starter to any meal. The most sought-after are tomato (*tomaten*), onion (*uien*), oxtail (*ossenstaart*), and mustard (*mosterd*). Vegetarians should be aware that vegetable soup (*groentensoep*) often contains a type of meatball (*soepballen*) though some of these are soya-based. Cauliflower (*bloemkoolsoep*) can get pretentions when served with morels and oysters but head and shoulders above all of these is pea soup (*erwtensoep*, or simply *snert*).

Served in winter and hearty enough to be the main meal, *erwtensoep* is made with dried split peas, boiled at length with leek, celeriac, carrot, parsley, smoked sausage (*rookworst*) and a bit of bacon (*spek*) for flavour, then served with *katenspek*, a smoked bacon eaten cold like ham, on slices of dense, chewy rye bread (*roggebrood*).

Pub grub

Perhaps the commonest lunchtime pub standard is *uitsmijter* – often translated on an English menu, correctly but uninstructively as 'three fried eggs on bread'. Depending on the café, this can be overcooked eggs on processed white bread, with tasteless cheese and slippery, wet ham or, with some bacon, a bit of salad and melted grilled cheese a nostalgia-forming winner.

Uitsmijter

Then there is pub grub with colonial influence. In Indonesia, *satay* or *saté* means bamboo sticks threaded with delicate morsels of grilled meat, often served with chillied peanut sauce. In café-speak this becomes a giant metal skewer spearing industrial chucks of pork or chicken, served with chips and swamped in a puddle of thick, sweet peanut goo.

Pancakes (*pannenkoeken*) are popular, and come with a range of savoury as well as sweet fillings. Do not expect delicate lacy crêpes – these are thick and hearty, designed to keep draughts out and designed to be doused in syrup (*stroop*) before eating.

Filet americain is a form of steak tartare imported from Belgium – spiced raw minced beef. Do not order it medium rare.

Ethnic restaurants

As the British have adopted the curry from their colonial past, so the Dutch have the *rijsttafel* (literally 'rice table'). Served in restaurants designated Indonesian, often run by third or fourth generation descendants of Javanese immigrants, the dishes served have authentic origins but the dining concept is Dutch.

The core of a *rijsttafel* is based on West Sumatran *nasi padang*, in which you are served a dish of everything available, but only pay for what you eat. This being the Netherlands, the tweak is that you pay for the lot, with diners ordering one apiece – ordering fewer and sharing being frowned upon. Most include 15–20 dishes of variable spiciness, cooled with pickled vegetable (*atjar*) or spiked with chilli sauce (*sambal*). Much food is wasted and doggie bags jettisoned after breakfast.

Some Indonesian places offer the more manageable mixed rice (*nasi rames*), a one-plate variant involving rice with spoonful-sized portions of several other dishes.

Besides straight Indonesian cuisine, every Dutch town has a *Chinees-Indonesisch* restaurant serving an amalgam of Chinese and Indonesian cuisine that often falls short of either. The red-orange sauces that cover most dishes vary so little from one place to another that we suspect all are prepared in a giant central kitchen and then piped nationwide.

Indigenous restaurant food

Most but not all traditional Dutch dishes are designed to allow the locals to survive the winter gales that whip in off the North Sea.

Stamppot and *hutspot* are one-pot meals in which (usually) smoked sausage (*rookworst*), potatoes (*aardappelen*) and a vegetable, most commonly cabbage (*kool*) or curly kale (*boerenkool*) are boiled up together. The sausage is then temporarily removed while the rest is mashed with hot milk, butter and perhaps nutmeg. These domestic favourites appear increasingly in restaurants showing renewed confidence in local classics.

The Dutch share the German love of pig eating in various forms, either as pork

Cheese in evo...

(*varkensvlees*), ham or bacon (*spek*). If something appears meaty, but its origins are unspecified, it is probably pig. They eat 'everything but the oink', as the French say, accompanied at home by apple purée (*appelmoes*), which they also take with the enormously popular grilled, roasted or otherwise improved chicken (*kip*).

For a nation that in large part arose out of, and continues to share half its border with the sea, Dutch fishy delicacies are remarkably restrained.

Mussels (*mosselen*) are common in the late summer, when the new season for farmed shellfish begins, so they need to claw back income greater than that earned in the rest of the year by selling most of the crop to the Belgians. The largest stocks come from the Zeeland delta around the town of Yerseke (pronounced 'ear sucker'). Most are found steamed in the shell, in stock featuring celery and onion only (*natuur*), or in combination with white wine (*witte wijn*), cream (*room*), garlic (*knoflook*) or curry (*kerrie*). They are also found de-shelled, then fried in breadcrumbs like common fish.

Other fish dishes feature salmon (*zalm*), Dover sole (*slibtong*), lemon sole (*tongfilet*) or cod (*kabeljauw*), with occasional appearances for a local favourite, smoked eel (*gerookte paling*).

On the vegetable side much is grown, particularly in the massive acreage of greenhouses that light the way for pilots descending into Schiphol from the North Sea, but is of boy-band quality – good looking but insipid. One exception is white asparagus (*asperges*), seen mostly in May, particularly in Limburg, where most is grown. It is cultivated in the dark, inside mounds of earth beneath lightproof plastic sheeting, keeping the shoots colourless, the green variety being considered unsubtle and inferior.

Desserts and sweet things

Dame Blanche is vanilla ice cream with hot chocolate sauce and whipped cream. A good insight into Dutch restaurant psyche can be gained by asking for flavours other than vanilla.

Dutch fruit pies are legendary, particularly apple (*appeltaart* or *appelgebak*). The whipped cream (*slagroom*) offered alongside is usually from an aerosol. Traditional stone-baked tarts (vlaai) include the excellent fruit-filled Limburg (*Limburgse vlaai*) variety topped with a sweet lattice pastry, baked sweetened rice tart (*rijstevlaai*), and creamy variations on custard, egg and advocaat versions, which are personal favourites.

Cheese

The Netherlands is famous for cheese. We cannot work out why.

The days when Dutch cheese was Edam or Gouda have gone, thankfully. Yet the majority remain but variations on a few themes: firm, yellow and no more than moderately tasty, labelled and sold according to how long they have matured, occasionally containing seeds, such as cumin (*komijn*).

While there are no doubt craft producers starting to create or re-create soft, blue-veined or goat's cheeses, the Dutch reputation for cheese-making is more uni-dimensional.

Older versions are sharper and more flavoursome. Young cheese (*jonge kaas*) gets to sit around for a month; *jong belegen* for two months; mature (*belegen*) for four months; *extra belegen* for 7 or 8 months maybe; old (*oude*) for up to a year; and vintage (*overjarige*) for 18 months and longer. With age comes a darker, harder consistency and a crumbling graininess built on the formation of salt crystals.

We do not dislike Dutch cheese. It is just that in comparison to French, Italian, Belgian, Spanish or, and let's not be modest here, British, it is pretty dull.

DRINKING (OTHER DRINKS)

With Dutch beer nose-diving in originality in the latter half of the 20th century, it was inevitable that wine would rise, and so it has. Most restaurants stock a plausible variety though those sold by the glass in bars are, well, worthy of caution. There is a local wine industry beginning, but this is a tiny niche, yet to justify its prices.

In contrast, the Dutch spirits industry is massive, in more ways that one.

All gin is descended from *jenever*, named for the juniper berries used to flavour it. The origins of juniper-floured distilled alcohol are obscure, with references found as early as the 13th century, though its official launch date is 16th century.

There are two basic types, distinguished by process, not age. *Oude* (old) jenevers are made in the original style and must contain at least 15% grain distillate, while *jonge* (young) jenever has less than that and is made by the cheaper, industrial distillation process that processes neutral alcohol without flavour reference to its source. This is the process responsible for 'blended' whiskies and the rash of brightly coloured back bar bottles.

Those *oude* jenevers containing only grain-derived distillate are termed *graanjenever*. *Moutwijn* is entirely derived from distilled malt liquor and is equivalent to an unaged single malt whisky. *Korenwijn* (literally corn wine) is typically 50 to 70% malt-derived and usually aged.

It is a question of taste. If you want taste, choose something oude and drink it at room temperature, ideally in a specialist tasting room (*proeflokaal*), though not as a spirit chaser, for reasons expressed in the Dutch name for that, a *kopstoot*, or head butt.

In a traditional proeflokaal, shot glasses are poured to the brim. Before picking them up, lean forward to take a first sip (*nippen* or *slurpen*) without using your hands.

Distillers also produce a bewildering variety of fruit and herb liqueurs, which vary from the crystal clear, sickly sweet and 'chemical' to some perfectly lovely and sophisticated alcoholic fruit juices, the best of which have whole fruit steeped within them.

In the Netherlands, the collective name for bottled water is Spa, regardless of the brand, ordered as red (*rood*) for sparkling, blue (*blauw*) for still and green (*groen*) for in-between. Cola is 'cola', or 'cola light' if you prefer sugar-free and aspartame-rich. Ask for 'coca' and you may get you more than you bargained for.

At home and at work, the Dutch like to wash down food with milk (*melk*) or buttermilk (*karnemelk*), which seems odd to everyone else. This habit is rarer in cafés.

Despite the popularity of alcohol and its reputation for dope, the Netherlands' national drug of choice is caffeine. Dutch coffee is universally excellent and great care goes into its preparation. No business meeting or social gathering can commence without a regulation cup (or two), served with evaporated milk (*koffiemelk*). Decaffeinated is available in most places. Don't even consider asking for instant, which rarely appears except beside the kettle in some hotel rooms.

As regards tea, well, shall we just say that English or Indian entrepreneurs have thus far missed a major trick by allowing tasteless grit packaged in bags to flagship the world's most popular beverage in mainland Europe. Tea in the Netherlands is, in our opinion and perhaps literally, the dregs of the beverage world.

Jenever proeflokaal, Wijnand Fockink in Amsterdam

Brewing &

beer styles

THE beer revolution has achieved a great deal around the world in the past few decades, creating far greater awareness of the massive variations in the types of beer it is possible to make. In the process it has grown a new tradition of appreciating 'beer styles' for their unique properties and qualities.

Unquestionably, this assists a nascent craft brewing industry to assert its excellence by awarding itself prizes for this and that, each more clearly defined that it otherwise would be. Whether it adds much in the way of understanding is a different matter.

There follows a brief introduction to the art of understanding beer.

HOW BEER IS MADE

There may be tens of thousands of different beers in the world, but virtually all follow the same fundamental life cycle: growing, selecting and preparing the ingredients; mashing, boiling and filtering; fermentation and conditioning; packaging; selling; drinking; and returning the nutrients to the soil to start over.

The ingredients

Making a great beer requires skill. The first is to choose its four basic components: grain, hops, water, and yeast. Their infinite variety is down to subtle tweaks designed into them by the growers, maltsters, technicians and scientists.

Grain

Play around all you like, but no beer is beer without grain. This provides flavour, aroma, colour and texture – and sugar for the yeast to transform into alcohol. In principle, you can use any grain, though malted barley is the best suited to the task.

Barley contains plentiful starch, enzymes to convert that starch into sugar, and proteins to keep the yeast healthy. Malting is the process of allowing the grain to germinate before killing it off by flash heating and then roasting.

The grains are soaked in water for several days, then aerated to induce germination. They are considered 'fully modified' when the young roots reach the same length as the original kernel. By this stage the enzymes have developed enough to prepare the grain's sugars for optimum fermentation.

The next step is to roast the malt. The longer you roast, the darker it gets, and the darker your beer will be. Lightly-roasted malts are known as 'base' malts (such as Münchener, Pale Ale and Pilsener). Short-roasted 'toasted' malts add nuttiness. Darker 'roasted' or 'chocolate' malts add intense coffee and chocolate. In the case of 'crystal' malt, grains are added wet to the roaster and kept moist, forming caramelised sugars that do not ferment, adding sweetness to the beer.

Almost all beers contain barley, but other grains may be added as 'adjuncts', to introduce new textures and flavours. The most popular

Malting barley

is wheat, which besides affecting flavour, also gives a creamy stable head. Rye, oats and spelt and others are also used.

Less welcome are rice and maize, often used in industrial beers to add flavourless alcohol but seldom listed among the ingredients. While decent flavours can be coaxed from these their reputation is so tarnished that it is rarely worth trying.

Water

In terms of liquid, almost everything in a beer that is not alcohol, is water. Any unpolluted source will do, but the mineral content affects flavour and, historically, determined to some extent what kinds of beer worked where. In the UK, Burton-upon-Trent's water contains sulphates, perfect for modifying bitterness in British ales. Munich's water is low in sulphates, but rich in calcium carbonate, making hoppy beers unpalatable but softening malty dunkelweizens. In the Czech Republic, the waters of Plzeň and České Budějovice are virtually pure, ideal for delicate Pilsener and Budweiser lagers.

Yeast

Without yeast there is no beer. Add these micro-organisms to anything sweet and they start to convert simple sugars into alcohol, producing carbon dioxide gas as a by-product. Once the yeast have gorged on brewers' wort, they go dormant and sink, partially clarifying the beer as they plummet.

There are many thousands of yeast strains, each suited to working best under certain conditions, adding their own thumbprint flavours. Historically they are divided into two categories: top-fermenting ale yeast that work best at room temperature, and bottom-fermenting lager yeast that prefer a chill. A third way, mastered by the lambic makers of Belgium, is spontaneous fermentation, in which open tanks and oak casks attract natural yeasts from the atmosphere – or beers fermented like wines.

Above certain strengths typical beer fermenting yeast get alcohol poisoning and die, leading brewers to add wine yeast for their stronger beers.

Hops

Put grain, yeast and water together in the right way and you can make beer. However, this will be too sweet and grainy for most tastes and also tend rapidly to oxidise to malt vinegar. While various herbs and spices have been tried over the centuries, today's overwhelming people's champion is the hop. The bitter acids in its flowers (cones) make beer palatable. As a bonus, they are also antibacterial, and thus a natural preservative. Moreover, the hops contain essential oils that add a myriad of flavours and aromas, ranging from earthy, floral and fruity, to you name it.

There are hundreds of hop varieties, each with indiviual characteristics. German and Czech hops such as Saaz and Hallertau are floral and provide a crisper, cleaner taste. British hops like Fuggles or East Kent Goldings are earthier and spicier. Newer American hops such as Cascade or Amarillo add citrus bitterness, while from New Zealand varieties like Motueka and Nelson Sauvin come tropical fruits.

Ideally, all brewers would use whole (compressed) cones but these take up space in warehouses, wagons and brewhouses, making

ps on the vine

fine flour. The grist is then mixed with water, and this 'mash' is heated for 60-90 minutes in a mash tun. At a constant temperature of around 60-70°C it is mostly sugars that are extracted. Anything hotter speeds the process and makes it more rigorous, but releases dextrins that make beer taste sweet on the tongue as enzymes in saliva convert them to sugar in your mouth.

After mashing, the mixture is filtered to leave a high-sugar, hazy brown suspension called 'sweet wort' – which also contains proteins. The residual grain is then sparged, or rinsed in hot water to flush out more sugar.

At this stage, bittering hops are added and the brewing process begins, the sweet wort being boiled for another hour or so to release the hops' bittering and flavouring agents to make 'hopped wort', which is then cooled and filtered, sometimes by centrifuge, to remove residual solids. The more you take out, the more polished and less flavoursome the beer will be – the more you leave in, the hazier and more troublesome it will be.

Fermentation and conditioning

Cooled hopped wort is a drinkable, extremely sweet, non-alcoholic beverage. It is not beer. To complete the metamorphosis it must be transferred to a fermentation vessel and have yeast added.

Primary fermentation

Most modern fermentation vessels are closed stainless steel tanks that reduce the risk of infection. The first (or primary) fermentation will typically take between 3 and 7 days, during which the yeast converts most of the sugar to alcohol and CO_2. The more fermentable sugar, the higher the ABV.

Fermentation temperatures can be tightly controlled. Top-fermenting yeast, for making ales, collect at the top of the vessel in clumps, and are most content at 15-20°C. Warmer fermentation is faster and cheaper, but the yeast gets stressed and makes gunky phenolic flavours that have to be hidden by chilling the beer. Calm yeast will, in addition to alcohol and CO_2 produce a wide varieties of esters that add fruity and spicy flavours.

it more practical to use pellets, which are good substitutes when properly made. Powdered hops and extracts are also used, but like any ingredient, the more you process it, the greater the loss of finesse.

Other ingredients

Besides the big four ingredients, brewers may add a variety of other substances. Fruits and spices have been revived in recent years but experimental brewers love throwing in weirder stuff, that nowadays can range from vegetables to whey, or in the case of one Swedish brewer, beaver musk. All of which begs the question of how wine makers came not to do so.

The brewing bit

Base malts form the basis of every beer, including the darkest. If you used exclusively chocolate malt in stout it would be undrinkably harsh – 5% is all you need. Beers made with 100% malted grain can be overpowering at ABVs above 5%. For balance, brewers may replace up to 15% of the malt with cornflour, starch, syrup or sugar. Going higher saves money but thins the flavour.

Before yeast can get at the sugars in your grain it needs to be ground or cracked in a mill, to form grist: either coarse meal or

Bottom-fermenting yeast allowed to do their thing at temperatures around 10°C, which is rarely the case nowadays, sink lower in the fermentation tank and working slowly and efficiently to produce cleaner-tasting beers with less volatile by-products.

Some stronger ales may go through several fermentation steps using various yeast strains that work best at different alcohol levels.

Conditioning

Once primary fermentation is finished and the yeast have sunk, the beer is drinkable. Indeed with simpler beers the quicker that happens the better.

But like a good wine, beers will improve if given enough time and the right micro-organisms, allowing some character to develop before it is packed up and sold. Such 'conditioning' can happen in stainless steel lagering tanks, oak tuns and/or in its final container.

Conditioning with regular sacchromyces yeast, the type used for primary fermentation, will mostly complete fermentation that was a bit rushed. In a classic lager – nowadays a fairly rare beast – low temperature tank-conditioning at 3–4°C, ideally for about 12 weeks leads in effect to the microflora sweeping up those chemicals in beer that cause odd and sub-standard tastes. Those brews that condition far longer, usually at cellar temperature and sometimes in oak casks or tuns, are mainly being conditioned by slower acting yeast, some actions of which are similar to what occurs to a long-cellared wine, while others are of a type that wine makers dread.

Finally, some brewers will induce further conditioning by adding fruit, part of the effect of which is to reawaken the yeast, though most modern fruit beers are created by simpler shortcuts, more along the lager and lime principle.

Packaging

However much or little a beer is conditioned at the brewery, it will at some point be packaged into a sealed keg, bottle, can, or on some occasions a cask or barrel that has a broachable seal.

To capture a beer at peak condition, it is simplest to pasteurise and recarbonate it, then have it drunk as soon as possible. However, even the tiniest amont of yeast will allow some continued conditioning in the container, which will continue developing the beer.

Some brewers bottle-condition beer by adding carefully calculated extra yeast to induce further (or secondary) fermentation. Add too much to a beer with a lot of residual sugar and the natural recarbonation may be excessive. Include any rogue or infected yeast and you may get a 'gusher', often smelling or tasting foul in addition to, well, gushing.

Control over the amounts of fermentable sugar and live yeast in a beer at this stage have become so precise in recent years that it is now possible to continue some secondary fermentation or conditioning in cellar tanks, sealed kegs and even, due to a particularly clever sleight of hand, in some cans. This practice has been spreading for some years but has yet to acquire the political importance, in the UK at least, of cask-conditioning.

Selling the beer

It does not matter how fantastic your drink is; if it does not look the part, few will be tempted.

Some amateurish bottle labels put you off before you start. On the other hand, look too slick and professional and you may be shunned. Our advice to buyers is to be wary of any beer where there is a lack of clarity on the label about its brewery of origin – place it back on the shelf and step away.

Something simple and clear works best, with a common image across the product range, precise information about where a beer was brewed and by whom, and maybe some non-promotional, useful facts and figures.

Choosing the right format is important. The same beer tastes different when presented in different forms, for reasons that are

part real, part imagination. Light, heat and oxygen damage beer, so sealed, darkened, heat-proof containers would preserve quality best, leaving all conditioning issues to one side. You have to know your audience.

Finally there is appearance. After any form of secondary fermentation, the yeast again settles to the bottom, becoming a sediment that if it mingles with the beer on pouring can add its own flavour, for better or worse. Persuading people that good beer need not be shiny can take a lifetime.

For larger brewers, who inevitably follow the shiny beads route, packaging becomes more important than product, though none will admit this openly. It is, after all, the look of the logo, bottle or advert that first catches a punter's eye.

If there were a dictionary definition of how to market beer to a global audience, it would read, simply: see Heineken. Did you really think those little smiley upturned 'e's in the name got there by accident?

BEER STYLES

If a world is ever created in which all beers are defined by their style, Michael Jackson and the other great beer writers will have lived in vain. Understanding beer styles is simply a shorthand way to gain an early understanding of the breadth and depth of possibilities in beer making.

There are few styles of beer that are native to the Netherlands. Most have been collected magpie-like from elsewhere. In the past, Dutch brewers wishing to create something other than pilsener imitated Belgian abbey beers or witbier. In the last decade, they have started following more global trends and started producing types of beer more associated with North America, Germany and, a century ago, the UK. As a result beer has become more adventurous and extreme. Where they will go next? Who knows?

Here are a few names with which to conjure, defined as for their current Dutch use:

Altbier: a lagered ale speciality of Düsseldorf in Germany, typically amber-coloured and 4.5–5.5% ABV.

Amber ale: similar to pale ale (qv), but typically less bitter, redder and 5–5.5%. Most are imitations of well-known Belgians.

Amber lager: dark lager modelled on an American steam beer, hoppier and more characterful than pilsener, typically 6%.

Barley Wine: generic British description of strong beers, 8% and up, historically finished with a wine yeast. Similar to a Belgian strong or massive ale, the terms have become interchangeable. The bulk are amber or brown, tending to be sticky-sweet to balance the alcohol.

Blond ale: light coloured ale made with pilsener malt (6–6.5%). A new Belgian style from the last two decades adopted in the Netherlands. Some can be great but all too many are bland and sweet, low in bitterness and largely indistinguishable from one another. We call these LBJs: Little Blond Jobs.

Bok or **Bock**: brown beers, traditionally bottom-fermented and 6.5–7%, for release on the first Monday in October. They now appear in September, occasionally year-round, and are often top-fermented. Also termed Bokbier or Bockbier, Herfstbok or Herfstbock. The tradition most likely originates from the habit of using up the old grain from the previous year in a harvest-time superbrew.

Dubbel: a brown ale (6.5–7%) of a type first popularly designated by the brewery of the Trappist abbey at Westmalle in Belgium, and much imitated so-called abbey-style ranges. Brewed with 'double' the malt, at their best a dubbel is rich and rewarding though too often there is excessive caramel sweetness. Probably related to British Double Brown, French Double and Italian Doppio Malto traditions.

Dubbelbok or **Dubbelbock**: a stronger version (8%+) of bok (qv).

Gueuze: see Lambic

Herfstbok or **Herfstbock**: see Bok

India Pale Ale or **IPA**: massively hoppy American style of medium strength pale ale (5.5-7%), originally derived from an English style of export pale ale bound for outposts of empire. Numerous sub-genres, including Red, Rye, Black, Double (DIPA) and Triple (TIPA) are starting to appear, all constructed with North American or Australian hops to the fore.

Kölsch: taken to mean a top-fermented, lagered blond ale (4.5-5.5%), of a type that originated from the German city of Cologne (Köln), though its use by other brewers within the EU is formally banned.

Kuit: a traditional Dutch style of pale mixed-grain ale, classically hopped only with noble hops (Saaz, Hallertau, Tettnanger or Spalt varieties), which has recently been revived. It should contain a minimum of 45% oats and 20% wheat or malted wheat. Typically 5-8% ABV, it is also found spelt Kuyt or Koyt.

Kriek: see Lambic

Lambic: a collective term for beers that are fermented like wines, which is to say without brewers' yeast being pitched into them. This family of 'spontaneously fermented' beers were perfected in Brussels and neighbouring Payottenland. Young lambic is typically fermented by 'wild yeast' for 4 to 12 months, old lambic for up to 3 years, starting musty and going on to develop citrus flavour and aromas of old bookshops, horse barns and tobacco pouches. In their locality, lambics are sometimes served on draught but are more common in other forms. Blended together, young (*jong*) and old (*oude*) lambics become Oude Gueuze, compared by some to champagne and by others to cider. If whole cherries are steeped in young lambic for 4 to 8 months you get Oude Kriek, or with raspberries Frambozen. Less common is Faro, draught lambic with added sugar. EU-protected 'oud' lambics must originate from Brussels and the surrounding Payottenland region, though other brewers around the world are experimenting with the principle, including the Dutch brewer Oersoep (page 65).

Lentebok or **Lentebock**: seasonal springtime golden blond beers (6.5-7%), formally called Meibock but rebranded since release moved forward to early April, which also broadens the linguistic gap with German Maibock lagers. Currently suffering from beer connoisseurs' aversion to sweet beer styles, but nonetheless no less authentic and capable of being alluring when they are.

LBJ: see Blond ale.

Meibok or **Meibock**: see Lentebok.

Oud Bruin (Dutch): low-alcohol (2-3.5%), dark malty concoctions that are typically overpoweringly sweet. Derived from the lower alcohol Donker lagers that were popular a century ago and related in principle to German *Malzbieren*, Belgian *tafelbieren* and British 'Invalid' stouts.

Oud Bruin (Flemish): 1980s designation of the oak-aged brown ales (4.5-7%) found in various parts of Belgian Flanders, featuring lactic sourness gained from a year or two of maturation in oak tuns. Similar in principle to Gulpener's lower ABV Mestreechs Aajt (p. 51).

Pale ale: derived from the much undersung classic, crisp and polished British ale style of the 19th century that once enjoyed global fame. Typically 4.5-5.5% with firm but balanced hopping in contrast to a hop-forward modern IPA.

Pils or **Pilsener**: bottom-fermented blond lager, typically 5% ABV. The use of the name was essentially deregulated by a Court in Munich in 1899. The preferred Dutch style is crisp and malty with low hopping, lots of pzazz but not much taste. It accounts for 90% of the Dutch beer market and should be ordered as 'pils', not 'lager'. The latter marks out an ignorant foreigner.

Quadrupel: a term invented in the 1990s to define a single product from Koningshoeven brewery that was stronger than dubbel and tripel, then picked up by beer enthusiasts seeking to be equally vague. Interchangeable, for now, with strong or massive ale.

Rauchbier or **Rookbier**: originally a type of smoked lager from the days before maltsters could control their kilns adequately, prominently preserved by some brewers in the German town of Bamberg in Upper Franconia. Nowadays the smoking is deliberate, malted barley being smoked with beechwood to give the beer (5-7%) the aroma of bonfire and a fruity, smoky taste.

Rosé: vile pink-washed witbiers created by marketing people to sell to those who don't like beer. Most are patronising alcopops. If Hell has a reception area for newly deceased beer lovers, this is what the Devil would serve as a welcome drink.

Saison: originally a low-alcohol pale ale brewed to quench the summer thirst of Belgian farm workers, now a middle strength (5.5-6.5%), refreshingly dry, near blond ale using a distinctive farmhouse yeast.

Schwarzbier: in Germany, a black lager typically for the East. Most Dutch versions are dryish ales (4.5-5.5%) with crisp, fruity overtones.

Scotch ale: heavy sweetish brown ale, around 8%, that the Belgians preserved long after the Scots had stopped drinking Wee Heavy, from which it is derived.

Stout: developed originally from dark ales called porter, stouts get their dark brown or black colouring from the inclusion of some roasted chocolate malts in the recipe. In their modern form they range from dry to sweet, come in every degree of bitterness, and gain depth and complexity with liquorice, coconut, vanilla, blackcurrant, cocoa or burnt coffee notes, tasting more authentic when derived from the malt and the yeast rather than added beans or essences. Lighter stouts begin around 4.5%, with their heavier-hitting Imperial cousins ranging from 8% upwards. Milk stout implies lactose, Irish or Oyster should mean salted and dry, and Oatmeal just that. Stout was brewed widely in the Netherlands in the 19th century, but went all-but-extinct in the 20th, though these days most Dutch brewers are following the American trend to revive the sort of strong stouts that used to be found all along the Scandinavian and Baltic coast from their origins in London and Burton-on-Trent to St Petersburg. Most are reasonable; some outstanding.

Tripel: a strong ale, usually golden-blond, its name implying that the mash contained three times the normal amount of grain. The designation was first popularised by the Trappist abbey of Westmalle in Belgium. Typically 8-9.5%, and widely copied in the Netherlands.

Vienna: deep amber lager with a slight malty sweetness, typically around 5%, featuring Vienna or Wiener malt.

Weizen: the generic term used for German wheat beers (5-6%). Top-fermented from a mash of unmalted wheat and malted barley, the banana and clove flavours coming from the yeast rather than the spicing. Many add Hefe- and some prefer Weissbier. Amber versions are known as Dunkelweizen or Dunkelweiss, literally dark white.

White beer: see Weizen and Witbier.

Witbier: the Belgian form of wheat beer, nowadays with added spices, typically coriander and dried orange peel. Normally 4.5-6%. Until recently almost all Dutch wheat beers were in this style, though the trend is swinging towards Germany. They can be refreshingly citrus, while the worst are intrusively sweet.

Winterbier: seasonal ales, often dark, heavy, and sometimes sweet. The nearer to Christmas the name, the higher the chance of heavy spicing. Strength tends to be 8% and up, to keep out the chill.

Other useful beer terms

ABV: stands for Alcohol By Volume, the routine measurement of a beer's alcoholic strength, often rendered an inexact science by the effects of secondary fermentation.

Alcoholvrij: any drink with less than 0.5% alcohol. The first such beers in the Netherlands were introduced by Bavaria in 1978. Not very appealing. We prefer water.

Dry-hopping: adding hops to a brew at some point after brewing is completed, generally occurs during or just after fermentation, increasing the hop aroma and flavour.

EBU or **IBU**: stands for European or International Bitterness Units, increasingly quoted on the label. A measurement of specific acids, the higher the number, the more bitter a beer will be. Wheat beers and industrial pils may be as low as 15-20 EBU, while an intense IPA could go beyond 60. A hoppy presence becomes more obvious at 30 and up.

High-density brewing: the technique of brewing to a higher ABV then diluting the beer with water before packaging, thus saving space and energy during production, at the expense of quality. Many of the canned winobeers are same brews undiluted, marketed as strong lagers for students and tramps.

hl: short for hectolitre, or 100 litres.

Radler: pilsener and lemonade, known to the British as shandy. The makers often claim real lemons are added, which is very sweet of them.

Trappist: beers that can be called an 'Authentic Trappist Product' must be produced under the supervision of the Trappist Order, within the walls of an abbey, and the proceeds from sale spent on charitable works or the upkeep of the Order. In practice there are currently 10 Trappist breweries: 6 Belgian, 2 Dutch, 1 Austrian and 1 American. Some Dutch café owners still offer grenadine syrup with the dark beers, a prospect that makes us shiver.

Wisseltap: a tap reserved for a guest beer.

The Dutch

BACK in 2002, the country's 40 beer producers made about 200 regular beers. Today's equivalent figures are 200 and 1100, with both still rising. This does not include one-offs.

Whereas new breweries used to appear at a sedate pace – say 2 or 3 a year – and were easily monitored, they now crop up at a rate of 20+ annually. More will doubtless have appeared between us going to press and the guide hitting the *straatjes*.

Not all have breweries, though more than 100 do, if not all of their commercial output is produced there. A few use other facilities for larger runs. There is a huge gulf in size between the largest and smallest. At the top end, Heineken's Zoeterwoude site is the largest beer production plant in Europe. At the other extreme, Oud Rijn's brewery is in a potting shed. Those who think of breweries the size of all-steel brewpubs and upwards may have to downgrade their concepts of scale.

The Netherlands also possesses an unusual number of individuals or companies that are legally classed as breweries, but who do not operate their own commerical facilities. Some still achieve greatness, despite this apparent handicap; others do not. For more on this thorny and divisive issue, see Brewers without breweries (pages 82–87).

SOCIALLY CONSCIOUS BREWERIES

Several Dutch breweries have taken it upon themselves to offer a social service, helping to rehabilitate those who have otherwise failed to find work. Some (like Dordrecht) employ the educationally or socially disadvantaged, who have found it hard to integrate into society. Others, most notably De Prael, have a workforce consisting mostly of people who have suffered major mental disorder. Their principle is that many jobs in a brewery are quite complex, yet easy to learn from experience, which gives people both the confidence and the skills to work constructively. We applaud their efforts.

Beer ratings

We are mean with our stars – and approximate too.

- ★ Pointless or inadequate: buy something else
- ★+ Could do better: try only as a tick
- ★★ Competent: buy once at least
- ★★+ Worth looking out for: buy when you can
- ★★★ Among the best in its class: take some home
- ★★★+ Among the Netherlands' finest Year-round: keep a stock
- ★★★★ Among the world's finest Year-round: keep a secret stock

DISCLAIMER: we do our best to keep tabs on every beer, producer and brewery, but new brands appear and existing ones evolve at a dizzying rate, with older brands disappearing just as suddenly. Let us know if you find something new and amazing at: **timskelton@hotmail.com**.

Dutch beers that are not

We have excluded two high volume but otherwise inconsequential "Dutch" beer brands, that are made abroad, their breweries of origin being long gone. These are Leeuw Pilsener, which now comes from Haacht in Belgium, and Oranjeboom Pilsener, which originated from the long-levelled Drie (or 3) Hoefijzers brewery in Breda but is now manufactured in Germany.

The Schelde brewery is a trickier issue. Originally based in Zeeland and so barely over the Belgian border that it is reached from a Dutch motorway junction, it maintains a distribution warehouse in Flevoland and an increasingly tenuous claim to Dutchness. However, as it is now listed in CAMRA's *Good Beer Guide Belgium* we consider it to have emigrated.

The opposite argument goes for the Urthel beers from De Leyerth, the bulk of which are produced in the Netherlands.

The Mongozo brand also claims Dutch nationality via its Boxmeer office but as the Huyghe brewery in Belgium lists them as their own, we exclude them.

right: *Modern Du[tch] brewing exploits [the] best of old and ne[w]*

brewing
industry

Independent breweries and brewpubs

Except where we have stated otherwise the brand name on any beer range, if any, will be the name of the brewery as it appears in the heading.

Alfa

Alfa Brouwerij
Thull 15-19, 6365 AC Schinnen
T 046 443 2888
www.alfa-bier.nl

Long-established bottom-fermenting brewery, founded in 1870 in rural South Limburg, and one of the largest independents. The focus remains on unadventurous larger-volume beers. Its superior unfiltered pils is only sold on tap in its two brewpubs (Amsterdam's Bierfabriek and Heerlen's Beerkompanie). Tours by arrangement.
YEAR-ROUND: malty sweet **Oud Bruin** (2.5%: ★+); average, unassuming **Edel Pils** (5.0%: ★+); superior, bitter unfiltered pilsener **Ongefilterd Puur** (5.0%: ★★+); flowery bittersweet **Super Dortmunder** (7.5%: ★★+); and winobeer **Super Strong 9.2** (9.2%: ★), which is strong but not super.
SEASONAL: sweetish **Lente Bok** (6.5%: ★★); and autumnal **Bok** (6.5%: ★★), which avoids sweetness and much else.

YEAR-ROUND: decently rounded blond **'t Leste Lot** (6.0%: ★★); bittersweet brown wheat **Skutehôn** (6.3%: ★★+); its lighter sister, dry and bitter white beer **Butenbiëntke** (6.5%: ★★); hoppy amber **Barnstiën** (6.5%: ★★+); fruity, dry stout **Bikkelha'd** (6.5%: ★★+); and sharply refreshing local ale **Bij 't Roaie Hek** (6.5%: ★★+), amber flavoured with cranberries.
ALSO: **Ballumer Sap** is a 'surprise' beer that appears occasionally, in different forms.

Amelander

Amelander Bierbrouwerij
Smitteweg 6, 9162 EC Ballum (Ameland)
T 0519 554365
www.amelanderbier.nl

Wadden Islands nanobrewery set up in 2010 by a husband and wife team, currently brewing 200 litres of beer weekly, in a barn. A proper shop with opening times may appear soon. Visitors welcome, but call ahead – the brewer is also one of the island's bus drivers.

Apeldoorn

Stadsbierbrouwerij Apeldoorn
Fabianusstraat 46, 7333 BE Apeldoorn
T 055 533 7249
www.stadsbierbrouwerij.nl

House brewery founded in 1999 in a south Apeldoorn suburb. Its small-scale production of **Apeldoorns** beers is becoming more adventurous. Beers mainly found in Apeldoorn; less common elsewhere. Visits by appointment.

YEAR-ROUND: spiced blond **Stadsbier**
(6.5%: ★★); lightly bitter blond **Bloot Bier**
(6.5%: ★★); golden clove-spiced amber
Martineus de Schijnheilige (7.0%: ★★+);
vanilla-tinted Tripel (8.5%: ★★); and rich,
bittersweet **Obama Honey Porter** (7.0%: ★★+).
SEASONAL: rounded chestnut-edged
Bockbier (7.5%: ★★+); and festively spiced
Christmas amber **Kerstbier** (6.2%: ★★+).

Bavaria

Bavaria NV, De Stater 1, 5737 RV Lieshout
T 0499 428111
www.bavaria.nl

The Netherlands' largest independent, founded in 1719, and run by the Swinkels family since
1764, making it the oldest family brewery too.
They went bottom-fermenting in 1924, introduced the world's first alcohol-free beer in
1978, and in 1989 produced the first Western
beer to be sold in the Soviet Union. They also
run and own the kit at the Koningshoeven
Trappist brewery (see page 57), where we
believe their top-fermented brands are made.
Group tours (Tu–Su) by arrangement.
YEAR-ROUND: liquidised cereal **Oud Bruin**
(3.0%: ★★), less sweet than some; anaemic
Premium Pilsener (5.0%: ★+), lacking much of
anything ; unpasteurised but not dry enough
pilsener **Swinckels' Volmaakt** (5.5%: ★+);
8.6 Gold (6.5%: ★+) is not 8.6%; and sweetish
strong lager **8.6 Original** (7.9%: ★+) ain't neither.
SEASONAL: top-fermented sweetish
Hooghe Bock (6.5%: ★★).
ALSO: there are alcohol-free 'beers' called
Original, Rosé, Lemon, Gold and Wit.

varia brewery,
eshout

Beijerse

Beijerse Brouwerij
Stravinskypad 45, 3261 WT Oud-Beijerland
T 06 2061 0166
www.beijersebrouwerij.nl

South Holland hobbyist who went pro in
2012. The brewery is in the owner's attic.
Production of **Beijers** beers is low, and
currently they are hard to source outside the
locality, but clock the website for ambition.
YEAR-ROUND: fruity, golden-blond **Weizen**
(5.3%: ★★) and four we have not tried –
Pilsener, **Red Amber**, **Wulpsblond** and a
tripel called **Lamoraal**.

Bekeerde Suster

Amsterdamse Stoombierbrouerij
De Bekeerde Suster
Kloveniersburgwal 6, 1012 CT Amsterdam
T 020 423 0112
www.beiaardgroep.eu

The Repentant Sister opened in 2004 on the
site of the city's first new wave brewpub,
Maximilians. Owned and run by the Beiaard
Group, which sells the beers on tap in all its
cafés. Brewing happens on Fridays. Can have
quality issues.
YEAR-ROUND: white beer **Witte Antonia**
(5.4%: ★★); fruity **Blonde Barbier** (6.2%: ★★);
and improving tripel **Manke Monnik** (7.2%: ★★).
SEASONAL: creamy **Meibock** (6.9%: ★+);
sweetish **De Gewaeghde Bock** (6.5%: ★★);
and brown winter **Vintrus** (8.5%: ★★).

Berghoeve

Berghoeve Brouwerij
Achteres 15, 7683 SX Den Ham
T 06 1827 8345
www.berghoevebrouwerij.nl

The husband and wife owners of this farm-house brewery in rural Overijssel are food nutritionists. Brewing since 2010, in their own 7.5-hl installation since 2013, their beers are gaining a great reputation by word-of-mouth and are increasingly available at home and abroad. Visits (Mo-Fr) by appointment.
YEAR-ROUND: darkly warming **1842 Hammer Brand** (4.0%:★★★) chilli porter, which punches above its ABV; hugely quaffable hoppy blond **Khoppig** (4.5%: ★★★); malty top-fermented **Hammer Pilz** (5.0%: ★★); black IPA **Donker-bruin Vermoeden** (6.0%: ★★★) blending hoppiness with burnt notes; disconcertingly amber **Hammer Blont** (6.0%: ★★); sharply dry dubbel **Goede Buur** (7.0%: ★★); pleasing imperial stout **Hammer Schout** (8.0%: ★★+); dry and lightly perfumed tripel **Verre Vriend** (8.0%: ★★+); and coriander-spiced hoppy blond **Vuurdoop** (8.5%: ★★+).
SEASONAL: fruity and bitter spring **Kriebels!** (7.5%: ★★); citrussy summer but strong white beer **Juffer Helena** (7.0%: ★★); rich, raisiny 7-malted **Windbuul Herfstbock** (7.0%: ★★+); warming, treacly Scotch ale **Mirrwinter** (7.0%: ★★★).
ALSO: they make amber **Helders Goud** (5.7%: ★★) for Hellendorn tourist office.

Berging

Berging Brouwerij
Impuls 147, 1446 WE Purmerend
T 06 2920 9585
www.bergingbrouwerij.nl

North Holland brewery established in 2013, brewing in occasional 200-litre runs, labelled by batch number as recipes vary. A work in progress, so our ratings are approximate. Thus far hard to source.

YEAR-ROUND: spiced wheat **Wit** (5.0%: ★★); dark amber **Ale** (5.5%: ★★); promising **IPA** (6.5%: ★★); dry, rounded **Blond** (6.7%: ★★); and a decent **Tripel** (8.5%: ★★).
SEASONAL: **Bock** (6.5%: ★★).

Beyerd

Brouwerij De Beyerd
Boschstraat 26, 4811 GH Breda
T 076 521 4265
www.beyerd.nl

Long established café that began brewing only for itself in 2004, starting with a resurrection of Drie Hoefijzers beer, which had disappeared when AB InBev closed the town's Oranjeboom brewery. Group tours by arrangement.
YEAR-ROUND: above-average **Dirk Urtyp Pilsener** (5.0%: ★★+); moderately successful cloned icon **Drie Hoefijzers Klassiek** (5.0%: ★★+) pilsener, occasionally prepared unfiltered as **Nassaubier**; fruity, burnt-edged **Schwarzbier** (5.0%: ★★+); too-sweet **Hefe Weisse** (5.5%: ★★); dry bitter **Blond** (6.8%: ★★); and seldom-seen **Tripel** (8%).
SEASONAL: autumnal **Herfstbok** (6.5%: ★★); and darkly fruity **Winterbier** (8.0%: ★★).

Bierfabriek

De Bierfabriek
Rokin 75, 1012 KL Amsterdam
T 020 528 9910
www.bierfabriek.com

Alfa-owned central Amsterdam brewpub, opened in 2011. Brews in 300-litre batches, weekly. Only sold in-house.
YEAR-ROUND: amber **Rosso** (5.8%: ★★); and porter **Nero** (6%: ★★) are slowly gaining confidence.

Boei

Bierbrouwerij De Boei
Rommelpot 11, 1797 RN Den Hoorn (Texel)
T 0222 314180
www.landgoeddebontebelevenis.nl

Wadden Islands nanobrewery founded in 2002 at the Bonte Belevenis farm museum, where the entry fee includes a tour of the brewery and on-site distillery. Brews in 5-hl batches, twice a month. Despite the tiny scale they have a cool room for bottom fermentation. All beers are bottled and only sold only in-house or at a local off-licence.
YEAR-ROUND: aromatic, flowery pilsener **Noorderzon 6** (6.0%: ★★), with honey to bump up the ABV; wheat ale **Dichte Mist** (6.0%: ★★); floral amber **Loodsbier 7** (7.0%: ★★+), with honey, elderberry, and sea buckthorn berries; dry, bitter tripel **Windkracht 8** (8.0%: ★★); and warming barley wine **Windkracht 10** (10.0%: ★★+).
ALSO: a super-strength **Windkracht 12** and a seasonal **Bock** are planned.

Bourgogne Kruis

Brouwerij Bourgogne Kruis
Wilhelminakanaal-Zuid 104
4903 RA Oosterhout
T 06 3964 8251
www.bourgognekruis.com

North Brabant nanobrewery, established in 2009 on the site of another that closed 50 years earlier, run by the same family. Its single beer is brewed in 7.5hl batches. A second is expected in 2014. Tours by appointment.
YEAR-ROUND: citrussy white beer **Goud van Tarwe** (5.0%: ★★).

Brand (Heineken) –
see global beer companies

Brouwcafé

Het Brouwcafé
Dr. Lelykade 28, 2583 CM Den Haag (Scheveningen)
T 070 354 0970
www.hetbrouwcafe.nl

Brewpub opened in 1996, overlooking the gentrified fishing harbour in the old port town of Scheveningen, now part of Den Haag. Production is 500 hl a year in 200-litre batches. Beers are in-house and occasionally seen at festivals. The brewer also makes his own Bijdehand beers here.
YEAR-ROUND: decent if lightweight **Scheveningse Stout** (5.0%: ★★); gently bitter blond **Frisse Wind** (5.3%: ★★+); strongly bitter honeyed blond **Bijtje** (5.5%: ★★); sweetish amber **Malle Mok** (5.5%: ★★); uncomplicated citrussy spelt **Speltje** (5.5%: ★★); weizen **Witte Wolk** (5.5%: ★★); reasonable **Blontje** (6.5%: ★★); bittersweet amber **Grundelers Mok** (6.5%: ★★); cinnamon-spiced amber **Speculaasje** (6.5%: ★★+); superior dubbel **Donker Genoegen** (7.5%: ★★+); and Cascade-hopped **Scheveningse Tripel** (7.5%: ★★).
SEASONAL: spring's fruity **Voorjaars Vreugde** (6.5%: ★★); autumn's caramelly **Brouw Bock** (6.5%: ★+); and warming, golden **Winters Verlangen** (7.5%: ★★).

Budels

Budelse Brouwerij
Nieuwstraat 9, 6021 HP Budel
T 0495 491369
www.budels.nl

Established in 1870 and now run by the fourth generation of the Arts family, this Brabant independent with a conscience and a generally reliable output has many beer lovers screaming for it to adopt a bit of

daring and imagination. They strive to be carbon neutral, and beers are brewed using renewable energy. Visits by arrangement.

YEAR-ROUND: the organic beers are overly honeyed blond **Honing** (4.5%: ★+); malty **Bio Pilsener** (5.0%: ★★); drinkably balanced wheat **Witte Parel** (5.0%: ★★); and warming barley wine **Zware Dobber** (8.5%: ★★+). Also, sticky sweet **Oud Bruin** (3.5%: ★+); vaguely malty **Pilsener** (5.0%: ★★); unbalanced malty amber **Batavier** (5.0%: ★+); above-average dry **Goudblond** (6.0%: ★★+); faintly sweet 'n' sour dubbel **Capucijn** (6.5%: ★★+); and coriander-spiced amber **Kolos** (7.5%: ★★).

SEASONAL: standard **Lentebock** (6.5%: ★★); and autumnal **Herfstbock** (6.5%: ★★).

ALSO: alcohol-free organic 0.0% Malt.

Burg

Burg Bier Brouwerij
Putterweg 45, 3851 GB Ermelo
T 0341 564934
www.burgbieren.nl

Founded in 1995, this small-scale Gelderland brewery is set between an adjacent beer shop selling its bottled beers and a brewery tap selling them on draught. Tours Sa 14.00; also We 15.00 (mid-May to mid-Sep); and Th 15.00 (Jul&Aug). Occasionally seen elsewhere.

YEAR-ROUND: fruity-edged wheat ale **Witte Pauw** (5.0%: ★★); fruity, malty and bitter hodgepodge **Veluws Blond** (5.5%: ★★); malty, caramelly unbalanced dubbel **Veluws Bruun** (7.0%: ★+); malty-sweet golden **Triple-B** (8.0%: ★★); and dark barley wine **Gulle** (9.5%: ★★), which has oomph but little else.

SEASONAL: fruity **Springbok** (6.0%: ★★); autumnal **Herfstbock** (7.0%: ★★); and vanilla and cocoa-tinged **Winterbok** (8.5%: ★★).

ALSO: they use Molen de Koe's own barley to make amber **Ermelo's Molenbier** (5.5%: ★★) for them.

Butcher's Tears

Butcher's Tears
Karperweg 45, 1075 LB Amsterdam
T 06 5390 9777
butchers-tears.com

Brewery with a Swedish brewmaster, with its own site in a former factory in Amsterdam South since 2013. Beers served in the brewery tap (We-Su 16.00-21.00), and increasingly available nationwide. Quality is always high, sometimes exceptional.

YEAR-ROUND: deliciously quaffable hoppy blond **Green Cap** (6.0%: ★★★), and its lighter sister **Night Cap** (5.5%: ★★+); lovely dry saison **Raggle Taggle** (6.5%: ★★★); fruity golden **Misery King** (8.0%: ★★+); and 'strong dark saison' **Ex Voto** (9.0%: ★★+).

ALSO: one-off heavily hopped spring and autumn bocks are made, more akin to IPAs.

Cambrinus

Stadsbrouwerij Cambrinus
Houtmarkt 56B, 7201 KM Zutphen
T 0575 546688
www.hanze-stadsbrouwerij.nl

This city-centre brewpub, founded in 2006 as the Hanze Stadsbrouwerij, was re-christened when the kit was moved to the back of the bar in 2013. Beers are only available on tap in-house. Quality is solid. Group tours by arrangement.

YEAR-ROUND: bitter amber **Torenwolf** (4.4%: ★★); malty bitter 'pils' **SjoS** (4.8%: ★★); sweet and sour weizen **Lipica** (5.0%: ★★); Belgian-style white beer **Witte Wolf** (5.2%: ★★); fruity **Framboosje** (5.3%: ★★) – Witte Wolf with raspberries and blackberries; safe blond **Liesje** (6.8%: ★★); caramelly dubbel **Broedertje** (8.0%: ★★); strong blond **Robert**

(9.0%: ★★+) with lychee hints; middling tripel **Droge Nap** (9.5%: ★★); and mighty **Magistraat** (12.5%: ★★+), a tangled witches' brew of alcohol, sweetness, walnut and aniseed.
SEASONAL: golden meibock **Willy** (5.8%: ★★) is overwhelmed by toffee; dubbelbock **Hanzebock** (8.2%: ★★) has caramel and vanilla notes.

Croy

Croybier
Croylaan 9, 5735 PB Aarle-Rixtel
T 0492 381348
www.croybier.nl

Lovely middle-of-nowhere Brabantine tavern brewery opened in 2011, but claiming a brewing heritage back to 1671 and beers made to 19th-century recipes. They have their own hop field. The draught beers (1671 and seasonals) are brewed here but we believe the bottled range comes from Van Steenberge in Belgium. Pre-booked tours (Sa 16.00) are free-ish – you have to buy four bottles beforehand.
YEAR-ROUND: unfiltered top-fermented pilsener **Croy 1671** (4.5%: ★★); nondescript **Blond** (6.5%: ★★); average **Dubbel** (7.5%: ★★); and banana & honey-tinged **Grand Cru Tripel** (9.0%: ★★).
SEASONAL: bitter spring **Croyale** (5.5%: ★★); dryly quaffable summer **Croyse Weizen** (4.5%: ★★); autumnal **Croyse Bock** (4.5%: ★★); and winter **Croy Stout** (5.5%: ★★).

Daendels

Daendels Brouwerij
Verlengde Parklaan 8, 8051 VB Hattem
T 038 444 6662
www.hattemerhuisbrouwerij.nl

Gelderland house brewery near Zwolle, founded in 2009, brewing in a 90-litre copper installation. Bottled beers are seen in some shops and local bars. Quality is generally good.
YEAR-ROUND: standard Belgian **Daendels Wit**

(5.5%: ★★); grassy sweetish **Blond** (6.5%: ★★); sharp-edged fruity **Dubbel** (7.0%: ★★); bittersweet **Tripel** (8.5%: ★★); and nicely balanced copper barley wine **Krachtig** (9.0%: ★★+).
SEASONAL: richly fruity **Bock** (7.0%: ★★+).

Dampegheest

Brouwerij Dampegheest
Achterweg 22, 1906 AG Limmen
T 06 5194 0176
www.brouwerijdampegheest.nl

Founded in 2008 in a North Holland village, brewing in 300-litre batches using homemade stainless steel kit salvaged from the dairy industry. Its beers are widely available locally in bottles; occasionally further afield. Tours by arrangement.
YEAR-ROUND: golden **Antje van Gerrebrandje** (6.0%: ★★), with marshmallow hints; dry, pleasantly rounded amber **Skoftig** (7.6%: ★★+); bittersweet blond **Merakels** (8.0%: ★★), with 30% whey 70% water; and chocolaty dark-brown barley wine **Zware Hufter** (10.0%: ★★).
SEASONAL: fruity, bitter **Ut 1e Kieft-ai Lentebock** (7.0%: ★★); summer **Zomerskarrel** (6.5%: ★★), with added mango; sweet 'n' sour autumnal **Bockbier** (7.5%: ★★); and sweetish wheat ale **Winterwit** (9.0%: ★★).

Doetinchem

Stadsbrouwerij Doetinchem
Grutstraat 31, 7001 BW Doetinchem
T 0314 820993
www.grandcafehendrixen.nl

Gelderland micro producing **Walters** beers
since early 2014. Only sold in the adjacent
taphouse, the HendriXen.
YEAR-ROUND: fruit-edged golden **Blond**
(5.0%: ★★); and a dryer **Amber** (5.0%: ★★).

Dommelsch (AB InBev) –
see global beer companies

Dordrecht

Stichting Stadsbrouwerij Dordrecht
Buddinghplein 20, 3311 BV Dordrecht
T 078 750 7227
www.stadsbrouwerijdordrecht.nl

City-centre nanobrewer founded in 2008, in
a building known to have housed a brewery
in 1533 and to have been a malt store well
into the 20th century. Brews 100-litre
batches weekly of its **Schapenkopje** beers.
Employs young people from disadvantaged
backgrounds to help jump-start their
careers. Pre-booked tours at 14.00, 15.00 &
16.00 (last Sa of the month).
YEAR-ROUND: floral-tinged **Blond** (5.0%:
★★); golden, malty, sweetish but balanced
Schapenscheerder (5.5%: ★★+); orange-
peel laden **Amber** (6.0%: ★★); and non-
sweet toffee-tinted **Dubbel** (6.5%: ★★).
SEASONAL: autumnal **Bockbier** (5.0%: ★+).

Drie Horne (3 Horne)

Brouwerij De 3 Horne
Marktstraat 40-A, 5171 GP Kaatsheuvel
T 0416 275666
www.de3horne.nl

North Brabant brewery, established in 1991.

Currently using two 7.5-hl kettles. Beers
widely available in shops; less so in bars.
Excess capacity is rented out to numerous
nomadic brewers. Visits by appointment.
They also sell brewing equipment in the
Gruithuys shop (Sa 10.00–17.00).
YEAR-ROUND: perfumed **Blondy** (5.3%:
★★); sweetish **Dobbelaer** (6.0%: ★★)
dubbel; spiced wheat **Kaats Witje** (6.0%:
★★); cherry **Kerselaer** (6.5%: ★★) with a
cocoa edge; sharply citrussy **Horns Wit**
(7.0%: ★★+) wheat ale; too-sweet
Mangootje (7.0%: ★+) leaves you wondering
what place mango has in beer; easy-drinking
Trippelaer (8.5%: ★★) tripel; and golden
honeyed **Wiegeleir** (8.7%: ★★).
SEASONAL: spring **Meibock** (7.0%: ★★)
balances caramel and bitter; autumnal
Horn's Bock (7.0%: ★★); rounded liquorice-
tinged **Wolluks Drupke** (7.0%: ★★+) winter
ale; and too-sweet amber **Meesbrees
Winter** (9.5%: ★+).

Drie Ringen

Drie Ringen
Kleine Spui 18, 3811 BE Amersfoort
T 033 465 6575
www.dedrieringen.nl

Long-standing central microbrewery,
operating since 1989 in a riverside building
beside a medieval gate. Their Amersfoorts
beers are reasonable, but unexpectedly
hard to source. Served in-house and in
several other Amersfoort bars. Reserve
group tours in advance.
YEAR-ROUND: lightly bitter,
quaffable **Blond** (5.0%: ★★);
malty, dry, kölsch-leaning
Cordeux (5.0%: ★★+); spiced
wheat **Wit** (5.0%: ★★); dry,
slightly bitter blond **Stadsbier
1259** (5.9%: ★★+); healthily non-
sweet amber **Dubbel** (7.0%: ★★);
golden **Tripel** (7.2%: ★★); and
refreshingly hoppy blond
Vuurvogel (7.5%: ★★+).
SEASONAL: standard **Bokbier** (6.5%: ★★).

AMERSFOORTSE
STADSBROUWERIJ
DE DRIE RINGEN
SINDS 1626

Emelisse craft pub-restaurant in Zeeland

EleganT

EleganT Bierbrouwerij
Tijmtuin 1, 2353 PH Leiderdorp
T 06 2271 5517
www.elegantbier.nl

Commercial homebrewer in a Leiden suburb since 2003. Their bottled EleganT beers available locally, and occasionally elsewhere. Reasonable quality, but variable. No tours. We infer the capital 'T' stands for Totty.

YEAR-ROUND: spiced brown **Nimf** (6.0%: ★+), with a metallic edge; fruity **Blondje van de Eerste Liefdesnacht** (6.5%: ★★) is more interesting; reasonable **Callgirl** (6.5%: ★★); and golden amber **Deerne** (6.5%: ★★), given sharpness from added 'berries'.

SEASONAL: golden **Springmeid** (6.5%: ★★); honeyed blond summer **Groupie** (8.5%: ★★+) has sour undertones; pleasantly burnt-edged dubbelbock **Bruintje** (7.0%: ★★+); and dark, warming, sweet **Winterprinses** (8.5%: ★★).

Emelisse

Brouwerij Emelisse
Nieuweweg 7, 4493 PA Kamperland
T 0113 370262
www.emelisse.nl

Now for something more serious. This 2004 craft brewery, based at a brewpub-restaurant in Zeeland, is an increasingly confident star of the Dutch beer scene. Named after a submerged village and housed in an old-look, new-build, it became seriously experimental when the current brewer, former chef Kees Bubberman, took over in 2007. He brews using a 10-hl copper kettle. IPAs are the house speciality, alongside a range of one-off brews. The **Emelisse** brands, which have become widely available nationwide and increasingly abroad, are frequently superb. Individual tours (Sa 15.30), but only by arrangement.

YEAR-ROUND: occasional, grapefruit-

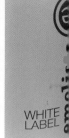

hoppy, light **2½** (2.5%: ★★★), astonishingly complex for one so slight; refreshingly malty **Oertype Pilsener** (5.0%: ★★+); blackcurrant hinted, spicy **Witbier** (5.0%: ★★); fruity-hoppy **Red IPA** (6.5%: ★★★) with a bergamot edge; sweetish hoppy **Blond** (6.6%: ★★+); warming copper **Dubbel** (7.0%: ★★); fruity, rich and intense **Rauchbier** (7.0%: ★★★) with beechwood-smoked Bamberg malt; hoppy, eminently drinkable **DIPA** (7.9%: ★★★+) with its strongly bitter finish; intensely bitter **Black IPA** (8.0%: ★★★+) with burnt notes; moreish classic coffee-laden **Espresso Stout** (9.5%: ★★★+); complicated golden **TIPA** (10.0%: ★★★+) with a complex blend of fruity, hoppy, malty, bitter, sweet and dry; lovely, smoky, deeply respected, Islay-barrel-aged **Black & Tan** (10.5%: ★★★+), a blend of the last beer and ... gorgeous **Imperial Russian Stout** (11%: ★★★+), which is so good you want it to meet your parents.
SEASONAL: ultra-hoppy **Lentebock** (7.0%: ★★★) veers IPA-ish; richly chewy **Herfstbock** (6.5%: ★★+) holds back on sweetness; accomplished **Imperial Dubbelbock** (11.0%: ★★★) trends towards imperial stout; and dark but too-sweet Winterbier (9.0%: ★★).
ALSO: the **White Label** series (★★★+ to ★★★★) of usually barrel-aged imperial stouts is seldom less than world class; while the Innovation series (★★★ to ★★★+) goes every which way, from saisons to smoked porters.

Erve Kots

Brouwhoes Lievelde
Het Hoofdkwartier van Frederik Hendrik
Eimersweg 4, 7137 HG Lievelde
T 0544 371691
www.ervekots.nl

Bottom-fermenting micro, more correctly known as Brouwhoes Lievelde, brewing in the Erve Kots open air museum since 1998. The museum shop, café and brewery can be accessed without tickets. Group tours by appointment. The focus is increasingly on their pilsener, other beers becoming rare. They also have a pub in nearby Groenlo.
YEAR-ROUND: highly competent flagship pilsener **Frederik Hendrik** (5.0%: ★★); and standard spiced white beer **Bokse Achterhoeks Witbier** (5.0%: ★★).
ALSO: Amber **Bokse** (5.0%) and blond **Stadsch Schemer** (6.0%) are scarce.

Fiddler

The Fiddler
Riviervismarkt 1, 2513 AM Den Haag
T 070 365 1955
www.fiddler.nl

City centre brewpub, originally opened in 1996 as the Firkin & Fiddler, closing in 2007 but re-emerging in 2012. Brews in 10-hl kit. The only Dutch brewery to make UK-style cask-conditioned ales as its regular range. Only available in-house.
YEAR-ROUND: lightly bitter pale ale **Albino Fox** (4.5%: ★★); not-very-bitter bitter **Lion's Den** (4.5%: ★★); easy-drinking red ale **Redhead** (5.6%: ★★); smooth stout **Black Mamba** (6.0%: ★★+); token 'Dutch' blond **Fuzzy Bear** (6.0%: ★★); and UK-style **Sea Lion's IPA** (6.2%: ★★+).
SEASONAL: delicious **Howling Wolf** (6.5%: ★★+) is an 'English bock'.

Fontein

Brouwerij De Fontein
Ondergenhouseweg 15, 6171 GW Stein
T 046 426 2858
www.brouwerijdefontein.nl

Semi-rural south Limburg farm brewery, founded in 2006, with a 5-hl installation. Besides their own range they brew to order for numerous bars and restaurants, and rent out excess capacity to others. Beers are sold in-house and in beer shops elsewhere. Quality is generally good. Group tours by appointment.

YEAR-ROUND: marshmallow-tinged **Steinder Wit** (4.9%: ★★); amber **Paladijn** (5%: ★★+) with homegrown lemon balm; safe **Limburgs Blond** (5.9%: ★★); chocolaty **Limburgs Dubbel** (6.4%: ★★); fruity amber **Cherubijn** (7.5%: ★★+) with lychee hints; straw-coloured citrussy **Sakamai** (8.4%: ★★), from Japanese sake rice; lightly fruity **Limburgs Tripel** (9.0%: ★★+); and amber barley wine **Ambrozijn** (10%: ★★), honeyed by their own bees.

SEASONAL: standard **Meibock** (6.5%: ★★); gently floral summer blond **Euleteul Zomer** (5.1%: ★★+) contains elderflowers; slightly thin autumn **Herfstbock** (6.5%: ★★); and golden amber **Euleteul Winter** (8.5%: ★★), with elderberry.

ALSO: commissioned beers include blackberry-flavoured **Inspirator** (6.3%), plus raspberry and linden blossom **Inspirator Zomerblond** (5.5%) for Heeze's

Kapellerput Hotel; **Vlaamsche Reus Blond** (6.1%) for the Wageningen café; and **Witte Jan** (5.2%) for the Centrum in Horst, among many others.

Friese

De Friese Bierbrouwerij
Snekerstraat 43, 8701 XC Bolsward
T 0515 577449
www.bierbrouwerij-usheit.nl

Friesland's first modern brewery, founded in 1985 in the hamlet of Uitwellingerga. It moved to its current site, a former food and drink technology college, in 1995. Their **Us Heit** beers are brewed in a 20-hl installation and they have their own maltings and whisky distillery. Pre-booked tours Th-Sa at 16.00.

YEAR-ROUND: malty **Twels Pilsener** (5.0%: ★★); dark-brown thirst quencher **Twels Speciaal** (5.0%: ★★); unsubtle amber **Buorren Bier** (6.0%: ★★); rounded wheat **Dubbel Tarwe Bier** (8.0%: ★★+); and **Elfstedenbier** (8.0%: ★★+), a warming bittersweet brown ale for when it's Frisian outside.

SEASONAL: sweetish autumnal **Twels Bokbier** (6.0%: ★★); and balanced amber winter **Kerstbier** (7.5%: ★★+).

ALSO: there is an alcohol-free beer, Nuchtere Heit; and **Dom Blondje** (6.5%: ★★), which we think is commissioned by Bert's Bierhuis of Utrecht.

Fontein, south Limburg farm brewery

Goeye Goet

Brouwerij 't Goeye Goet
Schelmseweg 89, 6816 SJ Arnhem
T 026 357 6111
www.openluchtmuseum.nl

Founded in 2007 in the impressive National Open Air Museum and based in an incongruously modern glass building next to a preserved 18th-century brewhouse. A visit is included with a museum ticket. Draught **'t Goeye Goet** beers are served at the Viersprong café, opposite. Their 75cl stone-effect bottles are sold at the brewery, the museum shop, and in Arnhem off licences.
YEAR-ROUND: refreshingly balanced **Pilsener** (5.0%: ★★+); simple spiced **Witbier** (5%: ★★); copper-brown sweet 'n' sour **Dubbel** (7.0%: ★★); and the **Tripel** (9.0%: ★★), which is too sweet and banana-heavy.
SEASONAL: standard spring **Lentebier** (6.5%: ★★); delicate golden summer **Oogstbier** (6.0%: ★★); sweetish autumn Herfstbock (6.5%: ★★); and warming, slightly treacly, black **Winterbier** (8.0%: ★★+).

Graaf van Heum
brewery, Gelde

Graaf van Heumen

Bierbrouwerij Graaf van Heumen
Rijksweg 232, 6582 AB Heumen
T 024 358 5960
www.graafvanheumen.nl

This out-of-town Gelderland brewery has had three lives since 1814. The first, Bergzicht, went bankrupt in 1920. The second, De Raaf, was among the first new wave start-ups in 1983, was expanded by big money in 1991 and closed by 1993. The current incarnation is a 2009 brewpub that brews most Sundays in distinctive 5-hl glass kettles in the main bar. The beers are sold in-house and are sometimes available bottled to take away.
YEAR-ROUND: dryish **Weizen** (5.0%: ★★) has faint toasted walnut hints; dark-brown **Donker** (5.2%: ★★); apricot-tinted grassy **Blond** (5.3%: ★★); and refreshing golden **Tripel** (7.6%: ★★+).
SEASONAL: average **Meibock** (6.7%: ★★); dry-hopped **Superieur** (6.4%: ★★+), also brewed in spring; caramel-heavy **Herfstbock** (6.4%: ★★); and dry copper-amber **Winterbier** (6.7%: ★★).

Groese Zwaluw

Museale Ambachtelijke Brouwerij De Groese
Zwaluw, Slijkstraat 12, 4503 BC Groede
T 0117 372414
www.het-vlaemsche-erfgoed.nl

The entire street housing this tiny Zeeuws-
Vlaanderen village brewery is a heritage
museum. Established in 2008 and staffed by
volunteers, they brew roughly four times a
year. Beers are sold in the museum shop,
and occasionally in the café across the street.
Each batch is different, so listings are
pointless, save to say that those we have
tried have been pretty competent (★★ > ★★+).

Grolsch (SAB Miller) –
see global beer companies

Gulpener

Gulpener Bierbrouwerij
Rijksweg 16, 6271 AE Gulpen
T 043 450 7575
www.gulpener.nl

Established family-run South Limburg
brewery, and one of the country's oldest,
founded in 1825. Defiantly independent,
despite SAB Miller owning a chunk, it lays
claim to be Europe's only sizeable brewer
fermenting 'all three' ways: top, bottom and
spontaneous – the last thanks to star-turn
Mestreechs Aajt. Otherwise its beers
miss a trick by staying doggedly
mainstream. Pre-booked tours start
from the Gulpener Bierhuys next door.
YEAR-ROUND: lovely, quaffable
sweet/sour wood-aged **Mestreechs
Aajt** (3.5%: ★★★), now on tap in
Gulpen and Maastricht; malty, sugary
Oud Bruin (3.0%: ★+); Oud Bruin and
Pilsener blend **Sjoes** (4.0%: ★+),
highlighting the worst of both; distinctly
average **Pilsener** (5.0%: ★+); crisper, better-
balanced **Chateau Neubourg** (5.0%: ★★);
organic, unpasteurised **Ur-Pilsener** (5.0%:
★★); classy dryish white beer **Korenwolf**
(5.0%: ★★+); solidly eco
Ur-Amber (5.3%: ★★); competent **Ur-Weizen**
(5.3%: ★★); shallow **Gerardus Wittems
Kloosterbier Blond** (6.0%: ★★); its better,
drier-edged sister **Dubbel** (7.0%: ★★); fruity
amber **Puurzaam** (6.5%: ★★) in 75cl bottles;
and sadly unchallenging amber lager **Dort**
(7.0%: ★★).
SEASONAL: sweetish malty spring **Lente
Bock** (6.5%: ★★); thinnish sweet autumnal
Herfstbock (6.5%: ★+); slightly better year-
old bock **Jaarling** (6.5%: ★★); and overly
sweet **WinterVrund** (8.5%: ★+), which is
better on tap (> ★★).
ALSO: **Korenwolf Rosé** (3.5%: ★) is the white
beer ruined by something pink and perfumed.

Gulzige Gans

De Gulzige Gans
Van Heutszsingel 90, 7741 EW Coevorden
T 0524 518772
www.degulzigegans.nl

The Greedy Goose is a commercial home
brewery in Drenthe, established in 2008,
where a husband and wife team make
weekly 100-l batches. Despite the low

output, quality is surprisingly high and their beers are found in numerous local shops and bars. Visits by appointment.

YEAR-ROUND: dry, malty, dark amber **Coevorder Vestingbier** (6.5%: ★★); gentle blond **Snaterwater** (6.5%: ★★); fruity bitter wheat ale **Spring in 't Veld** (7.0%: ★★+), with linden blossom and coriander; IPA **Vreemde Eend** (7.0%: ★★+) has restrained bitterness and grapefruit hops; golden-amber **Kasteelheer** (8.5%: ★★+) balances a fruity edge with a bitter finish; beefy tripel **Waggel** (9.0%: ★★+); rich and darkly moreish barley wine **Kachel** (10.0%: ★★+); and **Rook in de Kachel** (10.0%: ★★★), which adds smoke to the former.

SEASONAL: marshmallow-tinged autumn **Bokkige Bok** (7.0%: ★★).

Halve Maan

Bierbrouwerij De Halve Maan
Absdaalseweg 2, 4561 GG Hulst
T 0114 310660
www.halvemaan.com

Southern Zeeland brewery founded in 1991. Although there is brewing kit it is not used much, with most beers made elsewhere – possibly Belgium. They claim to brew still so we have given their beers the benefit of the doubt. For now. The lovely tasting room, a former station, is only open for groups. Visits by appointment.

YEAR-ROUND: unpleasantly sweet **Java Kriek** (3.5%: ★), like liquidised Black Forest gâteau; tedious pilsener **Java Premium** (5.0%: ★+); reasonable, spiced white beer **Zeeuwsche Witte** (5.0%: ★★); sweetish caramelly **Dubbele Java** (6.5%: ★+); characterless, allegedly vanilla-honeyed amber **Lazarus** (6.5%: ★+); overwhemingly sweet, spiced brown **Grof Geschut** (8.0%: ★+); and citrussy, unnecessarily restrained **Java Tripel** (8.0%: ★★).

SEASONAL: malty dubbelbock **Zondebok** (8.0%: ★★).

Heerlijkheid

Brouwerij de Heerlijkheid
Kerkbuurt 56, 3354 XK Papendrecht
T 078 644 0599
www.brouwerijdeheerlijkheid.nl

Nanobrewery and farm shop opened in 2011, across the river from Dordrecht. The 16th-century building once housed the lords of Papendrecht. Brews 300-litre batches, two or three times a month, surprisingly well. Bottled beers are sold in the shop, at one off licence in town and rarely elsewhere. Tours by appointment.

YEAR-ROUND: refreshingly fruity amber **Steegtbier** (4.2%: ★★); dry-hopped, hop-forward blond **Dijkbier** (4.8%: ★★+); and multigrained blond **Boezembier** (4.9%: ★★+), sweetened with apple and pear juice, and spiced with coriander and elderflower.

SEASONAL: **Broertje Bok** comes as bittersweet **Lentebock** (5.9%: ★★); and rounded, bitter chocolate, autumnal **Bock** (6.5%: ★★+), with chestnut hints.

Heineken – *see global companies*

Hemel

Stadsbrouwerij de Hemel
Franseplaats 1, 6511 VS Nijmegen
T 024 360 6167
www.brouwerijdehemel.nl

The country's oldest brewpub, founded in 1983 and always one of the best, expanding to serve many cafés in Nijmegen and beyond. Located in the Commanderie van Sint Jan, a 12th-century cloister, the brewhouse and a museum are in cellars below the café. Individual visits Sa&Su 13.00–17.00; groups on request. They also make vinegar and mustard, and have a distillery.

YEAR-ROUND: grassy, gently bitter top-fermented blond **Luna** (5.0%: ★★); well-rounded spiced wheat **Serafijn** (5.0%: ★★);

malty-nosed amber **Godelief** (5.0%: ★★), lacking the killer punch; fruity bitter tripel **Helse Engel** (8.0%: ★★+); and dangerously drinkable warming **Nieuw Ligt** (10.0%: ★★★), a amber barley wine that becomes sublime in its cellar-aged version, **Grand Cru** (12.0%: ★★★+).
SEASONAL: fruity summer blond **Mariken** (6.5%: ★★); smoky, fruity autumnal **Eikenbock** (6.5%: ★★+), matured in oak; lightly smoked, winter amber **Moenen** (6.5%: ★★+).
ALSO: quaffable spiced blond **Botterik** (6.2%: ★★), commissioned to sell in local cafés and elsewhere; tripel **Rooie Tiep Top** (8.0%: ★★+), for the Blaauwe Hand in Nijmegen; and **Hanenbeek** (10.0%) a beer commissioned for the village of Beek, brewed with their water.

Hertog Jan (AB InBev) –
see global beer companies

Hettinga
Zwolse Stadsbrouwerij Hettinga Bier
Esdoornstraat 3, 8021 WB Zwolle
T 038 466 2902
www.hettingabier.nl

Founded in 2008 at Zwolle in Overijssel, moving in 2013 to a new 5-hl capacity location, in a business complex north of the city centre. A tasting room may follow. The **Hettinga Bier** brands are solidly reliable, and increasingly available. Group visits by appointment.
YEAR-ROUND: top-fermented **Pils** (5.0%: ★★); spiced wheat **IJsselwit** (5.5%: ★★); its unspiced cousin **Zachte IJssel Weizen** (5.5%: ★★); competent amber **Agnietenbier** (5.5%: ★★); moreish malty and cocoa-tinged **Porter Robuust** (6.8%: ★★+); non-sweet **Hanze Dubbel** (7.0%: ★★); and pleasant but over-sweet **Hanze Tripel** (9.0%: ★★).
SEASONAL: bitter, coffee-tinged autumnal **Zwolse Bok** (6.5%: ★★+).

Heusden
Bier Brouwerij Heusden
Burchtplein 6, 5256 EA Heusden
T 0416 660039
www.kareltje.info

Established in 2002 as a brewpub occupying an attractive building in a picturesque town on the North Brabant bank of the Maas. Brewing in 175-litre batches may be waning. The beers are only sold in-house and take the same name as the owner's dogs, who are **Kareltje** 1 and 2. The brewpub also distills a range of liqueurs.
YEAR-ROUND: quaffable if unexciting **Blond** (5.0%: ★★); and clean-tasting spiced **Wit** (5.0%: ★★).
ALSO: **Kanjer** (6.0%) and **Amber** (6.0%) may have disappeared.

Hopper
Brouwerij D'n Hopper
Vaartstraat 55, 5171 JH Kaatsheuvel
T 043 450 3967
www.denhopper.com

Brabant-based husband-and-wife brewing team, established in 1996, and now using a 120-litre installation. Some larger runs are brewed at Drie Horne. Beers are sold in paper-wrapped 37.5cl bottles. Regulars at local festivals but otherwise hard to come by. The brand names are made by plonking a different word in the phrase **N'n** *Plonk* **Hopper**. Great, eh?
YEAR-ROUND: decent lightweight **Stoute** (5.0%: ★★); citrussy golden blond **Oer** (6.0%: ★★); drinkable wheat ale **Albin'** (6.0%: ★★); herbal hoppy pale ale **Bepruuvde** (6.4%: ★★); fruity **Blonde** (6.7%: ★★); oaked blond **Ge-Eikte** (7.6%: ★★); hoppy honeyed tripel **Gezegende** (7.7%: ★★); and amber barley wine **Klassieke** (9.0%: ★★).
ALSO: dubiously packaged **N'n Lekkele Hoppel** (6.5%: ★★) contains rice, Chinese yeast and 5-spice powder, ending refreshing with vague wafts of takeaway.

IJ

Brouwerij 't IJ
Funenkade 7, 1018 AL Amsterdam
T 020 622 8325
www.brouwerijhetij.nl

A pioneer of the Dutch beer revival, founded in 1985 in an old bath house with a popular brewery tap out front. In 2013 a second brewery opened at Zeeburgerpad 55, capable of a 40-hl brew run, trebling capacity. After decades of unpredictability, quality is finally on a roll, prompting a new series of interesting one-offs (often ★★★), identifiable by their black and white labels. All beers are organic and most are now widely available. Tours Fr-Su at 15.30 (in English) and 16.00 (in Dutch).

YEAR-ROUND: top-fermented **Plzen** (5.0%: ★★); bittersweet date and raisin tinted dubbel **Natte** (6.5%: ★★); lightly spiced white beer **IJwit** (7.0%: ★★); copper-brown **IPA** (7.0%: ★★+); slightly sharp-edged tripel **Zatte** (8.0%: ★★); chocolate-tinted barley wine **Struis** (9.0%: ★★+); and rich dark amber **Columbus** (9.0%: ★★+).

SEASONAL: standard blond meibock **PaasIJ** (7.0%: ★★); coffee-tinged autumn **IJbok** (6.5%: ★★); and dry, rounded amber winter **IJndejaars** (9.0%: ★★+).
ALSO: slightly smoky amber **Speciale Vlo** (7.0%: ★★) is commissioned by the Bierkoning in Amsterdam. One of the best one-offs was the wonderfully hoppy **IPA Ciel Bleu** (7.0%: ★★★), brewed for the Michelin-starred Amsterdam restaurant of that name, but seen elsewhere.

Jopen

Jopen Bier
Gedempte Voldersgracht 2, 2011 WD Haarlem
T 023 533 4114
www.jopen.nl

Although the company was established in 1994, brewing only returned to Haarlem in 2010 with the opening of the 20-hl capacity Jopenkerk, a brewpub in a decommissioned church. A new off-site location with a bottling line, second brewing installation and additional lagering tanks will move all production back to the city and increase output. The beers are getting broader recognition internationally and are now widely available across the country and increasingly in the export trade.

YEAR-ROUND: refreshing golden blond **Gerstebier** (4.5%: ★★); citrussy spiced white beer **Adriaan** (5%: ★★); intensely hoppy rye IPA, the almost classic **Jacobus RPA** (5.3%: ★★★); fruity bitter dunkelweizen **Malle Babbe** (5.5%: ★★); easy drinking **Extra Stout** (5.5%: ★★); flowery hoppy IPA **Mooie Nel** (6.5%: ★★+), in numbered batches; improving dry, hoppy blond **Hoppen** (6.8%: ★★+); strong brown original **Koyt** (8.0%: ★★), without its former sheen; bitter and characterful **Trinitas Tripel** (9.0%: ★★★); and fruity hoppy barley wine **Ongelovige Thomas** (10.0%: ★★★).
SEASONAL: improving spring **Lentebier** (7.0%: ★★+) has fruity tones and honey hints; multigrained autumnal **4-granen Bokbier** (6.5%: ★★★) is a class standout; simpler, but still above-average bock **Johannieter** (6.5%:

★★+); and the annually brewed barley wine Meesterstuk (10.0%: ★★+).
ALSO: golden amber **Mashing Pumpkins** (9.0%: ★★★) is a spiced pumpkin ale with 5 malts, brewed with SNAB.

Kaapse

Kaapse Brouwers
Katendrecht – Fenixloods, Rotterdam
T 010 414 6050
www.facebook.com/Kaapsebrouwers

New brewery set up in 2013 with the help of De Molen, in a warehouse in the Katendrecht district in the south of Rotterdam. One of the brewers, Aren Reijngoud, also runs the Boudewijn and Reijngoud cafés. A tasting room and beer store is expected in due course. One to watch.
YEAR-ROUND: lychee-laced American bitter **Karel** (4.9%: ★★+); ginger-tinged saison **Harrie** (5.6%: ★★+); black rye IPA **Bea** (6.0%: ★★+); fruity IPA **Carrie** (6.2%: ★★+); and too-sweet oatmeal stout **Gozer** (9.8%: ★★).

Kasparus

Bierbrouwerij Kasparus
Eggestraat 14, 8308 AB Nagele
T 0527 240877
www.kasparus.nl

Flevoland village brewery, founded 1994. Its bijou 30-litre copper kettle is for show – most brewing is done in 250-litre batches in the kitchen. They make a bewildering range, usually only available from the brewery and of variable quality. Lots of stuff with fruit in it. They also make beer liqueur.
YEAR-ROUND: crisp, top-fermented blond **Polder Pilsener** (5.0%: ★★); sharp, tangy, raspberry **Frambosia** (5.0%: ★★); passable blond **Schokkers Lust** (5.0%: ★★); and brawny dubbel **Schokkers Last** (8.5%: ★★).
ALSO: we have tried a dozen or more irregulars, some OK, others directionless and a few hiding horrors between fruit underlays and spice blankets; though we did like the darkly warming **Winter Vast** (8.0%: ★★+), with faint cherry hints.

Kemphaan

Brouwerij de Kemphaan
Kemphaanpad 8, 1358 AC Almere
T 036 532 3844
www.brouwerijdekemphaan.nl

It seems wrong that pan-flat Flevoland's brewers sometimes have to cling onto a cliff. Yet the 'Ruff' brewery (as in bird, not medieval fashion accessory), run by a local beer guild, has had to do that, first arriving in 2002 at a location that closed in 2004; re-opening in 2006 in a building shared with a restaurant, which promptly closed, throwing its future into doubt. When the restaurant re-opened under new management in 2012 that they were forced to relocate into an adjacent farm shop. They brew in 200-litre batches and have vague plans for a tasting room.
YEAR-ROUND: spiced wheat **Wit** (5.0%: ★★); refreshing lightweight **Blond** (5.5%: ★★); and overly sweet golden **Tripel** (8.5%: ★★).

Kievit

Trappistenbrouwerij De Kievit
Rucphenseweg 38, 4882 KC Zundert
www.zunderttrappist.nl

The Netherlands' second authentic Trappist
brewery, in the Maria Toevlucht retreat,
close to the Belgian border south of Breda.
It achieved its accolade of Authentic Trappist
Product (ATP) late in 2013, ensuring
commercial production as the world's ninth
or tenth official Trappist brewery, an American
abbey getting the nod on the same day.
No visits and no tasting room thus far.
YEAR-ROUND: the first brew is sweetish,
polished copper-amber **Zundert** (8%: ★★+),
showing great promise if not yet a bona fide
Trappist classic

Klein Duimpje

Bierbrouwerij Klein Duimpje
Hyacintenlaan 2a, 2182 DE Hillegom
T 0252 531186
www.kleinduimpje.nl

Klein Duimpje, or 'Tom Thumb' was founded
in 1996, and got its own premises in 2012,
somewhere in the the South Holland
bulbfields. Currently they brew in 5-hl
batches but should expand to 10-hl in 2014,
which we hope will stem their desire to
produce an absurdly broad range of beers
that are sometimes very good, more often
OK and occasionally not. Outsourcing to
Proef in Belgium should change when they
expand their lagering capacity. They are a
good crew, but need to shrink the range
and realise that less can indeed be more.
Meanwhile, a brewery tap is open weekends.
YEAR-ROUND: decently roasted bitter
Schwarz Blackbird (4.6%: ★★+); dryish blond
Gerstebier (4.9%: ★★); smoky, accomplished
Rauch Lager (5.1%: ★★+); so-so **Hillegoms
Tarwebier** (5.5%: ★★); dark-brown **Porter**
(5.5%: ★★+), with roasted edges rounded by
fruitiness; **Hazelnoot Porter** (5.5%: ★★+),
upped by hazelnuts; blackcurranty **Hillegoms
Kuyt** (6.0%: ★★); bittersweet amber **Dark Ale**

(6.0%: ★★); fruity, hoppy **American Pale Ale**
(6.5%: ★★+); a none too hot black IPA with rye,
BRIPA (6.5%: ★★); restrained **Smokey Porter**
(7.0%: ★★+); boring wheaty **Bollenstreek
Ale** (7.0%: ★★); revised **ZevenMijlsLaarzen**
(7.0%: ★★), now a golden IPA; smoky **Rauch
Weizen** (7.5%: ★★); a run-of-the mill **Dubbel**
(7.5%: ★★); a tripel **Blauwe Tram** (7.5%: ★★);
stronger tripel with myrtle **Gagel Tripel**
(8.5%: ★★); Christmas cake Scotch ale
Hillegomse Hangkous (8.5%: ★★);
longstanding but too-sweet **Erik de Noorman**
(9.0%: ★★); all-singing **Extreme Baltic
Coffee Choco Mocca Porter** (9.0%: ★★+);
all-dancing **Imperial Russian Stout** (10.5%:
★★+); and treacly but bitter barley wine
Elfeneenhalf (11.5%: ★★).
SEASONAL: honey-scented spring **Tulpenbok**
(7.0%: ★★); dry autumnal **Slobberbok** (7.2%:
★★); and bitterish Christmas amber
Kerstbier (8.5%: ★★).
ALSO: we know of two ex-beers threatened
with revival and two future ones planned.
Enough!! Surely! The Bierhistorie Delft
society commissions unhopped **Gruytbier**
(5.5%: ★★) and there are others like thinnish,
coffee'd **Jubilator Stout** (5.5%: ★★); juniper-
laced amber **Luyks Bier** (7.0%: ★★); middle-
of-the road **Mueselare** (7.5%: ★★); gently
hopped amber **Dubbel Gerste Bier** (7.5%:
★★+); and herbal winter **Kuyte Bier** (8.5%: ★★).

Koelschip

Bierbrouwerij 't Koelschip
Grace Kellystraat 21, 1325 HC Almere
T 036 537 5503
www.brouwerijhetkoelschip.nl

Flevoland nanobrewers since 1995, though
we suspect a few beers come from Sint
Servattumus or elsewhere. Some are of
dubious quality. They also distil spirits and
have made super-strength 'drinks' as part of
a game to create the world's strongest beer.
Our understanding of the EU rules is that
spiked and freeze-distilled drinks cannot
legally be designated as beer. Maybe better
to concentrate on the basics?

YEAR-ROUND: malty **Almere Blond** (5.0%: ★★); slightly sharp smoked **Rookbier** (5.0%: ★★); fruity-sour **Skyline Amber** (5.5%: ★+); hoppy amber lager **Hopfazupfa** (5.5%: ★★); sweet **Keltisch Blond** (6.9%: ★+); plain odd amber **IJsbier** (8.5%: ★+); and barley wine **Explosie** (13.9%: ★★), like a carbonated port. *SEASONAL:* off-balance gingered autumnal **Geitenbokbier** (8.5%: ★+) needs help.

Kollenburg

Stadsbrouwerij van Kollenburg
Korenbrugstraat 5-7, 5211 EG 's-Hertogenbosch
T 073 613 6915
www.stadsbrouwerijvankollenburg.nl

Nanobrewery founded in 1999 beside the Le Duc brewery tap. A 5-hl batch is brewed each week. Plagued with inconsistency and quality issues for years, but saved by a new brewer who cleaned it up and radically redesigned recipes. The 't Kolleke beers that once struck fear into our hearts can now be embraced.
YEAR-ROUND: improving dry, spiced wheat **Jonge Jan** (5.5%: ★★); dunkelweizen **Kleine Jan** (5.5%: ★★); dry fruity dubbel **Oude Jan** (5.5%: ★★); blond **Ome Jan** (6.5%: ★★) has become drier and more bitter; and golden-blond **Tripel** (7.5%: ★★) has lost its flaws.
SEASONAL: autumnal **Bock** (6.2%: ★★+) has oddly pleasant hints of coffee meringue; and annually brewed IPA **Jubileum** (6.8%: ★★+) is a rising star.

Koningshoeven

Bierbrouwerij De Koningshoeven
Eindhovenseweg 3, 5056 RP Berkel-Enschot
T 013 535 8147
www.latrappe.nl

What was for many years the Netherlands' first and only Trappist brewery was founded in 1884 at Schaapskooi Abbey on the outskirts of Tilburg. By 1970 it was producing only one beer, billed in those days as Abdij Pilsener, though it was conceivably a dry blond ale. With the revival of interest in the more traditional dubbel and tripel ales of the abbey brewery at Westmalle in Belgium, a brown dubbel and golden- or orange-blond tripel re-appeared under a variety of names including Tilburgs, Abdij Koningshoeven, Trappist Koningshoeven and eventually La Trappe. Ownership of the brewery and its brands flip-flopped between God and Mammon, as companies took ownership of the brewhouse, the production methods, the barnds and the distribution. Following

Schaapskooi Abbey

Koperen Kat

Delftse Stadsbrouwerij De Koperen Kat
Schieweg 15 H, 2627 AN Delft
T 06 4212 3398
www.koperenkat.nl

The Copper Cat, founded in 2011, is now located on an industrial estate south of Delft. They brew using a 300-litre installation bought from the former Vallei brewery of Leusden, near Amersfoort. A brewery tap is open weekends. Tours by arrangement. Beers are solid, and widely available in Delft and beyond.

YEAR-ROUND: malty bitter 'pils' **015** (4.0%: ★★); pleasingly bitter **Blonde Anouk** (5.0%: ★★+); lightly hopped amber **Princebier** (5.7%: ★★); and **Balthasar** (8.0%: ★★), a dry fruity tripel with a smoky side.

SEASONAL: flowery spring **Lentebock** (6.5%: ★★); dryish summer honeyed wheat ale Lindebier (6.5%: ★★+); autumnal **Herfstbock** (6.0%: ★★); and dark fruity winter ale, beautifully designated **Brrr...** (6.3%: ★★).

its purchase by Bavaria (see page 41) in 1998, it was stripped briefly of its Authentic Trappist status. However, this was reinstated after significant renegotiations, which put the Trappist Order technically back in overall charge of decisions about the production of any Trappist beers from a brewhouse that remains within the walls of the abbey. That said, Bavaria's top-fermented beers appear to be made here and a few other brewers have been seen brewing here. There have also been significant advances in the beer range in recent years, regardless of who has been responsible. Beers are currently sold as **La Trappe**. Pre-booked tours happen Fr-Su year round and daily Apr-Oct.

YEAR-ROUND: malty organic not-a-kölsch **Puur** (4.7%: ★★); citrussy wheat Witte Trappist (5.5%: ★★); oddly uninspiring **Blond** (6.5%: ★★); disappointing by Trappist standards **Dubbel** (7.0%: ★★); enjoyably dry amber **Isid'or** (7.5%: ★★+); golden **Tripel** (8.0%: ★★+) with bitter orange hints; and amber barley wine **Quadrupel** (10.0%: ★★+), which has warming alcohol, and gains massive complexity in its **Oak Aged** version (10%: ★★★+). The latter can improve to world class (★★★★) with cellaring.

SEASONAL: decent, if slightly thin **Bockbier** (7.0%: ★★).

ALSO: we are not sure who commissions sweet, dull **Tilburg Dutch Brown Ale** (5.0%: ★+) or **Kroon Pils** (5.0%: ★★), which is for its former home village of Oirschot.

Kromme Jat

Stadsbrouwerij De Kromme Jat
Sontweg 26, 9723 AT Groningen
T 06 5470 8537
www.krommejat.nl

Groningen province's only real brewery, founded in 2011. They brew in 200-litre kettles on an industrial area east of the city centre. The beers are reliable, and appear under the oddly multilingual brand **Golden Raand**. Easily obtained locally, but less common further afield. No visits.
YEAR-ROUND: satisfyingly dry **Amber** (6.0%: ★★+); faintly straw-tinted **Blond** (7.0%: ★★); bittersweet warming **Tripel** (8.0%: ★★); and rounded, fruity **Pagode** (9.5%: ★★+), brewed with whisky malt and lagered in Islay barrels, yet almost smokeless.
SEASONAL: rich autumnal **Ramskop Bock** (6.0%: ★★).

Kuipertje

Brouwerij 't Kuipertje
Appeldijk 18, 4161 BH Heukelum
T 0345 611839
www.hetkuipertje.nl

Hard-to-find brewery on the northwest outskirts of a tiny Gelderland village. This one-man concern was founded by Frits Kuiper in 1987 and is now run by his son Henk. It remains wilfully uncommercial, an approach we love. The brewery tap, open on Saturdays, is just about the only reliable place to try the beers, though they are occasionally seen at festivals and in shops.
YEAR-ROUND: rounded golden **Blondie** (6.5%: ★★); the subtly banana-dabbed **Dunkelweizen** (6.5%: ★★); and bittersweet amber winter barley wine **Nachtvorst** (10.0%: ★★).

Leckere

Brouwerij De Leckere
Molensteyn 3 D, 3454 PT Utrecht (De Meern)
T 030 231 2343
www.deleckere.nl

Organic brewer founded in an Utrecht suburb in 1997. Between themselves and Budel every health-food shop in the country is covered. Quality has varied over the years but newer arrivals show more pizzazz – a trend we hope will continue. Excess capacity is rented out to other brewers.
YEAR-ROUND: malty **Premium Organic Pilsener** (5.0%: ★+); standardly spiced white beer **Witte Vrouwen** (5.0%: ★★); dark amber **Willibrord** (5.0%: ★★); blond, dry-bitter **Gulden Craen** (5.2%: ★★); nicely rounded dubbel **Crom Hout** (6.5%: ★★+); pleasingly hoppy **IBA** (6.7%: ★★+), termed 'International Blond Ale'; accomplished hop-forward **IPA** (7.5%: ★★+); sweetish golden tripel **Paulus** (7.5%: ★★); too-sweet tripel **Razende Swaen** (8.0%: ★★); and malty brown barley wine **Blauwe Bijl** (10.0%: ★★).
SEASONAL: sweetish dubbelbock **Rode Toren** (8.5%: ★★); and heavy, sweet, alcoholic, copper barley wine **Winterbier** (10.0%: ★★+) with bold fruity hops.

Leidsch

Leidsch Bier
Flevodwarsweg 35a, 2318 BX Leiden
T None
www.leidschbier.nl

One-man operation founded in 2004 by brewer Jan-Willem Fukkink, who expanded his 90-litre facility in Leiden to 300-litre in 2013. Larger runs of the Aaipiejee and Blond are still outsourced to Proef in Belgium. The beers are good, sometimes great, but sell out quickly. Visits by appointment.
YEAR-ROUND: competent dry, bitter **Blond** (6.5%: ★★); lovely rounded hoppy **Aaipiejee**

(6.4%: ★★★), as an IPA should be; refreshing, slightly bitter **Weizen** (5.6%: ★★); above-average **Kuit** (6.0%: ★★+); and highly accomplished chocolaty dark **Morsporter** (6.1%: ★★★).
SEASONAL: rich and complex fruity **Pumpkin Raisin Bock** (7.1%: ★★+); and **Kerstbomenbier** (6.3%: ★★+), with added star anise and floral pine needles, like a mince pie placed in a blender with a Christmas tree.

Lindeboom

Lindeboom Bierbrouwerij
Engelmanstraat 52–54, 6086 BD Neer
T 0475 592900
www.lindeboom.nl

One of the country's five longer-running and larger independents, founded in 1870 on the outskirts of a small Limburg village, close to the Maas river. As with the other four (Alfa, Bavaria, Budel & Gulpen), while they appear happy to start pushing out into a wide stable of beers with different brandings, the willingness to take a risk and make assertive modern styles is simply not there yet. If they decided to go into making a range of bolder off-lager styles we know they would make a killing. As for now, no tours or exploration.
YEAR-ROUND: too-sweet, too-malty **Oud Bruin** (3.8%: ★+); anaemic, oddly sweet **Pilsener** (5.0%: ★+); copper-amber Dusseldorf-isch altbier **Venloosch Alt** (5.0%: ★★); matching run-of-the-mill spiced **Wit** (5.0%: ★★); and **Gouverneur** 'abbey' beer brands, blond, grassy and fruity **Speciale 140** (5.5%: ★★); up-market hooker (no flaws, no class) **Blonde** (6.5%: ★★); caramel and vanilla dubbel **Brune** (6.5%: ★★) with a bitter finish; and too-sweet **Triple** (8.2%: ★★).
SEASONAL: undistinguished seasonal **Herfstbock** (6.5%: ★★); and **Dubbelbock** (7.5%: ★★), which has the bare bones of character.

Maallust

Maallust
Hoofdweg 140, 9341 BL Veenhuizen
T 0592 388971
www.maallust.nl

Microbrewery founded in 2011 in the former grain mill of a Drenthe colony, to which the 19th-century poor were deported. Beer is brewed once or twice a week in an impressive 15-hl installation, is turning out solid and reliable and enjoying growing availability. The brewery tap keeps regular hours. Tours by arrangement.
YEAR-ROUND: refreshingly rounded **De Kolonist Weizen** (5.0%: ★★); impressively bitter, amber **De Vagebond Vienna** (5.0%: ★★+), a rare Dutch version of a Vienna lager; malty bittersweet **De Weldoener Blond** (6.5%: ★★); and grassy **Zware Jongen Tripel** (9.0%: ★★+), which evokes images of summer meadows.
SEASONAL: autumnal **Veldwachter Bock** (6.7%: ★★+) has porter-like cocoa hints; and winter barley wine **1818** (10.0%: ★★★) has aniseed and banana riding waves of warming alcohol.

Maar

Dorpsbrouwerij De Maar
Maar 2, 6454 AM Jabeek
T 046 442 5882
www.dorpsbrouwerijdemaar.nl

Farmhouse brewery, established in 2003 in a tiny Limburg village near the German border. Beers are sold in porcelain-stoppered bottles salvaged from the former Leeuw brewery in Valkenburg. A new taphouse has made the beers more available. Otherwise they are sold in a few local pubs, and through De Kruik off licence (Kerkstraat 330, Brunssum). Group tours on request.
YEAR-ROUND: pleasantly rounded **Jabeeks Blond** (5.0%: ★★); lightly bitter amber **Genhoots Genot** (6.5%: ★★); stronger and better amber **Bengelder Bengel** (7.5%: ★★+), beefed up by dates; and citrussy white-leaning **Witte Juffer** (7.5%: ★★), made with unmalted rye rather than wheat.
ALSO: decent tripel **De Blauwe Krokodil** (8.0%: ★★) is commissioned for De Kruik (above).

Marckensteijn

Marckensteijn
Markt 30, 4503 AH Groede
T 0117 371511
www.marckensteijn.com

Based at a café, the Drie Koningen, in a sleepy south Zeeland village. Re-opened in 2012 by two beer enthusiasts named Marc and Stijn (geddit?), after a predecessor closed in 2011. Thus far the beers have numbers for names and are sold mainly in the pub, on tap and in 75cl bottles.
YEAR-ROUND: standard blond **Nr 1** (6.5%: ★★); fruity-edged dubbel **Nr 2** (6.5%: ★★); competent but undemanding tripel **Nr 3** (7.2%: ★★); solid amber **Nr 4** (6%: ★★); and malty house pilsener **Nr 10** (5.5%: ★★).
ALSO: one-off brews are sold as **Verassingsbier** (surprise beer).

Markies

Brouwerij de Markies
Statenlaan 299, 5223 LG 's-Hertogenbosch
T None
www.brouwerijdemarkies.nl

North Brabant nanobrewery established in 2011, brewing up to 100 litres per session in 25-litre batches. Occasionally seen in local bars, shops and at festivals but generally to find. Their brand, **Ons Vergist** means both 'Our Mistake' and 'Our Fermented'.
YEAR-ROUND: thinnish **Is Stout!** (5.0%: ★★); dry, rounded tripel wheat beer **Signature** (7.0%: ★★); amber **Grand Cru** (9%: ★★); and strongly hoppy wheat beer **Hop d'r op en d'r Over** (8.0%: ★★+).
ALSO: a 6% IPA is on the way. **Met Lef** (7%) is made for Restaurant Lef in Helvoirt; and **Gebroken Wit** (5.5%) for Crème Coffee & Pastry in 's-Hertogenbosch.

Maximus

Brouwerij Maximus
Pratumplaats 2A, 3454 NA Utrecht (De Meern)
T 06 8345 0013
www.brouwerijmaximus.nl

Confident new brewery founded in 2011 by
Marcel Snater, the brewer of Snaterende
Arend. It moved in 2012 into a purpose-built
site with a tap room, in a western Utrecht
suburb. Brews about three times a fortnight
in 15-hl batches. Rising stars on the national
scene, with increasing availability and
splashes of brilliance. One to watch.
YEAR-ROUND: lemon-tinged bitter **Saison**
(5.0%: ★★); superbly hoppy world-class
American amber lager **Brutus** (6.0%: ★★★+);
immensely likeable IPA **Highhops** (6.0%:
★★★); floral, hoppy, bitter pale ale **Pandora**
(6.0%: ★★★); darkly bitter nicely constructed
Stout 6 (6.0%: ★★+); and **Stout 8** (8.0%:
★★★), its alluringly imperial big sister.
SEASONAL: malty, bitter **Lentebier** (6%: ★★);
and dry, unassuming **Bock 7** (7.0%: ★★).
ALSO: hoppy IPA **Kamikaze** (6%: ★★+) is
made for the België café in Utrecht.

Merciless

Merciless Brewing
Overtocht 43, 2411 BT Bodegraven
T 0172 610826
www.facebook.com/MercilessBrewing

Established in 2013, Merciless is the tearaway
alter ego of De Molen, whose brewer Menno
Olivier and business partner John Brus get to
play on the windmill brewery's transposed
5-hl installation. This allows them to make
limited editions of extreme brews, with
names and labels aimed thus far at heavy
metallers. Beers are sold through De Molen's
beer shop in numbered 75cl
bottles. Expect to be shocked and
challenged, not just by the names.
YEAR-ROUND: the range varies but
can include IPA light **Human**
Sacrifice (4.2%); sour red **Rotting**
Carcass (6.0%); strong wild ale
Teeth Grinding (10.0%); imperial
IPA cum barley wine **Fast Decay**
(10.6%: ★★★); richly warming
imperial stout **Painful Death**
(11.2%: ★★★+); freeze-distilled
oak-aged ice bock **Blood Stains**
(20.0%); and **Epitaph** (19.0%),
similar but with dry hopping.

Mieghelm

Huisbrouwerij Mieghelm
Venkant 17-19, 5271 SP Sint-Michielsgestel
T 06 5316 2986

North Brabant house-brewery, established
in 1994 and brewing in a 10-hl copper
installation. Despite the kit size, they only
brew a few times a year, so output is low.
Beers are rare outside the local area, though
the semi-retired brewer is a festival regular.
YEAR-ROUND: fruity amber **Abraham Licht**
(5.0%: ★★); simple wheat **Withelm** (5%: ★★);
and sweetish **Mieghelm Tripel** (7.0%: ★★).
SEASONAL: dark spring **Brabants Buikske**
(7.0%: ★★) has sharp currant notes;
autumnal **Bokkendonks Bokbier** (7.0%: ★★)
passes muster, but lacks body.

Molen

Brouwerij De Molen
Overtocht 43, 2411 BT Bodegraven
T 0172 610848
www.brouwerijdemolen.nl

One of the world's great new craft breweries. With its reputation as unassailable as it is well-earned, it is hard to believe that this amazing enterprise was only founded in 2004, and in a small Protestant town of sober tastes. Brewmaster Menno Olivier has become a standard bearer for the Dutch beer revolution. Originally brewed in the windmill-cum-restaurant just up the way, which is now a separate building but houses bastard child Merciless (above), demand forced a huge expansion into new facilities on a small industrial estate. They now brew in 50-hl batches and are already having to expand their space as fast as effort allows. Their beers are found nationwide and across the diaspora of high-end craft brew importers around the world. Besides the 22 regular **De Molen** brands below, they also produce a relentless stream of one-offs that space prevents us including. Visit during the Borefts Beer Festival in September or else make tours by arrangement.

YEAR-ROUND: intensely fruity hoppy amber **Amerikaans** (4.5%: ★★★); light and bitter thirst quencher **Op & Top** (4.5%: ★★★+); dry, citrussy and bitter pale ale **Citra Single Hop** (4.8%: ★★★); full-mouthed big-hitting porter **Hamer & Sikkel** (5.2%: ★★★); multigrain amber **Licht & Lustig** (5.2%: ★★+), with a grapefruit edge and strong bitterness; world-beating IPA **Vuur & Vlam** (6.2%: ★★★★); supremely sour oak-aged brown ale **Lief & Leed** (6.2%: ★★★+), to turn your face inside out; glorious quadruple-hopped rye IPA **Brood & Spelen** (7.1%: ★★★+); bittersweet dark amber 'English' ale **Molenbier** (7.5%: ★★+); darkly rich smoked **Bloed, Zweet & Tranen** (8.2%: ★★★); bitter, fruity, smoked and chillied **Rook & Vuur** (8.2%: ★★★); floral hoppy IPA **Amarillo** (9.2%: ★★★+); coriander-spiced tripel **Heen & Weer** (9.5%: ★★★); and golden barley wine **Bommen & Granaten** (15.2%: ★★★), laden with sugary sweetness and intense alcohol, like drinking a hand grenade.

ALSO: one-offs and occasionals include no fewer than eight imperial stouts & porters, such as **Spanning & Sensatie** (9.8%: ★★★) with sweetness and bitter coffee; rich, intense and chocolaty **Hemel & Aarde** (10.0%: ★★★+); **Hel & Verdoemenis** (10.2%: ★★★+) with smoky coffee; chocolate-laced **Mooi & Meedogenloos** (10.2%: ★★★+); beautifully understated, treacly **Rasputin** (10.4%: ★★★★), with cocoa; deeply moreish star turn, vanilla and coffee-tinged **Tsarina Esra** (11.0%: ★★★★), which gets even better in its oak-aged **Reserva** incarnation; absurdly brilliant **Kopi Loewak** (11.2%: ★★★★), which adds those coffee beans that have passed through a civet; and the relatively restrained **Mout & Mocca** (11.6%: ★★★).

Mommeriete

Brouwerij Mommeriete
De Oostermaat 66, 7783 BX Gramsbergen
T 0524 562511
www.mommeriete.nl

Founded in 2004 by husband-and-wife brewers Gert and Carina Kelder, Mommeriete moved its altogether quieter brilliance to its current canalside spot in an Overijssel village in 2008. Brewing takes place in copper kettles. Their beers are consistently very good, and appear increasingly in better beer shops, and at some festivals but are best appreciated at their idyllic brewery tap, a former lock-keeper's house, open daily, just up from the station. Tours by arrangement.
YEAR-ROUND: malty-edged **Klokhenne's Weizen** (5.0%: ★★); lightly hopped, rustic and entertaining **Blond** (6.0%: ★★★); fruity hoppy **IPA** (7.0%: ★★★); bittersweet honeyed **Scheerse Tripel** (9.0%: ★★+); voluptuous barley wine **Vrouwe van Gramsbergh** (9.5%: ★★★), with alcoholic toffee notes and a bitter backtaste; and moreish, smoky barley wine **Heer van Gramsbergen** (11.0%: ★★★), the male of the species.
SEASONAL: delightful, hoppy, bitter and complex **Meibock** (7.0%: ★★★); rich, smoky and fruity autumnal **Rookbock** (6.7%: ★★+); full-bodied, dry **Gramsberger Dubbelbock** (7.5%: ★★+); and darkly warming **Winterbier** (8.5%: ★★★), with some chestnut.

Naeckte Brouwers

De Naeckte Brouwers
Weverij 5, 1185 ZE Amstelveen
T 020 789 5689
www.naecktebrouwers.nl

Formed in 2012, the Naked Brewers opened their own 10-hl brewery on a business park in Amstelveen in late 2013. Group visits (max 10 people) possible on request. The full range was still rolling out, but those we have tasted show promise.
YEAR-ROUND: hoppy blond **Hoppix** (6.8%: ★★); dry-edged saison **Zonnegloed** (6.8%: ★★); bitter, cocoa-laced imperial stout **Leprechaun** (8%: ★★+); and full-bodied spicy tripel **NIMF** (9.0%: ★★+).
ALSO: In the pipeline are a kuit called **Elser** (6.8%); **Chinook** (7%) IPA; **Naeckte Non** (8%) dubbel; **Naeckte Bock** (8%) for autumn; winter saison **Noorderlicht** (8%) and **Elegast** (10%) barley wine.

Natte Cel

Huisbrouwerij De Natte Cel
Prins Willem Alexanderlaan 8
1611 EV Bovenkarspel
T 0228 512451
www.denattecel.nl

Nanobrewers established 2008 in a North Holland village close to Markermeer lake. The only beer appearing in quantity, Skeetje, is generally brewed at Proef. The others are made in-house and appear, mostly locally, in 75cl bottles.
YEAR-ROUND: multi-grained blond **Skeetje** (6.0%: ★★+), with a rounded fruity edge; blond apricot-tinged **Kruimeldief** (5.5%: ★★); spiced white **Cipiertje** (6.0%: ★★); tart and fruity blond **Veelpleger** (6.0%: ★★); soft, sweet **Blonde Ann** (7.0%: ★★); peaty citrus **Whiskey Honey Ale** (7.5%: ★★+), from whisky-soaked wood chips; dry herbal tripel **Vrije Voeten** (8.0%: ★★); fruity-edged porter **Gladjanus** (8.5%: ★★); and distinctive tripel **Zware Jongen** (8.5%: ★★+).

Noord-Hollands

De Noord-Hollandse Bierbrouwerij
Molenwerf 22 E, 1911 DB Uitgeest
T 0251 213771
www.dnhbb.nl

Noord-Hollandse was founded in 2012 and
began brewing their **Uitgeester** beers in 5 or
10-hl batches three times a month in their
own kit a year later. Spare capacity is rented
out to homeless brewers. The beers are
widely available in beer shops and at festivals.
Tours by arrangement.
YEAR-ROUND: tangy **Amber 950** (6.4%: ★★);
spiced dry blond **Engeltje** (6.0%: ★★); and
Duiveltje (8.5%: ★★+), a heavyweight
bittersweet amber Scotch ale.

Oersoep

Oersoep
Waalbandijk 20, 6541 AJ Nijmegen
T 06 2506 4611
oersoepbrouwerij.nl

Founded in 2012, Primordial Soup moved to
a former soup factory in January 2014. The
larger 10hl installation should help increase
output several-fold and provide room to
expand their impressive wood-aged range.
Mainly organic beers are brewed in 'lines', or
broad styles, rather than as permanent

brands. Every batch is different and
differently named, rendering individual
ratings pointless. Nonetheless, most are
5–6% ABV and reliably ★★★ to ★★★+.
A tap house and shop are open on Fridays.
YEAR-ROUND: the **Bruisend en Blond** beers
are intensely hoppy farmhouse IPAs; the
Saison beers are just that and may merge
with the former into a single **Farmhouse
Ales** line; **Donker en Diep** beers are stouts,
occasionally with added fruit; and the sour
and complex **God is Goed** line is wild and
wood-aged for up to four years, including
both aged brown and lambic styles.

Oijen

Speciaalbierbrouwerij Oijen
Oijense Bovendijk 61, 5394 LA Oijen
T 0412 492217
www.speciaalbierbrouwerij.nl

Small farmhouse brewery near the Maas in
North Brabant, serving mostly its own
taphouse and restaurant. Going since 2002,
they brew their **Oijen** beers in 200-litre
batches, weekly in winter, more in summer.
Spare capacity is rented out to others.
The pigs in the pens by the car park and
the resident chickens are fed on spent
brewery grain. Tours on request.
YEAR-ROUND: tasty blond filtered draught
Pilske (5.0%: ★★+); reasonable **Blond**
(6.0%: ★★); bitter, slightly sour **Donker** (6%:
★★); fruity hoppy **IPA** (6.0%: ★★+);
caramelly chestnut-brown **Amber** (6.0%:
★★); and super-strong blond barley wine
Kaboem (10.0%: ★★), which has too much
barley.
SEASONAL: sweet but not cloying **Bockbier**
(6.5%: ★★+).
ALSO: cherried **Heren van Malsen
Kersenbier** (6.0%: ★★+) is made for a fruit
company; odd novelty **Autarkia Shii-take
Bier** (6.0%: ★+) for a mushroom vendor;
Cranberry Bier van Tosse (6.0%: ★★) for
a store in Oss; and blond **Garlic Queen
Knoflook Bier** (6.0%: ★★) – really – for a
restaurant in Amsterdam.

Oirschots

Brouwerij Oirschots Bier
Koestraat 20, 5688 AH Oirschot
T 0499 572002
www.oirschotsbier.nl

The De Kroon brewery was founded in 1665
in this Brabantine village and operated in
this guise until it was bought out by Bavaria
and closed in the 1990s. In 2002 it was
resurrected by former owner-brewer Gerard
de Kroon and turn into a small-scale brewing
museum making beers for the locals in
150-litre batches. However, plans are afoot
to open a 10-hl installation and expand the
characterful brewery tap to include a
restaurant. Watch this space.
YEAR-ROUND: bitter amber **Egelantier**
(6.0%: ★★); and above-average blond
Kempenlier (7.0%: ★★).
SEASONAL: balanced sweet and dry **Meibock**
(7.5%: ★★); and liquorice-tinted **Bokbier**
(7.5%: ★★).
ALSO: a summer white is expected in 2014.

Ootmarsummer

Ootmarsummer Bierbrouwerij Heupink & Co
Eerste Stegge 11, 7631 AE Ootmarsum
T 06 2538 3691
www.othmarbier.nl

Founded by two friends in 2012, when one of
them inherited a 10-hl copper kettle, fermentation and lagering tanks and a bottling line
from his father, who we infer was a pretty
serious home brewer. Currently brewing its
Othmar beers in an edge-of-town industrial
building, they brew two or three times a
month. The plan is to move into the town's
castle, currently being restored, and open a
tap house there. Opens on Friday (15.00–18.00)
for visits and tastings.
YEAR-ROUND: malty top-fermented pilsener
Goud (5.3%: ★★); refreshing **Weizen** (5.8%:
★★); increasingly clever, peaty smoky
Rauchbier (6.2%: ★★+); lightweight **Stout**
(6.9%: ★★+), which improves in the cellar;
and sweetish malty **Tripel** (8.9%: ★★).

Pauw

Bierbrouwerij De Pauw
Achterbroekweg 1, 7731 PN Ommen
T 0546 671363
www.pauwbier.nl

Remote farm brewery in a thatched barn, 20 minutes' walk from the nearest road! The brothers who founded it in the 1990s were both born on the farm and moved the brewery there in 2011. They brew in 5-hl batches 'in the old way', using scales, thermometers, a watch and 'common sense'. All the barley used is homegrown. A small on-site shop (daily 10.00 until sunset) sells ice cream and beer, occasionally via an honesty box, and has glasses, a bottle opener and table outside. Visits by arrangement but bring a map and boots.

YEAR-ROUND: strongly citrus, spiced **Wit** (5.0%: ★★); lightly honeyed **Blonde Trots** (6.5%: ★★); fruity dry **Bokbier** (6.5%: ★★); rounded dubbel **Pauw's Trots** (6.5%: ★★); and sweetish amber barley wine **Zwaar Bier** (8.0%: ★★+), with aniseed notes.

SEASONAL: the Wit is sold as **Zometrots** in summer, the Bok as **Herfsttrots** in autumn and the Zwaar as **Wintertrots** in winter.

Oudaen

Stadskasteel Oudaen
Oudegracht 99, 3511 AE Utrecht
T 030 231 1864
www.oudaen.nl

City-centre brewpub in a historic canalside manor house, operating since 1990. The café-restaurant occupies the upper floors, with the attractive brewhouse hidden in the wharf-level basement. Most of the beer is sold upstairs, on tap. Group visits by appointment.

YEAR-ROUND: top-fermented pilsener **Linteloo Gold** (5.0%: ★★+) has more character than many; soft unfiltered white **Ouwe Daen** (5.0%: ★★); crisper filtered white **Jonge Daen** (5.0%: ★★); and inoffensive little brown job **Dubbele Daen** (6.9%: ★★).

SEASONAL: standard spring **Lentebock** (6.5%: ★★); honey-sweetened autumn **Herfstbock** (6.0%: ★★); and malty **Winterbock** (6.5%: ★★).

Oude Rijn

Brouwerij De Oude Rijn
Rijndijk 269, 2394 CE Hazerswoude-Rijndijk
T 06 5171 6271
www.deouderijn.nl

Licensed hobby brewer since 2009 making occasional 50-litre runs from organic ingredients in a garden shed. Spiced wheat **Witte Bruno** (5.1%); blond **Bruno** 5.2 (5.2%); dubbel **Bruno 7.5** (7.5%); and triple-hopped tripel **Bruno 9** (9%) are rarer than hen's teeth.

Pelgrim

Stadsbrouwerij De Pelgrim
Aelbrechtskolk 12, 3024 RE Rotterdam
(Delfshaven)
T 010 477 1189
www.pelgrimbier.nl

Established above-average brewpub
on the historic quayside at Delfshaven,
opened in 1996. Brews in 10-hl runs
roughly once a week, mostly for the
taps on the bar. Quality is reliable to
very good. They also use the beer to
make mustard, pâté, chocolates,
cheese and syrups. Group tours by
appointment.

YEAR-ROUND: dry amber altbier **Pelgrim
1580** (4.8%: ★★+); smooth-edged, drinkable
white **Rotterdams Witbier** (5.5%: ★★+);
fruity, bitter but less regularly available
Delfshaven IPA (5.5%: ★★★); and lightly
bitter **Mayflower Tripel** (7.8%: ★★).
SEASONAL: banana-edged spring
Lammetjesbier (6.5%: ★★); sharply
refreshing summer wheat **Zonnelief** (5.8%:
★★+) with raspberry; sweetish autumn
Bockbier (7.0%: ★★); beefier, more complex
Dubbelbock (9%: ★★+); and intense treacly
Winterbier (10.5%: ★★+), which has
liquorice hints.
ALSO: Very Special Old Pelgrim, or **V.S.O.P.**
(7.8%: ★★★+ to ★★★★) is an occasionally
brewed stonker of a dark, chocolaty dubbel,
aged five months in wood, gaining a vanilla hit.

Pimpelmeesch

Stichting Dorpsbrouwerij de Pimpelmeesch
Ginderdoorstraat 4a, 4861 CC Chaam
T 0161 491615
www.pimpelmeesch.nl

Rural brewery created in 2010 within a
lovingly restored North Brabant farmstead.
Brews in 6-hl batches around five times a
month. A recent expansion of lagering
capacity should assist in increasing output.
The adjacent brewery tap is technically a
separate business. Tours by appointment.

YEAR-ROUND: sweet-edged weizen
Chaams Tarwebier (5.5%: ★★);
multigrained oversweet blond **Baken
van Breda** (6.0%: ★+); better blond
Zilverpel (6.5%: ★★); balanced
Chaamse Dubbel (7.0%: ★★);
outstandingly hoppy IPA **Goudpel**
(7.0%: ★★★); and increasingly dry
Chaamse Tripel (8.5%: ★★).
SEASONAL: copper-amber barley wine
Chaams Winterbier (8.5%: ★★+),
with a portery character.
ALSO: Rye ale **St Jans Rogge** (6%:
★★) is made for Landgoed de
Hoevens in Alphen; **Biesbosch Bier** (6%: ★★)
for an off licence in Made; and blond **Toontje
Schoen** (6%: ★★) for the brewery tap.
Tarwebier also appears as **Heisse Weissen**,
Dubbel as **Vurige Non**, Tripel as **Blonde Snol**
and Winterbier as **Dubbel-D**.

Prael

Brouwerij De Prael
Oudezijds Voorburgwal 30
1012 GD Amsterdam
T 020 408 4470
www.deprael.nl

An extraordinary work rehabilitation scheme based at the edge of Amsterdam's Red Light District, for people who have survived significant mental illness. Its head brewer and guiding light, Fer Kok, is also a fully qualified mental health professional. It began in 2002 and has gradually expanded to include a shop (daily 12.00–19.00) and brewery tap. Group tours and 'brew yourself' days are possible. Organic cheeses are also made using house beers. The beers, which are mostly named for Dutch crooners from the 1960s, have grown steadily in quality and confidence.

YEAR-ROUND: glorious milk stout **Zwarte Riek** (4.9%: ★★★), with macaroon hints; lightly bitter spiced wheat **Heintje** (5.4%: ★★); gently bitter blond **Johnny** (5.7%: ★★); a promising IPA named **Nick & Simon** (7.0%: ★★+), for two of the crew at the Wildeman café; adequate strong blond **Willeke** (7.5%: ★★); dry Scotch ale **Doe Maar** (7.7%: ★★); balanced bittersweet dubbel **Hepie & Hepie** (8.0%: ★★); faintly citrus tripel **Sjakie** (8.5%: ★★); bittersweet amber tripel **Mary** (9.7%: ★★); and malt-forward barley wine **Willy** (11.0%: ★★+), for cold evenings.

SEASONAL: blond meibock **André** (6.6%: ★★), with straw hints; rounded dubbelbock **Nelis** (7.7%: ★★); and its drier, smoky version **Nelis met Pijp** (7.7%: ★★+).

ALSO: they make **Ooievaar Bier** (7.5%: ★★) for the café of that name up the way.

Praght

Brouwerij Praght
Wisentweg 7, 8251 PB Dronten
T 0321 329321
www.brouwerijpraght.nl

Flevoland brewery in a mixed rural-industrial area. Founded in 2007, it offers work experience for the disabled and long-term unemployed. Beers are unfiltered, unpasteurised and *Reinheitsgebot* compliant. Solidly made and improving Praght Bier brews have become widely available in bottled form. A dog-walkers' snack bar next to the brewery doubles as a tap house and shop.

YEAR-ROUND: three-month lagered malty **Premium Pilsener** (5.3%: ★★); overly sweet golden-blond **Weissbier** (5.7%: ★★); slightly bitter spiced white **Pionier** (6.0%: ★★); solid dry-edged **Tripel** (8.0%: ★★); bitter chocolate and raspberry-tinted **Extra Stout** (8.0%: ★★+); and deceptively drinkable warming barley wine **Zware Blonde** (10.0%: ★★+).

SEASONAL: bittersweet spice fight **Lentebock** (6.5%: ★★); lightly refreshing **Zomerblond** (5.1%: ★★); autumn's smoky, dry, sweet and sour **Rookbock** (7.0%: ★★+); standout dubbelbock **Blackbox** (8.0%: ★★★), with burnt sugar, coffee and liquorice dabs; and bittersweet copper-amber **Winterbier** (8.0%: ★★).

Ramses

Ramses Bier
Thijssenweg 20a, 4927 PC Wagenberg
T 06 2951 7085
www.ramsesbier.nl

Set up in 2009 by eponymous brewer Ramses Snoeij, after he returned home from the US brimming with enthusiasm for, and an experience of, craft brewing. He got his own 15-hl capacity kit in 2013 to make beers in Wagenberg, north of Breda in North Brabant. To date his beers have been solidly in the Dutch Premier League, and should with luck turn him into a busy man. No tasting room or tours yet, though they will happen one day.

YEAR-ROUND: dryish kuit beer **Kuiter** (4.5%: ★★+); top-fermented organic lager **Ibis** (5.0%: ★★+); refreshing weizen **Moby Dick** (5.2%: ★★+); dry, satisfyingly bitter brown ale **Poolvos** (5.9%: ★★+); full-bodied, mocha-starting, fruity-bitter ending **Mamba Porter** (6.4%: ★★★); triple-hopped golden blond **Hop** (6.5%: ★★★), with Irish moss; all-round excellent IPA **Den Dorstige Tijger** (6.6%: ★★★+); superior dry-edged dubbel **Willem Bever** (6.9%: ★★★), and its superb, sharp, fresh-cherried variant **Eduard Bever** (6.5%: ★★★+); honeyed but balanced **Antenne Tripel** (9.0%: ★★★), with its intense bitter finish; and the lovely **Shire Stout** (9.0%: ★★★), which becomes even better as the barrel-aged **Stout met Hout** (9.6%: ★★★+). Chestnut ale **Notenkraker** (6.8%: ★★+) was

the first from the new brewkit.
SEASONAL: hoppier-than-most meibock **Zuiglam** (6.6%: ★★+); almost expresso-stout-like, uphopped autumn **Lambok** (6.8%: ★★+); and warming winter **IJsbeer** (8.8%: ★★★), a high-density aged version of Poolvos.

Rodenburg

Brouwerij Rodenburg
Rhabergseweg 9, 7224 NA Rha
(Bronckhorst)
T 0575 452149
www.brouwerij-rodenburg.nl

Middle-of-nowhere Gelderland brewery, founded in 2010 by expat Yorkshireman Steve Gammage. His **Bronckhorster** beers take their name from the local municipality and are brewed in 10-hl batches, twice or more weekly. Firmly on the national A-list, they are often superb and regularly win awards in international competitions. They are worth tracking down and are increasingly easy to source. The tasting room next to the kettles is open daily (12.00–17.00) in theory , but call ahead.

YEAR-ROUND: improving pilsener **Hooge Heeren** (5.0%: ★★+); superior weizen **Eigenweiss** (5.5%: ★★+); drier-than-most **Blond** (6.0%: ★★+); fruity hoppy **Royal Rha IPA** (6.0%: ★★★), with a strongly bitter finish; porterish **Dubbel** (7.0%: ★★), with coffee notes; dry-edged, subtly bitter **Angus Tripel** (8.5%: ★★+); intensely hoppy, moreish double IPA **Hoptimist** (9.5%: ★★★); treacly, rich and deliciously imperious **Night Porter** (8.0%: ★★★); a sticky subtle blend of majestic loveliness called **Midnight Porter** (12.0%: ★★★+); and **Terra Incognita** (12.0%: ★★★+), a superb rich, chewy and fruity barley wine.

SEASONAL: increasingly bitter spring **Lentebier** (7.5%: ★★+); dry blond **Summer Smile** (7.0%: ★★★), smoke-edged from whisky malt and designed for drinking with herring; hoppy bitter autumn **IJsselbock** (7.0%: ★★★); beefier but cruder **Dubbelbock** (9.0%: ★★+); and **Scrooge** (8.0%: ★★★), a seriously full-on dark Christmas ale that is a classic in the making.

Roos

Museumbrouwerij De Roos
Sint Sebastiaanstraat 4,
5081 ZG Hilvarenbeek
T 013 5055045
www.museumbrouwerij.nl

Modern North Brabant micro plant housed in a building known to have been the village brewery in the 19th century. This was restored by volunteers and re-opened as a museum in 2002, with the modern working-brewery alongside. Brews a wide range of beers in small quantities. Quality is variable though the best can be very good. Widely available in beer shops. The museum café is the brewery tap.

YEAR-ROUND: **Gemberbier** (5.0%: ★★), spiced with ginger and lemongrass; blond quaffer **De Roos** (5.5%: ★★); spiced wheat **Witte Roos** (5.5%: ★★); enjoyable light stout **Festivalbier** (5.7%: ★★+); directionless airheaded **Blonde Roos** (6.0%: ★★); brown **Dubbele Roos** (6.4%: ★+), spoilt by candy sugar; refreshingly balanced golden **Jubbelroos** (6.5%: ★★+); blond sweet and dry rye-based **Roggebier** (6.5%: ★★+), also as St Jansrogge; full-mouthed bittersweet dubbel **Rooie Fik** (6.5%: ★★); creamy, toffee'd, lightly bitter **Irish Red Ale** (7.0%: ★★); balanced amber **Konjel** (7.0%: ★★); spiced brown **Knuffel Bier** (7.0%: ★★), or Cuddle Beer, with a teddy on its label; underpowered **Bikse Tripel** (8.0%: ★★); and nicely honeyed tripel **Arnoldus** (8.3%: ★★+).

SEASONAL: unsurprising **Meibok** (6.5%: ★★); and matching autumnal **Herfstbock** (6.5%:★★).

Sallandse

Sallandse Landbier Brouwerij
Almelosestraat 2, 8102 HD Raalte
T 074 259 1311
www.sallandslandbier.nl

Founded in 2009 and operating in the basement of an events complex in a small Overijssel town. They brew in a 5-hl installation and have ample availability of lagering tanks, meaning they can rent out excess capacity to an increasing number of aspiring brewers – at least a dozen at the last count. They open their rather nice tasting room twice a week (*We & Sa 14.00–17.00*), with brewery tours and tastings at 14.30 & 16.00.

YEAR-ROUND: oddly pleasant **Witte Franciscus** (5.0%: ★★), tasting like a hay-flavoured fruit pastille; perfumed sweet **Blonde Johannes** (6.0%: ★+); dark amber malty **Donkere Henricus** (6.0%: ★★); standout flowery-hopped blond **Novello** (6.5%: ★★+), with a bitter finish; not-quite-sweet, fruity-edged **Lebuïnus Dubbel** (7.0%: ★★); and fruitier, sweeter **Lebuïnus Tripel** (8.5%: ★★).

SEASONAL: decent autumn **Bokkige Theodorus** (7.5%: ★★); and too-sweet red-amber **Rudolphus Winterbier** (8.5%: ★★).

ALSO: in season they make **Aspergebier** (4.8%: ★+), using asparagus, for Sallandse Aspergeland. It is as good as it sounds.

Schans

Bierbrouwerij De Schans
De Schans 17–21, 1421 BA Uithoorn
T 0297 522106
www.schansbier.nl

Sleepy small brewery in a sleepy North Holland commuter town, quietly going about its business since 1998, gaining a reputation for reliable quality without marketing splash. A wide range of brews come and go. We only list those seen recently. Can be hard to track down but worth it. They also distil their own jenevers and liqueurs and have a small beer shop next door.
YEAR-ROUND: dry **Triticale** (5.6%: ★★+), with 10% triticale, a wheat-rye hybrid; almost amber, malt-forward lightly bitter **Blond** (5.8%: ★★+); **Smoky** (5.8%: ★★), sadly lacking said smoke; beefy **Brown** (6.0%: ★★+), with warming cocoa, a hint of vanilla and background bitterness; bitter cocoa and coffe-laced stout **Spicy** (6.5%: ★★★); chocolaty, porterish **Classic Dubbel** (7.0%: ★★+); well-rounded **Saison** (7.0%: ★★+), with dabs of clove and ginger; **Van Vollenhoven Extra Stout** (7.0%: ★★+), a solid revival of an old Dutch institution; and richly rewarding strong stout **Imperial** (8.8%: ★★★), which starts out cocoa and finishes bitter.
SEASONAL: **Winter** (8.0%: ★★★) has imperial-stout quality with coffee overtones.

Sint Servattumus

Brouwerij Sint Servattumus
Ericastraat 11b, 5482 WR Schijndel
T 073 547 8956
www.sintservattumus.nl

Founded in 1996 and now housed in an industrial building on the edge of a small North Brabant town. They brew a massive range of beers with varying success. There is a strong and sometimes regrettable tendency to throw fruit of all sorts into the mash. More focus on a handful of star names might reap richer rewards. Excess capacity is hired out to several other brewers. Group tours by appointment.
YEAR-ROUND: pleasingly hoppy blond **Hopbelleke** (5.6%: ★★+); surprisingly good amber raspberry beer **Frambozen** (5.6%: ★★+), with an almost-triumphant tartness; yucky **Rosé** (5.6%: ★+), with grenadine; pleasant but odd blueberry juiced **Blauwe Bessen Bier** (6.0%: ★★); sourish appled **Un Appelke Vur d'n Dorst** (6.0%: ★★); tart, dark-brown **Vattumus** (7.5%: ★★); tangy amber **Knalbier** (7.5%: ★★); sweet liquoriced **Zoethouter Tripel** (8.0%: ★★); honeyed amber **Birre Bier** (8.5%: ★★); and **Skendels Kersenbier** (9.3%: ★★), with additional fermentation sparked by fresh cherry juice. The rye-based range of **Het Groene Woud Rogge** includes wheatless **Witbier** (5.6%: ★★) with a hint of apricot; and a simple but decent enough **Dubbel** (7.5%: ★★). A range of **Het Groene Woud Speltbier** includes blond, light **Enkel** (5.6%: ★★); wheatless spiced white **Witbier** (5.6%: ★★); sweet but highly drinkable **Stout** (6.5%: ★★+); sweet raisin-like **Dubbel** (7.5%: ★★); pleasingly under-sweet honeyed amber **Honingbier** (8.5%: ★★+); and a **Tripel** (8.0%: ★★) that lacks sparkle.
SEASONAL: unusually chestnut-coloured **Meibok** (6.0%: ★★); a sharp, fruity spelt branded autumnal **Bokbier** (7.0%: ★★); and dark **Winterkuninkske** (9.0%: ★★), a caramel vs burnt-edge fistfight in a glass.
ALSO: they make two spelt beers called **Kartuizer Gruytbier** for a local market, fruity blond **Enkel** (5.6%: ★★) having a whack of clove; and **Dubbel** (7.5%: ★★) getting a belt. For **Brandevoortse Hoeve** farm shop in Helmond they make fruity blond **Enkel** (5.6%: ★★); and **Stout** (6.0%: ★★), with strawberry juice.

Swambacchus

Brouwerij Swambacchus
Korte Brouwersstraat 3
6658 AC Beneden-Leeuwen
T 0487 594384
www.swambacchus.nl

Gelderland brewery in operation since late
2012. Beers are brewed once or twice a month
in 100-litre batches, but rarely found outside
the local area. We have yet to try them.
YEAR-ROUND: strong amber **Bôjum** (8.0%);
Drie Dijken Tripel (8.0%), wheat-based
Weterings Wit (5.5%); and a dark **Dubbel**
(8.0%).

Texelse

Texelse Bierbrouwerij
Schilderweg 214, 1792 CK Oudeschild
T 0222 320325
www.texelsbier.nl

Long-standing independent, operating in a
rural corner of Texel island since 1994.
Already among the largest of the little guys,
new brewing kit and a second bottling line
were added in 2013 to expand capacity
further. Their **Texels** beers are widely
available throughout the Netherlands and
they may have 100% coverage on Texel itself
– including the ferry. Walk-in tours are
possible throughout the year on a confusing
schedule – check the website – and the
brewery tap and shop are open on every
tour day.
YEAR-ROUND: slightly sweetish
dunkelweizen **Skuumkoppe** (5.0%: ★★);
spiced white **Wit** (5.0%: ★★); malty amber
Eyerlander (5.5%: ★★); the understated
sweetish **Dubbel** (6.4%: ★★); fragrant
amber weizenbock **Skimme** (6.4%: ★★);
golden blond **Goudkoppe** (6.0%: ★★), which
could do with being beefed up; and solid,
improving, recently up-hopped **Tripel**
(8.5%: ★★+).
SEASONAL: sweetish but appealingly off-beat
meibock **Springtij** (7.5%: ★★); solid,
dependable and full-bodied **Bock** (7.5%:

★★★); alleged dubbelbock **StormBock**
(10.0%: ★★+), which is more of a barley
wine; and slightly disappointing amber
Noorderwiend (7.5%: ★★), too thin and
sweet for cockle-warming on cold evenings.
ALSO: the winning hobby brewer from the
annual Groningen Bierfestival gets to
brew a full length batch here, sold as
d'Olle Grieze.

Troost

Brouwerij Troost
Cornelis Troostplein 23, 1072 JJ Amsterdam
T 020 737 1028
www.brouwerijtroost.nl

Brewpub in Amsterdam's De Pijp district,
producing in 10-hl batches since early 2014.
Beers sold in-house and at its sister, **Café
Kostverloren** (Tweede Kostverlorenkade 70,
www.cafekostverloren.nl).
YEAR-ROUND:
banana-tinged
Weizen (4.7%:
★★); a
lightweight
Blond (4.8%:
★★) for the
pils crowd;
and subtly
rounded **IPA**
(6.5%: ★★+).

Twentse

Twentse Bierbrouwerij
Tuindorpstraat 61, 7555 CS Hengelo
T 06 2127 4890
www.twentsebierbrouwerij.nl

Opened in 2008, in a renovated red-brick industrial building near the city centre, which also houses the Hengeler restaurant. Currently they brew roughly three times a week in a 5-hl kettle. Their **Twents** beers are available mostly in the surrounding Twente region of Overijssel, but can be found elsewhere – one batch having been spotted in a bar in Vientiane, the capital of Laos.
YEAR-ROUND: **Premium Pils** (5.0%: ★+), too watery to excite; significantly better, maltier **Oerpils** (5%: ★★); standard spiced white **Wit** (5.0%: ★★); overly sweet **Rosé** (5.0%: ★+); and simple but eminently quaffable **Amber** (5.5%: ★★+).
SEASONAL: slightly sweet autumnal **Bok** (6.5%: ★★).
ALSO: a honeyed Honing Tripel is in the works; while inexplicably their schwarzbier, Schwarz, a real star turn, sold poorly and had to be retired in 2013.

Van Moll

Van Moll
Keizersgracht 16a, 5611 GD Eindhoven
T 06 2459 4573
vanmolleindhoven.nl

Eindhoven's first commercial brewhouse for almost 60 years opened in 2013, housed in a city centre café created in some disused offices. Initial efforts have covered a wide range, all made in 100-litre batches. The beers are only sold in-house and the range is evolving. Shows early promise.
YEAR-ROUND: early standout, single-hopped blond quaffer **Eenvoud** (4.0%: ★★+); decent if thin stout **Conquistador** (4.6%: ★★+); cocoa-tinted black saison **Noir Desir** (4.9%: ★★); a pretty decent house **Pils** (5.0%:★★+); gently bitter blond **Toewijding** (5.2%: ★★+); quaffable lightweight IPA **Dolce Vita** (5.5%: ★★+); honey-tinged tripel **Scheepsrecht** (8.3%: ★★); and **Ons Blackie** (9.5%: ★★+), a chewy imperial stout.

Veluwse Heide

Veluwse Heidebrouwerij
Nieuwe Kazernelaan 2, Building 3, 6711 JC Ede
T 0318 785 428
www.veluwseheidebrouwerij.nl

Founded in 2011 and housed in the kitchens of a decommissioned military barracks. It uses the 60-litre stoves for brewing experiments and a proper 300-litre brewing kettle, used twice each session, to fill 6-hl fermentation tanks. Brews twice weekly. Its beers are available on tap in the on-site proeflokaal, and in 75cl bottles to take away. They are starting to be found elsewhere. Tours by appointment.
YEAR-ROUND: amber **Edenoartje** (5.5%: ★★); malty sweetish brown ale **Pegasus** (5.5%: ★★); and flagship golden **Veluws Heidebier** (6.2%: ★★+), made with local honey.
SEASONAL: sweetish **Lentebock** (6.0%: ★★); and caramel-tinged **Herfstbock** (6.2%: ★★).

Veluwse Schavuyt

Veluwse Schavuyt
Mariastraat 2H, 7311HL Apeldoorn

We suspect, but do not know, that when their new brewhouse is fully established, Veluwse Schavuyt's original Mariastraat location will cease brewing. This will hopefully leave the handsome Proef-Locaal Het Achterom, where the brewery was housed, to continue life as a beer bar. In this expectation we list all beers under Vlijt (below).

Vijfheerenlanden

Bier Atelier Vijfheerenlanden
Energieweg 17P, 4143 HK Leerdam
T 0345 618857
www.glassbier.nl

Established in 2012 on an industrial estate in this small South Holland town, the name of which was procured for a much-marketed cheese. They only brew their **Glassbier** brands from September to April, in 260-litre batches, with demonstrations and tastings on the first Sunday of each month (14.00–17.30). Other visits by appointment. Beers are rare outside the local area.
YEAR-ROUND: spiced white **Withut** (5.0%: ★★); dry blond **Hutters** (5.5%: ★★), with faint clove; caramelly dubbel **Zwarthut** (6.4%: ★★); summery light-blond **Owens** (6.5%: ★★); and fruity, slightly sweet **Tripel** (7.5%: ★★).

Vijfhuizen

Bierbrouwerij Vijfhuizen
Fortwachter 3, 2141 EE Vijfhuizen
T 023 565 0856
fortenbier.blogspot.com

One-man operation founded in 2011 and brewing 50-litre runs on a weekly basis to supply the restaurant 't Fort, located in the kitchen of an old fort near Haarlem that is part of the UNESCO-listed fortifications

ringing Amsterdam. Its **Fortenbier** brands take the names of military ranks, greater seniority denoting higher strength. Quality is usually commendably high.
YEAR-ROUND: refreshing light blond **Korporaal** (5.0%: ★★+); fruitier and drier quaffing blond **Sergeant** (5.4%: ★★+); malty, golden blond **Kapitein** (6.5%: ★★+); dark dubbel **Majoor** (6.6%: ★★+), with background cherry; golden tripel **Kolonel** (6.9%: ★★); and bittersweet Scotch ale **Generaal** (7.3%: ★★+).

Vlaardingse

Vlaardingse Bierbrouwerij
Hoogstraat 37, 3131 BL Vlaardingen
T 06 430 28355
vlaardingsebierbrouwerij.nl

Tiny start-up from 2012 occupying a former shop in the centre of the old herring port of Vlaardingen, west of Rotterdam. They brew in 120-litre batches, with larger runs commissioned from elsewhere. The plan is to upgrade to a larger installation in time. The beer is named for a local harbour, not a Star Trek character, and is found mainly in the town. YEAR-ROUND: lightly bitter amber pils **Vulcaan** (5.4%: ★★), which slips a warming glow into its tail.

Vlijt

Apeldoornse Bierbrouwerij De Vlijt (ABDV)
Vlijtseweg 130, 7317 AK Apeldoorn
T 06 1443 9518
www.veluwseschavuyt.nl

The new incarnation of **Veluwse Schavuyt**, opened in October 2013 in a renovated factory with a new 10-hl installation. With expansion has come a broadening of the range. The Veluwse Schavuyt brands are widely available in and around Apeldoorn, and increasingly beyond. A tasting room may arrive at some point.
YEAR-ROUND: dry, slightly thin **Pilsener** (5.0%: ★★); hazy fruity **Blond** (5.6%: ★★), with peach hints; and flagship **Amber** (6.5%: ★★), which tastes of gingerbread through added honey.
SEASONAL: slightly sweet **Bock** (6.5%: ★★).
ALSO: a Tripel will arrive in 2014.

Volendam

Bierbrouwerij Volendam
Morseweg 12, 1131 PK Volendam
T 06 5356 0875
www.bierbrouwerijvolendam.nl

Founded in 2000, on an industrial estate in an otherwise picturesque tourist town on the shores of the Markermeer, north of Amsterdam. They brew on a small scale with consistently good quality over the years. Their **'t Vølen** beers are found over much of North Holland but are less common elsewhere. They also distil their own whisky and liqueurs. Group tours by appointment.
YEAR-ROUND: spiced white **Witvoetje** (5.0%: ★★); dry golden **Zeebonck** (6.5%: ★★+);

sweetish dubbel **Bap** (7.0%: ★★); tripel **Ootje** (8.5%: ★★+), with some barley wine character; and the official barley wine, moreish **Pijtje** (10.5%: ★★+), which has raisin hints.
SEASONAL: **Vølenbock** (6.5%: ★★) counters sweetness with a sharpish finish.

Vriendenbier

Vriendenbier
Overtoom 3, 1851 VR Heiloo
T 06 5362 1894
www.vriendenbier.nl

Founded in 2012 by two guys who have been friends since schooldays. They brew in 160-litre batches in the former kitchens of a decommissioned mental health facility south of Alkmaar, which is becoming a centre for craft-based small enterprises. Only available locally thus far and not yet encountered by us.
YEAR-ROUND: Saaz-hopped malted wheat and pilsener malt **Wazige** (6.5%); and weizen **Wijze** (7%).
ALSO: an IPA (7%), Bok (7%) and Stout (7%) are planned.

Wageningen

Brouwerij Wageningen
Nudepark 99D, 6702 DZ Wageningen
T 06 3630 0440
www.brouwerijwageningen.nl

Brewing at De Hemel in Nijmegen before starting at their own installation in 2013 in an industrial building close to the Lower Rhine (Nederrijn). The brewers place emphasis on trying to source local ingredients wherever possible and have a penchant for unusual styles. Beers are mainly available in the Wageningen area, and at a few festivals. Visits by appointment. One to watch, maybe.
YEAR-ROUND: Cascade-hopped dry weizen **Hermelijn** (5.6%: ★★); and hoppy amber pale ale **Otto II van Gelre** (8%: ★★).
SEASONAL: their dunkelweizen dubbelbock **Mordicus** (7.0%: ★★+) appears during the winter.

Wittenburg

Stadsbrouwerij Wittenburg
Markt 25, 6901 AH Zevenaar
T 06 2050 8058
www.stadsbrouwerijwittenburg.nl

A handsome-looking small brewery installed in 2008 within a historic building on one of the oldest streets of the town centre. Its **De Jonkheer** beers are available on draught and in bottle at the brewery tap, and a few places around the town and beyond. A shop sells bottles and other local produce, and there are irregular but fairly frequent tour options posted on the website.

YEAR-ROUND: the superior oat-based blond **Stadsbier** (5.2%: ★★+); dry bitter oaty **Blond** (6.2%: ★★); above-average **Wit** (6.2%: ★★+); the cherry sour but sticky sweet **Dubbel** (7.0%: ★★); oddly sharpish **Stout** (8.5%: ★★); and a **Tripel** (7.8%: ★+) that had a sour edge we are not convinced was intentional.

Zeven Deugden (7 Deugden)

Brouwerij De 7 Deugden
Osdorperweg 578 achter, 1067 SZ Amsterdam
T 06 5164 8115
www.de7deugden.nl

Founded in 2009, the Seven Virtues is a confident brewery on Amsterdam's semi-rural western edge. Brewer Garmt Haakma is unafraid to use unusual spicing, usually with reasonable results. His 400-litre brewing installation may be expanded in the near future, though bottling by hand is what limits production. In fact it is a bottleneck. Visits by appointment.

YEAR-ROUND: assertive 5-malt amber **Arm+Zalig** (5.0%: ★★+); 3-grained white but non-wheat blond **Ruw+Bolster** (5.0%: ★★+); clove-laden dunkelweizen **Wijs+Neuzig** (5.0%: ★★★); chillied blond **Scherp+Zinnig** (5.0%: ★★+), with restrained warmth; rounded and superior **Dubbel+Dik** (6.5%: ★★★); accomplished dry **Stout+Moedig** (7.5%: ★★★); and cloved golden tripel **Scheepsrecht** (8.0%: ★★+).

SEASONAL: lovely **Spring+Bock** (6.5%: ★★+), with lemon balm; amber **Spring+Tijm** (6.5%: ★★★), freshened with thyme; and autumnal rich **Bock+Sprong** (7.0%: ★★+), with raisins.

And finally...

We have excluded from this listing two set-ups that almost brew commercially.

Proefbrouwerij Het **Vaghevuur** (**T** 06 2377 4197 – www.vaghevuur.nl) runs a micro-installation within the De Hemel brewery that does not brew regular beers but can be rented for large-scale home-brewing, brewing demonstrations or parties.

De **Wijkgaard** (**T** 0345 576391 – www.dewijkgaard.nl) meanwhile is a picobrewery within a home brewing shop on the village high street of Meteren in Gelderland. Many and varied beers under the Betuws brand have been made to order over the years, in 30-litre batches. An IPA called **Hopgenot** (7%) and their **Tripel** (8%) have proved the most enduring.

In the works

We are pretty confident that the following breweries will materialise soon after we hit the streets, or possibly even before.

Heerlen, near Maastricht, is promised a city-centre brewpub at **Beerkompanie** (Pancratiusplein 46; www.beerkompanie.nl), a modern café tied to and likely owned by Alfa (see page 40) not far from the site of the former Romein brewery.

The owners of Amsterdam's Bierfabriek brewpub plan to open another along similar lines in central Delft. **Bierfabriek Delft** (Burgwal 45–49, Delft) could be open by mid-2014.

Oldenzaal, north of Enschede, near the German border in Overijssel is promised its own 'stadsbrouwerij', the **Bombazijn** (Molenstraat 24; www.debombazijn.nl), as part of the redevelopment of its old city gardens.

Eindhoven is to get a second working brewery at an address that has yet to be confirmed, to open in late 2014. **Stadsbrouwerij Eindhoven** will double the city's portfolio of working breweries. Besides its own house beers, it will rent out excess capacity to several local homeless

brewers. The brewers from **Eijkenrode** (page 86) have a stake in it.

The North Brabant town of Helmond will soon be enjoying the first fruits of the **Kat** brewery (Ribbiusstraat 6; www.brouwerijdekat.nl), which had already trialled a 5.5% amber and 6.7% blond ales called De Kat. A white beer and a stout should follow. The plan includes sourcing local organic ingredients.

We are assured that despite having survived without a brewery since 2002, rural North Holland proto-brewers **Lepelaer** (**T** 0299 683722; www.lepelaer.nl) will open their own site at Midden-Beemster early in 2014 to make their **Beemster** beers, which had in the meantime been brewed at Proef in Belgium. These include faintly bitter **Blond** (6.0%: ★★); malty sweet golden **Tripel** (8.5%: ★★); autumnal over-caramelled old-school **Bok** (6.5%: ★★); and the better balanced dubbelbock **Bock Bock** (8.0%: ★★). No, really, that is its name.

At Den Helder in North Holland a rather different kind of new brewery should open from the people behind Olm Bier, a company that went out of business after Heineken sued them for filling its branded kegs with their beer. Returning as **Princen** (www.princenbrouwerijen.com) their first and possibly only beer is expected to be a high-volume, low-price 5% pils for the low expectations end of the market. Like the world needs this.

Although brewing since 2012 at Culemborg, at the north west corner of Gelderland, in 200-litre batches, organic specialists **Vrijstad** (Nijverheidsweg 6; www.brouwerijvrijstad.nl) had yet to launch a commercial beer by the time we went to press, though we expected their bottom-fermented märzenbier **Keller** (5.6%) to arrive any day.

Based near Utrecht, **RUIG** (Ruigenhoeksedijk 7, Groenaken; www.ruig.nl) should have launched their Blonde **Enigma** (6.0%) IPA by publication time.

Friesland-based **Admiraals** (www.admiraalsbierbrouwerij.nl) should release their first beers in May 2014.

Global beer companies

Although small breweries have transformed the global brewing scene in the past 20 years, six companies control roughly three-quarters of the world's beer. One began life in the Netherlands and another in Belgium.

AB InBev

The industrial behemoth that is the world's largest brewing company was formed when InBev, the 2004 creation of the merger of Belgian Interbrew with Brazilian AmBev took over American giants Anheuser-Busch in 2008. Many smaller breweries have been deleted along the way, usually with the loss of whatever star quality made them attractive in the first place. They calculate that their shareholders' interests are better served by producing simple products for the mass market than fine ones for people of taste.

Dommelsch

Dommelsche Bierbrouwerij
Brouwerijplein 84, 5551 AE Dommelen
T 040 208 7911 · www.dommelsch.nl

Brewing since 1744 in the Brabant village of Dommelen and controlled between 1950 and 1968 by the Snieders family, some of whom remain on the local Board. They only make two beers, each of them low on content and high on marketing. Production is 1,000,000 hl per year, so someone likes them.
YEAR-ROUND: woeful liquid breakfast cereal **Oud Bruin** (2.5%: ★+); and bog-standard dull **Pilsener** (5.0%: ★+).

Hertog Jan

Hertog Jan Brouwerij
Kruisweg 44, 5944 EN Arcen
T 077 473 2427 · www.hertogjan.nl

Ale brewery in the north of Limburg that began during the First World War in 1915 but was severely damaged in the Second. The crippling costs of reconstruction led to half a century of corporate pass-the-parcel. In 1995 the Arcen 'steam brewery' joined Interbrew, who renamed it Hertog Jan in 1998. Two decades later, sale conditions acquired along the way that demand it must remain an ale

brewery, allow it to remain incongruously in that role. We assume its Pilsener is either top-fermented or made elsewhere. Despite corporate ownership, it remains a lovely anachronism with a great little brewery tap.
YEAR-ROUND: uninspiring **Pilsener** (5.0%: ★★); reasonable **Weizener** (5.7%: ★★); ho-hum rather than oo-er **Oerblond** (6.2%: ★★); half-decent **Dubbel** (7.3%: ★★); amber not much **Karakter** (7.5%: ★★); the bitter-sweet **Tripel** (8.5%: ★★); and once-good, now unbalanced barley wine **Grand Prestige** (10.0%: ★+), which tastes like it has fallen downstairs.
SEASONAL: **Lente Bock** (7.2%: ★★) and **Bockbier** (6.5%: ★★) tick their respective boxes without shining.

Heineken

The world's third-largest brewing outfit officially came into being in 1864 when Gerard Adriaan Heineken bought a brewery in Amsterdam. It was the marketing genius of his grandson Alfred Henry 'Freddy' Heineken (1923–2002) that transformed a smallish family business into one of the most recognisable brands on the planet. They have been marginally more discreet than AB InBev in their disposal of smaller breweries acquired on the way to the top, though equally focussed on marketing high-profile industrial pilsener brands.

Brand

Brand Bierbrouwerij
Brouwerijstraat 2, 6321 AG Wijlre
T 043 450 8282 · www.brand.nl

The Netherlands' oldest brewery, with roots going back to 1340 and taken over by the Brand family in 1871. They have maintained some input since the 1989 Heineken acquisition. The brewery's 1937 copper brewing kit remains on show though it was replaced in 1981. Most of its production (98%) is sold domestically.

YEAR-ROUND: cloyingly sweet **Oud-Bruin** (3.5%: ★+); industrial-style blond lager **Premium Pilsener** (5.0%: ★★); far better, fuller-bodied, malty pilsener **Brand-UP** (5.5%: ★★+); citrus but over-sweet **Weizen** (5.3%: ★★); and malty bottom-fermented amber **Imperator** (6.5%: ★★).

SEASONAL: average **Lentebock** (6.5%: ★★); caramel-tinged bittersweet **Dubbelbock** (7.5%: ★★+); and treacly winter **Sylvester** (7.5%: ★★).

ALSO: the winner of an annual amateur brewing competition gets to brew a run of their creation commercially. The 2013 champion was complex, bitter, five-hopped, almost-tripel **Zwaar Blond** (8.5%: ★★+), which may become a fixture.

Heineken

Heineken Nederland
Burgemeester Smeetsweg 1
2382 PH Zoeterwoude
T 071 545 6111
&
Rietveldenweg 37
5222 AP 's-Hertogenbosch
T 073 620 9911
www.heineken.com

Heineken's Zoeterwoude plant is Europe's largest brewery, a colossus covering 30 hectares and producing 10 million hl per year – 60% of which is exported – of the regular pils, plus some export-only light versions. At 's-Hertogenbosch 6 million-hl per year of the same staple is produced, with other lines. Half the beer brewed in the Netherlands comes from these sites, where the aim is not to create exciting beers but consistent ones. The 'Mexican' brands Sol and Desperados are made here too and an alcoholic apple drink called Jillz. No tours.

REGULAR: watery mess **Lingen's Blond** (2.0%: ★+); unbalanced sweet **Heineken Oud Bruin** (2.5%: ★+); thin bland **Amstel Blond** (4.0%: ★); sickly pink mouthwash **Wiekse Rosé** (4.0%: ★); inexplicably popular simpleton **Amstel** (5.0%: ★+); unerringly competent but broadly pointless **Heineken**

(5.0%: ★★); maltier **Amstel 1870** (5.0%: ★★); faux Celtic amber **Murphy's Irish Red** (5.0%: ★★); half-decent white beer **Wiekse Witte** (5.0%: ★★); and disturbingly sweet **Amstel Gold** (7.5%: ★+).

SEASONAL: autumnal wheat-based **Heineken Tarwebok** (6.5%: ★★); and surprisingly good **Amstel Bock** (7.0%: ★★+).

SAB Miller

A string of high-profile international mergers and acquisitions has seen Castle Breweries of South Africa evolve gradually into a London-based multinational that is now the world's second-largest brewery company. One look at the brands they control – Fosters, Grolsch, Miller, Peroni and Pilsner Urquell to name a few – confirms that their core business focuses squarely on industrial blond lagers.

Grolsch

Koninklijke Grolsch
Brouwerslaan 1, 7548 XA Enschede
T 053 483 3333
www.grolsch.nl

The Netherlands' third-largest brewer traced its orgins to De Klok of Groenlo, founded in 1615. Grolsch came in 1922 following a merger and production moved to Enschede. They now occupy a large site just outside town. It was independent until SAB Miller acquired them in 2007.

YEAR-ROUND: supermarket lightweight **De Klok Blond** (4.8%: ★+); stuff-strutting **Premium Pilsner** (5.0%: ★★), rarely in porcelain-stoppered bottles; simpler pilsener **Kornuit** (5%: ★+); banana-tinged **Premium Weizen** (5.3%: ★★); and **Kanon** (11.6%: ★+), an alcoholic's wet dream.

SEASONAL: malty **Premium Lente Bok** (6.5%: ★★); caramelly **Premium Herfstbok** (6.5%: ★★).

ALSO: dull **Stender** (0.5%: ★+) is as good as we have tasted in its class.

Brewers without breweries

One feature of the Dutch brewing scene is the high proportion of individuals or companies that are registered with the Chamber of Commerce as a brewery company but who do not possess a brewery. We refer to them variously as beer makers or brewers without breweries, while the Dutch and Belgians prefer *brouwerijhuurders* (brewery hirers), though all agree that their real nature covers a wide spectrum.

At the ethical end of this group of nomads are skilled brewers who develop their own recipes, then either brew the beers themselves at someone else's site, or else collaborate actively in the design of their beers before another brewer makes them. The commonest reason for this is that they simply cannot afford the huge financial risks of leasing premises and investing in equipment. Included among these are some of the most talented and daring brewers in the Netherlands, whose products should be sought out.

More typical are beer makers who sketch out the brews they want and then take their ideas to a contract brewer, such as the famously flexible and talented gun-for-hire set-up at Proef in Belgium, who will turn the idea into a reality with whatever degree of input the customer is willing to input. The commissioners are not present during brewing or preparation, but they will have met with and discussed, what is to be produced and how. Some will even have test installations on which they do trial brews, choosing to use larger facilities for any commercial runs.

Sadly, giving everyone a bad name and blighting the concept are a few 'brewers' who simply order existing or slightly tweaked beers from others, then label them as their own. Look for the absence of information on the label about their origins. It is not so very long ago that anyone could contact the Bavaria brewery and order an industrial beer of any colour, strength and sweetness for delivery by the palate-load within a couple of weeks – provided the name was original.

It would be an impossible task to list every beer commissioner in the Netherlands here, but we have tried to include the most interesting and hope that from our descriptions you can glean what type of producer they are. In a scene that is progressing rapidly we will inevitably get it wrong sometimes, for which we apologise in advance to both readers and producers.

Arn

Bierbrouwerij De Arn
Strijplaan 168, 2285 HW Rijswijk
T 06 1099 2307
www.bierbrouwerijdearn.nl

Established in 2013 and brewing small quantities of two seasonal beers at Sallandse: bitter-hopped 7-malted dubbelbock **Bokkige Arn** (8.0%: ★★+); and darkly appealing **Winterse Arn** (9.0%: ★★+).

Bad Hair Brewing

Bad Hair Brewing
Kapellerie 7, 4421 KZ Kapelle
T 06 3613 9141
www.badhairbrewing.nl

Zeeland hobby brewers who gained a commercial licence in 2013, currently brewing at Sallandse, whence come: well-balanced triple-hopped IPA **Ut Bittere Eind** (6.5%: ★★+); and spiced, herbal, over-sweet **Stevug Tripel** (8%: ★★).

Bierderie

Bierderie
Zuideinde 74, 1541 CE Koog aan de Zaan
T 06 2292 1174
www.bierderie.nl

Husband and wife who began brewing in 2010 in a small North Holland town. Test brews are made in-house, with commercial runs brewed at De Molen. They intend to acquire their own brewery and currently focus on making one exceptional beer.
YEAR-ROUND: **Sprout** (9.0%: ★★★) is an imperial stout that is loaded with dark chocolate and coffee bitterness.

Bijdehand

Bijdehand Bierbrouwerij
Poldermolen 29, 2661 LB Bergschenhoek
T 06 1737 5153

In an unusual arrangement that began in 2012, Wesley Aarse, *brouwmeester* of the Brouwcafé in Scheveningen, hires the brewhouse at which he works to create his own beers for commercial sale.
YEAR-ROUND: amber **Provenier** (5.0%: ★★) is brewed for the Weeshuis café in Schiedam and elsewhere.
SEASONAL: rounded golden amber **Provenier Dubbellam** (7.8%: ★★+), the country's first dubbelmeibock; and liquorice-tinted **Provenier Dubbelbock** (7.8%: ★★+), its dark autumnal sister.

Blauwe IJsbeer

Bierbrouwerij De Blauwe IJsbeer
Vuurkruidstraat 3, 2965 CJ Nieuwpoort
T 06 5349 2330
www.brouwerijdeblauweijsbeer.nl

The Blue Polar Bear started out in South Holland in 2012 and currently has their beers brewed at De Hemel in Nijmegen.
YEAR-ROUND: refreshing weizen **Weijsbeer** (5.0%: ★★+); sweetish amber tripel **Mooie Weer** (8.0%: ★★); and tasty Scotch ale **Schotse IJsbeer** (8.0%: ★★+).

SEASONAL: an autumn blend of weizen and bock, **Weijsbeer Bock** (5.5%: ★+) may be revised.

Bours

Brasserie Bours
Terwestenstraat 4, 5613 HJ Eindhoven
T 06 4105 5274
www.brasseriebours.nl

One-man Eindhoven brewer since 2014. Beers available locally, and first efforts bode well.
YEAR-ROUND: gloriously hop forward American pale ale **Allure** (7.0%: ★★★); **Pas de Saison** (6.7%) launched as we went to press.

Breugem

Brouwerij Breugem
PO Box 9529, 1006 GA Amsterdam
T 06 1422 8459
www.brouwerijbreugem.nl

After his own brewery went to the wall in 2013, brewer Patrick Breugem rescued his **Saense** brands and had them made at Anders in Belgium, where they have yet to be perfected.
YEAR-ROUND: sweetish **Amber** (5.7%: ★★); as yet untried **IPA** (5.9%); slightly bitter **Blond** (6.3%: ★★); promising strong **Stout** (8%); and full-bodied, bitter finishing, golden **Tripel** (8.1%: ★★+).
SEASONAL: autumnal **Herfst** (7.0%: ★+) was a bit of a dog in year one; and winter's dark heavyweight quadrupel **Kracht** (11%).

Bru'd

Bru'd Beer
Nachtwachtlaan 363, 1058 EM Amsterdam
T 06 1070 1828
brudbeer.com

A new Amsterdam-based duo who, since 2013, have brewed at 7 Deugden, testing the waters for a promising beer. Organic, impressively dry and herbal blond **Hoppenheimer**

(5.0%: ★★★) has a careful hop recipe with dry-hopping to follow, ending up a bit like a kölsch on steroids. The plan is to stay semi-professional for now.

Ceaux

Ceaux Brew
Marnixlaan 244 b, 3552 HK Utrecht
T 06 4302 5021
www.ceaux.nl

Another hobby brewer with an intention to get his own brewhouse in due course is Ko Hendriks. He has started brewing at Kemphaan. His first effort is a highly promising, dry, hoppy, gloriously multinational weizen called **Bastard** (5.0%: ★★★), from German wheat, British yeast and American hops. A second is in the works.

Christoffel

Christoffel Bieren
Raadhuisstraat 28, 4835 JB Breda
www.christoffelbieren.com

One of the original pioneering Dutch micro-breweries, opening in 1986 with a double-hopped pilsener that challenged conservative tastes, spreading the range slowly and carefully. Sadly the business folded in 2013. The name has returned, but not the brewery, so the current range is made at Proef in Belgium and has yet to find its feet. So much so that we have held back our star ratings.
YEAR-ROUND: flagship double-hopped golden pilsener **Christoffel Bier** (6.0%); dunkelweizen **Wijs** (6.0%); and strong golden amber **Nobel** (8.7%).
SEASONAL: dry autumnal **Bok** (7.8%).

Compagnie

Brouwerij De Compagnie
Beurtschip 52, 1602 BA Enkhuizen
T 06 3067 3393
www.brouwerijdecompagnie.nl

The popular tourist destination of Enkhuizen in North Holland has no brewery so in 2012 a hobby brewer from one of its restaurants, the Mastenbar, decided to brew at Sallandse. His **Enkhuizen** beers are spiced **Wit** (5.0%: ★★), a pretty standard **Dubbel** (6.5%: ★★) and autumnal **Bock** (7.0%: ★★), only available locally thus far.

Davo

Davo Bieren
Hof van Adwaita 17, 7411 VR Deventer
T 0570 752669
www.davobieren.nl

An enthusiastic crew who have been brewing at Rodenburg since 2012 and hope to get their own kit 'soon'. Their beers are already found widely in beer shops.
YEAR-ROUND: refreshing, hoppy, clear white **Surf Ale** (6.4%: ★★+); bitter finishing **Hoppen Blond** (7.5%: ★★), with a syrupy aftertaste that dampens it; and a malty **Tripel** (8.5%: ★★).

Drentsche Schans

Drentsche Schans
Den Hool 4, 7845 TG Holsloot
T 0591 564160
www.drentscheschans.nl

If we believe the story, this remote set-up based in a Drenthe farming hamlet since 2002 sends its grain to Van Steenberge in Belgium, who turn it into beer for them to sell in regional bars and shops. Their on-site café is only open on Thursdays from 19.30 for darts nights, or for groups by arrangement.
YEAR-ROUND: mediocre **Pilsener** (5%: ★+); standard spiced white **Olde Witte** (5.2%: ★★); **Boeren Blond** (7.0%: ★★); and dubbel-strength amber **Turfsteker** (7.0%: ★★).

Duits & Lauret

Speciaalbierbrouwerij Duits & Lauret
Schoolstraat 77, 3451 AC Vleuten
T 06 1425 1923
www.duitslauret.com

Founded in a Utrecht town in 2009 by wife-and-husband team Daniëlle Duits and Marco Lauret. They develop recipes in their own 60-litre test kit at home and then order commercial runs from Proef, who create beers that are so good that they have won international awards.
YEAR-ROUND: gently bitter **Blond** (6.5%: ★★); and coffee-tinged, easy-drinking **Stout** (5.0%: ★★+).
SEASONAL: rounded meibock **Kiem** (6.5%: ★★); complex, wood-aged, smoked and peaty **Houtgerijpte Rook Dubbelbock** (7.5%: ★★★); warming and bitter chocolaty **Winterstout** (8.5%: ★★★), which develops Rochefort tones with cellaring; and end-of-year **TeVreden** (★★+ > ★★★), an annual one-off sold for charity.

Eanske

Brouwerij Eanske
Weverstraat 35, 7545 TJ Enschede
T 06 1267 9028
www.brouwerijeanske.nl

Oscar Moerman learned his trade at various breweries before starting this operation in 2013, brewing at Ootmarsummer. His first brew, **1325** (5.8%: ★★+) is an easy-drinking US-style pale ale.

Eem

Bierbrouwerij De Eem
Curacaolaan 10c, 3818 SE Amersfoort
T 033 461 6391
www.bierbrouwerijdeeem.nl

Founded in 2006 by Amersfoort-based Ruud van Moorst, who wants to brew in Eemgebied, near Naarden. Meanwhile his beers are brewed at five other breweries, growing in confidence, and widely available. He also brews house ales for innumerable cafés and assists the Tasty Lady collective (below) with marketing, distribution and advice.
YEAR-ROUND: lychee-hinted hoppy **Eem Blond** (6.2%: ★★); and fruity, rich brown Donker (7.0%: ★★+). Increasingly bitter blond **Xtreem Warrior** (4.6%: ★★+); golden malty-nosed **Centennial** (6.5%: ★★); blond **Chinook** (7.3%: ★★+), which is getting hoppier; and dry, bitter **Eem Stout** (7.5%: ★★+).
SEASONAL: balanced, above-average **Eem Bok** (7%: ★★+); darkly rich Christmas ale **Kerst** (7.5%: ★★★), with a bitter finish; and floral hoppy bittersweet **Xtreem Winter Red** IPA (7.5%: ★★+).

Egmond

Brouwerij Egmond
Sint Adelbertusweg 38, 1935 EM Egmond-Binnen
T 06 5537 0787
www.sanctiadalberti.nl

Founded in 2010, Egmond creates beers under licence by the Benedictine Egmond Abbey – making them the only non-Trappist Dutch brewers with a monastic connection. Currently their "90% organic" **Sancti Adalberti Egmondse** range is brewed at Proef in Belgium, though they are actively seeking funding for their own place.
YEAR-ROUND: uncharacteristically dry, bitter, triple-hopped wheat beer **Witte** (5.0%: ★★+), which divides opinion; more run-of-the-mill **Blond** (5.7%: ★★); cocoa-tinged bitter **Dubbel** (6.5%: ★★); and aromatic amber **Tripel** (7.5%: ★★), which is flavoured with coriander and lime blossom.
SEASONAL: dark-amber winter **Pastorale** (8.1%: ★★+).

85

Eijkenrode

Eikenrode Bier
Meerhovendreef 14, 5658 HA Eindhoven
T 06 1610 7614
www.eijkenrode.nl

Eindhoven-based brewers since 2012.
Beers are brewed elsewhere and becoming
increasingly available in the local area.
YEAR-ROUND: drinkable spiced white
Witte Dame (5.1%: ★★); overly banana'd
Eindhovens Blond (6.0%: ★★); sweetish
dubbel **Oude Haas** (7.0%: ★★); sweetish
golden tripel **EvoluWonder** (9.0%: ★★),
with a tad too much caramel in the finish;
and slightly bitter tripel **Heeren van
Eynthoven** (9.0%: ★★).

Epe

Epe Biercollectief
Laar Enk 4,8162 CH Epe
T 06 2335 3387
www.epebier.nl

Hobbyists who went pro in 2012 and brew at
De Molen and Sallandse, to a generally high
standard.
YEAR-ROUND: improving, imncreasingly dry
and burnt schwarzbier **Afschot** (5.5%: ★★),
occasionally found barrel-aged (★★★); fine
dunkelweizen **Duuster Wit** (6.2%: ★★);
fruity and fiercely bitter, wet-hopped IPA
Praotnat (6.2%: ★★★), which uses locally
grown US-strain hop cones in various
combinations.

Fontaine

Brouwerij La Fontaine
Vogelschordreef 8, 4551 MH Sas van Gent
T 06 1828 4547
www.brouwerijlafontaine.com

New brewers based in the Zeeuws-Vlaanderen
countryside since 2012, developing recipes
on in-house kit to be brewed at De Graal in
Belgium.

YEAR-ROUND: rounded blond **Belle & Elegante**
(6.5%: ★★); and wonderfully complex, fruity and
bitter amber IPA-ish **Belle & Forte** (7.0%: ★★★).

Gooische

Gooische Bierbrouwerij
PO Box 1300, 1200 BH Hilversum
T 035 642 6400
www.gooischebierbrouwerij.nl

One of two set-ups with near-identical names
headquartered in Hilversum. This one appeared in
2011. Recipes are developed in-house, but
brewed elsewhere. **Gooisch** beers are 100%
organic and usually feature buckwheat.
YEAR-ROUND: refreshing **Wit** (5.5%: ★★);
balanced bittersweet **Blond** (6.0%: ★★);
and dry schwarzbier **Zwart** (6%: ★★).

Gooische Biergilde

Het Gooische Biergilde
Reestraat 45, 1216 CP Hilversum
www.hetgooischbiergilde.nl

The other Gooische brewers, founded in 2012 to
make beers at Mommeriete and De Leckere, but
we think production has moved to Sallandse.
Plan to get their own brewery one day. Firstborn
Hilferts Blond (6.2%: ★★) was pretty average,
winter warmer **Gooische Bertus** (7.5%: ★★+) less
so. An amber ale called Vitusbier is in the works.

Goorsch Gruyt

Stichting Goorsch Gruyt Bier
Van Heeckerenweg 16, 7471 SH Goor
T 0547 261292
www.facebook.com/GoorschGruytBier

Overijssel brewers targeting a local market and hoping one day to brew in Goor. Their first beer, made to an ancient recipe at Enzensteiner in Germany, celebrated the town's 750th birthday. Oddly spiced **Goorsch Gruyt** (5.5%: ★+) has yet to be perfected.

Gouden Leeuw

Brouwerij De Gouden Leeuw
Jan Smuldersstraat 24, 5512 AZ Vessem
T 0497 591252
www.brouwerijvessem.nl

The Golden Lion, a village café in North Brabant, was a brewery until 1954, run by the grandmother of the owner of this beer company, which formed in 2011. **Beerze** beers are currently made at Anders in Belgium, but the long-term plan is to brew again in Vessem. *YEAR-ROUND:* lightweight blond **Beer** (5.5%: ★★); more complex stronger blond **Brave** (7.5%: ★★); and triple-hopped blond barley wine **Bold** (10.5%: ★★+).

Goudsche Leeuw

Stadsbrouwerij De Goudsche Leeuw
Volmolenhof 7, 2807 ES Gouda
T 0182 338211
www.stadsbrouwerijdegoudscheleeuw.nl

Conceived in 1999 and finally born in 2012, the Gouda Lion is run by a former Heineken brewer and an experienced business partner, brewing safe beers at De Leckere, mainly for the local market. *YEAR-ROUND:* sweetish spiced white **Goudsch Wit** (5.0%: ★★); blond **Erasmus Bier** (7.5%: ★★) needs more bitterness and less cane sugar; as does the syrupy **Goudsch Tripel** (8.0%: ★+).

Groningse

Groningse Bierbrouwerij
PO Box 5091, 9700 GB Groningen
T 050 318 3563
www.grunn-speciaalbier.nl

Set out on the road to good intentions but crashed. Beers are commissioned from breweries in Belgium and Germany, we think, and are then labelled misleadingly under numerous local-sounding brands. Some taste like the same beer with different labels. Quality seldom passes mediocrity and can be nasty, as if over-date bottles have been relabelled, inadvertently of course. *YEAR-ROUND:* the **Grunn** brands include **Goudhaantje** (5.0%: ★), a blond that tastes thin and metallic; white **Hoagelwit** (5.0%: ★+); difficult toffee amber **Rode Hoan** (5.0%: ★); slutty blond **Hopquell UP/Grunn UP** (6.0%: ★+); disappointing dunkelweizen **Hail en Zegen** (6.0%: ★+); and unbalanced sweet tripel **Dréidubbel** (8.5%: ★). *SEASONAL:* too-sweet autumnal **Bock** (7.0%: ★+). *ALSO:* beers branded **Dominikaner**, **Hunebed**, and **Zeevarder** seem remarkably similar; and don't get us started on **Kruisheren Helena Rosébier** (3.5%: ★).

Grootbier

Grootbier
Orgeldraaierspad 13, 1033 ZR Amsterdam
T 06 2632 4277
www.grootbier.nl

New as we went to press and brewing at Klein Duimpje, but included as their first beer made us want to be sure to try the other seasonal beers that they promise will follow. **Zon Saison** (6.0%: ★★★) is a lovely Cascade-dry-hopped summer ale.

Heyloo

Stichting Brouwerij Heyloo
E.J. Potgieterweg 6, 1851 CH Heiloo
T 072 533 4196
www.heyloobier.nl

North Holland team established in 2011. They develop the beers in-house on a 25-litre test kit then brew them commercially at De Schans, to sell mainly locally. *YEAR-ROUND:* coriander-spiced **Heilooër Blond** (7.0%: ★★); and too-vanilla **Ter Coulster Dubbel** (7.0%: ★★). *SEASONAL:* lightweight summer white **Midzomer Wit** (5.5%: ★★).

Hilldevils

Brouwerij Hilldevils
Plantagebaan 103, 4725 RB Wouwse-Plantage
T 06 2219 7086
New set-up in North Brabant making its first commercial runs at 3 Horne. **27-07 IPA** (6.0%: ★★) is extremely bitter.

Hoeksche Waard

Brouwerij Hoeksche Waard
PO Box 1559, 3260 BB Oud-Beijerland
T 0186 624904
www.hoeksch.nl

A South Holland team that has been making beer since 1998 and always meant to get their own premises but now seem to have dropped the idea. **Hoeksch** beers are brewed at De Leckere, and mainly sold locally. *YEAR-ROUND:* spiced **Wit** (5%: ★★); dry, but strangely over-malty dubbel **Eiken** (6.5%: ★★); bitter coriander-spiced blond **Molen** (6.9%: ★★); and full-bodied moreish tripel **1300** (8.0%: ★★+), with citrus and lychee hints. *SEASONAL:* golden **Winter** (9.3%: ★★) gives a warming blend of caramel and red berries.

HollandsGoud

HollandsGoud
Edisonweg 14a, 1821 BN Alkmaar
www.hollandsgoud.com

A North Holland team that split from now-defunct parent brewery Florindia in 2011. **HollandsGoud** beers are brewed commercially at Praght, or sometimes Schelde in Belgium and mostly sold locally. The long-term ambition is to brew in Alkmaar. *YEAR-ROUND:* reasonable **Blond** (5.0%: ★★); decent weizen **Witgoud** (5.3%: ★★); full-bodied sweetish tripel **Modderwater** (8.0%: ★★); and mighty barley wine **Noorderblond** (11.0%: ★★).

Hommeles

Brouwerij Hommeles
Fresiatuin 20, 3994 PJ Houten
T 06 1325 5615
www.brouwerijhommeles.nl

Set up in 2011 by three friends, one of whom – Jan Ausems – maintains the Dutch-language brewery website cambrinus.nl. Test recipes are brewed at De Ster windmill in Utrecht, with commercial brew runs at Sallandse. *YEAR-ROUND:* refreshingly fruity tripel **Goede Raat** (8.0%: ★★+), which survives the addition of apple, pear and elderberry; honeyed amber **Gluiperd** (8.5%: ★★+); and impressive imperial stout **Molotov** (9%: ★★+).

Huttenkloas

Huttenkloas
PO Box 303, 7550 AH Hengelo
T 074 259 0805
www.huttenkloas.nl

A Hengelo-based team that has been brewing since 2000, most recently at Sallandse. The plan remains eventually to have their own small-scale installation, we are told. *YEAR-ROUND:* competent white **Witbier** (5.2%: ★★); malty bottom-fermented blond

Goudbier (5.2%: ★★); dry and bitter triple-grain **Dubbel Kloat** (7.5%: ★★+); bittersweet strong blond Landbier (7.5%: ★★); and refreshingly light **Tripel Kloat** (8.0%: ★★+). *SEASONAL:* dark **Winterbok** (7.5%: ★★) has its character stifled by excessive sweetness.

Jantjes

Jantjes Bieren
Saxofoonstraat 80, 5402 CG Uden
T 0413 269361
www.jantjesbieren-uden.nl

Chummy one-man operation, brewing since 1993 in North Brabant, at Sint Servattumus or Mieghelm. Tastings are possible for small groups by arrangement, in the brewer's home. *YEAR-ROUND:* competent **Altbier** (5.5%: ★★); spiced **Witbier** (5.5%: ★★+); full-bodied **Amber** (5.5%: ★★); dryish cherried white **Kersenbier** (5.5%: ★★); malty-tinted **Blond** (6.0%: ★★); standard sweetish **Dubbel** (6.5%: ★★); overly sweet golden blond **Tripel** (7.0%: ★+); and self-explanatory **Barley Wine** (9.0%: ★★). *SEASONAL:* malty, fruity **Zomerbock** (6.5%: ★★); and sticky autumn **Bockbier** (7.0%: ★★).

Ketelbink

Ketelbink Bier
No official address, Rotterdam
www.ketelbinkbier.nl

This Rotterdam-based outfit, formed in 2013, brews its single beer at De Pelgrim, for sale in 75cl bottles. **Ketelbink Rotterdams Blond** (6.8%: ★★) has enough fruity sharpness to raise it above standard.

Keyzer

Bierbrouwerij de Keyzer
PO Box 5520, 6202 XA Maastricht
T 06 1052 0458
www.bierbrouwerijdekeyzer.nl

Set up in 2000 to preserve the memory of Maastricht's former 'steam brewery', De Keyzer, which closed in 1970. The original kit is still in place as a museum (Wycker Grachtstraat 26, Maastricht – see Beer Tourism). The beers are brewed to the old recipes at Proef. *YEAR-ROUND:* superior **Mestreechs Blont** (5.0%: ★★+), with 15 herbs and spices though clove and ginger dominate; middling amber **De Veldwachter** (5.1%: ★★); sweetish blond **Rolduc** (6.3%: ★★), which has a tenuous abbey link; and tasty amber **Double Saison** (6.5%: ★★+), to an 1881 recipe.

Kinhem

Kinhem
Bakkerstraat 7, 1973 PR IJmuiden
T 0255 531121
www.kinhem.nl

North Holland hobby brewers who went commercial in 2009, brew at Volendam, Noord-Hollandse and Klein Duimpje, and have longer-term plans to open their own brewery. *YEAR-ROUND:* nicely rounded, honeyed IPA **Konik** (6.0%: ★★+); dubbel-ish, bok-ish **Fazant** (7.0%: ★★); triple-hopped fruity blond **Hermelijn** (7.0%: ★★+), with background lychee; sweetish honeyed blond **Hooglander** (8.5%: ★★); and warming, copper barley wine **Wisent** (9.0%: ★★+).

Klaassens

Stadsbrouwerij Klaassens
Keizerstraat 13, 5911 JW Venlo
T 077 463 3287
www.cafedeklep.nl

Set up in 2012 by the owner of the Klep café in Venlo. **Venloos Paeterke** beers are brewed twice monthly at Fontein, and sold on tap in the pub. *YEAR-ROUND:* rich, fruity dark **Döbbel** (7.0%: ★★+); and robust golden **Triepel** (8.0%: ★★+).

Kompaan

Kompaan Bier
Helmersstraat 10, 2513 RX Den Haag
T 06 5260 1344
www.kompaanbier.nl

Running since 2012, Kompaan's 200-litre installation is larger than that of several commercial breweries, but is only used for recipe development. Commercial runs of the beers are brewed at various locations. By the time you read this they should have a tasting room (Helmersstraat 10, Den Haag).
YEAR-ROUND: malty pilsener **070** (5.0%: ★★) targets the local market; superior golden blond **20** (5.2%: ★★+); moreish stout-dubbel hybrid **45** (7.1%: ★★+), with bitter hops and cocoa hints; strongly bitter triple-hopped then dry-hopped IPA **58** (8.0%: ★★★); and excellent 'imperial stout with port' **39** (9.1%: ★★★).

Kraan

Brouwerij Kraan
Overtocht 6, 2411 BV Bodegraven
T 06 5736 8883
www.brouwerijkraan.nl

Bodegraven's third beer maker arrived in 2013, courtesy of the owner of the Speciaal Bierwinkel shop. He has a 200-litre installation for test brews that are commercialised at De Schans and Noord-Hollandse. Spicy blond **Kraanwater** 8.2 (8.2%: ★★) means 'tap water', but clearly isn't.

Levenswater

Brouwerij het Levenswater
Den Uylborch 27, 5241 HB Rosmalen
T 06 4834 5712
www.brouwerijhetlevenswater.nl

Small-scale brewer based near 's-Hertogenbosch since 2006, brewing their **Dikke Deur** beers at Sint Servattumus. Always rare, they seem to be getting scarcer.

YEAR-ROUND: flagship amber **Dikke Deur** (6.0%: ★★); competent but straight-laced **Stout** (6.0%: ★★); blond **LBJ Blont** (7.0%: ★★); raisiny strong **Dubbel** (8%: ★★); and sweetish fruity **Tripel** (9.0%: ★★).
SEASONAL: autumnal **Bokbier** (6.5%: ★★).

Leyerth

Brouwerij De Leyerth
www.urthel.com

Based both in Belgium, where they operate a tiny brewhouse with the right to sell commercially, and the Netherlands, where most of the brewing activity occurs. Run by an enterprising husband (marketing) and wife (brewing) outfit, their **Urthel** beers come mostly from Koningshoeven. Ales that once went down the wacky route have now settled down, with the range featuring hops instead of hair tonic.
YEAR-ROUND: decent saison **Saisonnière** (6%: ★★); intensely hoppy blond **Hop-It** (9.5%: ★★+); and powerful amber barley wine **Samaranth** (11.5%: ★★).

Liefde

Brouwerij Liefde
Ter Borghstraat 13, 5666 RA Geldrop
T 06 4170 4647
www.brouwerijliefde.nl

Antoinette van der Schriek's one-woman set-up in North Brabant has her testing beers on 25-litre in-house (or rather in-kitchen) kit since 2011 and then commercialising them in runs of 5 to 20 hl, most recently at Anders.
YEAR-ROUND: bitter blond **Intense Liefde** (6.0%: ★★); rounded imperial **Stoute Liefde** (8.5%: ★★+); and new barley wine **Ware Liefde** (10.0%).

Muifel

Muifelbrouwerij
Kerkstraat 30, 5351 EB Berghem
T 06 4056 0581
www.muifelbrouwerij.nl

North Brabant outfit established in 2006 by Martin Ostendorf, one of the Netherlands' more adventurous nomadic brewers, who specialises in big-hitters. Beers are made at Sint Servattumus, Proef and elsewhere. Easy to source, especially via beer festivals. Who needs a brewery when you are this busy? *YEAR-ROUND:* malty blond **Graaf Dicbier** (6.0%: ★★), with orange peel; rounded bitter amber **Berghs Bier** (6.5%: ★★+); pleasingly fruity hoppy **Muifel USA-IPA** (7.0%: ★★★); sweetish malty blond **D'n Ossekop** (7.5%: ★★); intensely hoppy **DIPA** (8.0%: ★★★), possibly a one-off; richly satisfying coffee-edged imperial stout **Black Bastard** (9.0%: ★★★); bittersweet tripel **Broeder Everardus** (9.5%: ★★+); barley wine **Zuster Agatha** (10.0%: ★★+) with sour cherry keeping the sweetness in check; and amber whisky malt heavyweight **Beerskey** (11.0%: ★★+), complete with peat smack.
SEASONAL: **Lentebock** (6.5%: ★★) is a bittersweet smoky fruity melting pot; autumnal **D'n Ossebock** (7.0%: ★★+) benefits from a subtler mix of sweet, sour and dry.
ALSO: the Zeewijck in IJmuiden buys beefy dubbel **1851 Bik & Arnold** (6.5%: ★★+), US-hopped white **1880 Blonde Kaairidder** (7.0%: ★★) and floral tripel **1865 Breesaap** (9.0%: ★★); bitter blond **Platte Thijs** (7.0%: ★★+) goes to a distributor in Hoorn; rounded raisiny dubbel **Kruijens Kracht** (8.5%: ★★+) to Wervin in Nieuwstadt; English-hopped blond **Bargs Pracht** (7.5%: ★★+) for Heinie Bosch in 's-Heerenberg; and various **Odulphus** beers for Gérard in Best.
ALSO: a US-hopped barley wine is coming, which may be their Winterbock.

Natte Gijt

De Natte Gijt
Mauritsstraat 35, 6006 EJ Weert
T 06 4495 4207
www.brouwerijdenattegijt.nl

Limburg-based Wet Goat was founded in 2011 and has brewed most of its beer at Anders, plus some at De Molen. Unafraid to experiment, their beers are steadily improving and increasingly available.
YEAR-ROUND: lovely floral hoppy IPA **Hop met de Gijt** (6.5%: ★★★); equally good, subtly smoked IPA **Vredesgijt** (6.8%: ★★★); moreish double IPA **Gijt UT?** (7.5%: ★★★); and burnt coffee-tinged hoppy imperial **Stoute Gijt** (8.8%: ★★+), which gains refined smokiness when **Barrel Aged** (★★★).
SEASONAL: rounded meibock **Gijtebok** (6.5%: ★★+).

Oedipus

Oedipus Brewing
Westerdok 274, 1013 BH Amsterdam
www.oedipusbrewing.com

Four friends connected through Amsterdam's Beer Temple went pro in 2011 to make beers commercially via Anders and De Molen, plus some interesting one-offs for special events in Amsterdam. Their own crowdfunded brewery will open on Westerdok later in 2014.
YEAR-ROUND: dry pale ale **Mama** (5.0%: ★★+), conjuring the spirit of Orval; rounded full-mouthed stout **Panty** (6.0%: ★★★); and

oddly spiced saison-white hybrid **Mannen Liefde** (6.0%: ★★+), with lemon grass and Szechuan pepper.

Oldskool

Oldskool Brewery
Cavallilaan 189, 5654 BD Eindhoven
T 06 2752 8036
www.oldskoolbrewery.nl

One-man operation based in Eindhoven, appearing commercially in 2013. Beers are developed at home in a 60-litre facility, then brewed commercially at Rodenburg or De Hemel. Thus far have come well-rounded, dry **Hopplukker IPA** (6.5%: ★★+) and herbal, banana-laced 'hopfenweizen' **Versnijder** (7.2%: ★★+).

Pampus

Brouwerij Pampus
Johan Huizingalaan 262-2, 1065 JM Amsterdam
T 06 2121 0088
www.facebook.com/BrouwerijPampus

Another newbie from friends who work at the Beer Temple and Arendsnest in Amsterdam. Early beers made at Sallandse show finesse, with dry-edged pale ale **Seeheld** (5.0%: ★★+), sharp and tangy milk stout **Melkmeisje** (5.0%: ★★+) and best so far, bitter juniper-spiced blond **Drenkeling** (5.5%: ★★★). Billed to come are Nathals pale ale, Blink IPA, Bombarde barley wine, and imperial stouts Nachtschot and Blekhol.

Peelander

Peelander Bieren
Verseputseweg 38, 4321 TD Kerkwerve
T 06 4433 0216
www.peelander.nl

From 1992 Peelander was a village-based hobby brewery but the original brewer sold the rather splendid name to the Spennekot Groep, which markets Zeeland products.

The beers are now made at an undisclosed location – we suspect Schelde but may be wrong.
YEAR-ROUND: dull **Pilsener** (5%: ★+); spiced **Wit** (5%: ★★); cherry soured copper-brown **Dubbel** (6.5%: ★★); citrussy **Tripel** (8.0%: ★★); and strong blond **Zeeuws Goud** (8.0%: ★★).

Phetradico

Phetradico Bieren
De Boskamp 16, 3828 VR Hoogland
T 06 1585 4513
www.phetradico.com

One-man creator of seasonal **Phoenix Hooglands** offerings, based in a suburb of Amersfoort since 2010 and brewing through Praght. The recipes are said to come from long-dead local brewery Phoenix Trading Company.
SEASONAL: bittersweet **Lente Bock** (7.5%: ★★); summery weizen **Zomer** (5.5%: ★★); sweet-edged **Dubbelbock** (7.5%: ★★); and bitter, malty brown **Winter** (7.0%: ★★+).

Raven Bone Hill

Raven Bone Hill Brouwers
Vincent van Goghlaan 163, 3141 KT Maassluis
T 06 5733 2123
www.ravenbonehill.nl

Beer makers based west of Rotterdam since 2010. The odd moniker derives from anglicising

the owners' surnames: Raaf (Raven), Bot (Bone), and Vreugdenhil. Recipes are developed in-house on 100-litre kit, then brewed at Ramses. The beers are always available in the Oporto in Maassluis, to which they are loosely affiliated, and sometimes elsewhere.
YEAR-ROUND: fruity amber **Masssluis Stadsbier** (6.7%: ★★+); and rounded bitter double IPA **Schaterhand** (7.8%: ★★+).

Rebels

Rebels Bierbrouwerij
Sint Lambertusstraat 1, 5221 BB Engelen
T 06 1268 0465
www.rebelsbieren.nl

This Brabant village hobby brewer has commercialised his beers via Sint Servattumus since 2011. Well-made brews that are easy to source locally.
YEAR-ROUND: dryish golden **Blond?** (5.0%: ★★+); Cascade dry-hopped IPA **Storm** (6.0%: ★★+); and **Stout!** (7.4%: ★★+), which starts cocoa and ends coffee.

Reuzen

Reuzenbieren
Burgemeester Maeijerstraat 22
5066 VL Moergestel
T 06 2650 4546
www.reuzenbieren.nl

Giants is a collection of Brabant hobbyists who began to produce beer commerically in 2010. Recipes are developed in-house. Larger runs were brewed at Proef, and more recently at Pimpelmeesch. A more professional approach was heralded when they rebranded the whole range as **ReuZ** in 2013.
YEAR-ROUND: lightweight **Dubbel** (7.0%: ★★); floral hoppy **Blond** (7.5%: ★★+); fruitier and hoppier **IPA** (8.5%: ★★+); and **Stout** (9.5%: ★★+), with strong cocoa, burnt coffee and imperial strength.
SEASONAL: raisiny **Meibock** (7.0%: ★★); and **Dubbelbock** (7.8%: ★★), which is almost derailed by a fruit-pastille edge.

Rooie Dop

Rooie Dop
Oudegracht aan de Werf 5, 3511 AL Utrecht
T 06 1891 4623
www.rooiedop.nl

Red Cap, launched in 2012, are the current poster boys of the Netherlands' nomadic brewing diaspora. Brewer Mark Strooker perfects recipes in a 20-litre 'bucket' in their wharfside cellar, but brew commercially at De Molen. They like to experiment and have a growing international reputation for beers that have become widely available.
YEAR-ROUND: Citra-hopped quaffable pale ale **24/7 Session Ale** (4.9%: ★★★); expresso-spiked porter **The Daily Grind** (6.5%: ★★+), like alcoholic iced coffee; superbly dry triple-hopped **Chica Americana IPA** (7.1%: ★★★+); complex floral and fruity double IPA **Ot the Explorer** (8.7%: ★★★); fruity hoppy **Utrecht Strong Ale** (9.1%: ★★+); and richly intense **Double Oatmeal Stout** (9.6%: ★★★), which gains warmth and desiccated coconut in its **Bourbon Barrel-Aged** incarnation (★★★+).

Roze Varken

Brouwerij Het Roze Varken
Trommelhof 17, 6852 TG Huissen
T 06 2278 3150
www.hetrozevarken.nl

Beers conceived in small town Gelderland and since 2013 produced at Veluwse Heidebrouwerij and Sallandse, originally for sale in 75cl bottles largely through the website but now on draught and in smaller bottles too. The first was strong amber **Knorretje** (7.2%: ★★), since followed by darker **Wintervacht** (7.2%). Set to come are white beer **Dageraad** (5.8%) and a summer blond **Zonpracht** (7.1%).

Sint Crispijn

Brouwerij Sint Crispijn
Sintcrispijnstraat 72, 5144 RE Waalwijk
T 06 4608 8771
www.brouwerijsintcrispijn.nl

One-man brewing operation in Brabant, another from the class of 2013. Beers brewed at Drie Horne include opaque, orange-fruity **Blond** (6.8%: ★★) and a hazy brown **Bock** (6.5%) that needed refinement. An IPA and Tripel will follow.

Sint Juttemis

Brouwerij Sint Juttemis
Fokkerhof 45, 5025 DT Tilburg
T 06 2242 6261
www.sintjuttemisbier.nl

Another saintly Brabantine brewer from 2013, this time Tilburg-based. Beers are brewed at Sint Servattumus and Oijen, and sold locally and at festivals. Thus far have come overly hoppy IPA **Flamboyant** (6.1%: ★★+); fruity dark dubbel-stout hybrid **Baldadig** (6.2%: ★★); and hazy brown **Frivool** (6.6%: ★★). Their autumnal **Bock** (6.5%: ★+) had too much banana.

SNAB

SNAB Bierbrouwers
PO Box 204, 1440 AE Purmerend
T 0229 248751
www.snab.nl

SNAB (Stichting Noordhollandse Alternatieve Bierbrouwers) has been making interesting beers since 1991. Leftfield from the start, many of their style revivals that once seemed revolutionary have become staples of the new wave. Quality remains good. They enjoy a long relationship with Proef. Available nationwide, with a stronghold in Purmerend. *YEAR-ROUND:* tasty amber **1410** (5.5%: ★★+); malty 'Strong English Bitter' **Otter S.B.** (5.6%: ★★); tangy smoked porter **Roock**

(6.5%: ★★+); excellent floral hoppy **Pale Ale** (6.2%: ★★★); sweetish honeyed **Koning Honing** (7.5%: ★★+); bittersweet red-amber barley wine **Speculator** (8.0%: ★★+); darker, richer barley wine **Maelstrøm** (9.2%: ★★★); and deliciously complex bittersweet imperial stout **Czaar Peter** (9.5%: ★★★). *SEASONAL:* autumn **IJsbok** (9.0%: ★★+) employs low-temperature lagering to freeze out water; **IJsbok Hout** is a white-oaked version of the same; and 'almost porter' winter **Ezelenbok** (7.5%: ★★+). *ALSO:* Mashing Pumpkins, brewed with Jopen (above).

Snaterende Arend

Brouwerij De Snaterende Arend
Amstel 51-L, 1018 EJ Amsterdam
T 06 5377 5717
www.desnaterendearend.nl

Originally begun in 2002 by Peter van der Arend, boss of the Arendsnest, with brewer Marcel Snater, who has carried it on. Beers were made at various locations, consistently well. With new commitments at Maximus (above), activities as Snaterende Arend have become sporadic but we are assured will not disappear.
YEAR-ROUND: lovely, hoppy IPA **Hopkoning** (6.0%: ★★+); floral, grapefruity, amber steam beer **Roodborst** (6.0%: ★★+); and mighty copper-brown barley wine **Stormvogel** (11.0%: ★★+).

Tasty Lady

Via Eem (see page 85)
www.tastylady.nl

This five-woman collective is pioneering beers designed by women to a female taste that will appeal to all, dismissing in a single move the idea that women should be offered light, soft, sweet or tasteless beers. They brew at various locations and are mentored by Eem (above), but do all the work themselves.

Regular: the original **Tasty Lady** (6.2%: ★★+) is a bitter spiced blond; and lightweight rookbier **Smoky Lady** (4.8%: ★★+) followed in late 2013.

Terschellinger

Terschellinger Bieren
Baaiduinen 32, 8884 HJ Baaiduinen (Terschelling)
T 0562 448797
www.terschellinger-bieren.com

Based on the island since 2011. Its **Scelling** beers are made with Terschelling grain by Wolf in Belgium but are rarely seen outside Friesland.
YEAR-ROUND: corn-based blond **Koan** (6.0%: ★★); not-quite-balanced sweet and sharp **Blond** (6.5%: ★★); and caramelly fruity **Stout** (8.5%: ★★).

Two Brew

Brouwerij Two Brew
Zandpad 44a, 3621 NE Breukelen
T 06 4781 5282
nijenrodebier.com

Small-scale outfit based near Utrecht since 2010. Their single beer is brewed irregularly at Proef in Belgium and rarely seen outside the local area.
YEAR-ROUND: strong amber **Nijenrode** (6.8% ★★).

Two Chefs Brewing

Sloterkade 82 1, 1058 HJ Amsterdam
www.twochefsbrewing.nl

Founded in 2012, by two chefs, who developed a recipe in-house for strongly hoppy IPA **Green Bullet** (5.7%: ★★+), then got it brewed at Sallandse.

Uiltje

Brouwerij Het Uiltje
Barrevoetestraat 17b, 2011 WN Haarlem
T 06 4308 2402
www.brouwerijhetuiltje.nl

Little Owl began life in 2012. Brewer Robbert Uyleman plays with recipes at home then takes them to Jopen, where he works, and hires the kit he uses in his day job to create commercial quantities.
YEAR-ROUND: triple dry-hopped pilsener **Dwerguil** (5.0%: ★★+); strongly hoppy American amber **Velduil** (4.5%: ★★+); excellent bitter black IPA **Bosuil** (6.0%: ★★★); increasingly bitter **Uiltje Pale Ale** (6.8%: ★★+); Scotch ale **Schreeuwuil** (8.0%); bitter double IPA **Steenuil** (9.0%: ★★+); lovely imperial stout **Ransuil** (10.5%: ★★★); and the stonking **Flaming Ass Owl** (11.2%: ★★★), an occasionally brewed richly smoked imperial porter with chilli.

vandeStreek

vandeStreek Bier
1e Atjehstraat 10, 3531 SK Utrecht
T 06 2755 7591
www.vandestreek-bier.nl

Crowdfunded brewers who launched in 2013 with beers made at De Leckere and Sint Servattumus. Hoppy white ale **Broeders** (6.3%: ★★) and coffee-tinged stout **Dark Roast** (7.8%: ★★+) are regulars, with the **Hop Art** series adding only one-off brews thus far. Long-term plans include a brewery with a tasting room.

Vijfhoeck

Bierbrouwerij De Vijfhoeck
Markt 7, 5701 RH Helmond
T 0492 537715
www.devijfhoeck.nl

The owner of the Il Borgo café on the market
square of Helmond in Brabant has revived
the connection of the 15th-century gabled
building with the Vijfhoeck brewery it housed
until 1915. The beer, bittersweet blond
Vijfhoeck's 1515 (6%: ★★) is made
somewhere in Belgium.

Volle Maat

De Volle Maat
L.C. van der Vlugtstraat 23
3822 WL Amersfoort
T 06 3176 2983
www.devollemaat.nl

Amersfoort-based operation whose beers
have been brewed commercially at Sallandse
since 2013. Thus far we have bitter-finishing
Hoogblond (6.5%: ★★), and rich, bitter,
black IPA **Tomahawk** (8.5%: ★★+).

Vriendschap

Brouwerij De Vriendschap
Kometensingel 383
1033 BK Amsterdam-Noord
T 06 1139 1675
www.brouwerijdevriendschap.nl

The Friendship is another 2013 start-up
dependent on Sallandse to realise ambitions
shaped on their home kit. Dry **Hopblond**
(6.2%: ★★+) contains wild hops from the
brewer's garden; and assuredly bitter **Puike
Pale Ale** (6%: ★★+). A plan for their own
brewery is at the paperwork stage.

Wispe

Wispe
Anna Horstinkstraat 20, 1382 MN Weesp
T 06 2451 4518
www.wispe.nl

North Holland organic brewer established
in 2009. Beers are currently brewed at
De Leckere and mainly sold locally.
YEAR-ROUND: average spiced **Wit** (5.0%: ★★);
and more interesting maltier **Blond** (6.0%: ★★).

Witte Klavervier

Witte Klavervier
Koestraat 33, 8011 NJ Zwolle
T 06 2200 1711
witteklavervier.nl

White Four-Leaf Clover is named after the
house where it has been based since 2011.
The building's brewing history goes back
to 1651. Full-scale runs of **Klavervier**
beers come from Schelde in Belgium.
YEAR-ROUND: refreshing oat-laden kuit
Koyt (5.8%: ★★+); similar, but hoppier
Schipluyden (6.2%: ★★+); fruity **Blond
Hoppenbier** (6.2%: ★★+), with local hops;
and smooth chocolaty **Poorter** (7.0%: ★★+),
gaining zing and raisins in its **BA** (for barrel-
aged) version (7.5%: ★★★), sold in hand-
numbered bottles.

Witte Leeuw

Brouwerij de Witte Leeuw
Beelhof 29, 8091 WP Wezep
T 06 3629 2689
www.brouwerijdewitteleeuw.nl

Husband-and-wife brewers who started in 2011 and have their beers brewed commercially at Schelde in Belgium.
YEAR-ROUND: hoppy blond **Amarillo Sun** (6.0%: ★★+); and three-grained, triple-hopped, double IPA **Stroatige Jannus** (7.5%: ★★+).
SEASONAL: grassy meibock **Smaragd** (6.2%: ★★); and autumnal bock **Oktober 23** (6.7%: ★★+).
ALSO: an altbier called **Alte Kameraden** (4.5%) and a tripel called **Hopus Dei** (7.5%) should arrive soon.

Zeeburg

Zeeburg
1e van Swindenstraat 433, 1093 GB Amsterdam
T 06 1153 2914
www.brouwerijzeeburg.nl

Established in 2009, Zeeburg are planning their own brewery, but to no specific timescale. Meanwhile their **Zeeburg** beers are brewed at Proef. A saison is set to arrive soon.
YEAR-ROUND: sweetish **Tripel** (8.2%: ★★); roasted malty **Dubbelbock** (8.2%: ★★+).

Zevende Hemel (7de Hemel)

Brouwerij de 7de Hemel
Klassenweg 13, 5975 PR Sevenum
T 077 467 3326
www.brouwerijde7dehemel.nl

Zevende Hemel, or Seventh Heaven, has been based in northern Limburg since 2006, originally brewing in nearby Horst and now at Proef. Solid, drinkable and widely available.

YEAR-ROUND: average blond **Wolkje** (6.5%: ★★); superior hoppy blond **Zonnestraal** (6.5%: ★★+); competent red **Avondrood** (7.5%: ★★); dry vanilla-tinged brown **Donder** (7.5%: ★★); standout hoppy blond **Hopla** (7.5%: ★★★), with prominent lychee; and rich, sweet warming Christmas amber **Vorst** (8.5%: ★★+).

We estimate that new proto-breweries are arising at the rate of about one every two or three weeks at present – which is absurd. We know of several others that will almost definitely have commercialised in the time between we went to press and hit the streets – including Rock City (www.rockcitybeers.com), Roodbaard (roodbaardbier.webklik.nl) and Santpoorts (www.santpoortsbier.nl). We suspect there will be a dozen more.

Major imported beers

The Netherlands' history as a trading nation is visible in its beer culture, where domestic brands have long wrestled for shelf space with imports from around the world.

This chapter is not intended as a comprehensive digest of every foreign beer sold in the Netherlands. Instead, it is a brief overview of those you are most likely to encounter – for better or worse. The reason for its heavy slant towards Belgium will become obvious when you walk into virtually any café.

We assume familiarity on the reader's part with some global brands. Beers such as Czech Pilsner Urquell, and a certain Irish stout, need no introduction from us.

We do not list all the products from the breweries listed below, preferring to list only those found commonly in the Dutch market.

For further ratings we recommend the *Pocket Beer Book 2015* by Stephen Beaumont and Tim Webb (Octopus Books: £12.99: ISBN 978-1-84533-916-6).

TRAPPIST IMPORTS

Trappist ales are among the commonest imported ales. Almost any bar menu with 50+ beers will include many of the Belgian ones, and the 2012 Austrian arrival Engelszell is making inroads too. We will be interested to see if the other newcomer, Spencer Trappist Ale from St. Joseph's Abbey in Spencer, Massachussetts, makes it over in due course.

Achel
Brouwerij der Trappistenabdij De Achelse Kluis (Hamont-Achel, Belgium; www.achelsekluis.org)
The newest Belgian Trappist brewery, opened in 1999. It is almost Dutch, since the abbey's small estate straddles the national border – marked with a white line across its courtyard. The brewery however falls firmly on the southern side, which is where they pay their taxes.
YEAR-ROUND: tasty **Blond** (8%: ★★+) is more tripel than the name hints; and very good dubbel **Bruin** (8%: ★★★).

Chimay
Bières de Chimay (Baileux, Belgium; www.chimay.com)
The second-largest Trappist brewery after Westmalle had to simplify its **Chimay** beers some years ago to streamline production, though it remains popular.
YEAR-ROUND: chocolate-brown 'sort of dubbel' **Rouge** (7%: ★★); decently dry **Tripel** (8%: ★★+), or Blanche; and strong dark **Bleue** (9%: ★★★), a former classic that can still be great (★★★+) when cellared in 75cl **Grande Réserve** format.
ALSO: they make amber **Mont des Cats**

(7.6%: ★★+) for the Trappist abbey of that name at Godewaersvelde in northern France (www.abbaye-montdescats.fr).

Engelszell

Stift Engelszell Trappistenbier-Brauerei (Engelhartszell an der Donau, Austria; www.stift-engelszell.at)
Austrian novitiate that restarted brewing in 2012, expanding the Belgian-Dutch Trappist duopoly.
YEAR-ROUND: light-amber **Benno** (6.9%: ★★+); and fuller-bodied brown **Gregorius** (9.7%: ★★+).

Orval

Brasserie de l'Abbaye de Notre-Dame d'Orval (Villers-devant-Orval, Belgium; www.orval.be)
Beautifully situated abbey in the far south of Belgium, known around the world for the eponymous beer that is 98% of its production and for its iconic bottle.
YEAR-ROUND: former world beater **Orval** (6.2%: ★★★+) was simplified for a time but remains a great dry amber, now regaining its brettanomyces-conditioned edge.

Rochefort

Brasserie de l'Abbaye de Notre-Dame de St. Remy (Rochefort, Belgium; www.abbaye-rochefort.com)
Of all the traditional Trappist brewers, **Trappistes Rochefort** seems the one most able to cope with rising demand without sacrificing quality. All three remain darkly moreish.
YEAR-ROUND: quaffable dark ruddy amber dubbel **6** (7.5%: ★★+); glorious house work-horse **8** (9.2%: ★★★+); and evening closer **10** (11.3%: ★★★★), a world classic in every sense.

Westmalle

Brouwerij der Trappisten van Westmalle (Westmalle, Belgium; www.trappistwestmalle.be)
In production since 1836 and the largest Trappist brewery. Probably the most common in the Netherlands, found in a high proportion of bars.
YEAR-ROUND: chocolate-brown **Dubbel** (7.5%: ★★★) and golden dry **Tripel** (9.5%: ★★★) were the originals, and still pretty much define their respective genres.

Westvleteren

Brouwerij der Sint-Sixtus Trappistenabdij (Westvleteren, Belgium; www.sintsixtus.be)
Reclusive rural brewers whose policy of making small amounts of beers that are hard to source has led inadvertently to a cult of adulation. Rated in some circles as the world's best beers, with anyone daring to suggest otherwise being prone to ridicule. Well they are damn fine, but they are not the best. Ridicule away. It remains to be seen what effect recent supermarket link-ups to raise cash for renovations will have on their untarnishable image.
YEAR-ROUND: relative lightweight floral **Blond** (5.8%: ★★★+); liquorice-tinted dubbel **Extra 8** (8%: ★★★); and **Abt 12** (10.2%: ★★★+), the dark barley wine that gets the geeks in a flap.

BELGIAN IMPORTS

It was the arrival of beers from more distinctive Belgian breweries in the 1970s that kicked off the Dutch beer revolution and inspired some of the country's pioneer brewers. Currently those imports that appear in bars are mostly from the safe end of the spectrum In time the more idiosyncratic beers that have made Belgium the world's most respected brewing nation are bound to spread.

Achouffe (Duvel Moortgat)
Brasserie d'Achouffe (Achouffe, Luxembourg province; www.achouffe.be)
Founded by an early beer rebel who rowed against the current, badging with gnomes instead of monks. Bought out by Duvel Moortgat in 2006 and omnipresent in Dutch beer bars.
YEAR-ROUND: simplified, but still decent coriander-spiced blond **La Chouffe** (8.0%: ★★+); dependable dark Scotch-ish **McChouffe** (8.0%: ★★); seasonal **Chouffe Bok 6666** (6.5%: ★★) gatecrashing the Dutch party; and winter's **N'Ice Chouffe** (10.0%: ★★+).

Anker
Brouwerij het Anker (Mechelen, Antwerp; www.hetanker.be)
Mechelen brewers with a documented history going back to 1369. A solid performer that manages both interest and reliable consistency in its **Gouden Carolus** brands.
YEAR-ROUND: journeyman amber **Ambrio** (8.0%: ★★); beefy brown Trappist-ish **Classic** (8.5%: ★★★); golden, strongly hopped, bittersweet **Hopsinjoor** (8.5%: ★★+); and balanced, dry golden **Tripel** (9.0%: ★★+).
ALSO: two **Cuvée van de Keizer** barley wines are brewed annually and sold in 75cl bottles. The hefty blue-label dark **Blauw** (11.0%: ★★★) improves (>★★★★) with cellaring; while simpler blonder red-labelled **Rood** (11.0%: ★★★) is less likely to do so.

Bocq
Brasserie du Bocq (Purnode, Namur; www.bocq.be)
Family brewers since 1858. Besides their own beers they brew a dizzying number by contract, including a few of the St-Feuillien range. Our list is the tip of the iceberg.
YEAR-ROUND: the **Gauloise** brands include refreshing **Ambrée** (5.5%: ★★); sweetish **Blonde** (6.3%: ★★); and clean, competent **Brune** (8.1%: ★★). Others are spiced white **Blanche de Namur** (4.5%: ★★); and herbal lightweight tripel **Deugniet** (7.3%: ★★).
ALSO: for the **Corsendonk** beer warehouse they make sweet-edged brown **Pater** (7.5%: ★★); and drier blond **Agnus** (7.5%: ★★).

Boon
Brouwerij Boon (Lembeek, Flemish Brabant; www.boon.be)
Of all the traditional lambic makers, Frank Boon has had the most impact on the Dutch market – mainly thanks to Palm's 50% stake and control of distribution. Whereas others are usually found only in good specialist shops and cafés, Boon's are found nationwide.
YEAR-ROUND: simple **Boon Kriek** (4%: ★★), the welcome mat for the hesitant lambic-curious; intensely fruity, sour and complex **Oude Kriek** (6%: ★★★+); gorgeous grapefruity **Oude Geuze** (7%: ★★★); and **Oude Geuze Mariage Parfait** (8%: ★★★+), a fabulous blend of the best casks in the brewery.

Bosteels
Brouwerij Bosteels (Buggenhout, East Flanders; www.bestbelgianspecialbeers.be)
Family brewer since 1791, responsible for two Belgian icons.
YEAR-ROUND: sweet amber **Pauwel Kwak** (8%: ★★), less memorable than its stand-mounted coachman's glass; superior spicy **Tripel Karmeliet** (8.5%: ★★+); and vivacious, pungent highly carbonated blond barley wine **DeuS** (11.5%: ★★★), for serving in champagne flutes.

Brabandere

Brouwerij de Brabandere (Bavikhove, West Flanders; www.brouwerijdebrabandere.be) Family brewers who make a host of beers, only some of which are common in the Netherlands. Formerly named Bavik, the brewery was rebranded in 2014 to mark its 120th anniversary.

YEAR-ROUND: the **Petrus** brands include sour **Oud Bruin** (5.5%: ★★), a blend of brown and oak-aged ales, nothing like the sweet Dutch style; amber **Speciale** (5.5%: ★★), in the soft sweet style; malty **Dubbel Bruin** (6.5%: ★★+); dryish **Blond** (6.6%: ★★); run-of-the mill **Tripel** (7.5%: ★★); and striking, sour, oaked **Aged Pale** (7.3%: ★★+), originally only for the US market. Spiced white **Wittekerke** (5%: ★★) is a decent effort, though its sweet medicinal sister **Rosé** (4.3%: ★) is nastiness personified.

De Ranke

Brouwerij de Ranke (Wevelgem, West Flanders; www.deranke.be) Reassuringly consistent new-wave Belgian brewer, founded in 2005, and hop-forward since some years before the trend. All their beers are consistently very good.

YEAR-ROUND: deliciously spicy **Saison de Dottignes** (5.5%: ★★★); outstandingly bitter pale ale **XX Bitter** (6.2%: ★★★+); blond ale and lambic blend **Cuvée de Ranke** (7.0%: ★★+); herbal hoppy tripel **Guldenberg** (8.5%: ★★★+); and tasty dark **Noir de Dottignes** (9.0%: ★★★).

Dochter van de Korenaar

Brouwerij De Dochter van de Korenaar (Baarle-Hertog, Antwerp; www.dedochtervandekorenaar.be) Founded in 2007 by a Dutchman, in a Belgian part of the anomalous enclave of Baarle-Hertog, which is surrounded by the Netherlands. We would love to claim it as Dutch, but hey ho. Once elusive, their sometimes experimental brews are becoming easier to track down.

YEAR-ROUND: golden saison-ish **Noblesse** (5.5%: ★★+) sometimes appears as stronger, dry-hopped **Extra-Ordinaire** (7.0%: ★★★);

lovely golden hoppy IPA **Belle Fleur** (6.0%: ★★★+); smoky amber **Bravoure** (6.5%: ★★+); spicy rye-based, hoppy tripel-ish **Finesse** (8.5%: ★★+); and dark brown almost-porter **Embrasse** (9.0%: ★★+), which gains depth if not subtlety in oak-aged form.

Dolle Brouwers

De Dolle Brouwers (Diksmuide, West Flanders; www.dedollebrouwers.be) Founded in 1980, the Mad Brewers are significantly less mad than most brewers, having found what they are good at – making characterful ales – and sticking to it.

YEAR-ROUND: dark-blond **Arabier** (8.5%: ★★+); sour-edged brown **Oerbier** (9.0%: ★★+); deliciously honeyed Easter **Boskeun** (10.0%: ★★★); and powerfully rich Christmas barley wine **Stille Nacht** (8.5%: ★★+).

Dubuisson

Brasserie Dubuisson (Pipaix, Hainaut; www.br-dubuisson.com) Family brewery since 1769, mainly known for making insanely strong barley wines.

YEAR-ROUND: **Bush** beers include filtered winolager **Blonde** (10.5%: ★★); flagship sweet **Ambrée** (12.0%: ★★+); caramel-laced **Noël** (12%: ★★), the Christmas turkey; and wonderfully complex **Prestige** (13%: ★★★+), oak-aged Ambrée reseeded and sold in 75cl bottles. They also make spicy, sweetish blond **Cuvée des Trolls** (7%: ★★).

Dupont

Brasserie Dupont (Tourpes-Leuze, Hainaut; www.brasserie-dupont.com) Farmhouse brewery founded in 1844, family-run by Duponts since 1920. They have a deserved reputation for excellence, largely thanks to their unique house yeasts.

YEAR-ROUND: dry, herbal and glorious **Saison Dupont** (6.5%: ★★★★), the last word in farmhouse saisons; slightly softer, dry **Moinette Blonde** (8.5%: ★★★+) is almost as good, defining what a strong blond should be; spicy **Moinette Brune** (8.5%: ★★+) pales only beside its housemates; and dry-hopped amber **Avec les Bon Voeux** (9.5%: ★★★), another corker.

Duvel Moortgat

Brouwerij Duvel Moortgat (Breendonk, Antwerp; www.duvelmoortgat.be)
Established in 1871, and now among Belgium's largest independents. Growth was achieved partly by buying other brewers, including the beer conditioning works of Liefmans in East Flanders. Unaffiliated to any chain, flagship Duvel is sold in virtually all Dutch cafés, making it the country's single most widespread beer – a marketing coup.
YEAR-ROUND: bland lager **Vedett** (5%: ★+) is targeted at the young; all-conquering hero, strong blond **Duvel** (8.5%: ★★★) remains annoyingly good despite its ubiquity; but more complex hugely hopped **Duvel Triple-Hop** (9.5%: ★★★+) reminds us how good it was. The **Maredsous** brands include balanced blond **6** (6.0%: ★★+); sweetish dubbel **8** (8.0%: ★★+); and unsubtle turbocharged tripel **10** (10.0%: ★★). The **Liefmans** brands are brewed at Breendonk. Odd, sugary **Fruitesse** (4.2%: ★+) is a synthetic-tasting fruit drink that expresses its confusion when served on the rocks; while much nicer, sour, cherry-laden **Cuvée Brut** (6%: ★★+) is, like the oak-aged, sour brown **Goudenband** (8%: ★★+) finished at Liefmans in Oudenaarde (www.liefmans.be).

Haacht

Brouwerij Haacht (Boortmeerbeek, Flemish Brabant; www.haacht.com)
Despite being Belgium's largest independent, only part of its range appears north of the border. Some would claim that is a good thing.
YEAR-ROUND: **Leeuw Pilsener** (5%: ★+), a bland recreation of the bland Dutch original;

mediocre **Keizer Karel** (or Charles Quint) golden-blond Goudblond (8.5%: ★★) and dark-amber Ambrée (9%: ★★); and **Tongerlo** beers **Blond** (6.0%: ★★), dark sugary **Bruin** (6.0%: ★★), standard **Tripel** (8.0%: ★★), and a spiced **Christmas** (6.5%: ★★) – none worth writing about.

Halve Maan

Huisbrouwerij De Halve Maan (Bruges, West Flanders; www.halvemaan.be)
Historic brewery on the Bruges tourist trail, condemned to museum status for years. Brewing resumed properly in 2007 and bravery arrived in 2013. New brands will come.
YEAR-ROUND: safe **Brugse Zot Blond** (6.0%: ★★); its dark sister **Dubbel** (7.5%: ★★); and beefier **Straffe Hendrik Tripel** (9.0%: ★★).

Huyghe

Brouwerij Huyghe (Melle, East Flanders; www.delirium.be)
Brewery near Ghent dating from 1906 and making a huge (60+) range of beers, many to commission. Like other brewers who make too wide a range, quality fluctuates across the portfolio. Its pink elephants denote its star brand.
YEAR-ROUND: easy-going spiced blond **Delirium Tremens** (8.5%: ★★), less great than the marketing claims; simpler brown **Delirium Nocturnum** (8.5%: ★★); and golden **La Guillotine** (8.5%: ★★), the only thing cutting-edge about it being the name. Its **Mongozo** beers use exotic fruits to make odd-tasting sweet drinks, the least bad of which may be **Palmnut** (7.0%: ★+).

Koninck (Duvel Moortgat)

De Koninck (Antwerp, Antwerp; www.dekoninck.be)
Iconic city brewer since 1833, De Koninck failed to catch the bus to the beer revolution and had to be bailed out by Duvel Moortgat in 2010. Not dead yet.
YEAR-ROUND: flagship **De Koninck** (5.0%: ★★) once defined the classic Belgian speciaal; average **Tripel** (8%: ★★), occasionally making it over the border; as does amber **Winterkoninck** (6.5%: ★★).

Lefèbrve

Brasserie Lefèbvre (Quenast, Wallonian Brabant; www.brasserielefebvre.be)
Family-run independent brewery, founded in 1871, sometimes guilty of taking its eye off the quality ball.
YEAR-ROUND: the **Floreffe** range of abbey beers includes boring **Blonde** (6.3%: ★+); dull dark **Double** (6.3%: ★+); lightly spiced **Triple** (7.5%: ★★); and aniseed brown **Prima Melchior** (8.0%: ★★), which does somewhat better. Others include sweet spiced **Blanche de Bruxelles** (4.5%: ★★); plain golden tripel **Moeder Overste** (8%: ★★); honeyed golden amber **Barbãr** (8%: ★★); darker honeyed winter **Barbãr Bok** (8%: ★★); and hoppy golden **Hopus** (8.3%: ★★+), arguably the house standout.

Lindemans

Brouwerij Lindemans (Vlezenbeek, Flemish Brabant; www.lindemans.be)
Family brewers since 1811, making only lambics but tending to send mostly the sweet commercial variety north. Their two sharp, light Cuvée René oude beers are rarely seen here.
YEAR-ROUND: the current **Lindemans** imports are sticky, cherry-laden **Kriek** (4%: ★★) and barely alcoholic raspberry **Framboise** (2.5%: ★★) each needing to be more tart; better dark-amber **Faro** (4.5%: ★★); disappointing filtered sweet **Gueuze** (5%: ★+).

Omer

Brouwerij Omer Vander Ghinste (Bellegem, West Flanders; www.omer.be)
Fifth generation family brewery that dabbles in brettanomyces fermentation. Known as Bockor since 1977, it reverted to its historical name in 2014.
YEAR-ROUND: **Kriek Max** (3.5%: ★+) and **Rosé Max** (4.5%: ★) are its tackiest sweet fruit beers; while dryish blond Duvel-oid **Omer** (8.0%: ★★+) is a sign of their new attitude.

Palm

Palm Breweries (Steenhuffel, Flemish Brabant; www.palm.be)
Second-largest Belgian independent, founded in 1747. The Speciale is almost as omni-present in the Netherlands as Duvel (above).
YEAR-ROUND: **Palm** flagship amber **Speciale** (5.2%: ★★); darker **Dobbel** (5.5%: ★★), is similar but beefed up for winter; clean-tasting amber **Royale** (7%: ★★); and single-hopped amber **Sauvin** (4.6%: ★★). Their **Steenbrugge** beers **Wit** (5%: ★★), **Dubbel Bruin** (6.5%: ★★), **Blond** (6.5%: ★★), and **Tripel** (8.5%: ★★) all contain gruut, a herbal blend, but still hog the safe middle ground. Dry pilsener **Estaminet** (5.0%: ★★); and safe **Brugge Tripel** (8.2%: ★★) also appear.

Proef

Proefbrouwerij (Lochristi, East Flanders; www.proefbrouwerij.com)
State of the art modern brewery with academic links, which has cornered the market in contract brewing, mostly for homeless brewers and commercial breweries that want to test out an idea, plus beer commissioners. Standards are generally high. For those brewed for Dutch companies, see above.
YEAR-ROUND: their own **Reinaert** range includes standard **Amber** (7%: ★★); more impressive golden **Tripel** (9%:★★+); and enjoyable brown barley wine **Grand Cru** (9.5%: ★★+). For Belgian commissioner **Viven** they make a great hoppy **Porter** (7%: ★★★) and even hoppier **Imperial IPA** (8%★★+), among others.

Rodenbach (Palm)

Brouwerij Rodenbach (Roeselare, West Flanders; www.rodenbach.be)
The leading exponents of sour, oak-aged ales, bought by Palm in 1998, who caused a near riot by fixing the barrels. Beers are conditioned in oak tuns at the brewery for up to two years.
YEAR-ROUND: regular **Rodenbach** (5.0%: ★★), a soft blend of young brown and oak-aged ale; sharply sour, minimally sweetened, complex **Rodenbach Grand Cru** (6.0%: ★★★+) is made from undiluted aged beer from different tuns, for balance.

Saint-Feuillien

Brasserie Saint-Feuillien (Le Rœulx, Hainaut; www.st-feuillien.com)
Originally founded in 1873 and closed for a

decade before reappearing in full 19th century splendour in 1988.
YEAR-ROUND: spicily delicious **Saison** (6.5%: ★★★); rounded dry **Blonde** (7.5%: ★★+); complex golden **Triple** (8.5%: ★★+); and top-of-the range aromatic strong tripel **Grand Cru** (9.5%: ★★★).
SEASONAL: spicy **Christmas Cuvée de Noël** (9.0%: ★★+).
ALSO: dark, burnt-edged **Brune** (7.5%: ★★+) is made by du Bocq (above).

Schelde

Scheldebrouwerij (Meer, Antwerp; www.scheldebrouwerij.nl)
Founded in Zeeland in 1993, the international removal vans came in 2007 and moved it slightly north but very east, across the border into Belgium. The concept has not changed much and the beers remain pretty good.
YEAR-ROUND: pale ale **Mug Bitter** (5.0%: ★★); blond **Strandgaper** (6.2%: ★★); dubbel-like **Dulle Griet** (6.5%: ★★); maltier blond **Lamme Goedzak** (7.0%: ★★+); newer standout, dry-hopped tripel **Hop Ruiter** (8.0%: ★★★); simpler coriander-spiced tripel **Zeezuiper** (8.0%: ★★+); unsubtle barley wine **'n Toeback** (8.0%: ★★); and dark **Oesterstout** (8.5%: ★★), which gets pumped over oyster shells.
SEASONAL: autumnal **Wildebok** (6.5%: ★★).

Sint Bernardus

Brouwerij St. Bernard (Watou, West Flanders; www.sintbernardus.be)
Originally founded in 1946 to brew Westvleteren clones called St Sixtus on a commercial scale, it has since developed its own range.
YEAR-ROUND: **St Bernardus** beers include above-average spiced **Wit** (5.5%: ★★+); fruity dubbel **Pater 6** (6.7%: ★★+); rounded bitter **Tripel** (7.5%: ★★★); peardrop-tinted 'double dubbel' **Prior 8** (8.0%: ★★★+); and superb dark barley wine **Abt 12** (10.5%: ★★★+), which can warm like a Rochefort. Also, spiced brown **Grottenbier** (6.5%: ★★+), said to be aged in caves.

Slaghmuylder

Brouwerij Slaghmuylder (Ninove, East Flanders; www.witkap.be)
Family brewery since 1860, with an unpronounceable name for many. Fortunately, their exported range **Witkap Pater** makes for easier branding.
YEAR-ROUND: aromatic blond **Stimulo** (6.0%: ★★+); burnt-caramel-tinted **Dubbel** (7.0%: ★★); and complex, spicy **Tripel** (7.5%: ★★★).

Van Den Bossche

Brouwerij Van Den Bossche (Sint-Lievens-Esse, East Flanders; www.paterlieven.be)
Mid-size family brewery, primarily known in the Netherlands for its **Pater Lieven** 'abbey' range.
YEAR-ROUND: spiced **Wit** (4.5%: ★★); agreeably complex **Blond** (6.5%: ★★+); superior dark **Bruin** (6.5%: ★★+); and gently spiced **Tripel** (8.0%: ★★)
SEASONAL: chocolate-laden **Kerst Pater Special Christmas** (9.0%: ★★+).

Van Eecke

Brouwerij Van Eecke (Watou, West Flanders; www.brouwerijvaneecke.be)
Respected brewery established in 1862 in the village at the heart of West Flanders hop yards.
YEAR-ROUND: citrussy **Watou's Witbier** (5.0%: ★★+); unassuming but tasty hoppy pale ale **Poperings Hommelbier** (7.5%: ★★+); and the Kapittel range of abbey beers, including ordinary dubbel **Pater** (6.0%: ★★); rich dark tripel **Prior** (9.0%: ★★★); and sweetish amber **Tripel Abt** (10.0%: ★★+).

Van Honsebrouck

Brouwerij Van Honsebrouck (Ingelmunster, West Flanders; www.vanhonsebrouck.be)
Commercially minded brewery founded in 1900 and somehow missing the plot of where Belgium fits in the global beer revolution.
YEAR-ROUND: the missable **St Louis** range includes cherried **Kriek** (4.5%: ★+); and an off-beat **Gueuze** (4.5%: ★+), made with the right stuff in the wrong way, ending with overly sweet simplicity. Brigand (9.0%: ★★) is a strong blond; and the **Kasteel** range includes blond **Hoppy** (6.5%: ★★), which isn't

very; airheaded **Blond 7** (7.0%: ★★); ruby-red **Rouge** (8.0%: ★★+), with syrupy fruit; unsubtle punch-in-the-face heavyweights blond **Tripel** (11.0%: ★★) and dark **Donker** (11.0%: ★★); and **Cuvée du Château** (11.0%: ★★+), which they imply is cellared for ten years.

Van Steenberge

Brouwerij Van Steenberge (Ertvelde, East Flanders; vansteenberge.com) Long-standing family brewer with a wide but shrinking range, with even more brewed, or at least relabelled under contract. The regular Dutch visitors are limited. *YEAR-ROUND:* the **Augustijn** beers are above-average **Blond** (7.5%: ★★+), shining above the normal peroxide set; less-distinguished dubbel **Donker** (7.0%: ★★); and souped-up but simpler blond **Grand Cru** (9.0%: ★★). Strong blond **Piraat** at Duvel-strength **9°** (9.0%: ★★) may be disappearing while the **10.5°** (10.5%: ★★) gets a revamp to push it closer to more serious dark, spicy barley wine **Gulden Draak** (10.5%: ★★★). *SEASONAL:* autumn **Leute Bokbier** (7.5%: ★★).

Verhaeghe

Brouwerij Verhaeghe (Vichte, West Flanders; www.brouwerijverhaeghe.be) Family-run brewery since 1880, making several decent brews, though only one is widely available in the Netherlands. *YEAR-ROUND:* precocious **Duchesse de Bourgogne** (6.2%: ★★★+), a devilishly lovely sweet 'n' sour brown ale blended from beers matured in oak for many months.

Other Belgians

The above list is necessarily selective. For a fuller look at Belgian beer we recommend *Good Beer Guide Belgium* by Tim Webb & Joe Stange (CAMRA Books: 7th edition March 2014). To source other good Belgian brews in the Netherlands you will need to track down the top beer shops and specialist cafés. As a simple rule, if you encounter any lambics from Drie Fonteinen (3F), Oud Beersel, Girardin, Cantillon, de Cam or Tilquin; or ales from Struise, Kerkom, Senne, Rulles, or Cazeau, just plunge right in.

GERMAN IMPORTS

It is hardly a surprise, but behind Belgium the commonest Dutch imports originate from across its only other land border, with Germany. The best of those that are easily accessible tend to be Bavarian weizens.

Three big name German lagers have cornered the imported pilsener market, one being AB InBev-owned Beck's (see Big group imports below). The other two are **Warsteiner Premium Verum** (4.8%: ★★), an easy-drinking clean pils from North Rhine-Westphalia; and **Bitburger Premium Pils** (4.8%: ★★), from Bitburg near the Luxembourg border, which is arguably the better but still merely OK.

More interesting are the breweries below:

Erdinger

Erdinger Weissbräu (Erding, Bavaria; www.erdinger.de) The world's largest weizen brewer, founded in 1886, and likely the one with the biggest share of the Dutch market. *YEAR-ROUND:* uncomplicated, misty **Erdinger Weissbier** (5.3%: ★+) is an entry-level weizen, which may explain its popularity.

Paulaner (Heineken-ish)

Paulaner Brauerei (Munich, Bavaria; www.paulaner-brauerei.de) Founded in 1649, with Heineken taking a 49.9% stake in 2001. Their reach has increased as their excellence has wavered. Most Hacker-Schorr brews are also made here. *YEAR-ROUND:* reliably safe **Paulaner** beers include cloudy **Hefe-Weissbier Naturtrüb** (5.5%: ★★); its duskier sister **Hefe-Weissbier Dunkel** (5.3%: ★★); and the more impressive dubbelbock **Salvator** (7.9%: ★★). **Hacker-Schorr** brands include rounded **Hefe-Weisse** (5.5%: ★★); and unobtrusive dark **Dunkle Weisse** (5.3%: ★+).

Heller-Brau Trum

Heller-Bräu Trum (Bamberg, Bavaria; www.schlenkerla.de) Heroic Upper Franconian brewery founded in 1678, though its legendary Schlenkerla tavern, from which the beers take their name, traces its roots further back. It is globally famous for its smoked beers, one of which is common in the Netherlands.

YEAR-ROUND: **Aecht Schlenkerla Rauchbier Märzen** (5.1%: ★★★+) is a gloriously unsubtle black, bottom-fermented smoked lager, often imitated but rarely bettered.

Weihenstephan

Bayerische Staatsbrauerei Weihenstephan (Freising, Bavaria; weihenstephaner.de) Bavarian brewery with half a claim to be the world's oldest, claiming a history of sorts back to 1040. Nearly a millennium later the beers are still good.

YEAR-ROUND: flagship **Weihenstephaner Hefe Weissbier** (5.4%: ★★★) has more banana than a small Caribbean island; darker **Hefe Weissbier Dunkel** (5.3%: ★★) holds back on banana and adds chocolate; dubbelbock **Korbinian** (7.0%: ★★) adds subtle maltiness; and rounded weizenbock **Vitus** (7.7%: ★★+) balances everything with bitter citrus.

UK IMPORTS

For years the only Anglo-Irish beers found in the Netherlands were in imitation British or Irish pubs designed to lure the unfussy expat and stag party tourists, who knew no better. Most were either over-carbonated keg ales of the type that caused CAMRA to come into being, or dull Irish stouts.

Times have changed. And while the horrors still exist, some cask-conditioned ales manage the journey across the North Sea and Britain's nascent craft beer brewers have a foot in the door. Indeed one punk entrepreneur is already in up to their knees.

Of the established brewers, Fullers of Chiswick is the only one appearing with any regularity, respect for its products being boosted by its wonderful annual limited-edition **Vintage Ale** (8.5%: ★★★ > ★★★★).

Two lesser but oft-seen bottled ales are Wychwood/Marston's dark bitter **Hobgoblin** (5.2%: ★★), and Greene King's all-too smooth **Morland Old Speckled Hen** (5.2%: ★+).

BrewDog

BrewDog (Ellon, Aberdeenshire; www.brewdog.com) Established as recently as 2007, this wire-haired Scottish terrier is gradually taking over the world – making enemies and influencing people everywhere. With finely judged marketing and more luck that any brewer deserves, it is no surprise they have made a splash in the Netherlands, where the entrepreneurial spirit gets applause rather than sneers. The secret weapon at present is their beers, which are either good or LoL, occasionally both. Centuries ago, when the English wanted an empire they sent the Scots out to get it for them. Some things never change.

YEAR-ROUND: unusually restrained golden blond **Dead Pony Club** (3.8%: ★★+); similar but less great **Trashy Blond** (4.1%: ★★); increasingly refined grapefruit bomb **Punk IPA** (5.6%: ★★+); impressive imperial stout **Riptide** (8%: ★★★); full-on bitter citrus **Hardcore IPA** (9.2%: ★★★+); and beautiful but absurd cranberry stout **Tokyo*** (18.2%: ★★★★). More interesting London brewers like Meantime and The Kernel are starting to appear in top bars, but less frequently than we would like to see.

US IMPORTS

In contrast to the British beer revolution the American one has made real headway in the Dutch market. Among the better imports are Anderson Valley's bittersweet **Hop Ottin' IPA** (7.0%: ★★★); Alaskan's deliciously fruity **Smoked Porter** (6.5%: ★★★+); and Left Hand's creamy **Milk Stout** (6.0%: ★★★). Two brewers wave the Stars & Stripes more vigorously.

Anchor

Anchor Brewing Company (San Francisco, California; www.anchorbrewing.com) Founded in 1896, and one of the foundation-stone stories of why modern beer is as it is. Saved from extinction by an alternative son of a wealthy family, its modern form came in to being in the 1970s, and is perhaps the

original craft beer standard bearer.
YEAR-ROUND: flagship **Steam Beer** (5.6%: ★★★) showed the world how to make amber lager with true depth; genre-defining **Liberty Ale** (5.9%: ★★★) was an early IPA; and **Old Foghorn** (8.8%: ★★★) did the same for acceptable barley wines.

Flying Dog

Flying Dog Brewery (Frederick, Maryland; flyingdogales.com)
Aspen, Colorado brewpub that relocated to Maryland in 2008. They may not be the greatest American new wave brewer, but they have the best Dutch distribution.
YEAR-ROUND: hoppy pale ale **Doggie Style** (5.5%: ★★); citrus-central **Snake Dog IPA** (7.1%: ★★★); and subtler fruity IPA **Raging Bitch** (8.3%: ★★★).
ALSO: marvellously dry **Farmhouse IPA** (7.5%: ★★★) is fermented with a saison yeast for In de Wildeman in Amsterdam.

BIG GROUP IMPORTS

There once seemed to be an unspoken agreement that AB InBev and its predecessors would not push its major Belgian pilseners north into the Netherlands, and Heineken would not try to encroach south into Belgium. Then the gloves came off.

AB-InBev subsidiaries

The world's largest brewing corporation is now an inescapable part of the Dutch beer landscape. As well as its Dutch producer Dommelsch, dull pilsener **Jupiler** (5.2%: ★+) appears all over, though equally yawnsome **Stella Artois** (5.2%: ★+) remains rarer. Their **Becks** (4.8%: ★+) comes from Bremen, probably, while from Spaten-Franziskaner-Bräu of Munich comes dependably unremarkable cloudy weizen **Franziskaner Hefe-Weissbier** (5%: ★+). What is it about big brewery companies that compels them take the guts out of so many once-decent beers?
The group's **Leffe** brands are average dubbel **Brune** (6.5%: ★★); vacuous **Blonde** (6.6%: ★+); better blond **Royale** (7.5%: ★★);

uncouth amber **Radieuse** (8.5%: ★★); and oddly characterless heavyweight **9°** (9%: ★+).
From its smaller Hoegaarden brewery come white **Hoegaarden** (5%: ★+), a shadow of itself, tripel wannabe **Grand Cru** (8.7%: ★★), and chocolate-brown **Verboden Vrucht** (8.8%: ★★), which has gone all village idiot.
Its **Belle-Vue** sweetened lambic brands, cherried **Kriek** (5.2% ★+) and sweet, bland **Gueuze** (5.2%: ★+) seem to be slipping slowly away, thankfully.

Heineken subsidiaries

The Affligem brewery in Opwijk (Belgium) was taken over in effect by Heineken in 1999, but remains an ale brewery and has retained some originality. Thanks to shared distribution they are found commonly in the Netherlands. The **Affligem** brands are **Blond** (6.8%: ★★), **Dubbel** (7%: ★★) and **Tripel** (8.5%: ★★+) are all reliable examples of their genres, the latter being the standout. The **Postel** brands are bittersweet **Dobbel** (7%: ★★); and marginally more interesting **Tripel** (8.5%: ★★).
While Heineken keeps the bulk of its Alken subsidiary's output, such as Maes Pils and Cristal Alken, out of the Netherlands it takes in the **Mort Subite** fruit lambics. Ghastly **Pêche** (4.5%: ★) confirms peach is not a valid beer flavour; the regular **Gueuze** (4.5%: ★★) and **Kriek** (4.5%: ★+) taste artificially sweetened; while the **Oude Gueuze** (7.2%: ★★★) and **Oude Kriek** (6.5%: ★★★) are better by a universe breadth, but rare.
In the true spirit of the new Europe, we think the **Grimbergen** range of 'abbey beers' is brewed for this Dutch-owned Belgian operation by the Danish-owned French-based brewery Kronenbourg – a far cry from when Napoléon closed and sacked Grimbergen abbey. The main imports are reliably unremarkable **Dubbel** (6.5%: ★★); duller **Blond** (6.5%: ★+); and almost interesting **Tripel** (9.0%: ★★).
Also seen are flabby white **Brugs Tarwebier** (4.8%: ★+) and Duvel-wannabe tripels **Judas** (8.5%: ★★) and marginally better **Hapkin** (8.5%: ★★).

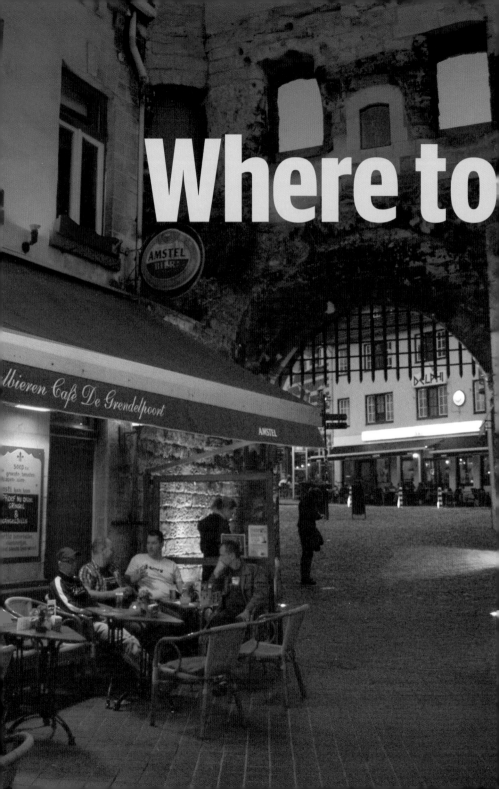

Where to

There follows a selection of Dutch beer outlets that we believe represents the best of the best, as it stood at the beginning of 2014.

find beer

The Netherlands has a rapidly growing beer culture, we are a tiny operation and not yet well known, and it takes time to turn researched words into a book, so we are bound to be out of date – though not by much, we hope.

If you find somewhere as good or better for beer than the places we list, or else that those we favour have been closed or ruined, please let us know via **timskelton@hotmail.com**.

WHAT WE LIST

We have included both drinking venues and places to buy beer to take home. Here are the standards we apply.

Beer cafés

A few exceptional cases notwithstanding, our arbitrary cut-off to define a bar, tavern, kroeg or eating house as a specialist beer venue is that 40 or more beers appear on its menu. A good selection of Dutch beers helps but is not essential.

Taphouses

All those breweries or beer makers that have a brewery taphouse or proeflokaal, literally 'tasting room', with regular and reliable opening times, should find it listed among the venues, regardless of how many other beers are served.

Beer stores

For beer shops and warehouses, the qualifying standard is 300 or more beers, unless we decided to make an exception.

HOW WE LIST IT

The selection is ordered alphabetically by province, then by town, and finally by venue name. For some towns we sweep up any oddities and near misses under 'Other venues' at the end of the full listings. Any shops and warehouses then appear at the end of the town listing under 'Beer to go'.

We have Anglicised some province names by changing Noord- to North and Zuid- to South.

We have also imposed the English alphabet by placing 'ij' between 'ii' and 'ik', instead of the Dutch convention of placing it between 'x' and 'z', which we only do when the preferred local spelling is with an old-fashioned 'y'.

Pub names have usually been simplified, dropping pronouns and other qualifiers. Hence 't Kuipertje becomes Kuipertje, In De Wildeman becomes simply Wildeman, and so on.

Opening times

Many bars list their hours simply as 'From 11.00' or similar, and stay open so long as someone is buying (and not misbehaving). Alternatively, if it gets quiet or the person in charge is getting bored and wants to go home, they can shut early. We try to list all closing times that are earlier than midnight.

UNDERSTANDING DUTCH CAFÉS

Where we use the term brown café, or kroeg, we mean a traditional café of that type that before the smoking ban had been browned by tobacco smoke. They will have some or all of the following: a wooden floor; dark wood tables, chairs and other fittings; smoke-stained walls and ceilings. The ambience kind of grows from there.

Blaauwe Ha Nijmegen

Etiquette

Dutch cafés are generally convivial paces but the staff have this annoying habit of assuming that everyone knows how to behave.

If you need to order at the bar it is usually obvious. The vast majority of cafés have table service so someone will come to take your order eventually, though attracting a waiter's attention is an art form, especially on a crowded terrace in summer. Staff have special training in how to look busy while scanning a room or terrace attentively, without actually spotting any of the sea of thirsty punters frantically waving at them.

In many parts of the world if you say that you would 'like a beer' a brief explanation will follow of the options. In the Netherlands, it will lead to the appearance of a small (20 cl) glass of industrial pilsener, poured fast until its foamy head spews over the top of the glass, to be flattened a deft flick from a white plastic spatula, the undrunk liquid going straight down the drain, and put in front of you.

If you want a particular beer, find a menu and ask for it by name. Then, when the waiter fails to understand your effort to prounce it in Anglo-Dutch, point and say, "That one." The Dutch speak English far better than English speakers attempt Dutch.

Many bars will serve you a pint (500ml) if you ask, though in doing so the word 'tourist' will appear on your forehead as a virtual tattoo. The arguments for drinking from small glasses are that you can finish them before they get warm – industrial pils fares badly at any temperature where the flavour becomes apparent – and people drink more of them.

Finally, many traditional pubs have a bell by the bar. Do not ring this. Unless that is you intend to buy everyone inside a drink, as that is the signal you will just have given.

Is there any interesting beer?

Even with the rise of craft beer, pilsener remains the overwhelmingly dominant species. The major brewers share the market between them. Market-leader Heineken is particularly prevalent in its North and South Holland homeland; Grolsch rules the eastern Netherlands; Bavaria is strongest in North Brabant; and AB InBev crops up everywhere, although they are now fond of promoting decidedly ordinary Jupiler ahead of home-grown names.

The bulk of cafés are owned by these same big boys and while not excluding products from other brewers altogether, only a few competitors are allowed. In the majority of cases this means a handful of Belgian abbey beers or real Trappist ales if you are lucky, plus a few familiar standard imports to bring the range up to around 15. This is typical of 90% of the country's bars.

Warning signs that you may be in for disappointment include plasticised generic beer menus, or beers on chalkboards being hailed simply as 'wit', 'tripel' or 'dubbel' etc, without reference to a specific brewer – a sure sign of disinterest. In contrast, cafés with a good range of beers are happy to make a song and dance about it. Look for boards on the street advertising the numbers in stock; or big chalkboards covering most interior walls.

Age limits

The minimum drinking age in bars used to be 16 but rose to 18 in January 2014. There are no age restrictions on children entering bars, although common sense applies – taking a toddler into a local boozer at midnight is certain to raise eyebrows. On the other hand, many larger places provide play areas and games to distract youngsters while mum and dad sup.

Smoking

In 2008 smoking was banned, though an exemption slipped in meaning that small bars where the landlord works alone got an option to allow smoking if they so choose. This loophole is set to change and it is about to become illegal to smoke in any bar or café, except in specially designated separate rooms with no table service.

It remains to be seen how well the law will be applied in practice. To understand the Dutch history of introducing laws and then ignoring them, see prostitution, cannabis and others.

Hemel, Nijmegen

Food

Where we describe a place as selling 'snacks' we mean the likes of *bitterballen,* or a hefty plate filled with cubed cheese and/or salami, while the term 'nibbles' means nothing larger than a small side dish of nuts.

Tipping

Tipping in bars is optional. If only buying drinks, it is perfectly acceptable to pay the exact amount. In restaurants, or if ordering food in a café, round up the bill to any convenient amount, adding no more than 5 to 10%.

SHOPS

We have been happy to list all the beer shops with a range that really impresses us.

Elsewhere, there are three major chains of retail stores that sell beer. The best by far and the place to head when touring is **Mitra** (www.mitra.nl), which has well over 200 outlets nationwide, most of which sell 100+ beers and some far more, as seen in our listings.

The largest chain, Gall & Gall (www.gall.nl) thus far carries a far less inspiring list – we have not found a single store meriting a special mention. Faring somewhat better is the 100-strong chain of independently titled Uw topSlijter stores (www.uwtopslijter.nl), many of which are OK beer-wise, and a couple – Zonneveld in Massluis and Drankenservice Gouda - beery enough to get their own listing with us.

Besides these physical beer shops and others in our listings, there are several web-only stores, most of which will only deliver within the Netherlands. The ones we know are:

De BierBoet – www.bierboet.nl
De Bierloods – bierloods.nl
De Biermeester – www.debiermeester.nl –
  sells unusual UK beers
Het Biermoment – www.hetbiermoment.nl
Biernavigatie.nl – www.biernavigatie.nl
Het Bierpaleis – www.bier-paleis.nl
Bierlab – bierlab.nl – *subscription service, whereby you have packages of surprise beers delivered every 1, 2, or 3 months.*

Drenthe

Now a flat, sparsely populated (pop. 490,000), largely agricultural province, back in the Bronze Age Drenthe was relatively crowded. Visible evidence of this are the 53 megalithic tombs, or dolmens (*hunebedden*) – built around 3,500 BC – that still dot the countryside.

In recent history, before World War II the Dutch government built a camp near Hooghalen to house Jewish refugees fleeing Hitler's Germany. Without irony, after the Nazi occupation began it was turned into a transit camp for Dutch Jews being shipped the other way, to concentration and extermination camps further east. Anne Frank went to Auschwitz on the last train to leave in September 1944.

This is deeply Protestant province and for nine years from 1993 had no breweries at all. This is changing slowly but the provincial capital Assen has yet to acquire its first beer destination.

LARGEST CENTRES: **Emmen** (110,000), **Assen** (67,000), **Hoogeveen** (55,000)

MORE INFORMATION: in.drenthe.nl

BREWERIES: **Gulzige Gans**, *Coevorden*; & **Maallust**, *Veenhuizen*

OTHER BEER MAKERS: **Drentsche Schans**, *Holsloot*

Coevorden, Drenthe

EMMEN
🔗 Emmen

Drenthe's largest city (pop. 110,000) is a classic example of 20th century Dutch town planning. It only appeared in the 1950s, as modern suburbs that had been built around farming communities expanded and merged. Its zoo, Dierenpark Emmen (www. dierenparkemmen.nl), attracts 1.5 million visitors per year.

Brasserie
Hoofdstraat 53 · T 0591 616675
www.debrasserie.nl
Fr from 09.00; Su from 11.00; others from 10.00

Large café on the main square, with a terrace and conservatory. Inside, a British telephone box doubles as a smoking room. A Heath Robinson series of interconnected ceiling fans are all driven by a single belt. Food served all day. The 50 beers are dominated by safe Belgians. Upstairs an old-fashioned all-wood bar is billed as the Tempelier Belgian beer café but is only open on Saturdays from 22.00 and has the same range.

COEVORDEN
20km SW of Emmen off N34
🔗 Coevorden

Small town (pop. 36,000) whose name means a river crossing for cattle, so Oxford in English or Bosphorus in Turkish. Around 1650 its castle was among the most powerful in Europe. The ancestors of 18th century British explorer George Vancouver, who gave his name to the Canadian city and province, came from here (Van Coevorden). A handy touring base for the Mommeriete tap and brewery in Gramsbergen (see Overijssel) and the rest of the region.
HOTEL TIP: **Talens** ★★★, Sallandsestraat 51 (T 0524 516251; www.hoteltalens.nl), or for something grander, try the castle (www.kasteelcoevorden.nl).

No full entries but **Miracle** (Bentheimerstraat 20 – T 0524 523434 – www.eetcafemiracle.nl – *Closed Mo; Su 16.00-22.00; Tu 11.30-22.00; We 10.30-22.00; others 10.30-24.00*) has a mock Art Deco interior and 30+ beers, while **Vancouver** (Friesestraat 9 – T 0524 855 148 – www.stadscafevancouver.nl – *Closed Mo&Tu; others from 14.00*) has good food and occupies a lovely stepped gable house dating from 1631.

Vancouver, Coevorden

GASTEREN
9km NE of Assen

Tiny village (pop. 400) on the 58 bus route from Assen.

BEER TO GO: Shop **Bierboe 't ij k Uit de Wildeman** (Westeinde 10 – **T** 0592 231421 – *Closed Su-Th; Fr 14.00-19.00; Sa 11.00-17.00*) is the domain of Henk Eggens, who founded In De Wildeman in Amsterdam, and now sells 80+ well-chosen beers from his garage. Will open at other times by appointment.

HOOGEVEEN
44km NE of Zwolle off A28 exit 26
 Hoogeveen

A quiet provincial town (pop. 55,000) that remained fenland until the railways arrived. Its wide, grid-like street pattern reflects canals formed by peat cutting, which were filled in sixty years ago.

Dégust

Hoofdstraat 38 · **T** 0528 233475
www.degust.nl
Closed Mo&Tu; others 15.00-24.00

Excellent beer café-restaurant on the main square, whose landlord learned his craft at Amsterdam's Arendsnest. The tiled floor interior has an 'ancient and modern' feel and includes a champagne rack. The food (*17.00-22.00, snacks until 23.30*) is great. Dishes use beer as a key ingredient. It has won awards for beer and food pairing. The menu had only 50 beers listed on our last visit but there were 120+ in stock. The Dutch-dominated range has many unexpected delights. The wine list is almost as long.

*OTHER **HOOGEVEEN** BEER VENUES:*

Friendly rock café **De Lijst** (Hoofdstraat 34 – **T** 0528 277747 www.cafedelijst.nl; *Closed Tu; Su from 18.00; others from 16.00*) has only 25 beers but occasional gems on tap.

Majesteit (Grote Kerkstraat 8 – **T** 0528 261899 – www.biercafedemajesteit.nl –

Closed Mo; others from 16.00) has colourful murals, chandeliers, wooden-beamed ceilings, and 35+ beers that almost deserve a full entry.

MEPPEL
25km NNE of Zwolle off A32 exits 1-3
 Meppel

The God-fearing townsfolk of Meppel (pop. 31,000) were once known as Meppeler Muggen (Meppel midges), due to an apocryphal tale that they once mistook a swarm of midges for the church tower being on fire.

If in town, central **Beurs** (Grote Kerkstraat 3 – **T** 0522 251661 – www.eetcafedebeurs.nl – *Su from 11.00; others from 08.00*) comes closest to a beer café, with a 30-odd range.

BEER TO GO: **Mitra Kisjes** (De Putstoel 2 – **T** 0522 255923 – www.mitrakisjes.nl – *Closed Su; Mo 12.00-18.00; Fr 09.00-21.00; Sa 09.00-17.00; others 09.00-18.00*) is one of the better in the national chain, with 300+ beers, and strong emphasis on Dutch brewers.

Dégust, Hoogeveen

RODEN

18km SW from Groningen off N372

Provincial town (pop. 15,000) with no decent pubs, but a great beer shop to compensate.

BEER TO GO: Sister of the like-named Groningen outlet, **Van Erp Dranken** (Raadhuisstraat 11 – **T** 050 501 0501 – **www. vanerpwijn.nl** – *Closed Su; Mo 13.00-18.00; Th 09.00-21.00; Sa 09.00-17.00; others 09.00-18.00*) stocks 500+ beers, with many Dutch options and 75cl choices. The range of single malts is also good.

VEENHUIZEN

15km W of Assen on N919

Spread out village (pop. 800) with a unique history as Europe's only 'colony within a country'. In the 1820s the Maatschappij van Weldadigheid (Society for Benevolence) bought the land to house and provide work for the poor, who worked blocks of farmland, most of which remain as they were. When the society went bust the land passed to the Justice Department, who turned it into a penal colony, with three prisons. Visit the National Prison Museum (Nationaal Gevangenismuseum,

www.gevangenismuseum.nl) and get a peek inside an actual working jail. The whole colony may soon become a UNESCO World Heritage site. Get there by bus 14 from Assen.

Maallust

Hoofdweg 140 · **T** 0592 388971
www.maallust.nl
Shut Mo; others 10.00-18.00

Brewery and tap in a former mill. Watch your head on the wooden beams. Above is a circular conference room, if you have a meeting planned. Simple lunches feature bread baked with spent brewer's grain, and cheese made next door. There is also apple pie, plus snacks. All the house beers are available on tap and in bottle, and for sale in gift packs.

Maallust Brewery and tap with conference room (below)

Flevoland

Created mostly on land reclaimed from the IJsselmeer and Markermeer in the 1950s and 60s, the Netherlands' newest province (pop. 400,000) only became official in 1986. Its two cities are not much older, Lelystad being founded in 1967 and Almere in the 1970s. We would love to tell you that town planners found room for picturesque squares surrounded by cafés but this would not be true.

Flevoland cafés have yet to get the beer message. It has more breweries than decent beer bars. Almere, now the country's 7th largest city, has none. Provincial capital Lelystad is no better. We hope to be proved wrong one day soon. Beer consumer group PINT gained a Flevoland branch in 2013, and Almere now hosts a beer festival, so the corpse is twitching.

Not everything is modern urban planning. The train between Almere and Lelystad passes through the Oostvaardersplassen nature reserve, an area used for 'rewilding' large herds of deer, and Europe's largest population of wild horses.

LARGEST CENTRES: **Almere** (196,000), **Lelystad** (76,000)

MORE INFORMATION: www.ookflevoland.nl

BREWERIES: **Kasparus**, *Nagele;* **Kemphaan**, *Almere;* **Koelschip**, *Almere;* **Praght**, *Dronten*

DRONTEN

30km W of Zwolle off N307

Dronten

Modern provincial town (pop. 41,000) founded in the 1960s.

Dorpsboerderij Dronten

Wisentweg 5a · **T** 0321 329332
www.dorpsboerderijdronten.nl
Closed Su (Oct-May); Mo-Sa 09.30–17.00; others 13.30–17.00

Small café west of town beside the Praght brewery, serving as its tap despite belonging to a neighbouring farm. Take bus 21 or 22 to Drieslag. This a dog-walkers' snack bar so do not expect grandeur. Counter service, then sit on the terrace. Two tap beers and half a dozen in bottles, all from next door. Bottles to take away. Do not feed the spaniels.

NAGELE

27km NE from Lelystad off N352
Village (pop. 2,000) in northern Flevoland. Take bus 345 from Lelystad to the Domineesweg stop, then call the pub and they will pick you up.

Kasparus

Eggestraat 14 · **T** 0527 240877
www.kasparus.nl
Closed Mo; others from 15.00 (times may vary)

Brewery tap on a remote industrial estate. The front resembles a warehouse, but the back has a rural canalside terrace. Inside, the wood and chipboard pub sometimes doubles as a cinema. To the side is a separate, vinyl-floored dining room. Reserve ahead to eat. Food (from 18.00) is cooked by the brewer's Hungarian wife, and reflects her origins. All available house beers are sold, which could be 15+, plus a few Hungarian or German imports.

Friesland (Fryslân)

The Netherlands' most independent province (pop. 646,000), and the only one with a local language that enjoys equal official status with Dutch. It includes four of the populated Wadden Islands – Vlieland, Terschelling, Ameland and Schiermonnikoog.

Frisian history pre-dates the Romans. Before it was conquered by the Franks in the Middle Ages, its influence had at times stretched as far as modern Belgium and northwest Germany. Today what remains is sustained by agriculture and tourism.

Its most famous event is the Elfstedentocht, a 200km ice skating marathon in which 16,000 racers speed through 11 towns along frozen canals. Because it requires a prolonged cold snap it does not happen that often – the last was in 1997.

A long history of conservative Calvinism meant having any form of fun was once frowned upon. This prompted an ancestor of this book to suggest fostering beer culture here was like 'trying to whisk honey'. We can report that while that honey has not yet reached the soft peaks stage, the mixture has become frothier.

And yes, this is where the cows came from.

LARGEST CENTRE: **Leeuwarden** (97,000)
MORE INFORMATION: www.visitfryslan.nl
BREWERIES: **Amelander**, *Ameland;* **Friese**, *Bolsward*
OTHER BEER MAKERS: **Terschellinger**, *Terschelling*

BALK

40km SSW from Leeuwarden off N359

Small Fries town (pop. 3,800) with one long main street, spliced lengthwise by a canal. Halfway along is Friesland's beeriest pub. Take bus 47 from Sneek.
HOTEL TIP: the **Teernstra**★ (below) has basic rooms.

Teernstra

Van Swinderenstraat 69 · **T** 0514 601013
www.hotelteernstra.nl
Daily from 10.00

Hotel, restaurant and café with bench seating outside, and a canalside terrace over the road. The largely wooden interior is divided in two: to the left is a locals' bar with billiards table; to the right a more formal restaurant (from 17.00). Empty beer bottles and enamels dominate. Lunch (until 17.00) and snacks are served in the bar. Maallust and De Molen feature prominently on the 90+ beer list.

Us Heit brewery, Bolsward

BOLSWARD

27km SW from Leeuwarden off A7 exit 18

Small town (pop.10,000) on the Elfstedentocht skating route, home to the province's oldest brewery. Take bus 92 or 350 from Leeuwarden.

Us Heit

Snekerstraat 43 · **T** 0515 577449
www.bij-usheit.nl
Closed Su-We; others 12.00–21.00

Friese brewery tap in a former food and drink technology college. You can drink in the first-floor tasting room, the former canteen, where a mural covers one wall, and brewing equipment is scattered about. A separate restaurant with a terrace on the ground floor serves lunches, high beer (as opposed to high tea), and dinners cooked using local ingredients. Four or 5 tap beers are available in each area. Bottles are sold in the shop.

*OTHER **BOLSWARD** BEER VENUES:*

Central canalside **Wijnberg** (Marktplein 5 – **T** 0515 572220 – www.wijnbergbolsward.nl – *daily from 08.00*) has 20+ beers, including some from Friese.

HARLINGEN

27km W from Leeuwarden off N31
Harlingen (Harlingen Haven for the ferry)

Small attractive harbour town (pop. 15,500) awash with fish restaurants, its ancient quays stretching into its shopping heart, lining the streets with sailing boats. Worth stopping off at if heading to the islands.

Old-school local **Skûtsje** (Heiligeweg 70 – **T** 0517 416768 – www.harlingen-skutsje.nl – *closed Mo; Tu-We from 19.00; others from 15.00 in theory*) has a nautical theme and 30 beers.

JOURE

29km S from Leeuwarden off A6 & A7 exit Knooppunt Joure

Neat provincial town (pop. 13,000) with one long main street. It has a history of clock making, and was the original home of the Douwe Egberts coffee company. Take bus 199 from Sneek or Heerenveen.

If you get thirsty shopping (see below), the **Stam** (Douwe Egbertsplein 3 – **T** 0513 414918 – www.cafe-destam.nl – *Mo&Tu from 19.00; others from 16.00*), just around the corner, is a brown café with table football and 20 beers.

BEER TO GO: Box of delights **Lekker Bier De Bierwinkel** (Kolkstraat 2a – **T** 0513 410190 – www.lekkerbierdebierwinkel.nl or www. bier-winkel.com – *shut Su&Mo; Fr 11.00-21.00; Sa 10.00-18.30; others 11.00-18.30*) stocks 1,000+ beers from all over and has an on-line store.

Lekker Bier De Bierwinkel, Joure

LEEUWARDEN
🚉 Leeuwarden

The provincial capital (pop. 97,000) is a pleasant place with canal-lined streets. This was the birthplace of Margaretha Zelle, the exotic dancer known as Mata Hari, who was shot as a spy in 1917. Much of her life is vague, but secret files are set to be de-classified in 2017. Another famous son was graphic artist MC Escher, he of those 'impossible' drawings with endless staircases. For a different kind of perspective try the Fries Museum (www.friesmuseum.nl) of local history.

HOTEL TIPS: **Bij de Waagsbrug**, Nieuwestad 135 (**T** 06 2466 4499; www.bijdewaagsbrug.nl) is a central 2-room B&B; while the up-market **Oranje**★★★★ Stationsweg 4 (**T** 058 212 6241; www.edenoranjehotel.nl), opposite the station, sometimes offers good deals.

Markies

Groot Schavernek 19 · **T** 06 4125 9568
www.de-markies.nl
Closed Su&Mo; others from 16.00

Compact café with a terrace on a small square, 200m west of the centre. The building was once a garage, then a pils swillers' hangout, before turning beery in 2010. It may change name to the Manke Monnik to disasssociate itself from its past. Beer blackboards take up most wall space, relegating the beer enamels to the ceiling. Snacks only, though these are substantial. The 60-odd beers are well chosen, with short shrift given to crowd-pleasers. The Dutch list features Friese and Emelisse.

Stroohoed

Eewal 72 · **T** 058 212 7499
Daily from 19.00 (hours 'flexible')

The Straw Hat is one of those reassuring places that has not changed much since the earth cooled. The name derives from a former owner's fondness for Buster Keaton's straw hat. If you walk in when it is quiet, a comforting musty smell hangs in the air. This old creaky-floored brown café stretches across three tatty rooms. The front bar has a piano; the centre contains the billiards table; and the back has old British station signs.

Throughout are wooden UK pub signs salvaged from the era before branding. Food is international snacks. The 85+ beers stick largely to safer Belgians, although Dupont is there. Prices are kept low to attract students and nurture the next generation.

*OTHER **LEEUWARDEN** BEER VENUES:*

To find the wonderful **Ossekop** (Uniabuurt 8 – **T** 058 212 3082 – www.ossekopleeuwarden.nl – *Closed We&Su; others from 20.00-ish*), look for the ox's head (ossekop) in the window. Once the meeting room of a city guild, it has changed little since 1912. To protect the décor, in particular the dusty taxidermied birds and beasts, the curtains stay shut and the lights low. If you like 1960s/70s rock music you will find a kindred spirit in the affable host. Only two beers but the guest tap can hold interest.

Ossekop, Leeuwarden

MIDSLAND (on Terschelling)
25km NW from Harlingen by ferry

Historically, Terschelling (pop. 4,700) has been a popular spot for shipwrecks. With few trees on the windswept island, most farms and barns were built using salvaged timber. To this day things falling off container ships still wash up here, though the main income is tourism, and much of the land is a nature reserve.

Mention this quietly, but in 1666 the English fleet sailed into West-Terschelling harbour and destroyed 150 ships, burning the town to the ground for an encore. Many locals considered the Great Fire of London later that year as divine retribution. It also provoked one of the most famous defeats inflicted by the Dutch on the English outside of a football stadium, when Admiral De Ruyter sailed up the Medway in 1667 to ransack Chatham.

Buses ply the only main road, but check timetables as they stop early. Midsland (pop. 900) is 5km east of the ferry port. *HOTEL TIP:* **Wapen van Terschelling** ★★ (below) has basic rooms. The **Stormvogel** (Midslanderhoofdweg 32, **T** 0562 448797 www.destormvogel.nl) has B&B rooms and apartments – the owner runs the Terschellinger brewery.

Wapen van Terschelling

Oosterburen 25 · **T** 0562 448801
www.twapenvanterschelling.nl
Summer: daily from 10.00 (closes 22.00 Su).
Winter: closed We; Fr 10.00–24.00; Sa 10.00–01.00;
others 10.00–22.00

A two-room beer café with a terrace on the main street. Wood abounds inside. The left side dining room is beer-themed, with enamels everywhere. Conversely, the walls in the main bar area carry enamel grocery adverts, and the ceilings are hung with kitchen utensils and musical instruments. A ship's figurehead mermaid also gets thrown into the mix. An extensive food menu includes pancakes. 'Local' Terschellinger and Texel feature among the 80+ beers.

NES (on Ameland)
10km NW from Holwerd by ferry

In the 1870s, Ameland (Amelân) – one of the larger Wadden Islands – was briefly connected to the mainland by a dyke, which was breached in a storm in 1882 and never repaired. The spit leading to Holwerd ferry port is all that remains. This was also one of the last places in Europe liberated by Allied forces at the end of World War II. Being of limited strategic value, the occupying forces were not forced to surrender until June 2 1945, four weeks after hostilities had officially ended!

Today Ameland is mainly sand dunes and farmland, with birdwatching the main draw. Nes (pop. 1,200) is its second-largest village, ferry port and tourist hub.

HOTEL TIP: **Hofker** ★★★, J. Hofkerweg 1 (**T** 0519 542002; www.hotelhofker.nl) is comfortable, central, and 10-minutes' walk from the ferry.

Nes Café

Van Heeckerenstraat 10 · **T** 0519 542760
www.nes-cafe-ameland.nl
Closed Tu&We (Jan-Mar); Th 16.00–22.00 (Jan-Mar);
others from 10.00

It is a café and it is in Nes, so what else could they call it? The front terrace is warmed by decorative gas fires. Inside are a bar area designed primarily for drinking, and a semi-conservatory for dining. Each has a red-painted, wooden ceiling. Centre stage among the beer pumps is a model of Ameland's distinctive lighthouse. A shelf behind the counter inevitably contains instant coffee jars. Foodwise, the house speciality is organic steak cooked in a 'Green Egg' barbecue. The 40+ beers include several from Amelander. Good whiskies too. Often open till 04.00.

OENTSJERK
12km NE from Leeuwarden on N361

Small village (pop. 1,750) known by its Fries name, more formally Oenkerk in Dutch. Bus 51 from Leeuwarden passes through.

It Wapen fan Fryslân

Rengersweg 51 · **T** 058 256 1747
www.kafee.nl
Fr&Sa from 11.00; Su&Mo from 16.00;
others from 14.00

Main road village local, with a terrace. The carpeted interior has a billiard table, dartboards, a cast-iron stove backed with Delft tiles. They have *Hammerschlagen*, a game that originated at the Munich Oktoberfest and involves banging nails into a tree stump, ideally without ending up in hospital. Rolls and snacks are available all day. The bottles on the wall make choosing from the 70 beers easy. Ask what is available from the collection of cellared 75cl bottles, some of them 20 years old.

Gelderland

Geographically the Netherlands' largest province (pop. 2,000,000) and a beerhunter's paradise. It is divided into three vague regions, with its main cities running down the middle like a zipper.

To the north and west is the Veluwe, an undulating region of heathland and the forests of the Hoge Veluwe national park, home to the Kröller-Müller Museum (www.kmm.nl) and its collection of Van Goghs. The southwest, based round the major rivers is more industrial. The east, bordered on two sides by Germany and known as the Achterhoek, literally back corner, feels more pastoral and remote.

Home to some of the country's best breweries, beers, and bars, Gelderland should be built into any beer-finding national tour.

LARGEST CENTRES: **Nijmegen** (165,000), **Apeldoorn** (157,000), **Arnhem** (150,000) & **Ede** (68,000)

MORE INFORMATION: www.gelderland.nl

BREWERIES: **Apeldoorn**, *Apeldoorn*; **Burg**, *Ermelo*; **Cambrinus**, *Zutphen*; **Daendels**, *Hattem*; **De Vlijt**, *Apeldoorn*; **Doetinchem**, *Doetinchem*; **Goeye Goet**, *Arnhem*; **Graaf van Heumen**, *Heumen*; **Hemel**, *Nijmegen*; **Hoofdkwartier van Frederik Hendrik**, *Lievelde*; **Kuipertje**, *Heukelum*; **Oersoep**, *Nijmegen*; **Rodenburg**, *Rha*; **Veluwse Heidebrouwerij**, *Ede*; **Veluwse Schavuyt**, *Apeldoorn*; **Vrijstad**, *Culemborg*; **Wageningen**, *Wageningen*; **Wittenburg**, *Zevenaar*

OTHER BEER MAKERS: **Epe Bier Collectief**, *Epe*; & **Witte Leeuw**, *Wezep*

APELDOORN

Apeldoorn

Modern provincial town (pop. 157,000). The Dutch royal family liked the area enough to build a country seat here: Paleis Het Loo (www.paleishetloo.nl). Besides that, lovers of history and twee architecture will be disappointed. Railway nuts should note that on summer weekdays a steam train (www.stoomtrein.org) runs between here and Dieren.

HOTEL TIP: **Paris★★★**, Raadhuisplein 5-7 (**T** 055 522 1822; www.paris.nl) has simple rooms above a central café.

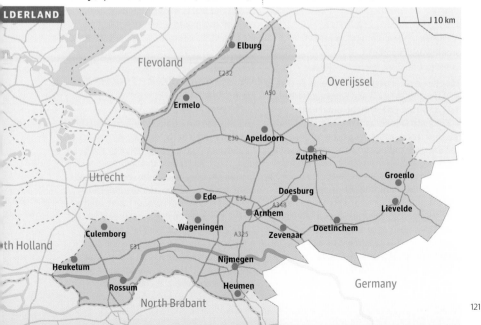

Achterom

Mariastraat 2H · **T** *none*
www.proef-locaalhetachterom.nl
*Closed Mo-Th; Fr 15.00–20.00; Sa 14.00–20.00;
and 1st Su of month 13.00–18.00*

Brewery tap and quiet haven, a few steps
down an alleyway off the main drag, in a
building dating from 1910. The interior is an
elegant drawing room, replete with
chandeliers. Behind this is a conservatory,
and further back a peaceful garden. No
food. Beers are from the house Veluwse
Schavuyt range, which is gradually moving
to De Vlijt.

Graaf van Vlaanderen

Hoofdstraat 165A · **T** 055 576 7701
www.degraafvanvlaanderen.nl
Sa&Su from 14.00; others from 16.00

The Duke of Flanders is a popular café with a
terrace, on the square. The single-room
interior is home to four tile murals depicting
the seasons. Elsewhere is darkened wood,
and fading pictures of artists. Snacks only,
apart from one changing evening special.
The 80+ beer list is 100% Belgian, but
includes Dupont and St Bernardus. They
also have a decent range of jenevers.

Kater

Hoofdstraat 174A · **T** 055 521 7086
proeflokaaldekater.nl
Closed Mo&Tu; Sa&Su from 14.00; others from 16.00

The Hangover is part of a small empire that
includes the SAS café and Finnegan's Irish
bars on either side, and the Graaf van
Vlaanderen (above) across the street. This is
the Dutch one, with partly bare-brick walls,
and a terrace out front. Some interior seating
has been rescued from old trains, complete
with luggage racks. Behind these is a wooden
pulpit. Pride of place at the rear goes to a
framed collection of 300 beer mats, some
over 50 years old. Food is snacks, but you can
sometimes get a meal delivered from one of
the neighbours – dependent on which is
least busy. All 55 beers are Dutch, including
Emelisse, De Molen and Rodenburg. They
also have 300 jenevers and Fries whisky.

*OTHER **APELDOORN** BEER VENUES:*

Brown café **Nieuws van Apeldoorn**
(Leienplein 12 – **T** 055 522 0566 – www.
nieuwsvanapeldoorn.nl – *Closed Mo; others from
15.00*) almost reaches 40 beers and a full entry.

ARNHEM

Arnhem

The site of the infamous battle in 1944 that
was "a bridge too far", Arnhem (pop. 150,000)
suffered heavy damage during World War II,
which left fewer than 200 houses intact.

In the 19th century it had been a genteel
resort, and today its biggest USP is its parks.
It also has the country's only trolleybus
network.

Just outside town is the Netherlands Open
Air Museum, about which more below, with
houses, farms, and factories imported from
across the country, and including a brewery.

TRIVIA FOR FILM BUFFS: the 1977 movie
A Bridge Too Far featured the bridge in
Deventer, as Arnhem's destroyed one was
rebuilt to a different design. And Audrey
Hepburn went to school here.

HOTEL TIP: **Blanc ★★★**, Coehoornstraat 4–8
(**T** 026 442 8072; www.hotel-blanc.nl) has
modern rooms and is convenient for the
station.

Caspar

Elly Lamakerplantsoen 2 · **T** 026 840 3524
www.caspararnhem.nl
Daily from 09.30

Literally the wrong side of the tracks, but
worth it. North of the railway, 200m west of
Velperpoort station, or 10 minutes' walk east
from the main station, this chic modern café
has lampshades made from recycled glass-
ware, floor-to-ceiling windows (offering
unimpeded views of passing trains), and a
leafy terrace. Food runs from breakfast on.
Little among the 100+ beers is run of the
mill. Guest taps sometimes include aged
Krieks, and there are many lambics among
the bottles. Emelisse leads the Dutch way,
and there are several Italian imports.

Meijers

Beekstraat 2 · **T** 026 370 7462
www.cafemeijers.nl
Mo-We 08.00–19.00; Th-Sa 08.00–02.00;
Su 13.00–19.00

A city institution developing its beery credentials. The building dates from 1895 and has
been a café for more than 80 years. The
dark-stained wood interior seems unchanged,
but actually stems from a 1970s renovation.
The terrace is popular as it catches the
afternoon sun. Beyond simple lunches it is
snacks only, plus homemade fruit pies.
The 50+ beers include the tasty house brew
dhr. Meijers Tripel (7%), from Rodenburg.

Moortgat

Ruiterstraat 35 · **T** 026 445 0393
www.moortgat.nl
Sa from 12.00; Su from 16.00; others from 15.00

Long-standing beer champion in an old brick
corner house that looks like a barn with a
terrace. Amiably rough-edged with battered
furniture, it has smoke-darkened brewery
and film posters pinned to the ceiling. There
is a billiard table at the back. Toasties and
snacks only. The 120+ beers are listed on a
hotchpotch of randomly scattered chalkboards. If you need order in your life, there is
a laminated menu. The list is strong on German
Weizen, rauchbiers and Belgian lambics.

Moortgat,
Arnhem

Viersprong

Schelmseweg 89
Nederlands Openluchtmuseum
T 026 357 6111 · www.openluchtmuseum.nl
Closed from November to March; others 10.00–17.00

Farmhouse café opposite the Goeye Goet
brewery and its de facto tap. To reach it you need
a ticket for the Open Air Museum, which repays
the investment before you get there. The
museum tram stops by its terrace. The building
dates from 1700, with the atmospheric interior
looking as it would have done in 1900. A tiled-
floor parlour has rustic furnishings. The
handsome ceramic and brass beer tap is German.
Food is snacks and sandwiches. The superior
Goeye Goet pils is a constant on tap, backed up
by a couple of seasonals from across the way.

BEER TO GO: **Van Pernis** (Prinsessestraat 34 – **T**
026 442 1918 – www.slijterijvanpernis.nl – *Closed
Su&Mo; Sa 09.30–17.00; others 09.30–18.00*) is a cellar-
like backstreet shop just east of the centre,
stocking 400+ well-chosen beers.

CULEMBORG

25km SE from Utrecht off N320
🚃 Culemborg

Provincial market town (pop. 27,000) with a
grand main square. This was the birthplace of
Anthony van Diemen, governor of the Dutch East
Indies, who sent Abel Tasman to find 'the great
southern continent', and briefly had Tasmania
(Van Dieman's Land) named in his honour.

Poortwachter

Everwijnstraat 27 · **T** 034 551 3627
www.tapperijdepoortwachter.nl
Closed Mo&Tu; others from 12.00

Characterful bar with a terrace on the square,
adjoining the 1350 Binnenpoort gate. The café
building was a barracks, prison, brewery and
someone's home, before gaining its current role.
The split-level interior has Delftware tiles on the
walls and an impressive beamed ceiling.
Decoration includes a carousel horse and some
old leather briefcases. They serve a full food
menu, and 40 beers. Corporate names dominate
the taps, with the bottles more impressive.

DOESBURG

18km E from Arnhem off N317

Well-preserved Hanseatic city (pop. 11,500). Its historic heart has several museums and monuments, including the Waag (below). One museum celebrates the fact this was once the Dutch mustard capital (www. doesburgschemosterd.nl). Take bus 26 from Dieren, or 29 from Arnhem.

Waag

Koepoortstraat 2-4 · **T** 0313 479617
www.waagdoesburg.nl
Daily from 10.00

The 1478 weigh house is the country's oldest café – an annex has served beer for over 500 years. The impressive red-brick stepped gable building has wooden window shutters, and a terrace looking across at the near-identical town hall. The barn-like interior has high ceilings and plaster walls, with lattice windows. Giant scales hang from the ceiling. Next door a modern addition serves dinners. Bar food (11.30–21.30) runs to steaks and fondues. The 50+ beers include the full La Trappe range.

Waag, Doesburg

DOETINCHEM

30km E from Arnhem off A18 exit 3
🚄 Doetinchem

Tidy market town (pop. 45,000) in the Gelderland Achterhoek.

HendriXen

Grutstraat 31 · **T** 0314 820993
www.grandcafehendrixen.nl
Closed Mo&Tu; We&Th from 16.00;
Fr&Sa from 15.00; Su from 14.00

Popular grand café doubling as the Doetinchem tap (the brewhouse is a separate building at the rear). There are terraces front and back; inside, dark wood, brass and chandeliers abound. Food stretches from snacks to full restaurant meals. Besides the house Walters beers, most of the 20+ options are industrial standards.

EDE

20km WNW from Arnhem off A12 exit 24
🚄 Ede-Wageningen

Provincial town (pop. 68,000) that prospered thanks to its army barracks. These fell into disuse after national service ended, and one now houses a brewery.

Veluwse Heidebrouwerij

Building 3
Nieuwe Kazernelaan 2 · **T** 0318 785428
www.veluwseheidebrouwerij.nl
Closed Mo; Fr&Sa 10.00–22.00; others 10.00–19.00

This brewery tap used to be the barracks kitchen. From the station, walk north along Stationsweg, turning right at the lights (Berkenlaan). Follow the road to the left, then take the bike path heading right for 300m – on foot from the centre is 15 minutes. The bar contains cushions made from army blankets, and ex-military light fittings. Pictures recall Operation Market Garden, the code name for the Arnhem offensive. Snacks and occasional main dishes. They have 3 or 4 house house brews on tap, plus crowd pleasers. Bottles to take home too.

ELBURG

20km SW from Zwolle off N309

Well-preserved medieval town (pop. 22,600), founded in the 9th century. Its grid layout dates from the end of the 13th century, when is was rebuilt after a flood. The town's beers include **Elburgs Admiraal** (9%), a hoppy barley wine made at Sallandse by local hobbyists in collaboration with De Eem.

Haas

Jufferenstraat 21 · **T** 0525 681737
www.restaurantdehaas.nl
Closed Mo; Su from 13.00; others from 09.30.

Huge central complex that includes a kids' play area and banqueting hall. The carpeted bar has high stucco ceilings and chandeliers. To one side is a swish restaurant and at the front a terrace. Simple lunches are served in the bar. The grander evening restaurant (until 21.00) has everything from snails and mussels to things with legs. Several Dutch choices lurk among the 40+ off-the-peg Belgians, including **Elburgsch Gappie Tripel** (6.5%), from De Eem, to an old recipe.

ERMELO

22km NE from Amersfoort on N303
🚉 Ermelo

Provincial town (pop. 26,000) with a beer café, brewery and shop, all in a neat row.

Hazeburg

Putterweg 43 · **T** 0341 564745
www.hazeburg.nl
Closed Mo; Sa from 11.00; Su 15.00–21.00; others from 15.00

This wood-dominated café is both a specialist beer outlet, and the Burg brewery tap. There is a terrace out front and an open wood fire inside. Simple lunches are available until 17.00 and heartier dinner dishes to 21.00. Snacks come all day. Five of fourteen taps are from the brewery, while the 70+ bottles have a more Belgian slant.

BEER TO GO: **Burg Bierwinkel** (Putterweg 45 – **T** 0341 564934 – www.burgbieren.nl – *Closed Su; Mo 13.00–18.30; Fr 09.30–21.00; Sa 09.00–17.00*)

others 09.30–18.30) next to the brewery and café, is the Netherlands' hugest beer shop and stocks 1,250+ beers, including swathes of hard-to-find Dutch options.

GROENLO

30km SW from Enschede off N18

Small town (pop. 10,000) in the Achterhoek, not far from the German border. Take bus 73 from Winterswijk. Not worth a specific journey but for those with an interest in beer history worth a detour if visiting Erve Kots (see Lievelde, below).

Central **Huys van Frederik Hendrik** (Markt 4-6 – **T** 0544 461691 – www.frederikhendrik.com – *Closed Mo; Sa&Su 15.00–24.00; others 16.00–24.00*) was a 1904 post office, and is owned by the nearby Erve Kots museum and brewery.

Lange Gang (Kevelderstraat 15 – **T** 0544 464860 – www.langegang.nl – *Closed Mo-We; others from 16.00, from 12.00 in Jul&Aug*) was the Brouwerij de Klok, Grolsch's original 1615 incarnation. Brewing ceased in 1922, but the building remains a restaurant and has a brewery museum in its cellar.

HEUKELUM

10km NE from Gorinchem off N848

Small village (pop. 2,000) that flips back and forth between Gelderland and South Holland – currently the former - but reliably on the bus 73 route from Leerdam or Gorinchem.

Kuipertje

Appeldijk 18 · **T** 0345 611839 or 06 1748 3105
www.hetkuipertje.nl
Sa only 14.00–19.00

Semi-rural brewery tap, 1 km WNW from the village centre. Getting here without a car requires creativity, but residents know it if you ask. The dilapidated brick building could use TLC. It has a door but in summer the accepted practice for moving twixt terrace and the slightly musty bar area is to shortcut through the window. Crisps only. The draught beer list is whichever house brews are available, plus a bought-in pilsener. Bottles sometimes available for off-sales.

HEUMEN

10km S from Nijmegen on N271

🚉 Mook-Molenhoek

Heumen is a village in Gelderland, Molenhoek a village in Limburg. The target bar and its brewery is clearly in Molenhoek yet still in Gelderland. Confusion passes for fun here. Bus 83 from Nijmegen is a better option than the train station, a 15-minute walk away.

Graaf van Heumen

Rijksweg 232 · **T** 024 358 5960
www.graafvanheumen.nl
Sundays only: 12.00–19.00 (closed sometimes – check website)

Brick barn brewpub in a building that has in its time been three different breweries. The field beside the terrace is used for flying demonstrations by raptor enthusiasts – American Eagles swoop past occasionally. Inside the bar is dominated by two glass brewing kettles, and there is a wood-burning stove in winter. Snacks and apple pie. There are 4 or 5 draught house beers, and occasionally 75cl bottles for sale. There is a 4-beer tasting option.

LIEVELDE

32km SW from Enschede off N18

🚉 Lichtenvoorde-Groenlo

Small village (pop. 1,500) in the heart of nowhere.

Brouwhoes

Eimersweg 4 · **T** 0544 371691
www.ervekots.nl
Daily 10.00–20.00 (Shut Mo, Nov to Easter)

From the station, walk 500 m north along Lievelderweg, then 500 m west on Eimersweg. In 1627 this was the temporary headquarters of Frederik Hendrick, Prince of Orange – a fact used by brewery publicists. This is the tap. Part of the Erve Kots open air museum, but accessible without a ticket. The atmospheric several-roomed interior has low oak-beamed ceilings and brick floors. Period furnishings feature a mangy stuffed fox, cast-iron sewing machines, and a massive open fireplace with Delftware tiles. The terrace is cobbled. Food is pancakes, plus other light meals. Beers are the house pilsener, plus seasonal brews. Bottles are sold in the museum shop.

*Brouwhoes
Leivelde, p
the Erve Ko
open air me*

NIJMEGEN

🚉 Nijmegen

Three cheers for Nijmegen, pound-for-pound possibly the nation's beeriest place. Gelderland's largest city (pop. 165,000) is also the Netherlands' oldest. Mentioned in the first century BC, when there was a Roman military camp nearby, it celebrated its 2,000th birthday in 2005. Although few ancient remains are visible today, there are fragments of city wall, and the Valkhof Museum (**www.museumhetvalkhof.nl**), which contains Roman artefacts.

In 1944 the city was bombed accidentally by American planes, who thought they were over the German town of Kleve. The error caused major damage to the centre, which has never really regained its former grandeur.

Every July Nijmegen hosts the International Four Day March (Nijmeegse Vierdaagse), a tortuous event entailing walking 30–50 km each day. Forget about finding a hotel room at that time – as 40,000 people participate. *HOTEL TIP:* **Hemel** (below) has two suites. **Credible★★**, Hertogstraat 1 (**T** 024 322 0498; www.in-credible.nl) is a quirky, central, designer hotel.

Beij Ons

Daalsedwarsweg 21 · **T** 024 323 7020
www.beijons.nl
Daily 11.00–02.00

Modern corner café 500m south of the centre, half way to/from Jos (below). The split-level bar is dominated by a huge photo of old brewery workers enjoying the product. It has a small terrace, and occasional live music. Lunches are simple. Daily-changing dinners are more upmarket – there is game in season. Snacks are available all day. The 70+ beers include several American and Dutch choices, with at least one tap from De Hemel.

Blaauwe Hand

Achter de Hoofdwacht 3 · **T** 024 323 2066
www.indeblaauwehand.nl
Mo&Tu 14.00–24.00; Sa from 11.00; others from 12.00

Historic café near Grote Markt, with a small terrace and loads of atmosphere. It is the town's oldest bar, dating from 1542, though it was rebuilt after the war, not that you

would guess. Dark wood dominates. Food is served, mainly on the first floor given the cramped nature of the lower bar. Lunches until 16.00; Alsace flammkuchen (pizzas with cream instead of tomato) until 20.00; snacks all day. The 45 beers include the house **Rooie Tiep Top**, commissioned from De Hemel.

Brink

Grote Markt 32 · **T** 024 323 3033
Daily early until late

Modern café that does not appear to have set hours, but is usually open from breakfast time onwards. This is a high-ceilinged bar with a large terrace. Food is typical Dutch café fare, served all day. The 60+ beer list is the best of the row of cafés lining the square. Taps are largely corporate, but the bottles include US and UK imports.

Deut

Koningstraat 36 · **T** 024 323 8110
www.cafededeut.nl
Daily from 10.00

One-room beer café, with a terrace on a small square. Smoke-darkened ceilings, ageing wallpaper, candlelit tables, and assorted bric-a-brac create an atmosphere of fin-de-siècle kitsch. Rolls available 11.00–16.00; snacks continue until 20.00. The beer list of 70+ finds room at least one De Hemel among the 12 taps. Several lambics lurk among the bottles.

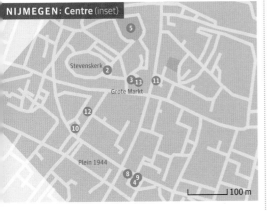

NIJMEGEN: Centre (inset)

Hemel, Nijme

Hemel

Franseplaats 1 · **T** 024 365 6394
www.restaurantdehemel.nl
Mo 12.00–18.00; others 12.00–24.00

The Netherlands longest-established
microbrewery is set in a 12th-century
cloister. The brewery occupies the cellar
of the ivy-clad building, while the bar and
restaurant are above. The cobbled terrace is
a peaceful retreat. Inside, the pictorial clock
on one wall of the flagstone-floored bar is a
work of art – the workings are on the far side
of the room. Lunch and high tea are served
12.00–17.00; dinner from 17.30; and snacks
throughout. Six house beers appear on tap,
with others available in the bottle and to
take away. The Hemelse Proeverij is a taster
of all the draught options.

Jos

Daalseweg 309 · **T** 06 2267 4739
www.cafejos.nl
Closed Mo & Christmas week; Su 14.00–20.00;
others from 15.00

On a leafy residential square with a terrace
round two sides, Jos is the kind of corner
local that reaffirms your faith in corner locals.
It is a 15-minute walk south along Daalseweg,
or bus 8 to Badhuis (keep going, passing left
of the Badhuis theatre). The L-shaped interior
has beer memorabilia everywhere. Snacks
and toasties only. The 170 beers always
include one tap from De Hemel. Emelisse
and Jopen, plus Danish, UK and US imports
supplement the Belgians. If that does not
finish you off, the 130 whiskies and 15+
cognacs will.

Kluizenaar

Burghardt van de Berghstraat 96
T 024 322 1235
www.dekluizenaar.nl
Sa&Su from 13.00; others from 14.00

The Hermit is a residential local with a small
terrace, just south of the centre. The inside
is an oddity – note the chandelier, the stag's
head sporting a cowbell, and the TV at the
back that always shows the same scene (see
it, you'll understand). Then look through
the small glass window in the door to the
right, where a 'hermit' sits writing at a desk
in his cell. Standard lunches expand to tapas,
spare ribs and fondue in the evening, served
in a separate dining area. Snacks all day.
The 50+ beers include De Hemel's Botterik,
originally brewed exclusively for bars in this,
the Bottendaal district.

Mug

Pauwelstraat 9 · **T** 024 845 2673
www.cafedemug.nl
Closed Mo; Su 13.00–20.00; Tu&We 13.00–24.00;
others 13.00–02.00

Cosy one-room local with carpeted tables
within and a small terrace on a central shopping street. Food is soups, toasties, snacks
and apple pie. Tea and coffee are served in
china cups. The 40+ beers have enough
highlights to warrant a visit, not least those
from Oersoep. Schelde's **Mug Bitter** is on tap.

Opera ⑨

Koningstraat 34 · **T** 024 323 2197
www.cafedeopera.nl
Daily from 10.00

Modern 'mock Art Nouveau' café and
neighbour of the Deut (above), with a terrace
on a small square. Its walls and ceilings are
painted in 'stone effect' beige, while wall
photos show iconic celebrity poses. We do
not get the Opera connection – it certainly is
not the music. Lunches and snacks available
until 20.00. The 55 beers have just enough
Dutch, British and US interlopers to balance
Belgian dominance.

Samson ⑩

Houtstraat 4 · **T** 024 323 3023
www.cafesamson.nl
Su from 12.00; others from 10.00

Central café named after the family who
moved their café here in the 1950s. It is a
several-roomed, semi-dark warren, with a
terrace out front. Light meals served all day.
Help yourself to the peanuts in the bowl on
the bar. Its 100+ beers run it a good second in
the 'best in town' stakes. Well-chosen guests
can be spectacular. Permanent fixtures include
Oersoep. There is also a 'port of the month'.

Tout ⑪

Grotestraat 6 · **T** 06 4838 6780
www.stadscafetout.nl
Daily from 14.00

Just off the main square. Formerly the Nieuwe
Maan, it has changed hands, but retained
beeriness. The small single room café has
stained glass windows at the back and a bijou
terrace out front. Food is soups, toasties and
snacks. The 80 beers offer few surprises,
though the taps do change regularly. Some
beers at discount price on Thursday nights.

Van Ouds ⑫

Augustijnenstraat 33 · **T** 024 323 3625
www.cafevanoudsnijmegen.nl
Closed Mo; Sa&Su from 13.00; others from 16.00

Smallish friendly local on a pedestrianised
street just south of Grote Markt, dominated
by dark wood and white-painted walls.
Snacks only, but these use products from
local suppliers. The 55+ beers find room for a
few Dutch and several other imports besides
the Belgians. There is a decent range of 75cl
bottles and a good wine list too.

*OTHER **NIJMEGEN** BEER VENUES:*

On the main square, **Camelot** ⑬ (Grote Markt
37 – **T** 024 322 6426 – www.cafecamelot.nl –
Sa from 10.00; others from 11.00) is a fine grand
café with 30 beers. By the time we appear,
so should **Oersoep** ⑭ (Waalbandijk 20 –
T 06 2506 4611 – oersoepbrouwerij.nl – *Fr only,
16.00–23.00*), Primordial Soup's brewery tap and
shop *(16.00–20.00)*, at the back of an industrial
complex, near the river 1.5 km from the centre
and station, just off the no. 5 bus route.

ROSSUM

15km N from 's-Hertogenbosch off N322

Sleepy riverside village (pop. 2,700).
Take bus 49 or 267 from Zaltbommel.

De Pub (Morrison's)

Waaldijk 1 · **T** 0418 513662
www.morrisons.nl
Closed Mo-We; Su from 15.00; others from 16.00

To find this dykeside place, look for the In
Petto bistro sign. The pub is around the back
on the floor below, with a sheltered terrace.
This compact wooden bar was an Irish pub,
and the old name Morrison's still appears on
the sign. We are not aware of food beyond
nibbles, but there is that bistro. The Irish
connection among the 50+ beers stops at two
global brands on tap. Only the draught choices
are advertised. They also stock 70 whiskies.

WAGENINGEN

18km W from Arnhem on N225

Provincial university town (pop. 37,500), one
of the largest places in the country not on
the rail network, Ede-Wageningen station
being 7 km to the north, a 15-minute ride on
bus 88. From Arnhem take bus 52. At the
end of the war, the German surrender in the
Netherlands was negotiated and signed in
the Hotel De Wereld (5 Mei Plein 1), now a
national monument.

Vlaamsche Reus

Hoogstraat 21 · **T** 0317 412834
www.vlaamschereus.nl
Sa from 14.00; others from 15.00.

The Flemish Giant has been a specialist beer
outlet since 1984, and is a founding member
of ABT. It has a terrace on a small square,
and beer memorabilia everywhere inside –
from enamels to cans, via Germanic glasses
and steins, to 75cl bottles dangling above
the bar. Food is scarce, but may contain nuts.
If you want to see a proper beer menu, ask
for the bier bijbel, a weighty metal-bound
tome containing detailed descriptions of the
140+ brews. Most are Belgian, with a good

choice of lambics. A couple of the 14 taps are British real ale pumps, and bottled imports include several Fuller's Vintage Ales.

Zaaier

Herenstraat 33 · **T** 0317 410806
Closed Mo; Fr&Sa from 15.00; others from 16.00

The Sower is a small central café with a terrace around several sides. It goes for a combi old and new theme, with agricultural equipment and saws rubbing shoulders with hand-painted murals and music posters. Snacks only. Among the mainly Belgian 60+ beers are a few UK imports. They also stock plenty of jenevers.

ZEVENAAR

15km SE from Arnhem off A12 exit 29
Zevenaar

Quiet provincial town (pop. 32,000), badly damaged in the war and rebuilt from scratch.

Nostalgie

Weverstraat 1-3 · **T** 0316 344205
www.biercafe-nostalgie.nl
Closed Mo; Tu-Th from 19.00; others from 14.00

Locals' bar down a side street off the main square. The modern terrace has bright cushions. Inside a proliferation of wood gets a contemporary touch with a lick of purple paint. They host occasional live music. Nibbles only. The 50 beers are not listed - ask, or peer behind the bar into the chiller cabinets. On our last visit some were from nearby Rodenburg, but none from Wittenburg, 200m away.

Proef & Zijn

Markt 25 · **T** 06 2050 8058
www.stadsbrouwerijwittenburg.nl
Closed Su&Mo; Fr 10.00-18.00; Sa 12.00-18.00; others 10.00-16.00

Simple brewery tap to the right of the entrance to Wittenburg brewery. To the left is a small farm shop. The high-ceilinged café is mainly wood, with a red-balustraded mezzanine. Food is fruit pies, soup and quiche. Four house beers are on tap, and in bottles.

ZUTPHEN

22km SE from Apeldoorn off N345
Zutphen

Attractive town (pop. 47,000) with Hanseatic connections. The chapter house of St. Walburgis church houses one of only five surviving medieval libraries in Europe. Books are chained to ancient desks, just as they were centuries ago to prevent them being nicked.

Cambrinus

Houtmarkt 56B · **T** 0575 546688
www.hanze-stadsbrouwerij.nl
Closed Mo; others 10.00-24.00

Brewpub on Zutphen's main drag, in a row of places with lively terraces. It was the Hanze Stadsbrouwerij until a 2013 rebranding. The interior is dominated by the copper brew kettles at the rear. The brewery is relatively new, but the cellars are 800 years old. Food (from 12.00) is all-encompassing, from snacks to steaks. There is also a monthly beer and food pairing menu. The 15+ beers include 6 house taps. Try them all with the tasting menu.

Cambrinus, Zutphen

OTHER **ZUTPHEN** BEER VENUES:

Camelot (Groenmarkt 34 - **T** 0575 511804 - *Fr&Sa from 12.00; others from 14.00*) has mock-medieval shields and banners, and a mural depicting the round table, but its 35+ beers are hardly the stuff of Arthurian legend, stopping it just short of a full entry.

Groningen

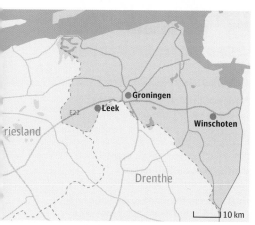

Groningen
Leek
E22
friesland
Winschoten
Drenthe
10 km

Outside the provincial capital, Groningen (pop. 580,000) feels far from anywhere. To the east is German Lower Saxony; to the north the Wadden Sea. It is flat and agricultural, mainly comprised of reclaimed sea marsh. Its flatness creates an awful lot of sky.

The east has a long history of political class struggle – from 1982 to 1990 the municipality of Beerta boasted the country's first and only Communist mayor.

Despite its rich history, the province only has one proper brewery.

LARGEST CENTRE: **Groningen** (195,000)

MORE INFORMATION: toerisme.groningen.nl

BREWERY: **Kromme Jat**, *Groningen*

GRONINGEN
Groningen

During the Middle Ages, Groningen – the biggest city in the north (pop. 195,000) – was a regional power base, operating as a semi-independent state within the Hanseatic League. Today it is a university town with 25,000 students. The recently rebuilt Groninger Museum (www.groningermuseum.nl) has some of the country's best contemporary art. Other eclectic museums are devoted to maritime history, comics, and tobacco.

The student angle, and its relative remoteness, mean Groningen has a thriving nightlife. There are two beer festivals here each year: the larger, in April is in the historic Martinikerk, which somehow escaped damage in the war.

If arriving by train, the station café is among the grandest anywhere – sadly demoted to a global franchise coffee house. *HOTEL TIP:* **University** ★★★, Kleine Kromme Elleboog 7B (**T** 050 311 3424; www.rug.nl/hotel) is a modern central hotel run by the University of Groningen, and next door to the Pintelier (below).

Koffer
Nieuwe Blekerstraat 1 · **T** 050 313 6251
www.dekoffer.nl
Daily from 16.00

In a residential neighbourhood just west of the centre, this unassuming simply furnished local could easily slip under the radar of the casual imbiber, but is an ABT member and worth seeking out. Snacks only, though some are substantial. There is a good Dutch showing among the 150+ beers, with De Molen, Ramses, local Kromme Jat and more, plus several US and UK imports.

Pintelier
Kleine Kromme Elleboog 9 · **T** 050 318 5100
www.pintelier.nl
Daily from 15.00

Down a side street called Little Crooked Elbow, this ABT café has been a beery institution since 1999. It has a small terrace to one side. The large but narrow smoke-yellowed and dimly lit interior is decorated with beer enamels and some of those oversized bottles. Music is easily drowned by conversation. Snacks only. The 100+ beers include an impressive 23 taps, half of which rotate regularly, which is where most highlights lie. The bottled range is largely Belgian.

Goudkantoor, Groningen

Toeter

Turfsingel 6 · **T** 050 312 4499
www.cafedetoeter.nl
Mo&Tu from 19.00; We&Th from 16.00;
Fr&Sa from 15.00; Su from 18.00

Large ABT café just north of the centre, with a canalside terrace and a music theme in sound (mostly rock) and vision (instruments on the ceiling). Food is pizzas, kebabs and snacks. The 125+ beers include the house **Toeter Blond** (6%), commissioned from Mommeriete. Beers from no fewer than nine nations featured among its 16 taps on our last visit. They also stock 300 single malts, which can be sampled on various 5-shot tasting planks. Beers and whiskies are half price after 22.00 on Sunday.

OTHER GRONINGEN BEER VENUES:
Filling one side of the main square, the nation's largest café, **Drie Gezusters** (Grote Markt 36/39 – **T** 050 312 7041 – www.driegezustersgroningen.nl – *Su-Mo from 11.00; others from 10.00*), is really several bars interconnected at the back.
In a glorious 1635 stepped gable building, the former tax office, **Goudkantoor** (Waagplein 1 – **T** 050 589 1888 – www.goudkantoor.nl – *Su 12.00-18.00; Mo from 12.00; others from 10.00*), lists local Kromme Jat among its few beers. Worth checking out for its Art Deco interior and good food, the **Ugly Duck** (Zwanestraat 28 – **T** 050 312 3192 – www.ugly-duck.eu – *Mo 16.30-23.00; Tu&We 12.00-23.00; Su 13.00-23.00; others 12.00-24.00*) manages 35 beers.
Opened in 1923, **Wolthoorn & Co** (Turftorenstraat 6 – **T** 050 312 0282 – www.cafewolthoorn.nl – *Fr&Sa from 15.00; others from 16.00*) is a lovely old café with a flock red wall-papered back room that appears unchanged.
BEER TO GO: **Mitra** (Vismarkt 36 – **T** 050 313 3654 – www.mitra.nl – *Closed Su; Mo 13.00-18.00; Tu 10.00-18.00; We 10.00-20.00; Th 09.00-21.00; Fr 09.00-20.00; Sa 09.00-17.30*) is among the best in the chain, with 300+ beers – quite why they need different hours every day is beyond us. Meanwhile, **Van Erp Dranken** (Grote Kromme Elleboog 16 – **T** 050 312 6414 – www.vanerpwijn.nl – *Closed Su Mo 13.00-18.30; Sa 10.00-17.00; others 10.00-18.30*) stocks 500+ beers.

LEEK

20km WSW from Groningen off N372
Provincial town (pop. 10,500), reached by buses 306 and 319 from Groningen.

Oude Bank

Tolberterstraat 6 · **T** 0594 512017
www.cafedeoudebank-leek.nl
Closed Tu; Sa from 14.00, Su from 15.00, others from 16.00

This large, old-fashioned town centre local, dominated by its billiards table, was once beerier than now, and even had a beer shop next door. No more. Food is snacks only, with toasties. No longer worth a specific journey but if you are in the area its 30+ beers with 10 taps are above average for the north. The bottled selection can feature De Molen.

WINDSCHOTEN

36km E from Groningen off A7 exit 47
Winschoten
Sleepy town (pop. 18,000) that is almost in Germany.

Carambole

Blijhamsterstraat 2 · **T** 0597 424190
www.carambole-winschoten.nl
Closed Mo&Tu; We&Th from 19.00; Fr&Sa from 15.00; Su only for events

Long-standing café just south of the main square. Carambole is a type of billiards played without pockets, where you score by cannoning or 'caroming' your ball off others. The back room, used nowadays mainy for music functions, once had many tables but only one remains. The front bar, dimly lit by mosaic glass lamps, has gentlemen's club comfy armchairs and barrel tables. Snacks only. The beer list fluctuates between 50 and 80. Reflecting its location, the standouts are German, not Belgian.

Limburg

Long thin Limburg (pop. 1.1 million) is 110 km from north to south, but at is narrowest point separates Belgium from Germany by a mere 5 km. Along its length is the widening river Maas and its valley. The northern portion is flat farmland, while the far south is that most un-Dutch of things, hilly.

Being the most Catholic, least Calvinistic part of the country, Limburg likes to enjoy itself. Its long history of beeriness is reflected in the presence here of many of the better and longest-standing breweries.

The south is particularly good for beer bars too, which is not mirrored in the more industrial central areas around Roermond, Sittard and Geleen.

Limburg is also (in)famous for its pre-lent carnaval, which every village celebrates with fervour. If you do not like fancy dress, excruciating oompah music and (allegedly) watered down beer, avoid the area at this time.

The local language Limburgs has semi-official status, but attempting to master it is pointless – every village has its own dialect, each less intelligible than the last.

LARGEST CENTRES: **Maastricht** (121,500), **Heerlen** (88,500), **Roermond** (57,000)

MORE INFORMATION: vvvlimburg.nl

BREWERIES: **Alfa**, *Schinnen*; **Brand** (Heineken), *Wijlre*; **Fontein**, *Stein*; **Gulpener**, *Gulpen*; **Hertog Jan** (AB InBev), *Arcen*; **Lindeboom**, *Neer*; **Maar**, *Jabeek*

OTHER BEER MAKERS: **7ᵈᵉ Hemel**, *Sevenum*; **Natte Gijt**, *Weert*

ARCEN

15km N from Venlo off N271

Small village (pop. 2,200) with a brewery and a castle. From Venlo bus 83 runs to the village and or alternatively for the brewery take bus 29 to Broekhuizen Hoogstraat, then catch the free ferry across the Maas. The castle grounds (www.kasteeltuinen.nl) are among the Netherlands' finest formal gardens, first laid out in the 16th century.

Hertog Jan Proeverij

Kruisweg 43 · **T** 077 473 9160
www.hertogjanproeverij.nl
*Closed Mo&Tu, Sa 11.00–24.00;
others 13.00–20.00 Oct-Mar, 11.00–22.00 Apr-Sep*

Brewery tap near the Maas, 1 km north of the village. Linked by an umbilical pipe to the brewery, though we doubt much beer passes along it. The café's Germanic feel is

Hertog Jan Proe Arcen

enhanced by the 2,000 steins hanging from the ceiling. Simple lunches are served until 17.00; more elaborate fare until 19.30 (20.30 Fr&Sa). Some dishes are prepared with beer. The 50+ beers include 11 taps, roughly half house brews, half Belgian.

GULPEN
16km WSW from Maastricht on N278

Attractive village (pop. 3,600) with a large brewery at its heart. Take bus 50 or 150 from Maastricht.

Zwarte Ruiter
Markt 4 · **T** 043 450 4635
www.herbergdezwarteruiter.nl
Closed Tu; others from 10.00

The Black Knight is Gulpener brewery's public taphouse. The large café has a terrace on the square, a winter garden at the rear, and food until 21.00. There is copper piping aplenty and they claim their tap beers are piped in directly from the brewery. Draught Mestreechs Aajt, matured in the vats visible through glass, was also first available here. Beyond the house range are a handful of others, notably from Val-Dieu from just over the Belgian border.

HEERLEN
25km ENE from Maastricht off A79
Heerlen

Provincial town in the nation's bottom right-hand corner (pop. 88,500), and part of Parkstad Limburg, an agglomeration of 220,000 souls. Although it has Roman connections, the town only grew during a 19th century coal mining boom. The mines are now long gone, their slag heaps planted with greenery and appearing as newly honed hills.

Beerkompanie
Pancratiusplein 46 · **T** 045 571 1877
www.beerkompanie.nl
Daily from 11.00

Large, multi-roomed brewpub on the site of the former Romein brewery. The copper brewing kit on the mezzanine should be operating by the time we appear. There is already a Burgundian restaurant in the basement and a large terrace. One bar is made entirely of beer crates, Bacchus heads adorn columns, and a yellow and white mosaic wall at the back depicts a giant beer. Food is served all day. Until the house beers arrive(d), the beer list was from owners Alfa, including their better unfiltered pils, **Puur**. Some tables have a self-tapping facility.

Lange Jan
Bongerd 3 · **T** 06 5581 1896
www.langejanheerlen.nl
Su from 15.00; Tu from 10.00; Closed We; others from 13.00

Tall Jan is named after the chimney of an old power station that was a local landmark before being demolished in 1976. The high-ceilinged tiled-floor café has a terrace on a central market square. Walls are covered in beer bottles and enamels, and photos of miners and the aforementioned chimney. Light shades above the bar are modified beer kegs. A dozen types of toastie, plus rolls and soups, are available until 18.00; snacks until 22.00. The 75+ beers always include one from Jopen and a US import from Anchor among the 12 taps. The bottled choices feature De Molen, Natte Gijt, and Emelisse, as well as US and UK imports.

HORST

17km NW from Venlo via A73

🚆 Horst-Sevenum (3 km south)

Small, northern Limburg town (pop. 12,000). Buses 60 and 69 connect the centre and its station.

Cambrinus

Venrayseweg 94 · **T** 077 398 3009
www.cafe-cambrinus.nl
Closed Tu-Th; Su from 15.00; others from 19.00

Small, friendly local on a busy residential street, 500 m north from the centre. It had its own brewery until 2010, when the emhasis switched to music. Above a gas hearth, a cartoon painting depicts a naked Cambrinus bathing in a vat of beer. Walls are hung with photos of musicians. The stage in the corner hosts live music every Sunday (www.cambrinusconcerten.nl). There is a beer garden at the back. Snacks only. The 100+ beer list, displayed on a chalkboard, is a joy. Among the bottles is everything from local 7de Hemel, whose beer recipes were developed here.

Centrum 🚲

Wilhelminaplein 13 · **T** 077 398 6001
www.hetkleinstecafevanhorst.nl
Closed Mo; Tu from 08.00; We&Th from 19.00; Fr from 14.00; Sa&Su from 10.30

Small café with a large terrace on a square. Green and black tiled floors and coloured chairs make a refreshing change from brown. Walls are hung with old photos of Horst, and food packaging. Statler and Waldorf from the Muppets watch you from above the bar. Food is snacks and homemade apple pie. The best of the 70 beers are found among the 12 taps, which include the house spiced white beer, **Witte Jan** (5.2%), commissioned from De Fontein. They are not afraid to experiment. There are 75 whiskies too.

JABEEK

14km NNW from Heerlen off N274

Quiet hamlet (pop. 750) that feels miles from anywhere, 500 m from the German border. Take bus 36 from either Sittard or Heerlen.

Maar

Maar 2 · **T** 046 442 5882
www.dorpsbrouwerijdemaar.nl
Closed Mo; Sa&Su 11.00-18.00; others 13.00-18.00

Brewery tap on a quiet village backstreet, with a grassy terrace in the shade of an apple, pear and cherry orchard. It is an old brick farmhouse with wooden-beamed ceilings and checked tablecloths. The brewery is visible through a window. Simple meals are available. The beers are two or three from the house on tap, plus a bought-in pilsener. Bottles are sold to take away.

MAASTRICHT

🚆 Maastricht

One of the Netherlands' oldest and most attractive cities, Maastricht (pop. 122,000) is a popular spot for signing treaties, as well as being a Premier League beer destination. It straddles the Maas, with the station on one bank and the old town on the other.

The Romans built the first river crossing here in 50 AD, which lasted until 1275, when it collapsed killing 400 people. The current one, the St Servatius pedestrian and cyclists' bridge, is somewhat sturdier.

The 10th century Romanesque St Servatius Basilica dominates the Vrijthof square. Onze Lieve Vrouwebasiliek (Basilica of Our Lady) was begun around the same time. Parts of the old city wall still stand, with the 13th century Helpoort gate the country's oldest. Even the tourist office (VVV) is the 15th century former town hall and law courts.

The town's beer culture is so steady that the VVV carries a leaflet advising on where to find Mestreechs Aajt. In July, Maastricht is the epicentre of the pre-lent carnival – dress up, or leave town.

HOTEL TIPS: **Poshoorn** ★★ (below) has basic rooms, within convenient staggering distance of most places.

Falstaff

St. Amorsplein 6 · **T** 043 321 7238
www.cafe-falstaff.com
Daily from 10.00

Lively café between the river and the Vrijthof, with a terrace on a tiny square. White walls downstairs are hung with art, and crystal chandeliers dominate. An upper mezzanine is for evening diners. Food begins with breakfast and runs through lunch (until 17.00), to burgers, pasta and more for dinner. Tapas is available 15.00–24.00. The 60 beers are predominantly Belgian, with two taps and several bottles as guests.

Frape

Het Bat 7 · **T** 06 4865 8918
Closed Tu; Mo 10.00–20.00; We 09.00–20.00; Th 15.00–22.00; Fr&Sa 09.00–24.00; Su 11.00–20.00

A slice of beer heaven by the Maas, with a river view terrace. This simple tiled-floor brown café has a DVD fire in winter, and empty bottles lining shelves and windowsills. Pasta, omelettes and similar are served until 19.00; snacks at other times. The beer list is a gem, running to 500+. Only 150 are advertised on the menu, so convey your wishes to the knowledgeable landlord and he will find something to suit. Most top Dutch beers seem to be available including from De Molen, Emelisse, and Rodenburg. Besides a huge choice of Belgians, other imports come from the UK, US and Germany.

Knijnspiep

Muntstraat 45 · **T** 043 321 4065
www.knijnspiep.nl
Fr&Sa 10.00–02.00; Su 15.00–23.00; Mo 12.00–19.00; others 10.00–23.00

The Rabbit Hole is a narrow-fronted old bar steps from the tourist office, on a shopping street too narrow for a terrace. This place is typically Maastricht, kneading Burgundian ingredients into a Dutch brown café. Dimly lit with bare brick walls, crystal chandeliers hanging from a wooden-beam ceiling, sepia photos for decoration, and crooners on the stereo. Snacks only. The 40-ish beers throw up a few oddities, and the tiny bar finds space for a dozen taps.

Naovenant

Helmstraat 16b · **T** 043 750 1695
www.naovenant.nl
Closed Tu; Mo from 12.00; others from 11.00

Unassuming popular local, with a cramped terrace a few steps north from the Vrijthof square. Snacks only. The 60+ beers try to stick 'local' as far as possible, which in this case means more Belgian Limburg than Dutch. That means room for a few from Kerkom, a rarity in the Netherlands. There are also several lambics, including from Drie Fonteinen (3F).

Poshoorn

Stationstraat 45–47 · **T** 043 321 7334
www.poshoorn.nl
Daily from 10.00

Lively ABT pub with a large terrace, on the road from the station to the centre. Old newspaper is used as wallpaper in the L-shaped interior, but is largely obscured by pictures, bottles, cabinets and so on. Simple lunches expand to evening steaks and satay, dishes using local ingredients. The 50+ beers include 13 taps, among which are several Limburg locals. The house **Parel van Wiek** tripel (8%) is brewed by Kerkom in Belgium.

Pothuiske

Het Bat 1 · **T** 043 321 6002
www.pothuiske.nl
Closed Mo; Tu&We 10.00–24.00; Su 10.00–21.00; others 10.00–02.00

By the St Servatius bridge, this riverside beer café with a cosy terrace is named after the fact that for many years – starting in the mid-15th century – a boiling cauldron was kept on the premises, to provide safe drinking water to the locals. The tiled-floor interior goes for wooden bench seats, and beer adverts cover wood-panelled walls. Barrels above the bar pretend to be the tap beers. Food, served all day, includes the house special Geuldals Engeltje – ham and vegetable stew. The 75+ beers stray mainly Belgian, but there are a few Limburg locals. Opens on Mondays (10.00–19.00) in summer.

Take One

Rechtstraat 28 · **T** 043 321 6423
www.takeonebiercafe.nl
Closed Tu&We; others from 16.00

Quirky corner café, full of beer, just east of the river. Its walls and bar are buttoned with thousands of bottle tops, with beer mats higher up. Food is peanuts. Legendary landlord Peet Seerden has run the place since 1983 and is likely to have an opinion about what you will want to drink – be prepared to stand your ground if you disagree but have your reasons well-prepared. The range of 170+ is worth the fight. La Trappe is left holding the Dutch fort, but there are several German Weizen on what is otherwise a sea of Belgians, ranging from Dupont and De Ranke to a good showing of lambics.

Thembi

Dopplerdomein 20a · **T** 043 361 3621
www.thembi.eu
Daily from 14.00

Bustling café on a housing estate. Take bus 1, 5, or 57 to Randwycksingel/VGZ, one block north, or walk 500 m west from Maastricht Randwijk station. Décor is functional and modern, with a view of houses from the terrace. There is occasional live music. Dinner is served 16.00–22.00; snacks and tapas all day. The impressive beer list of 250+ makes pleasing reading. Limburg is well represented, including Fontein's Beluga beer, otherwise brewed for the Michelin-starred restaurant of that name. The bottled range has some hard-to-find Belgians, like Dochter van de Korenaar, with Emelisse and Ramses from closer to home. American and British imported IPAs also abound.

OTHER MAASTRICHT BEER VENUES:

Lovely **Bobbel** (Wolfstraat 32 – **T** 043 321 7413 – www.debobbel.com – *Th-Sa 10.00–22.00; others 10.00–21.00*) has sandy floors, marble tabletops and counter, a brass coffee machine that is a work of art, and a beer list that as yet is not.

Claiming to be the nation's smallest café, **Moriaan** (Stokstraat 12 – **T** 043 321 1177 – www.indemoriaan.nl – *Closed Mo; Tu&We 12.00–22.00; Th 12.00–23.00; Fr&Sa 10.00–22.00; Su 11.00–21.00*) has operated since 1905 in a building dating from 1564, and stocks 30 beers.

All dark brown and creaky floors, the **Ouden Vogelstruys** (Vrijthof 15 – **T** 043 321 4888 – www.vogelstruys.nl – *daily from 09.30*) is the most characterful place on Vrijthof square. Beside the like-named bridge, **Servaas** (Corversplein 10 – **T** 043 321 7669 – www.servaascafe.nl – *Sa from 11.00; Su from 12.00; others from 10.00*) has an up-and-coming range of good Dutch beers.

BEER TO GO: In a western suburb, **J. van Wissem & Zonen – Acht Zaligheden** (Erfprinsbastion 40 – **T** 043 354 1550 – *Closed Su; Fr 09.00–18.00; Sa 09.00–17.00; others 10.00–18.00*) is a large drinks warehouse, stocking 250+ beers.

MECHELEN

20km E from Maastricht off N278

Not to be confused with the Belgian city, this quiet village (pop. 2,000) is blessed with two great pubs, adjacent to each other. It also has several attractive half-timbered houses. Take bus 50 from Maastricht, 61 from Gulpen, or 57 from either.

Kroeën

Hoofdstraat 23 · **T** 043 455 1262
www.cafeindekroeen.nl
Closed We; Mo&Fr from 15.00; Tu&Sa from 12.00; Th from 12.30; Su from 11.00

Just downhill from the church, the Crown has the village water pump on its terrace. Plastic ivy decorates the bar of the light-painted interior. Beer bottles line up in the windows. In the same family for five generations, it only went beery in 2009. Light meals are available, plus a few dishes named after beers. The 130+ brews cover the entire range of European Trappists, and several Limburg breweries. US and UK imports also appear.

Pintje

Hoofdstraat 25 · **T** 043 455 9079
www.tpintjemechelen.nl
Closed Tu; others from 11.00

The Wee Pint also has a terrace on the main road beside its beerier neighbour. Inside is a charming warren of wooden-floored rooms, with a wood-burning stove in most. Food runs the full gamut from snacks to lunches and plate meals. Stocking a respectable 50 beers, Dutch interests are dominated by nearby Gulpener, and there are some from Belgian, but equally local, Val-Dieu.

OSPEL

10km NW from Weert off N275

Small village (pop. 3,500) next to a great country pub. To reach the latter, take bus 61 from Weert to 'Meijelsedijk 16', then trek 1 km west-ish along Schepensgraaf, onto Schinkelsweg and finally Casseweg.

DorpsHerberg

Casseweg 1a · **T** 0495 641356
www.dedorpsherberg.nl
Closed Tu; others from 11.30 (open daily in Jul&Aug)

Lovely middle-of-nowhere café and pancake house with fields on most sides. Birdsong fills the terrace. The bar area is crammed with old food tins, tea caddies and whisky cases. There is a small conservatory. Lunches (weekends only in winter) and dinners (daily until 21.00) feature pancakes. Asparagus and strawberries appear in season. Dishes have beer pairing suggestions. The 50+ well-chosen beers contain plenty of Dutch, including the house **Doospels Dubbel** (6.5%), brewed in collaboration with Natte Gijt, and a decent selection of 75cl bottles.

SITTARD

25km NE from Maastricht off A2 exit 48
Sittard

Small provincial town (pop. 38,000) with a picturesque market square, although the beery interest lies closer to its station.

Onder de Linden

Stationsstraat 25 · **T** 046 204 8005
www.dezaaksittard.nl
Fr&Sa 11.00-01.00; Su 13.00-23.00; others 11.00-23.00

Unassuming local with a large terrace containing no linden trees, despite the name. The cosy bar area has an abundance of dark wood, and there's a glass-roofed winter garden dining area at the rear. Lunches *(from 12.00)* include – oddly – English breakfast. Dinners served 16.00-21.00; snacks at other times. The 55 beers feature several Dutch choices, with Jopen and Liefde standing out.

STEIN

16km NNE from Maastricht off A2
Beek-Elsloo (3 km south)

Small town (pop. 12,000) next to a colossal chemicals plant that is fortunately obscured from its brewery, the highpoint of central Limburg.

Fontein

Ondergenhousweg 15 · **T** 046 426 2858
www.brouwerijdefontein.nl
Closed Mo&Tu (all year) and We-Fr (Sep-Mar); others 10.00-22.00

To reach this cosy, semi-rural brewery tap in a renovated farmhouse, take bus 12 or 112 from Beek-Elsloo station to Omphaliusstraat, then head 800 m WSW. Its inner bar has a wood-burning stove. Beside it is a semi-glazed conservatory with chandeliers. There is also a courtyard terrace. Simple meals and local Limburgs vlaai fruit tarts are served. Bread from a local bakery uses their spent brewing grain. Most of the expansive house range is available, eight on tap with the rest in bottle. Only the industrial pils is not brewed here. Bottles are also sold for takeaway.

VALKENBURG
12km ENE from Maastricht off A79
🚆 Valkenburg

Picturesque town (pop. 6,000) in the Geul valley. A tourist hotspot since the railway arrived 160 years ago. Apart from the country's oldest-surviving railway station, visitors come to see the hilltop ruins of Valkenburg castle, and several 'grottoes' that are actually disused stone quarries dug by the Romans. One of these, Fluweelengrot, hosts a subterranean Christmas market.

Grendelpoort 🍺
Muntstraat 17 · **T** 043 601 2640
Closed Mo&Tu; others from 12.00

Lovely beer café with a terrace on a pedestrianised street, beside the like-named 14th century gate, complete with portcullis. The shelves inside are crammed with beer bottles. Snacks only, except for the special monthly 5-course dinner, paired with beer. The 200+ beers are a delight but you may have to ask – the menu only covers the standards. Better things lurk in the shadows. Three house beers – dry Gringel Blond (7.5%), roasted-edged dubbel Duustere Gringel (7.5%), and Christmas ale Gringel Bells (ho ho) – are brewed for them at Proef. These are served in two-part glasses that have a pottery base modelled on Gringel Well, which once stood nearby.

Grendelpoort, Valkenburg

Pumpke
Daalhemerweg 2 · **T** 043 601 3721
Closed Mo&Tu; Sa&Su from 12.00; other from 19.00

The Little Pump is a friendly brown café with a small roadside terrace, around the corner from the Municipal Caves (Gemeentegrot). The interior is filled with the usual tat, leaning heavily towards musical instruments, with some religious statuary (nod to grotto), a ceramic stove and an old water pump. Lace doily lampshades add a cosy touch. Food runs to toasties, baguettes and soup. The 60 beers are almost entirely Belgian, but include Duchesse de Bourgogne on tap, several from Kerkom, and – perhaps inevitably – Grottenbier from St Bernardus.

VENLO
60km E from Eindhoven off A67
🚆 Venlo

Quiet provincial town (pop. 36,000) on the German border, best known as the railhead linking to the German network, but blessed with one very good reason for stopping off …

De Klep 🍺
Keizerstraat 13 · **T** 077 463 3287
www.cafedeklep.nl
Closed Mo&Tu; others from 14.00

From the station, head down Keulsepoort, take the second left, then the alley going right at the end to find this exceptional beer café in the shadow of a church alongside which its terrace runs. The interior has an ecclesiastical theme, with iconography, pews and statues. A stove provides non-denominational heat. The front café is dark wood, while a larger olive-painted tasting room lies behind. Both feel old but were actually purpose-built in 2012. Snacks only. There are many Dutch highlights on the 100+ beer list, including the house Klaassen range, brewed at Fontein by landlord Louis Klaassens. Downstairs the cellar is visible through glass, as is the 'executive cellar', which currently consists mainly of Trappist ales aged for 20+ years.

VIJLEN

15km S from Heerlen off N278

The country's highest village (pop. 1,500). Take bus 61 from Gulpen or Vaals. The country's highest point (a massive 321m above sea level) is 5 km SE at Drielandenpunt, where the Netherands, Belgium and Germany meet.

Hijgend Hert

Harles 23 · **T** 043 306 2499
www.boscafe.nl
Mo-Th (winter) 11.00–19.00; others 11.00–21.00

This self-styled 'mountain hut' (260m above sea level) is one of the country's cutest pubs but a bugger to reach by public transport. From the village it is a bracing 2km walk up a side road. A huge terrace roamed by chickens has sweeping countryside views. An outer conservatory has wood-burning stove, boar's head, and antler light fittings low enough to take out an eye. The stone-walled cabin bar within has an open hearth lit most days, filling the air with wood smoke. The food menu is extensive. Two of its 45 beers, Hert Blond and Bruin, are commissioned from nearby Grain d'Orge in Belgium.

Hijgend Hert, Vijlen

VOERENDAAL

4km W from Heerlen off A79
Voerendaal

Small village (pop. 3,000) near Heerlen.

Pintelier

Valkenburgerweg 33 · **T** 045 575 3214
www.herbergdepintelier.nl
Closed Tu&We; Mo&Th 16.00–01.00; Fr 14.00–02.00; Sa 12.00–02.00; Su 12.00–01.00

A large brown corner local, 1 km south of the station, with a terrace at the back. The interior has a floral ceiling hand painted by a local artist, an old stove, and an upright piano. There is a full food menu. The 100+ beer list is all Belgian, except for Hertog Jan and La Trappe, and the house blond Pintelierke is brewed in Watou.

WEERT

30km SE from Eindhoven off A2
Weert

Mid-sized industrial town (pop. 49,000) that prospered thanks to the railways and canals.

Dennenoord

Voorhoeveweg 2 · **T** 0495 532 884
Sa from 13.00; Su from 10.00; Shut Mo; others from 14.00

Rural café 2 km west of Weert station. Walk or take bus 173 to Geurtsvenweg/Ijzeren Man. Its USP is a large lakeside terrace, where you will be serenaded by birdsong and frogcroak, even if the view is partially spoiled by a fence. The interior is simple brown with beer fridges down one wall. Snacks only. There is plenty among the 50+ beers to maintain an interest. The house Iezere Menke amber is brewed by the landlord at Boelens in Belgium.

North Brabant

North Brabant (Noord-Brabant), or Brabant for short, is among the largest and most populous provinces (pop. 2.5 million). South of the big rivers it is unrelentingly flat, and outside the major towns is largely farmland, broken up by canals, with some fen and heathland.

Although a bastion of Catholicism, the people of Brabant were never as zealous as those further south, so for much of its life it was a buffer zone keeping the warring branches of Christianity apart, though its boundary with Belgium, especially around modern-day Baarle-Hertog/-Nassau is a lesson in how not to draw a border.

Brabant is among the beeriest regions of the country, with the highest concentration of production breweries. It also – to our non-scientific eye – has the best array of country pubs. If in doubt, aim for the church in any village, and there could be a decent watering hole close by, ready to replenish the sins of the repentant.

LARGEST CENTRES: **Eindhoven** (219,000), **Tilburg** (207,000), **Breda** (178,000), **'s-Hertogenbosch** (143,000), **Helmond** (89,000), **Roosendaal** (78,000), **Oss** (57,000), **Oosterhout** (54,000), **Bergen op Zoom** (53,000)

MORE INFORMATION: vvvbrabant.nl (in Dutch)

BREWERIES: **Bavaria**, *Lieshout;* **Beyerd**, *Breda;* **Bourgogne Kruis**, *Oosterhout;* **Budels**, *Budel;* **Croy**, *Aarle-Rixtel;* **Dommelsch** (AB InBev), *Dommelen;* **Drie Horne**, *Kaatsheuvel;* **Heusden**, *Heusden;* **Hopper**, *Kaatsheuvel;* **Kat**, *Helmond;* **Kievit**, *Zundert;* **Koningshoeven**, *Berkel-Enschot;* **Markies**, *'s-Hertogenbosch;* **Mieghelm**, *Sint-Michielsgestel;* **Oijen**, *Oijen;* **Oirschots**, *Oirschot;* **Pimpelmeesch**, *Chaam;* **Ramses**, *Wagenberg;* **Roos**, *Hilvarenbeek;* **Sint Servattumus**, *Schijndel;* **Van Kollenburg**, *'s-Hertogenbosch;* **Van Moll**, *Eindhoven*

OTHER BEER MAKERS: **Eijkenrode**, *Eindhoven;* **Gouden Leeuw**, *Vessem;* **Liefde**, *Geldrop;* **Muifel**, *Berghem;* **Oldskool**, *Eindhoven;* **Reuzen**, *Moergestel*

AARLE-RIXTEL

17km ENE from Eindhoven off A270

Residential village (pop. 5,800).

Croyse Hoeve

Croylaan 9 · **T** 0492 381348

www.croysehoeve.nl

Su from 12.00; others from 17.00
(open from 12.00 on Sa in Jul/Aug)

Croy's brewpub is a large rural tavern 1.5 km
SW from the village. Bus 25 from Helmond
lands you at Verliefd Laantje, from which it
is a 1.8 km walk W down De Grote Overbrug.
The flower-filled terrace looks onto the
brewery's own hop field, and Kasteel Croy.
The nearby 16th century castle gatehouse is
a B&B. The pub interior has an open hearth
and copper brewing kettles – the real stainless
steel kit is in a back room. Food (to 21.00)
includes dishes made with the house beers.
Four or five beers are usually on, with
bottles for takeaway.

Croyse Hoeve, Aarle-Rixtel

BAARLE-NASSAU

27km SW from Tilburg off N260

Two towns and countries all wrapped into
one – three-quarters is Dutch Baarle-Nassau,
the rest Belgian Baarle-Hertog. Take bus 132
from Tilburg or Breda to find this bizarre
medieval mess of boundary disputes that
centuries of effort have failed to simplify.
Individual plots of land belong to different
countries, creating Belgian enclaves in the

Netherlands, and enclaves within enclaves.
National flags on the house numbers are
invaluable, and street markings inform you
when you cross borders, which happens
often. The whole set up is endearingly crap.
Despite everything, national characters
shine through: Belgians houses look scruffier,
Dutch homes better tended. The local
brewery, Dochter van de Korenaar, is run by
a Dutchman, in Belgium, though if he moved
the brewhouse a few metres down the same
road it would be Dutch.

BEER TO GO: One of the world's oddest beer
shops, **Biergrens** (Molenstraat 26 (NL), or
Molenstraat 98 (BE) – **T** 013 507 7878 (NL) –
www.debiergrens.be – *Closed Mo; Sa 10.00-*
17.00; Su 10.00-16.00; others 10.00-18.00)
straddles the border, with two separate
addresses and phone numbers. We suspect
tax may have a hand in this. We would love
to see them start two sets of opening times.
A line on the floor tells you where you
stand. Its 300+ beers are mainly Belgian,
strong on gueuzes and 75cl bottles.

BERGEIJK

21km SW from Eindhoven off N397

Dormer town (pop. 8,700) for Eindhoven
and Tilburg commuters. Take bus 172 or 174
from Eindhoven.

Hofkaemer

Hof 18 · **T** 0497 571396

www.hofkaemer.nl

Closed Mo&We; others from 10.00

A friendly village local with a terrace by the
bandstand, and a secluded garden at the
rear. The cosy front bar has a wood-burning
stove, and one wall consisting entirely of
wooden drawers. At the back is a larger
dining area. The restaurant – light lunches
and more substantial dinners – uses
Brabantine ingredients where possible and
dishes come with recommended beer
pairings. Around half the 60 beers are from
small local breweries, and even the wine list
has a couple of Dutch options.

BERGEN OP ZOOM

16km WSW of Roosendaal off A58 exit 27

Bergen op Zoom

Attractive town (pop. 53,000), the name of which implies hills, conspicuous by their absence, but actually refers to way an ancient dyke built up naturally and kept out the surrounding marshland. Or something like that. Star attraction is the Markiezenhof (www.markiezenhof.nl), a beautiful brick palace built in 1485. The town still claims a link to Schelde brewery, despite its relocation to Belgium in 2008.

HOTEL TIP: **De Draak** ★★★★, Grote Markt 36 (**T** 0164 252050; www.hoteldedraak.nl) is the Netherlands' oldest hotel, dating back to 1397.

Provoosthuis

Potterstraat 36 · **T** 0164 257978
Mo-We from 19.00; others from 13.30

One block west of Grote Mark, this impressive brick and stone building, dating from 1783, was once the town garrison provost's house, and a military court and prison. Nowadays it is a pool and snooker hall, with five tables. Décor is limited to a few enamels and a pair of old skis above the bar. No food, except for occasional barbecues in the leafy beer garden at the rear. Besides La Trappe, its 70 beers are mainly Belgian, with interesting options including Boon lambics.

*OTHER **BERGEN OP ZOOM** BEER VENUES:*

Decorated with everything from carousel horses to human skeletons, **Lokomotiefke** (Grote Markt 11 – **T** 0164 250321 – www.locomotiefke.nl – *shut Mo; others from 15.00*) is billed as a curiosities café. The beers are more obvious.

BEER TO GO: **Bierwinkel** (Halsterseweg 110 – **T** 0164 255606 – www.de-bierwinkel.nl – *Closed Su; Fr 09.00-21.00; Sa 09.00-17.00; others 09.00-18.00*), a large drinks warehouse 2km N of the centre, stocks 250+ beers.

BERKEL-ENSCHOT

6km ENE from Tilburg off A65 exit 2

Dormer town (pop. 10,000) near Tilburg, but do not be fooled. While officially within the municipality, its famous monastery is 6km to the south, on the road between Tilburg and Moergestel, and closer to each of these. Bus 141 from Tilburg passes its entrance.

Koningshoeven

Eindhovenseweg 3 · **T** 013 572 2650
www.latrappe.nl
Daily 11.00-19.00; 17.30 (Nov-Mar)

The Koningshoeven Trappist brewery tap is a purpose-built thatched barn beside the monastery, with a huge terrace. Inside is a high-ceilinged refectory with leather couches. Simple lunches (12.00-17.00) use organic local ingredients, including monk-made breads and cheeses. Snacks available all day. The beer list is the abbey's own La Trappe range, on tap or in bottle. Bottles are also sold in the abbey shop.

BLADEL

27km WSW from Eindhoven off N284

Modern village (pop. 9,800) with a charmless main square. Take bus 150 from Eindhoven.

D'n Bel

Markt 50 · **T** 0497 383323
Closed Mo; Fr&Sa from 15.00; Su from 14.00; others from 18.00

The dartboard and large TV screen give this loud, modern pub a sports-bar feel. With the music turned up high, the only respite can be on the terrace outside on the square. No food. The 100+ beers compensate. There are several local Brabant offerings, and the Belgian majority has unusual finds such as Dolle Brouwers and Viven.

BOXTEL

25km NW from Eindhoven off A2 exit 25
🚆 Boxtel

Neat commuter town (pop. 24,000). In 1794, the Battle of Boxtel was part of a failed Anglo-Austro-Dutch attempt to invade Napoléon's France via Flanders. One of the British brigade commanders was a certain Lt-Col Arthur Wellesley, later the Duke of Wellington.

Becoloth

Rozemarijnstraat 2-2a · **T** 0411 673673
www.becoloth.nl
Fr from 10.00; Sa&Su from 15.00; Mo from 16.00; others from 11.30

Several-roomed beer café a few steps from the Markt, with a small terrace. The right hand side can be quieter than the left at weekends. At the back is a 'courtyard' winter garden with a Roman villa theme. Cherubs adorn the semi-bare brick walls elsewhere. Snacks only. The 130 beers find room for some local Brabant and other Dutch brews among the otherwise Belgian list, with a few German Weizen.

BREDA

🚆 Breda

Brabant's third city (pop. 178,000) is ringed by canals, and parks roamed by feral chickens. The centre has a medieval elegance despite a 1534 fire that left only 150 buildings standing. The Grote Kerk, under construction at that time, is one of the country's finest Gothic cathedrals.

Among the more noteworthy visitors was King Charles II, who spent much of his time in exile here during Cromwell's Commonwealth. It was his Declaration of Breda in 1660 that pardoned any enemies who recognised his restoration to the English throne. Five years later he was fighting the Second Anglo-Dutch War. There's gratitude for you.

On the first weekend in September Breda hosts International Redhead Day, a global gathering of thousands of people of the ginger persuasion.

Beyerd

Boschstraat 26 · **T** 076 521 4265
www.cafedebeyerd.nl
Closed We; Sa from 12.00; others from 10.00

Some 400m E of the centre, the popular and long-standing Carillion is a founding member of ABT and since 2004 a brewpub. It was opened in 1967 by Piet de Jongh and is still run by his sons, Orson and Mikel. The front terrace seems perpetually full. Inside, traditions are upheld with carpeted tables and a billiard table at the rear, although it is normally too crowded for anyone to play. A back room is the brewery and a restaurant (evenings only). Lunches and snacks are served in the bar. The 125 beers include 14 taps, of which 3 or 4 are house brews. Elsewhere the menu has a reasonable Dutch selection and is strong on Belgian lambics.

Bierreclamemuseum

Haagweg 375 · **T** 076 522 0975
www.bierreclamemuseum.nl
Su only 12.00-23.00

A warren of a pub that doubles as a free museum, packed to bursting with beer memorabilia. It is 3.5km southwest of the centre - a standout oddity in a quiet suburb. From Breda station, take bus 4 (to Princenhage) as far as Nieuwe Heilaarstraat. Backtrack 10m and head left into Haagweg. You cannot miss it - it is the one with the blue truck and British telephone box on the terrace. It has a beer garden at the back. There is sometimes live music from 17.00. Snacks only. The 55 beers are mainly Belgian, but there are a few Dutch options.

Boterhal

Grote Markt 19 · **T** 076 889 8180
Closed Mo; others from 11.30.

Popular drinking hole with a terrace on the main square. The former butter exchange spreads over two large floors, but still gets packed. Loudish music attracts a younger crowd. Lunches served until 16.00. Dinners are sold in 'tapas' portions, so you'll need more than one. Almost a quarter of the 100+ beers are on tap but with the exception of the five guests poured from showy copper tanks, most are predictable. The bottles are much better, including Emelisse and De Molen, plus several US and UK imports.

Don Qui-John

Haagsemarkt 20 · **T** 076 514 7669
www.donqui-john.nl
Closed Mo; others from 11.00

Suburban café-restaurant 4km SW of the centre, near the Bierreclamemuseum (above). Follow the directions to the latter, but turn right into Haagweg, not left. The sleek modern interior has minimalist wood furnishings. The restaurant is similar, but adds tablecloths and wine racks. Lunches (until 17.00) are standard Dutch. The restaurant dinner menu is grander. The 40+ beers are well chosen, and strong on Dutch brewers: Leidsch, Emelisse, Maximus and Ramses have all been spotted. It has a streetside terrace.

Zeezicht, Breda

Kleine Wereld

Grote Markt 59 · **T** 06 3819 0975
www.cafedekleinewereld.nl
Closed Mo-We; others from 16.00

Cutesy step-gabled café beside (and below) the looming walls of the Grote Kerk, the Small World has a tiny conservatory and an equally tiny front terrace. The compact interior has bright white walls, with wood elsewhere. Snacks only. The 50+ beer range is not bad, with several from Brabant, plus US and UK imports.

Sam Sam

Grote Markt 2 · **T** 076 522 7526
www.samsambreda.nl
Daily from 10.00

Long-standing café that re-launched in a beerier direction in 2013, with a distinctly Dutch slant. Diagonally opposite the Zeezicht (below), they have adjoining terraces. The interior has Art Deco & Nouveau hints. Food is simple meals and borreleuken, or beer snacks. The bulk of the 80+ beers are from Dutch breweries, with a 'Craft Beer' tap reserved for limited editions from small ones. They also specialise in jenevers.

Zeezicht

Ridderstraat 1 · **T** 076 514 8248
www.cafezeezicht.nl
Daily from 10.00

Corner bar on the Grote Markt with a terrace round two sides. Inside is a casual all-round light-brown café. Simple lunches are served downstairs *(11.00–17.00)*; more elaborate dinners in the upstairs restaurant *(17.00–22.00)*. Beerwise this is a treasure trove. Almost half the 80+ choices change seasonally, with Dutch brewers forming a large minority. They have good selections of whiskies and wines. The one thing the Sea View does not have is a sea view, but then you are 80km from the coast…

OTHER **BREDA** BEER VENUES:

Bruxelles (Havermarkt 7 – **T** 076 521 5211 – **www.bruxelles.nl** – *daily from 12.00*) ticks boxes for its cosy interior and open fire, but its 35+ beers lack standouts.

BEER TO GO: South of the centre the **Bierhuis** (Van Goorstraat 5 – **T** 076 522 8394 – www.hetbierhuis.nl – *Closed Su; Sa 09.30–17.00; others 09.30–18.00*) stocks 300+ beers, with many US imports and 75cl bottles.

BREDA (Ginneken)

Southern Breda suburb, once a separate village, now swallowed up. Take southbound bus 7 to Viandenlaan.

Moeke

Ginnekenmarkt 17 · **T** 076 560 7020
www.moekebreda.nl
Closed Tu (winter); others from 10.00

Beside the 1792 former town hall, this imposing brick building has a terrace on a picturesque market square, and a beer garden behind. The high-ceilinged interior was once a hotel lobby. Lunches are served 12.00–17.00; dinner 17.00–21.00 (*until 22.00 Th-Sa*); snacks all day. The 55 beers are exclusively Belgian, with several Trappists and Anker beers among the standouts. A couple of doors down, frozen-in-time brown café **Boerke Verschuren** (Ginnekenmarkt 13 – **T** 076 565 3220 – *daily from 10.00*) has carpets on some tables, in-laid games boards on others, and gingham curtains. Dull beer but you cannot win 'em all.

CHAAM

13km S from Breda on N639

Sleepy village (pop. 3,800) pronounced 'Kaam', which is logical in neither Dutch nor English. A former raspberry capital, it now makes its living from tourism and has numer-ous campsites. Take bus 132 from Breda.

Toontje Schoen

Ginderdoorstraat 4 · **T** 0161 496610
www.toontjeschoen.tonschoenmakers.nl
Closed Mo all year & Tu-Fr (Oct-Apr); others 10.00-20.00

A 20-minute walk south from the village bus stop, the de facto Pimpelmeesch tap is not linked officially to the brewery though

physically there is only a glass wall between them. It is a restored 18th-century thatched *langgevel* farmhouse. One end used to house the farmer and the other livestock. Wooden beams dominate. The terrace is opposite fields, with the background lowing of cows coming from nearby sheds and pastures. Snacks include apple pie and ice cream. Only Pimpelmeesch beers, among them the house Toontje Schoen blond.

DONGEN

16km NW from Tilburg off N260

Small commuter town (pop. 22,000) that once had a leather industry. Bus 127 from Tilburg or Breda passes the pub below.

Janssen & Janssen

Hoge Ham 59 · **T** 0162 319 850
www.eetcafejanssenenjanssen.nl
Closed Mo; others from 11.30

English-speakers familiar with Tintin will know Janssen & Janssen as The Thompson Twins, as becomes evident when you enter this vast village local, with no fewer than three bars in interconnecting rooms, a beer garden at the back, and a front terrace opposite the unusually large-domed St Laurentius church. There is live music some nights, and a full food menu. The 120+ beers are Belgian led, but there are several Dutch choices, and US and UK imports.

EINDHOVEN

Eindhoven

Despite receiving city rights in 1232, the Netherlands' fifth city (pop. 219,000) remained a backwater until a certain Gerard Philips began manufacturing light bulbs here in 1891. Its subsequent growth is almost entirely down to the global electronics giant that his family business became, even if nowadays most manufacturing has relocated to the Far East and the factories have been converted to leisure facilities. To see what they used to make, visit the Philips Museum (www.philips-museum.com).

Major war damage led to a radical redesign – for which read flattening – of the city centre, and few old buildings remain. Modern Eindhoven now views itself as a design capital, which manifests itself in some unusual buildings – for example the Evoluon, or The Blob.

Recent years have seen a healthy flowering in this former beer desert, and after a gap of 60 years a brewery is in town once again. A second is in the offing.

HOTEL TIP: **Lumiere** ★★★, Hooghuisstraat 31 (**T** 040 239 4950; **www.hotellumiere.nl**) is a modern central boutique hotel.

Baron

Kleine Berg 26 · **T** 040 296 0099
www.cafedebaron.com
Su from 13.00; others from 12.00

Popular beer café with a streetside terrace. Inside is all beer enamels and mirrors, with a large chandelier. Lunches are served in the bar; snacks all day. Dinners are served from 18.00 on the mezzanine above. The 150+ beers change on every visit as when stocks run out they are replaced on the owner's whims. It is heavily Belgocentric, with a few Dutch options. About a quarter of the range comes in 75cl bottles. There is no menu – just check the stack of glass-fronted chiller cabinets to the right of the bar.

Bierprofessor

Stratumseind 33 · **T** 06 5535 5572
www.bierprofessor.nl
Closed Mo; Fr from 16.00; Su from 18.00; others from 20.00

Stratumseind – 'the Strat' – is a notorious street of bars, with over 40 lining up shoulder to shoulder. Most are crap and aimed at students, with loud music and indifferent beer. This exception at its northern end is a small café with a tiny terrace. Snacks include 'Dutch Balls' – we assume they mean *bitterballen*. The beer list has reached 180 and is rising slowly. They have a printed menu but the bottles on the wall give a

more up-to-date idea of what is avaialble. Chiefly Belgian, the range from smaller Dutch brewers is improving.

Bolle Boel

Stationsplein 2 · **T** 040 245 5331
www.eetcafebolle.nl
Daily from 11.00

Large and loud modern café with a conservatory and terrace opposite the station, and three glitter balls inside that indicate which way the volume knob is going. It appears to be striving for a mock-British pub look. There is occasional live music. A full food menu is served. Perhaps best avoided at night if you are looking for somewhere to chat quietly. Its 55 beers include several from De Prael. US imports jostle for space among the Belgians.

Jack

Stratumseind 55 · **T** none
www.cafethejack.nl
Fr&Sa from 15.00, Su from 14.00, others from 19.00

This tatty, rough-edged rock café is another oasis of beeriness on the Strat. Concrete floors, table football and darts for frills, and occasional loud live music. A small terrace provides some relief at such times. No food we believe. The standouts among the 65+ beers are a good choice of bottled IPAs and stouts, including several Dutch versions, and a number of US and UK imports.

Spiegelbeeld

Dommelstraat 22 · **T** 040 243 4441
www.hetspiegelbeeld.com
Closed Mo; others from 17.00

The Mirror Image takes its name from its two unrelated, follically challenged co-owners. During restaurant hours (until 22.30), the low-lit intimate café functions as a tapas bar, serving international snackettes. The focus at those times is on food, so drinkers are expelled from tables to prop up the bar. There is a terrace at the front. The 125 beers include some unusual guests on tap. Various multi-beer menus are offered.

Van Moll

Keizersgracht 16A · **T** 040 848 7255
www.vanmolleindhoven.nl
Closed Mo; Tu&We 17.00–01.00; others 15.00–01.00

Modern central brewpub in former offices, with an industrial chic minimalist interior. Some of its lamps were originally runway lights from Eindhoven Airport. The brewery is in the cellar. Snacks only. The 65+ beers vary regularly. Three of the 12 taps are from the house. Other taps and bottles pluck the best from top Dutch and imported brewers.

Van Moll, Eindhoven

*OTHER **EINDHOVEN** BEER VENUES:*
The **Centraal** (Markt 8 – **T** 040 245 2689 – www.centraaleindhoven.nl – *Su from 11.00; others from 10.00*) has 30 beers, the best range on the main square.

In a rare old building, dating from 1685, the **Little One** (Jan van Lieshoutstraat 26 – **T** 040 243 8995 – *Closed Su; Sa from 21.30; others from 17.00*) is a tiny local with dusty bric-a-brac everywhere.

In a former industrial area northwest of the centre, barbecue restaurant **Ketelhuis** (Ketelhuisplein 1 – **T** 06 8724 7348 – www. ketelhuis.com – *Closed Tu&We; others from 17.30*) has a small but well-chosen selection of 25 international beers, while to its west, **Sala Thai** (Staringstraat 31 – **T** 040 243 4101 – www.restaurantsalathai.nl – *daily 17.30–22.30*), is possibly the world's only restaurant combining excellent Thai food with De Molen beers.

Loud and popular **Sgt Peppers** (Stratumseind 49 – **T** 040 244 4934 – *Closed Su&Mo; others from 20.00*) has a beer list approaching 40 that fails to light fireworks.

BEER TO GO: In a shopping complex west of the centre, **Van Bergen** (Hurksestraat 44 – **T** 040 252 5856 – www.mitravanbergen.nl – *Mo 13.00–18.00; Tu-Th 10.00–18.00; Fr 10.00–20.00; Sa 09.00–17.00*) is Mitra's beeriest outlet, stocking 600+, alongside 250 whiskies.

HELMOND

14km E from Eindhoven, on N270
Helmond

A medium-sized town (pop. 89,000) with a castle from 1350 that is one of the nation's better-preserved. It houses the town museum (**gemeentemuseumhelmond.nl**).

Lokaal 42

Markt 42 · **T** 0492 830043
www.lokaal42.nl
Closed Mo&Tu; Sa from 12.00; others from 15.00

Small music café with a terrace on the market square. The interior is dominated by the stage, used Sunday afternoons and occasional evenings. There is a full food menu. We have been promised that there is a plan to expand the current 40+ beer list but for now the standouts are half a dozen offerings from Texel.

BEER TO GO: **Biermoment** (Schorfhoeve 4 – **T** 06 5143 4820 – www.hetbiermoment.nl) stocks several hundred Dutch beers. Technically web only, they will sell from the garage if you turn up – but call first between 10.00 and 12.00 to be sure.

's HERTOGENBOSCH

's-Hertogenbosch

Brabant's attractive provincial capital (pop. 143,000) is known universally by its colloquial name, Den Bosch ('denn boss'). The impressive 1530 St John's Cathedral was even grander before the western tower burned down in 1830.

The city's most famous son is Hieronymus Bosch – he of the nightmarish medieval visions in paint. His statue stands on the Markt square. Also there is the 13th-century De Moriaan, the nation's oldest brick house. If you are looking for a lazy pub crawl, make a beeline for Korenbrugstraat, where three of our entries sit handily in a row.

Gouwe Sleutel

Koninginnenlaan 28 · **T** 073 689 0789
www.cafedegouwesleutel.nl
Mo-We from 17.00; others from 14.00

This friendly local boozer 200 m north from the station has Roccoco-leaning décor, tiled floors, and a wooden-beamed ceiling. It is largely populated by regulars of an evening. Food is snacks only. The 'almost' 100 beers include a refreshingly wide range of Dutch choices, among which are De Molen, Ramses and Muifel.

Hertog

Hinthamerstraat 83 · **T** 073 614 0550
www.tapperijdehertog.nl
*Closed Mo; Tu from 15.00; Su from 12.00;
others from 10.30*

Convivial café a block north of the cathedral, with a billiard table as its central feature. Photos on the wall suggest this is somewhere to avoid during carnival. Food runs from baguettes to schnitzels and spare ribs. Besides La Trappe, the bulk of the 45 beers are standard Belgians, but guest beers occasionally provide pleasant surprises.

Le Duc

Korenbrugstraat 5 · **T** 073 613 6915
www.cafebarleduc.nl
Su from 12.00; Mo from 13.30; others from 11.00

Long-established beer café and the tap of the Van Kollenburg brewery. This popular place and its small terrace get crowded at peak times. Interior bric-a-brac has a general aquatic theme (fishing nets and a canoe), and there is a bijou mezzanine at the rear.

A full food menu is served, but reserve tables at weekends as space is limited. The 70+ beers are mainly Belgian, with a reasonable range of lambics. Six of the 12 taps are house Kolleke brews.

M'n Tante

Korenbrugstraat 7 · **T** 073 613 4030
Sa&Su from 12.00; others from 16.00.

My Aunt is a modern light brown café with a small and often packed terrace, part of a trilogy of joys on Korenbrugstraat. Black and white photos of ladies (aunts?) adorn the walls. Raucous chatting drowns out any hint of background music. Snacks only. The list of 75 is top-heavy with Belgians, though there are a couple from 't IJ.

Paultje

Lepelstraat 31a · **T** 073 612 4441
www.tpaultje.nl
Closed Mo; Tu&We from 18.00; others from 13.00

Around the corner from Korenbrugstraat, this unprepossessing new kid, with suspended polystyrene ceilings within and a terrace without, only opened in 2013, but immediately threw down the gauntlet. Snacks only. The 250+ beers include numerous Dutch choices, led by Emelisse and De Molen. The imports are equally impressive: strong on Belgian lambics and German Weizen, as well as multiple US and UK representations.

Root Scharlaken

Kolperstraat 4 · **T** 073 613 5009
www.rootscharlaken.nl
*Closed Tu; Sa from 09.00; Su from 11.00;
Mo from 12.00; others from 10.00*

The antidote to all things modern, this is a small, friendly and very local Brabant café with a bijou terrace just off the Markt. Walls are hung with classic album covers. Come on the first Sunday of the month for singalong time – lyric books are provided. Accompaniment comes from an accordionist. Food is peanuts. 60+ beers include 't IJ and La Trappe, plus a few US imports, and several vintages of Het Anker's Cuvée van de Keizer in 75cl bottles.

Terminus

Boschveldweg 15 · **T** 073 613 0666
www.hotel-terminus.nl
*Closed Mo; Fr&Sa from 14.00; Su 14.00–20.00;
others from 16.30*

Self-styled Scottish folk pub with a billiard
table, a block north of the station. Opened
in 1961, not a great deal has changed. The
furniture is struggling, and the carpet sticky.
Bric-a-brac includes musical instruments,
steins, and a carved pulpit. Posters
advertising music festivals grab your
interest, then you realise they happened
years ago. There is occasional live folk
music. Snacks only. The 90 mainly Belgian
beers are strong on Trappists. Scottishness
comes from 3 Belhaven brews on tap, and
200 whiskies.

Veulen

Korenbrugstraat 9a · **T** 073 612 3038
www.hetveulen.nl
Fr&Su from 14.00; Sa from 11.00; others from 15.00

Just like its neighbours (above), this bustling
beer café is often standing room only inside
and on the terrace. The interior is largely
wood and mirrors. Snacks only, but including
snails. Among the 55+ beers are a few from
La Trappe, and a house beer that occasionally
changes style and brewer, but last we looked
was a 6.5% IPA brewed by De Eem.

*OTHER **DEN BOSCH** BEER VENUES:*
Open since 1917, characterful tiny local
Bonte Palet (Hinthamerstraat 99 – **T** 073 613
2532 – *Closed Mo&Tu; others from 15.00*) has
peanut shells on the floor and carpeted
tables.

*Kareltje,
Heusden*

Kareltje

Burchtplein 5–6
T *Café*: 0416 660039 · *Herberg*: 0416 660560
www.kareltje.info
*Pub: Closed Mo&Tu (all year), We (winter);
Th&Fr (winter) from 18.00; others from 12.00
Restaurant: Closed Mo (all year), Tu (winter);
We&Th (winter) 17.00–23.00; others 12.00–23.00*

Possibly the only brewery and tap to share
its name with its resident spaniels. Kareltjes
1 and 2 patrol the pub, the restaurant, and
the terraces in between. The compact two-
room pub is cuter and older, with copper pipes
going everywhere. The restaurant seems
more brown café. Food (last orders 21.00) is
only served inside the latter but you can eat
on either terrace. There are usually two
house brews among the 30+ beers. There is
also a range of house liqueurs. Opens at
10.00 on Sundays in summer.

*OTHER **HEUSDEN** BEER VENUES:*
The lovely harbourside **Havenzicht** (Vismarkt
2 – **T** 0416 662723 – www.havenzicht.nl –
Sa&Su from 10.00; others from 11.00) is the
perfect spot for a brew with a view.

HEUSDEN

15km WNW from 's-Hertogenbosch off N267

Take bus 135 from 's-Hertogenbosch to this
attractive, fortified village (pop. 1,500) with
cobbled streets. Its little harbour by the
Maas has a backdrop of wooden drawbridge
and windmill – as Dutch as you can get
without a woman in clogs selling tulips, and
a man lobbing an old bicycle into the water.

HILVARENBEEK

10km S from Tilburg off N269

A town in name (pop. 8,600) but with a
village green (the Vrijthof) at its heart –
albeit without the crack of leather on willow.
Take bus 142 or 143 from Tilburg.
HOTEL TIP: **Sint Petrus** ★★, Gelderstraat 1
(**T** 013 505 2166; www.sintpetrus.nl) is beside
and run by the Taverne Paulus (below).

Gouden Carolus

Gelderstraat 20 · **T** 013 505 3178
www.goudencarolus.nl
Su 13.00–21.00; others from 19.00

Corner local south of the Vrijthof, with a billiard table, instruments and marionettes hung from the ceiling, and a hearth. Hanging on a back wall is a line of green bottles – insert your own gag. Two antique porcelain beer taps sit atop the bar. Snacks only. The 40 beers include – unsurprisingly – the full range of Gouden Carolus from Het Anker in Belgium, as well as La Trappe, and some from local De Roos.

Paulus

Gelderstraat 3 · **T** 013 505 5833
www.tavernepaulus.nl
Su from 15.00; others from 16.00

Lively tavern at the south end of the village green, with a small terrace. At the back is a conservatory with ceiling fans tickling the vines growing there. In between is more oak than you can shake a stick at: tables, floors, pillars and ceilings. Leather armchairs at the front gather around a gas-effect fire, and there is a second fireplace further back. Food is served until 22.00; snacks until 24.00. There is a full range of La Trappe among the 50+ beers, plus several from De Roos.

Roos

St. Sebastiaanstraat 4 · **T** 013 505 5045
www.museumbrouwerij.nl
Closed Mo&Tu (all year), We&Th (Sep-Jun except school holidays); others 13.00–17.00

Brewery tap and museum café just north of the Vrijthof. You do not need a ticket to reach the bar, in a wooden loft. Like the museum and brewery it is staffed by volunteers, hence the limited hours. Food is nuts only. There are 4 house beers on tap, plus whatever's in stock from the large bottled range. Bottles are also sold for takeaway.

*OTHER **HILVARENVEEK** BEER VENUES:*

Gelegenheid (Vrijthof 26 – **T** 013 505 1403 – www.degelegenheid.nl – *shut Mo; Tu-Th from 16.00; others from 13.00*) has a picturesque terrace, a rear garden courtyard, and 30 beers including De Roos.

KAATSHEUVEL
15km N of Tilburg via A261/N261

Small town (pop. 16,000) known for the Efteling amusement park (www.efteling.com) and in some circles for the 3 Horne brewery. Take bus 136, 300, 301 or 302 from Tilburg.

Roestelberg

Roestelbergseweg 2 · **T** 0416 333079
www.de-roestelberg.nl
Closed We (Sep-Jun); Mo from 11.00; others from 09.15

Country pub 4km from Kaatsheuvel and Waalwijk, beside the Loonse & Drunense Duinen, an area of inland dunes. The expansive terrace is within touching distance of the sand. There is no convenient bus. The massive interior seems set up for coach parties. Stars of the food menu are the sixty different pancakes *(until 17.00)*. The rest of the kitchen closes at 19.00 *(20.30 in Jul&Aug)*. The beer list, presumably under instructions not to upstage the batter, officially stops at 59 but guests may nudge it over. The house **Roestelaere** (7%) is a hoppy amber from nearby 3 Horne.

KNEGSEL
12km WSW from Eindhoven

You do pronounce the 'K' of this leafy village (pop. 1,300). Bus 494 between Veldhoven and Vessem passes through – get to the former from Eindhoven.

Kempen

Het Groen 14 · **T** 040 205 5032
www.dineecafedekempen.nl
Daily from 10.00

Large central modern café with black slate floors, stylish furnishings, a gas-effect hearth, and large terraces front and back. Lunches and dinners are served, with snacks in between. Besides Budels, most of the interest among the 45-odd beers is Belgian. St Bernardus, Het Anker and Achel feature, as do occasional US imports.

LIESHOUT

15km NE from Eindhoven off N615

Brabant village (pop. 4,300), utterly dominated by the country' largest independent brewery. Most locals probably know someone who works there. Take bus 121 or 122 from Eindhoven.

Moorees

Heuvel 5 · **T** 0499 425585
www.bavariabrouwerijcafe.nl
Sa&Su 12.00–22.00; Mo 17.00–22.00; others 10.00–22.00

Modern brasserie with two terraces, 100 m from the Bavaria brewery and effectively its taphouse. Modern furnishings miss no opportunity to promote the house brand. The only nod to tradition is the billiard table in the bar. Lunch and dinner is served, some dishes cooked with beer. Besides the house range, there are also most beers from La Trappe, a pie in which Bavaria also has several fingers.

MADE

12 km N from Breda, off A59

Small commuter town (pop. 12,000) near Oosterhout. As the latter has no rail link, the easiest approach is bus 123 from Breda.

The Pub

Kloosterstraat 36 · **T** 0162 690590
thepubandchurchill.nl
Daily from 10.00

This English pub and beer garden opened at the end of 2013, complete with Chesterfield sofas and open fireplaces. Food – fish & chips

and steak and ale pie – is British pub grub. Rare in the Netherlands, the taps feature several British real ale pumps. The casks are visible in the open cellar. The 50-ish bottled selection includes local Brabant offerings.

MOERGESTEL

7km ESE from Tilburg, off A58

Small town (pop. 6,000) that functions as a sleepover for Tilburg workers. Those who prefer not to drive take bus 141.

Veerkes

Sint Jansplein 3 · **T** 013 513 2405
www.deveerkes.nl
Closed Mo&Tu; We&Th from 19.30; Fr&Sa from 15.00; Su from 10.00

Friendly local with a terrace on the main square. The latter would be more attractive were it not a car park. The interior has worn tiled floors and green-painted walls. Snacks and toasties only. The 60 list includes two dozen changing guest bottles, posted on a separate board. The core range includes nearby La Trappe and Reuzen.

OIJEN

25km NE from 's-Hertogenbosch off N329

Small village (pop. 1,100) on the south bank of the Maas.

Oijen

Oijense Bovendijk 61 · **T** 0412 492 217
www.speciaalbierbrouwerij.nl
Daily 12.00–23.00. Oct-Mar: Shut Mo&Tu

Nearer Macheren than Oijen – take bus 296 from Oss to Macheren Dorpstraat and it is a 15 minutes' walk NW to this rural brewery tap. The snug café within was once a cattle shed, and has wood-burning stove, gingham curtains, and a higgledy-piggledy charm: hams and sausages hang in a corner, forks and spoons are attached to lampshades. Watch your head on the low door. The roomier restaurant was a hay barn. There is a conservatory and a terrace too. There is a full menu, or 'Hap&Tap' snacks. Two or 3 house beers are on tap, with maybe a dozen in the bottle, also sold as takeaway.

Buitenlust, Oirschot

OIRSCHOT
17km NW from Eindhoven off A58

Small town (pop. 11,000) with cobbled streets and a disproportionately large church. The village green has been turned into a leafy car park. But you will be here for the beer, on the country's most extraordinary list. Take bus 141 or 142 from Best.

Buitenlust
Spoordonkseweg 5 · **T** 06 4190 4295
www.cafebuitenlust.nl
Su from 12.00; others from 15.00

Unassuming local with a large terrace, in a quiet residential area north of the centre. Not where you would expect to find the most extensive beer list in this book. Inside is a large bar with a billiard table at the back, and live music some nights. There is a short lunch menu and sometimes evening dishes on request. Beyond that, there are snacks. The 9 tap beers include La Trappe and guests but behold the bottled range. By the end of 2013 this had reached 600, with the (possibly over-ambitious) aim of building over time to 1500. De Molen and Emelisse lead the Dutch way. Imports come from the US and pretty much every notable European brewing nation. It has to be done.

Vingerhoeds
Oude Grintweg 90 · **T** 0499 571334
www.cafevingerhoeds.nl
Closed Mo (all year), and Tu-Th (Oct-Mar); Fr 14.00–18.00 (Oct-Mar); Su 10.00–22.00 (23.30 Apr-Sep); others 10.00–18.00

The Thimble is 3.5km north of Oirschot and the nearest bus stop. By local tradition, each village's last building, such as this, was an 'open house' where folk fortified themselves before facing the perils of the woods and marshes. It was also a hangout for tramps, hawkers and other undesirables. Named after the family who own it. They have erected a statue in honour of their most acclaimed forebear, landlady Mieke Vingerhoeds, who wore clogs, refused to serve anyone in shorts, and ruled here from 1925 until her death aged 90 in 1989. The rustic 1920s tiled-floor interior has a wood stove, a built-in bed, and – yes – a collection of thimbles. Simple lunches are available. Around half the 80+ beers are German.

OTHER **OIRSCHOT** BEER VENUES:
Oud Brabant (Markt 14 – **T** 0499 575509 – www.oudbrabant.nl – *Closed Tu; others from 11.00*), a cosy café on the main square, serves local Oirschots beers among its short list.

OISTERWIJK
11km E from Tilburg off N65
Oisterwijk

Small town (pop. 19,000) with a tree-lined avenue – De Lind – running through its heart. There is a picturesque fenland nature reserve to the south of the town.

Boshuis Venkraai
Bosweg 162 · **T** 013 528 2396
www.boshuisvenkraai.nl
Su 09.00–19.00; others 10.00–19.00

Woodland café, 2.5km south from the station. Follow Stationsstraat to its end, through several name changes, then turn

Boshuis Venkraai, Oisterwijk

right and left into Wierdsmalaan. Continue on the forest path even when the road runs out and you will find this wonderful place. The terrace is surrounded by trees, fens and lily ponds. The bijou interior is typical brown café, with carpeted tables. Simple meals are served until 18.00. The beer list has shrunk to 45 in recent years, but it is worth visiting for its setting alone. Jopen and 't IJ are the best of Dutch. The house Blonde Kraai (6.5%) comes from Bocq in Belgium.

Gelagh

Lindeplein 3 · **T** 013 522 0127
www.proeflokaaltgelagh.nl
Closed We; Mo&Tu from 16.00; Th&Fr from 15.00;
Sa&Su from 11.00

Large two-roomed beer café, 200 m from the station, built to the owner's specifications in 2009. The wood-panelled walls granted it instant authority. There is a terrace out front. It hosts live music some nights. Simple lunches are served until 16.00; snacks all day. The 135 beers include local Reuzenbieren – this is their unofficial home – as well as numerous Belgian lambics and oak-aged ales, plus UK and US imports. Alternatively there is an impressive range of 200+ malt whiskies.

OOSTERHOUT

10km NW from Breda off A27

Large town (pop. 54,000) without a station. Take bus 10, 127 or 127 from Breda.

Beurs

Klappeijstraat 4 · **T** 0162 453477
www.cafedebeurs.nl
Daily from 11.00

Expansive beer café with a terrace, on a street of bars near the main square. The interior contains a billiard table, dresser and fireplace, and a British telephone box. If you need the time in Chobe, Botswana, the row of clocks on the wall will tell you – or would if they were wound. Ceiling fans give the whole a whiff of colonial club. Snacks includes sausage rolls. The 240+ mainly Belgian list includes Dutch

options from Jopen and Texels, plus a few UK imports. The house Beurs Blond is Belgian. The selection of whiskies touches 100.

ROOSENDAAL

Roosendaal

Provincial border town (pop. 78,000), the last railway stop before Belgium. Fans of tacky ostentation should nip into the Passage shopping mall and check out the Milano Café.

Captain Cook's

Markt 17 · **T** 0165 599669
www.cooks.nl
Su from 12.00; others from 09.30

Popular grand café with a large terrace and beer garden at the rear and front terrace on the Markt. Typically 'mockened', with dark wood, polished brass, and loud music. Lunch and all-day tapas are served downstairs; dinner in the upstairs restaurant from 17.00. Many Trappists number on its list of 50, with 3 or 4 guest taps. Apart from a few portraits of Hawaii's first celebrity murder victim, we are unsure of any links it may have with the famous British explorer for whom it is named.

Caruso

Nispensestraat 21 · **T** 0165 583458
www.caruso.nl
Closed Mo&Tu; others from 15.00

Friendly corner café with a terrace on a busy street, 200m SE of the Markt. The interior is filled with pot plants, and posters advertising Caruso-themed concerts. A lighter rear area has a glass roof. Apple pie and snacks are served 15.00–22.00; dinners from 17.00. You can order high tea, high beer, or high wine. Among the 40+ beers the house blond **Caruso** (6%), is commissioned from Schelde. It stocks a fair selection of single malts.

Sjoes

Markt 16 · **T** 0165 564345
www.sjoes.nl
Closed Tu; Mo&Th from 19.00; Sa from 13.00;
others from 14.00

Z'Onder Zeil, Steenbergen

This large boozer with a terrace on the Markt is one of few on the main square to focus on beverages rather than food. Red walls and stucco ceilings add a touch of 'not brown'; the wooden seats are even cushioned. There is table football at the rear. Snacks only. The 55 beers are largely Belgian, with a few interesting choices. The 'high beer' tray is snacks with 3 or 6 tasting glasses.

SINT-OEDENRODE

15km N of Eindhoven off A50 exit 9

Neat, prosperous commuter town (pop. 18,000) on the 156/157 bus route from Eindhoven.

BEER TO GO: **Van Boxmeer** (Deken van Erp-straat 20 – **T** 0413 4751333 – debierkelder.nl – *Closed Su; Mo 10.00–18.00; Fr 09.00–20.00; Sa 09.00–17.00; others 09.00–18.00*) is a treasure-trove off-licence, stocking 300+ beers – strong on 75cl bottles and lambics – with more of them ageing in their cellars, and a huge choice of single malts.

STEENBERGEN

15km NW of Roosendaal off N259

Small town (pop. 12,000) in NW Brabant near the Zeeland border. Take bus 101 or 111 from Bergen op Zoom. Its harbour's connection to the Zeeland delta made it an important medieval port. Wing Commander Guy Gibson of Dambusters fame and his co-pilot Jim Warwick are buried in the Catholic cemetery and have streets named after them. They lost their lives near here in 1944, when their Mosquito crashed on the way home from a raid.

Z'Onder Zeil

Kade 3 · **T** 0167 538399
www.zonderzeil.nl
Closed Tu&We; Mo&Th 16.00–23.00; Fr&Sa 16.00–24.00; Su 14.00–23.00

This friendly nautical café is by a pleasure boat harbour, with a lovely waterside terrace. The interior has a boating theme, with ships' bells, sails, lanterns, wheels, and seashells in oil lamps. Karel the dead parrot perches on the bell – even though he is no more and has ceased to be. Eat in the bar or in the separate dining room. The 50 beers are well chosen, a high proportion are guests with Dutch represented by the likes of Emelisse and Duits & Lauret.

TILBURG

Tilburg

Brabant's second city (pop. 207,000) and stepping off point for the Efteling theme park. For quieter pastimes, the National Textile Museum (www.textielmuseum.nl) reflects its heritage as a centre of the wool trade. Tilburg was also one of the first Dutch cities to develop a healthy new beer culture, with plenty of decent pubs, old and new.

HOTEL TIP: **City★★★**, Heuvelring 128 (**T** 013 535 1355; www.cityhoteltilburg.nl), a small modern central hotel, two doors from our first entry.

Buitenbeentje

Heuvel 15a · **T** 013 536 0466
www.kafeebuitenbeentje.nl
Daily from 15.00

Delightfully scruffy café with a terrace on a street full of otherwise trendy bars. Inside, an elaborate but peeling brown stucco ceiling almost gets lost amid the tat. Furniture is (barely) functional. The bar is sunken: to sit at it you perch on oddly low 'high' stools; if you order standing up, the bar staff are staring at your midriff. There is live music some Sundays. Bar nibbles only. The 150 beers come from all over: local La Trappe and 3 Horne, plus plentiful Belgian lambics, and German and British imports. Only a handful are listed on the wall. There is also a decent whisky list.

Burgermeester Jansen, Tilburg

Burgermeester Jansen

Piushaven 22 · **T** 013 545 1008
www.burgemeesterjansen.nl
Closed Mo; Su from 14.00; others from 15.00

Mayor Jansen is a cavernous one-room bar with a terrace beside a gentrified industrial harbour. Large front windows also look out at the water. Nautical maps hang on the walls. Food is soups, toasties and snacks. The 100+ list is a joy. Four taps are guests. Of most interest among the bottles is a changing selection of UK and US imports – the menu is the row of empties on the right-hand wall. They also stock around 15 British perries and ciders, plus a great many international whiskies.

Hoegaarden

Piusplein 2 · **T** 013 720 0622
www.hoegaardentilburg.nl
Su from 12.00; shut Mo; others from 10.00

The livery and name leave you in little doubt who the building's owners are, but do not judge this book by its cover. With a terrace on a small square, this huge café has Art Deco and Nouveau touches, not least among the eclectic light fittings. A full food menu includes mussels in season and the beer is on the march too, having passed 200 at our last visit. While it is Belgocentric, only a few

are from its corporate sponsor. There are local Brabant beers, several German Weizen, plenty of guests, and the house Amai range: a Blond, Dubbel, and Tripel brewed (we believe) by nearby Reuzen.

Jack's

Tuinstraat 81 · **T** 013 542 6322
www.cafejacks.nl
Closed Mo; Sa from 20.00; Su from 19.30; others from 17.00

Basic local two blocks south of the station. A bar area at the front gives way to sporadic seating at the back, with three dartboards. Beer enamels adorn otherwise plain walls. Foodwise, one evening main is offered. The 50-ish list fluctuates with the moment, as a large proportion are guests, advertised on the wall. Ask about what else is on.

Kandinsky

Telegraafstraat 58 · **T** 013 544 4924
www.biercafe-kandinsky.nl
Daily from 15.00

Long-standing beer oasis and ABT member since 1992, 300m SE from the station. This one-room corner bar has plentiful beer memorabilia, and a few seats outside that

Kandinsky, Tilburg

pass as a terrace. Food is snacks and toasties. The 200+ beer list has remained a feature for years. Heavily slanted towards Belgium, Dutch brewers are slowly making inroads, among them local St Juttemis. And no, we do not know why it is named after a Russian expressionist painter – except that it gives them an excuse to make a funky doodle out of the café logo. NB: may shut for two weeks in July.

Lambiek

Wilhelminapark 66 · **T** 013 536 4351
www.kaffeelambiek.nl
Fr&Sa from 15.00; Su from 14.00; others from 16.00

Large and friendly local boozer opposite the Wilhelminapark, 700 m north of the railway (head right out of the station, then turn right under the tracks at the lights). The typical brown interior consists of a pool table, dartboard, and fruit machines surrounded by dog-eared furniture. A collection of guitars on one wall hints at musical leanings: Friday's on vinyl; Saturday's mostly live. Food is snacks and toasties. The 95+ beers are mainly Belgian.

Little Devil

Stationsstraat 27 · **T** 013 545 2140
www.littledevil.nl
Closed Mo; Sa from 15.00; Su from 13.00; others from 17.00

Rock café 100m south from the station, feeling like a regular brown café with a pool table when there is no live music. No food that we know of, beyond the food of love, in which case play on. The beer list gets refreshed every few months. It was 45 last we looked, with several Dutch, American and Germans breaking up the Belgian monopoly.

Spaarbank

Noordstraat 125 · **T** 013 543 8331
www.stadscafedespaarbank.nl
Su from 12.00; others from 10.30

Trendy high-ceilinged corner café two blocks south of the station, with a front terrace spilling over the road into a tiny parklet, and

a beer garden at the rear. The Savings Bank (its former life) has two semi-separate bars. The back one has a wood-burning stove, while the front has seating rescued from trains. Simple lunches *(until 17.00)*, dinners *(17.00-21.30)* and snacks all day. Emelisse leads the limited Dutch selection among the 55+ otherwise-Belgian beers.

Zomerlust

Oisterwijksebaan 15 · **T** 013 542 5292
www.cafezomerlust.nl
Closed Tu; Sa from 11.00; Su from 10.00; others from 12.00 (15.00 Nov-Mar)

One of the Netherlands' first and best loved specialist beer cafés, the Summer Madness is a must-visit. Around 3km SE from the station, either take a taxi or a good map. Family-run since 1936, it lies just beyond the canal that marks Tilburg's eastern border. Its terrace overlooks fields. The lovely interior is lit by candles and Art Deco lamps, and warmed by a coal-burning stove. Breakfast is served on Sundays; lunches in summer only. No dinner, except for a book-ahead set menu on Fridays. Snacks at other times. The 70 beers always feature local 3 Horne on tap.

*OTHER **TILBURG** BEER VENUES:*

Sprawling **Anvers** (Oude Markt 8 – **T** 013 583 3533 – **www.oudemarkt.nl** – *Su-Mo from 11.30; others from 10.00*) is a warren with 35 beers. **Slagroom** (Piusplein 6a – **T** 013 582 0070 – **www.slagroomtilburg.nl** – *daily from 10.00*) has just short of 40. Popular 'Oirish' pub **Clancy's** (Korte Heuvel 44-45 – **T** 013 545 1837 - **www.clancystilburg.com** – *Sa from 12.00; Su from 14.00; Mo from 18.00; others from 16.00*) has 250 whiskies and 40 beers – the latter just too safe to warrant a full entry.

BEER TO GO: **T-Drinks** (Winkelcentrum Heuvelpoort – **T** 013 580 1126 – **www.tdrinks.nl** – *Closed Su; Mo 13.00-18.00; Th 10.00-21.00; Sa 10.00-17.00; others 10.00-18.00*) stocks 250+ beers, with a good regional Dutch selection, and 600+ whiskies.

VESSEM
15km W from Eindhoven

Quiet village (pop. 2,100). Take bus 16 or 150 from Eindhoven to Veldhoven, then the 492 or 494 to the village.

Gouden Leeuw

Jan Smuldersstraat 24 · **T** 0497 591 252
www.brouwerijvessem.nl
Closed Mo; Su from 10.00; others from 11.00

A large village complex with terraces front and back – the latter overlooks a hop field. In between is a modern café-restaurant, with a theatre at the back, and a brick cellar that can be hired for parties. Food runs through lunches, high tea, dinners, and snacks. The 45 beers include the house Beerze brews, which may eventually be brewed here. There is also a small B&B next door.

Gouden Leeu Vessem

WAALWIJK
16km N from Tilburg off N261

Another large-ish town (pop. 46,000) that lacks a rail connection. Take bus 136, 300 or 301 from Tilburg. The town is laid out in a grid that with many prominent buildings built in the 1920s and 30s, lending it a curiously modernist feel.

Jay's

Markt 8b · **T** 0416 858 910
www.jayswaalwijk.nl
Mo&Tu from 19.00; others from 13.00
(winter: We-Fr from 15.00; Sa&Su from 14.00

Lively modern beer and music café on the main square, with a terrace far larger than the part-brick, part-wood, partly wallpapered bar. Food includes 14 different burgers in various sizes. If you finish the 1kg one and live, it is free, and your photo is displayed on a wall of shame. The beer list is heavyweight too, with around 220. The menu is ordered by style, and has plenty of Dutch, UK and US stouts and porters, and numerous Belgian lambics and German Weizen.

ZUNDERT
16km SW from Breda on N263

Brabant village (pop. 7,700), home to the eponymous brewery. Bus 115 from Breda to Berkenring gets you closest to the café below, still a 1.5km walk away – bring a map.

Den Hoek

Rucphenseweg 14 · **T** 076 597 2300
www.den-hoek.com
Closed Mo&Tu; We&Th from 16.00; Fr&Sa from 15.00; Su from 14.00

An unassuming semi-rural local just beyond the village's western outskirts, the Corner has a growing culinary reputation. Lunches and dinners (until 21.00) are often seasonal and have suggested beer pairings. Unsurprisingly, the 75+ beers include local Zundert. There are also plentiful lambics and US imports, plus De Molen and Emelisse from closer to home.

Jay's, Waalwijk

North Holland

North Holland (pop. 2.7 million) is divided into two unequal halves by the IJ lake and the series of canals and locks linking the IJsselmeer to the North Sea, which allow ludicrously oversized cruise ships to reach Amsterdam.

The smaller southern half runs from Haarlem to Hilversum and is densely populated. The area around the watery divide is largely heavily industrial dockland. Things get quieter and more agricultural the further north you travel up the peninsula that separates the IJsselmeer from the North Sea.

At the tip of the mainland you can continue by ferry to Texel, the largest and westernmost of the Wadden Islands. Alternatively, veer northeast across the Afsluitdijk – one of the greatest 20th century engineering marvels. The 32km dyke opened in 1933, turning the inlet that was the Zuiderzee into the 1,700 sq km IJsselmeer, Western Europe's largest freshwater lake – itself later split in two by the dyke from Flevoland to Enkhuizen that created the Markermeer.

Considering Amsterdam's role in the international beer trade over centuries, it is no surprise to find the province has a high concentration of breweries, though contrary to popular belief, none of those is Heineken.

LARGEST CENTRES: **Amsterdam** (800,000), **Haarlem** (153,000), **Alkmaar** (95,000), **Hilversum** (86,000), **Amstelveen** (84,000), **Purmerend** (79,000), **Zaandam** (73,000), **Hoofddorp** (73,000), **Hoorn** (71,000), **Den Helder** (56,000), **Heerhugowaard** (51,000)

MORE INFORMATION: www.noord-holland.com; www.iamsterdam.com

BREWERIES: **Bekeerde Suster**, *Amsterdam*; **Berging**, *Purmerend*; **Bierfabriek**, *Amsterdam*; **Boei**, *Den Hoorn (Texel)*; **Butcher's Tears**, *Amsterdam*; **Dampegheest**, *Limmen*; **IJ**, *Amsterdam*; **Jopen**, *Haarlem*; **Naeckte**, *Amstelveen*; **Natte Cel**, *Bovenkarspel*; **Noord-Hollandse**, *Uitgeest*; **Prael**, *Amsterdam*; **Princen**, *Den Helder*; **Schans**, *Uithoorn*; **Texelse**, *Oudeschild (Texel)*; **Troost**, *Amsterdam*; **Vijfhuizen**, *Vijfhuizen*; **Volendam**, *Volendam*; **Vriendenbier**, *Heiloo*; & **Zeven Deugden**, *Amsterdam*

OTHER BEER MAKERS: **Bierderie**, *Koog aan de Zaan*; **Breugem**, *Zaandam*; **Egmond**, *Egmond-Binnen*; **HollandsGoud**, *Alkmaar*; **Kinhem**, *IJmuiden*; **Oedipus**, *Amsterdam*; **Pampus**, *Amsterdam*; **SNAB**, *Purmerend*; **Snaterende Arend**, *Amsterdam*; **Zeeburg**, *Amsterdam*; **Uiltje**, *Haarlem*

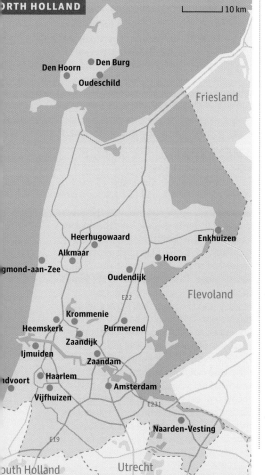

NORTH HOLLAND

10 km

Den Hoorn Den Burg
Oudeschild
Friesland

Heerhugowaard Enkhuizen
Alkmaar Hoorn
gmond-aan-Zee
Oudendijk
Flevoland
Krommenie
Heemskerk Purmerend
Zaandijk
Ijmuiden Zaandam
ndvoort Haarlem
Vijfhuizen Amsterdam

Naarden-Vesting

outh Holland Utrecht

ALKMAAR
≈ Alkmaar

Pronounced with a gap between the Al and the kmaar, this attractive rag-bag of cobbled streets and occasional canals attracts more people to its Friday cheese market (Apr-Sep: 10.00-12.30) every year than live here (95,000). Expect vendors in traditional costume to mug about rolling industrial cheeses theatrically for the camera-wielding hordes. More thematic is the National Beer Museum (see beer places to visit).

Boom 🍺
Houttil 1 · **T** 072 511 5547
www.proeflokaaldeboom.nl
Su&Mo from 14.00; others from 13.00

Semi-cellared beer café with a canalside terrace, just off the main square and below the beer museum. At night, overhead lamps contribute barely more light than a candle on tables. Chalkboards, beer bottles and enamels cover most walls. Live jazz (last Thursday of the month). Snacks only. The list of 50 changes regularly – 25% Dutch; the rest Belgian.

Kleine Deugniet
Koorstraat 12 · **T** 06 5278 5991
Closed Mo&Tu; Sa from 14.00; Su 14.00-22.00; others from 16.00

Small central local with a tiny terrace, a few paces from the Grote Kerk. The Little Rascal is a modern bar with beer enamel-strewn whitewashed walls, cow hide bar stools, and limited seating elsewhere. Food is snacks and toasties. The 50 beers are exclusively Belgian with few surprises, though the guest taps can be interesting.

*OTHER **ALKMAAR** BEER VENUES:*
Flemish restaurant **Vrolijke Pater** (Paternosterstraat 6-8 – **T** 072 512 9377 – www. devrolijkepater.nl – *Closed Mo; others 14.00-22.00*) cooks with beer, suggests beer pairings, stocks 30 for drinking, and has plastic grapes on the walls from its previous incarnation as a Greek eatery.

BEER TO GO: In a shopping mall north of the centre, **Hekeltje de Mare** (Europaboulevard 59-61 – **T** 072 562 2611 – www.hekeltje-slijterijen.nl – *Closed Su; Mo 13.00-18.00; Fr 09.00-21.00; Sa 09.00-17.00, others 09.00-18.00*) stocks 300+ beers. Dutch offerings including dozens from De Molen. A town centre branch (Laat 129) is less well-endowed.

AMSTERDAM
≈ Amsterdam Centraal (CS), Amstel, Lelylaan, Sloterdijk

The Dutch national capital and its largest city (pop. 800,000). For many tourists the city is simply a hub for loveless sex and the smoking of semi-illicit herbs. Others know it as a cutesy old fashioned place criss-crossed by canals and cobbled streets that are a bugger to walk along. This is also home to the world's most intolerant cyclists – their furious muttering and impatient bell tingling greeting the presence of half a toe on their bike path, in contrast to refusing pedestrian rights to cross the road on a green signal.

We apologise for the area outside the otherwise magnificent Centraal Station, which has become a grim mêlée of lost tourists, wheelie luggage, construction work (for the north-south Metro line), drug addicts, pickpockets, sex museums and pizzerias. Plough on through, suitably zipped, to reach

Boom, Alkmaar

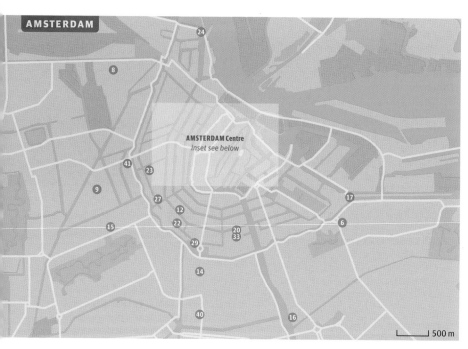

Beer Temple, Amste

the real Amsterdam, and you'll understand why you came.

With a hatful of great cafés, it should be first on the team sheet when compiling a Dutch – or indeed European - beer tour, part of its charm being the longevity of some of its best bars in this most cosmopolitan of cities. *HOTEL TIPS:* stay in Haarlem ... or Zaandam ... or anywhere but here. The good places fill up quickly and are far from cheap; and the most affordable places are usually rubbish.

Arendsnest

Herengracht 90 · **T** 020 421 2057
www.arendsnest.nl
Daily from 14.00

A Mecca for beer lovers, the Eagle's Nest is an elegant bar beside the stately Herengracht canal. The Eagle is Dutch beer icon Peter van der Arend, who also runs the Beer Temple (below). The original intention was to have an exclusively Dutch beer list with at least one from every brewery. That was never easy even when it opened in 2000 and there were only 35. Nowadays it would be impossible. Most of the 30 taps change regularly. The 100+ bottles cover stalwarts like De Molen, Emelisse and Mommeriete, as well as showcasing obscure micros that are hard to find elsewhere. Light meals and snacks are available. They also stock 75 liqueurs and jenevers, and 25 single malts.

Arendsnest, Amsterdam

Beer Temple

Nieuwezijds Voorburgwal 250 · **T** 020 627 1427
www.beertemple.nl
Daily from 14.00

Contrasting with the Arendsnest (above), Peter van der Arend's 'other' bar focuses on imports. There is a small terrace, while the inside goes for Americana. Gather round the bar to swap notes, or contemplate from the rear mezzanine. Décor includes a display of old pump handles from previous guest beers. Snacks include cheeses, dry sausage and beef jerky. The 100+ beers include 30 changing taps, though one constant is house blond **Tempelbier** (6%), brewed at Jopen. The rest is primarily American, although Scandinavian, Italian and other imports get a look in. There is an 'open bottle' evening on the first Monday of each month, where you can sample new arrivals for €10 — reserve ahead.

Bekeerde Suster

Kloveniersburgwal 6 · **T** 020 423 0112
www.debekeerdesuster.nl
Daily from 12.00

The Reformed Sister is a brewpub with a small terrace just off Nieuwmarkt. The expansive low-ceilinged interior has a mezzanine above and copper kettles at the rear. Lunches and full dinners are served (until 22.30) - some of the latter cooked with beer. Beyond the house brews, the remaining 50 beers are mainly Belgian.

Belgique

Gravenstraat 2 · **T** 020 625 1974
www.cafe-belgique.nl
Daily from 14.00

Almost lost down a side alley off the main shopping drag, the Belgique is possibly the country's smallest specialist café. Its terrace consists of two benches. It can be standing room only inside. Food is toasties and snacks. The 50+ beers are, as the name implies, all Belgian. Several of the 8 taps are guests.

Bierfabriek

Rokin 75 · **T** 020 528 9910
www.bierfabriek.com
Sa&Su from 14.00; others from 16.00

The Beer Factory brewpub and its small terrace are on the main drag just south of Dam square. The brewing kit takes centre stage in the large modern interior. Some tables have metered taps for self-pouring. Others have free peanuts. Food includes char-grilled chicken with homemade bread. Two of its three beers are brewed on site, the other being unfiltered Puur pilsener from the owner, Alfa.

Biertuin

Linnaeusstraat 29 · **T** 020 665 0956
www.debiertuin.nl
Daily from 11.00

Near the Tropenmuseum, the Beer Garden's beer garden is in truth a terrace. Inside, bare brick walls down one side add a certain rusticity. On the opposite wall, bookended by palm-shaped lamps, a sign says: 'God save the beer'. There is a full food menu, with snacks all day. The 40 beers feature several from 't IJ, around the corner, and the bulk of the 11 taps are Dutch.

Brabantse Aap

Spui 30 · **T** 020 622 5110
www.debrabantseaap.nl
Daily from 11.00

Until rebranding in 2012 this was the Beiaard, and it remains that group's flagship. It enjoys a prime location on a square where tourists and local shoppers converge. Be skimmed by trams passing the terrace, or seek refuge in the conservatory. The ramshackle interior has retained its pre-makeover charm. It has a full lunch and dinner menu. The 50-ish beers include 16 taps, among which are 3 or 4 from the group's Bekeerde Suster brewery.

Brabantse Aap, Amsterdam

Brel

Van Hallstraat 37 · **T** 020 341 5341
www.cafe-brel.nl
Daily from 15.00

This easy-to-find suburban boozer near the Westerpark is opposite the western terminus of tram 10. The minimalist terrace is a line of chairs on the busy pavement. Inside is rough and ready, with a few stools, some fruit machines, and that is it. Food is snacks, sometimes running to soup. The 40 Belgian beers scrape a full listing, with a few noteworthy entrants such as Duchesse de Bourgogne.

Brouw

Ten Katestraat 16 · **T** 020 223 8569
barbrouw.nl
Daily from 12.00

Modern craft beer bar with a small streetside terrace, opened in late 2013 in the Oud-West district. The simple, minimalist interior is dominated by blueboards on the walls advertising the food and drink options. Both show a distinct North American influence. The former will appeal to carnivores: smoked barbecue meats, pulled pork and ribs being the house specials. 60+ beers are dominated by US imports such as Anchor and Flying Dog, but De Molen is also present, as are the UK's Thornbridge and Norway's Nøgne Ø. A second branch will appear at Beukenplein 17 in East Amsterdam by publication time.

Butcher's Tears

Karperweg 45 · **T** 06 5390 9777
www.butchers-tears.com
Closed Mo&Tu; others 16.00–21.00

New brewery tap in southern Amsterdam. Take tram 2 to Amstelveenseweg then head south, then take the first right after the roundabout. It is signposted along a run-down street, in a former industrial area. The café is bright, with whitewashed brick, tiled walls, and art. Bench seating inside and on the terrace is functional. Food is cheese with Swedish crispbread, reflecting the brewer's nationality, plus help-yourself homemade bread. All the house beers are available in bottle and on tap.

Dwars

Egelantiersstraat 24 · **T** 020 625 5306
www.restaurantdwars.nl
Closed Tu&We; others 17.30–23.00

Intimate restaurant in the heart of fashionable Jordaan. The modern Dutch cuisine has high aspirations: the hope is to make this the first beer-themed eatery with a Michelin *Bib Gourmand*. Expect prices to rise if they succeed. All dishes come with recommended beer pairings. The expanding beer list should pass 60 by the time you read this. Exclusively Dutch, it features a strong showing by local North Holland and Limburg brewers – the latter betraying the chef's origins.

Elfde Gebod

Zeedijk 5 · **T** 06 3062 6373
www.hetelfdegebod.com
Closed Su-Tu; others 18.00–01.00

The 11th Commandment ('thou shalt enjoy life') is a long-running beer café at the north end of Zeedijk. Religious artefacts are dotted around the wood-panelled interior, and church pews line one side. Watch out for the step, halfway towards the rear. Food is nibbles only. The 70 beers are exclusively Belgian, but feature standouts such as St Bernardus and De Ranke.

Elfde Gebod, Amsterdam

Genootschap der Geneugten

Kerkstraat 54 · **T** 020 625 0934
www.cafegdg.info
Closed Mo; Fr&Sa 16.00–02.00; Su 17.00–24.00;
others 18.00–01.00

Just north of Leidseplein, the Pleasure Club
is a lively old brown café with Art Deco
pretensions that attracts a mixed bag crowd
of old and young. No food. The 45+ beers
are largely Belgian, but do feature some star
turns from Dupont and De Ranke. There are
also 40 jenevers and local spirits.

Gollem

Raamsteeg 4 · **T** none
www.cafegollem.nl
Fr-Su from 12.00; others from 16.00

Originally opened in 1974, the capital's first
specialist beer café had an enforced rest due
to licensing problems from 2010 to 2012, but
is now back in business. The cramped
wooden interior is standing room only at the
front, with some tables on a raised area at
the back. Most wall space is given over to
old beer bottles and numerous blackboard
menus. No food. The 200+ list, once heavily
biased towards Belgium, is now admitting
Dutch flag bearers such as De Molen – an
important sign of the times.

Gollem,
Amsterdam

Genootschap der Geneugten, Amsterdam

Gollem (De Pijp)

Daniel Stalpertstraat 74 · **T** none
www.cafegollem.nl
Daily from 16.00

Gollem's first sibling, in the trendy De Pijp
district, suffered the same licensing failure
as the mothership and was closed for two
years. Having sprung back into life it is again
a must-visit on the city beer circuit. Laid out
like a swollen version of 'Gollem 1', a bar
area at the front leads to a raised sitting area
behind. The large painting behind the bar is
of Cambrinus carousing. Snacks only,
although the hefty Trappist cheese board
stretches the definition somewhat. The
menu for the 140 beers is scattered round
the room on chalkboards, with Emelisse
starring on the Dutch side.

Gollem's Proeflokaal

Overtoom 160-162 · **T** 020 612 9444
www.cafegollem.nl
Fr-Su from 12.00; others from 13.00

Completing the trio of Amsterdam Gollems
(there is a fourth in Antwerp), the Tasting
Room is on a busy shopping street close to
the Vondelpark. There is a pavement terrace
outside and spacious brown café within.
Food includes daily specials, some cooked
with beer. Chalkboard menus list the 130+
beers. A previously strong Belgian slant has
softened, with star status now given to top
Dutch brewers such as De Molen and Oersoep.

Hesp, Amsterdam

Hesp 16

Weesperzijde 130–131 · **T** 020 665 1202
www.cafehesp.nl
Su from 11.00; others from 10.00

The Ham is a large beer café with a riverside terrace, close to Amstel station. It has been a café since 1897, as a glass panel inside celebrates. The spacious interior is largely wooden and candlelit. Food covers lunchtime wraps to dinner surf 'n' turf, with snacks served until midnight. The 70+ beers include 20 taps, many hosting guest options. The house **Hesp Blond** (6.2%) is brewed by De Eem. There are also several US and Italian imports, the latter from Birra del Borgo.

IJ 17

Funenkade 7 · **T** 020 528 6237
www.brouwerijhetij.nl
Daily 14.00–20.00

Popular brewery tap of Amsterdam's oldest operational brewery, just east of Artis Zoo. Pronounce it 'eye' and you are almost there. The windmill overlooking the terrace makes it easy to locate, but belongs to the neighbours. The café is a former bathhouse with tiled walls. Beer snacks only. All the house brews are sold on tap.

Lieve 18

Herengracht 88 · **T** 020 624 9635
www.restaurantlieve.nl
Fr&Sa 17.30–22.30; others 17.30–22.00

Belgian restaurant next door to Arendsnest (above). The interior is sumptuously and surreally decorated: Adam, Eve and the Virgin Mary rub shoulders with Chinese-stylised wallpaper depicting wild boar in the Ardennes. Decide between three menus – the 5-course 'Gastronomic'; 3-course 'Living Room' and 'Belgian Baroque' tapas. The 50+ beers are exclusively Belgian. Opt for the 'beer arrangement' and they will pair brews with each course.

Lost Property

De Leeuw van Vlaanderenstraat 33 · **T** none
www.lostproperty.cx
Th only from 21.00

One of Amsterdam's quirkiest bars. Head for Burgermeester de Vlugtlaan Metro station and take a street plan. Look for a ground floor apartment with a glass-walled front room that is an art exhibition and then is someone's kitchen behind it – this is the bar. There is a garden out back. No food. The number of beers can hit 35, depending on when they last went shopping, but the list has quality – one constant is Butcher's Tears, with whom the owners are linked.

IJ brewery tap, Amsterdam

Old Nickel (19)

Nieuwe Brugsteeg 11 · **T** 020 624 1912
www.oldnickel.com
Daily from 09.00

With sticky carpet and fruit machines
flashing away at the back, the crusty Old
Nickel is a place of many characters. Some
afternoons it may be semi-deserted, with
only the odd barfly at the counter for
company. Some evenings it transforms into
a convivial wood-panelled tavern, perhaps
with a live band playing in one corner. You
can stay in the hotel upstairs fairly cheaply,
but expect it to be basic. No food but 60
beers – half are Belgian with most of the rest
Dutch or German.

*er de Ooievaar,
Amsterdam*

Onder de Ooievaar (20)

Utrechtsestraat 119 · **T** 020 624 6836
www.onderdeooievaar.nl
Su from 10.30; others from 10.00

Under the Stork is a corner brown café with
large windows, and a small terrace beside the
Prinsengracht canal where it passes below
Utrechtsestraat. A collection of antique
spoons hangs in one corner. Food is confined
to lunch but served until 17.30. The beer
menu has risen slowly and now at 45+,
with some interesting finds from the
likes of Belgian Dupont.

Prael (21)

Oudezijds Armsteeg 26 · **T** 020 408 4469
www.deprael.nl
Closed Mo; Su 12.00–23.00; others 12.00–24.00

This split-level brewery tap's concrete
and industrial edge is softened by eclectic
furnishings. A lower bar area has brick
flooring, while the upper level seems
half café, half living room, with sofas
and armchairs. There may be live jazz on
Sundays. Dutch-influenced main dishes
are served until 22.00; snacks to 23.00.
Around 10 house beers are served on tap.

Spuyt (22)

Korte Leidsedwarsstraat 86 · **T** 020 624 8901
www.cafedespuyt.nl
Sa&Su from 14.00; others from 16.00

A few blocks east of cheesy Leidseplein,
this unassuming one-room café with a tiny
terrace is happy to stay off the lager-swillers'
radar and remain the preserve of discerning
beer lovers. Food is snacks and toasties.
The 100+ list is posted on the wall and gives
space to Dutch brewers such as 7 Deugden,
De Molen and Emelisse. Unusually it also
stocks 75cl bottles of **Trois Monts** (8.5%)
from the French brewery St Sylvestre.
There are tasting evenings every third
Monday of the month.

Spuyt, Amsterdam

Tripel

Lijnbaansgracht 161 · **T** 020 779 9442
No website
Daily from 16.00

Opened in late 2013, this canalside joint in the Jordaan district is a spin-off of the long-established Zotte. Marginally better-lit than its sister, the long, narrow, low-ceilinged bar goes for a similar candlelit ambiance. A counter runs down one side with beer menus and memorabilia lining other walls. A Belgian-oriented food menu is served. Like the mothership, the 200+ beers are all Belgian, but with more space available here, extra lip service is paid to progressive new wavers such as Dochter van de Korenaar.

Troost ㊵

Cornelis Troostplein 23 · **T** 020 737 1028
www.brouwerijtroost.nl
Daily from 11.00

Stylish modern brewpub in De Pijp, with a terrace out front, and a rear conservatory expected as we went to press. The brewery is visible through glass on one side. An extensive food menu *(until 22.30)* includes great homemade burgers. All beers are from the house. **Note:** electronic payments only (Dutch debit cards, plus MasterCard & Visa) – no cash accepted.

Westerdok

Westerdoksdijk 715/A · **T** 020 428 9670
www.cafewesterdok.nl
Closed Mo; others from 16.00

A 10-minute yomp (or take bus 48) west from Centraal station, this corner pub is another unsung hero. The back walls and ceiling slew half-timbered mock-Tudor, with illuminated windows showing medieval scenes. An upright piano gets a workout on occasion. Toasties and other snacks are available. The 80 beers are determined by the tastes of the expat British landlord. The chalkboards are usually out-of-date, so ask. In autumn the house bock has often been cellared for a year. Five of the 9 taps are dispensed through a ship's throttle.

Westerdok, Amsterdam

Wildeman ㉕

Kolksteeg 3 · **T** 020 638 2348
www.indewildeman.nl
Closed Su; others from 12.00

Founded in 1986 and a long-time ABT member, In de Wildeman is a place of pilgrimage for beer lovers the world over. A former jenever distillery, the two-room interior has tiled floors and olive-green walls, plus a rack of old spirits casks. The blessed absence of music adds to the communal hum of conversation and appreciative swigging. Bar snacks include stuffed vine leaves and kabbanossi – a kind of salami. On Saturday afternoons a travelling fishmonger drops in

to sell herring and smoked eel. The 270+ list is roughly half Belgian and nowadays one-third Dutch, with the remainder imported from all over. The ever-evolving range of 18 beers on tap is as cleverly chosen as you will find, often including several one-off, barrel-aged or tweaked versions of familiar names. A must.

Zilt

Zeedijk 49 · **T** 020 421 5416
www.cafezilt.nl
Daily from 17.00

This simple one-room café eschews tradition to go 21st century with high tables and stools, and cushioned seating in the window. The colour scheme drops brown in favour of dark blue-green and turquoise, with patterned wallpaper. Battered vinyl floors are more hole than vinyl, while behind the bar is imitation Kama Sutra erotic sculpture – we believe a copy of a Khajaraho original. No food, we think. Around 45 beers include Emelisse and 't IJ.

Zotte

Raamstraat 29 · **T** 020 626 8694
www.dezotte.nl
Daily from 16.00

The scarcely lit Fool is a block west of Leidseplein, with a small streetside terrace. Candles on the interior tables add atmosphere and the chance to get a partial glimpse at what you are drinking. Beer enamels abound. Music is mainly rock, there to reassure those who are old enough to remember the days when musicians were involved. The range of food (*until 21.30*) has expanded since its grungier days, and there is now a wide selection of Belgian mains. The 130 beers are also exclusively from south of the border.

OTHER **AMSTERDAM** BEER VENUES:
For the best and widest ranging guide to
Amsterdam's other beer bars we recommend
Around Amsterdam in 80 Beers by one Tim
Skelton, Cogan & Mater, £9.99 – available
from www.booksaboutbeer.com

The sumptuous Art Nouveau **1e Klas** ㉘
(Stationsplein 15 - Platform 2b, Amsterdam CS
- **T** 020 625 0131 - www.restaurant1eklas.nl -
daily 08.30-23.00) is to 19th-century station
cafés what the Taj Mahal is to mausoleums.

Styled as a Berlin living room café,
Brecht ㉙ (Weteringschans 157 - **T** 020 627
2211 - www.cafebrecht.nl - *daily from 12.00*) has
mismatched furniture and 25 German beers.

Family-run since 1798, tiny **Doktertje** ㉚
(Rozenboomsteeg 4 - **T** 020 626 4427 -
www.cafe-de-dokter.nl - *Closed Su&Mo; others
16.00-01.00*) is the city's smallest bar, with a
candlelit interior held together by cobwebs
and dust.

Timeless **Hegeraad** ㉛ (Noordermarkt
84 - **T** 020 624 5565 - www.cafehegeraad.nl
- *Su from 11.00; others from 08.00*) has carpeted
tables and a pissoir almost in the bar.

Ancient **Oosterling** ㉝ (Utrechtsestraat
140 - **T** 020 623 4140 - *Su 13.00-20.00; others
12.00-01.00*) has plentiful wooden casks, a
low-slung bar, and a sloping floor.

A.k.a. De Engelse Reet - or 'the English
Arse' - **Pilsener Club** ㉞ (Begijnensteeg 4 -
T 020 623 1777 - *Su; others from 12.00*) is a
characterful drinking hole with sandy floors,
smoke-darkened everything else, and no bar
- just a serving door at the back.

BEER TO GO: Among the country's finest
specialist beer shops, **Bierkoning** ㊴
(Paleisstraat 125 – **T** 020 625 2336 – www.
bierkoning.nl – *Sa 11.00-18.00; Su 13.00-18.00;
Mo 13.00-19.00; others 11.00-19.00*) somehow
finds space for 1,400 beers. One-third are
Dutch; the remainder global. If you become
Stendhalised, the enthusiastic staff can
make suggestions.

Open extraordinary hours, **Sterk** ㊶
(De Clerqstraat 1 – **T** 020 618 1727 –
www.sterkamsterdam.nl – *Fr&Sa 09.00-03.00;
others 09.00-01.00*) is a deli and late night
shop with an impressive range of 500 Dutch
and international beers.

THE JENEVER CONVENTION

An older tradition than the beer bars of Amsterdam is
that of spirits houses, a few of which are among the most
atmospheric bars in the city. A word to the unwary though,
if tempted to add these onto a pub crawl, do so at the
beginning, not the end. Wisdom is easier to bring to bear
on larger drinks.

The elegant and cultured **Olofspoort** ㉟ (Nieuwe
Brugsteeg 13 – **T** 020 624 3918 – www.olofspoort.com –
Closed Tu; Su 15.00-22.00; Fr&Sa from 15.00; others from 16.00)
has leaded windows, green-painted wooden walls,
and 200 drinks, albeit only 3 beers. A few paces down,
bijou **Ooievaar** ㊱ (Sint Olofspoort 1 – **T** 020 420 8004 –
www.proeflokaaldeooievaar.nl – *daily from 12.00*) has been
a jenever tasting room since 1782.

The unmissable and amusingly named jenever tasting
room **Wijnand Fockink** ㊲ (Pijlsteeg 31 – **T** 020 639 2695 –
www.wynand-fockink.nl – *daily 15.00-21.00*) has sanded
wooden floors, no seats, and a hatful of spirits. Equally
central is the **Hoppe** ㉜ (Spui 18-20 – **T** 020 420 4420 –
www.cafehoppe.com – *Fr-Su from 12.00; others from 14.00*)
head to the right to find its sandy-floored 1670 tasting room.

Bols-owned jenever tasting room **Drie Fleschjes** ㊳
(Gravenstraat 18 – **T** 020 624 8443 – www.dedriefleschjes.nl –
Su 15.00-19.00; others 14.00-20.30) has been serving since 1650,
though nowadays its locked private casks are mostly for show

*Private casks at
the Drie Fleschjes*

DEN BURG (on Texel)

On Texel Island, 20 mins by ferry from
Den Helder

Outside the tourist season, sheep far
outnumber people on Texel (pronounced
'Tessel'). Of the 13,600 permanent
residents, half are here in the island's main
village. It manages to retain a sleepy charm
even in summer. Buses run from the ferry
terminal and on to other points on the
island, but stop early.
HOTEL TIP: **Lindeboom**★★★, Groeneplaats 14
(**T** 0222 312041; www.lindeboomtexel.nl) is a
friendly place on the main square.

De Slock & De Hollebol

Parkstraat 36 & Hollebol 32-34 · **T** 0222 313161
www.deslock.nl & www.dehollebol.nl
*Slock: Sa from 15.00; Su from 12.00; others from 16.00.
Hollebol: Closed Su&Tu; Mo 10.00-15.00;
Sa 11.00-17.00; others 11.00-18.00*

Formerly the Grooten Slock and going for
over 50 years, these two separate-looking
institutions are umbilically linked via their
ownership, toilets and website. Friendly local
boozer the Slock (or Slurp) in Parkstraat is
wood-dominated and dark, with a small
conservatory, a billiards table and a few
nibbles. In contrast the neighbouring Hollebol
grand café, on Hollebol, is an airy addition
built in 2010 but in classic Jugendstil.
The same 40+ beers are available in both,
with a good selection of Texels.

Twaalf Balcken

Weverstraat 20 · **T** 0222 312681
www.12balcken.nl
Su from 17.00; others from 10.00

Just north of the main square, this ABT café
has evolved into Texel's best beer pub. The
front half is classic brown, with plentiful
wood. The back is a lighter atrium, with a
gas-effect stove, used as an exhibition space
for local artists. Lunches are served until
16.30. Several dishes on the dinner menu
feature local Texel lamb. The 60 beers
feature Texels, as well as Klein Duimpje
(who also made house beers Golfbreker,

Zwarte Schap, and Schering & Inslag).
Imports include several Belgian lambics.

DEN HOORN (on Texel)

Small village (pop. 450) in the SW of the
island, home to its 'other' brewery.

Bonte Belevenis

Rommelpot 11 · **T** 0222 314180
www.landgoeddebontebelevenis.nl
*Closed mid-Jan to mid-Feb; shut Mo&Fr (all year) &
Su (Sep-Jun); Su (Jul&Aug) 12.00-17.00;
others 10.00-17.00*

The proeflokkaal of the Boei brewery is the
café of the Bonte Belevenis farm museum,
1.5 km north of Den Hoorn. You need a ticket
to reach it but get a brewery and distillery
tour thrown in. The self-service café is rustic
rather than bar-like. British readers may
understand if we say 'National Trust'. Simple
meals feature home-baked bread. Three or
4 house beers are available in bottles, and
also sold in the museum shop.

EGMOND-AAN-ZEE

11km WSW of Alkmaar off N512

Tiny seaside resort (pop. 2,500) with a
lighthouse at the end of its main street.
Houses once stretched several hundred
metres further west but were swallowed by
the sea during a storm in 1741.
BEER TO GO: **Meijer** (Voorstraat 134 – **T** 072
506 1858 – www.slijterijmeijer.nl – *Mo 12.00-
18.00; Sa 09.00-17.00; Su 12.00-17.00; others
09.00-18.00*) has 200+ beers with good local
choices.

ENKHUIZEN

18km ENE of Hoorn, off N302
Enkhuizen

Picturesque West Fries harbour town (pop.
18,000) with oodles of history. It was an
important port until the Afsluitdijk cut it off
from the sea.

BEER TO GO: One of the better **Mitra** outlets (Westerstraat 91 – **T** 0228 321162 – www. mitra.nl – *Closed Su; Mo 13.00–18.00; Tu-Th 09.00–18.00; Fr 09.00–21.00; Sa 09.00–17.00*) stocks 300+ beers.

Mitra beer shop, Amsterdam

HAARLEM

Haarlem

The provincial capital (pop. 153,000) is one of North Holland's prettiest cities, dominated by St Bavo church, or Grote Kerk, which looms over the Grote Markt. Go inside to marvel at its impressive organ, proof that size is important.

Haarlem's most famous son was the painter Frans Hals. The museum named after him (www.franshalsmuseum.nl) contains a collection of old masters, housed in an old cloister. Founded in 1784, the Teyler's Museum (www.teylersmuseum.eu) is the country's oldest, housing what seem like the eclectic whims of an eccentric collector.

At its peak there were 60 breweries in Haarlem. Nowadays there is one, though it is a goodie.

HOTEL TIP: **Malts ★★★**, Zijlstraat 56–58 (**T** 023 551 2385; www.maltshotel.nl) is a small central B&B hotel.

Briljant

Lange Annastraat 33 · **T** 023 542 2925
www.cafebriljant.nl
Closed Mo&Tu; others from 16.00

Friendly one-room beer café down a residential street south of the centre. There is occasional live music, with an Open Mike night on the first Thursday of the month. Sunday is vinyl. Snacks only, though the beer tasting (17.00, second Sunday of the month) ends with a communal takeaway. The 55 beers contain an increasing proportion of Dutch, such as local Jopen and Uiltje, and guests from Ramses, De Molen and Klein Duimpje. The latter brews the house Briljant Bier (7.2%), a coriander-spiced tripel. There is also a fine range of single malts.

Briljant, Haarlem

Bruxelles

Lange Wijngaardstraat 16 · **T** 023 531 4509
www.cafebruxelles.nl
Daily from 17.00

Popular café down an alleyway off Smedestraat, just north of Grote Markt. There is a terrace at the rear of the first floor. Both levels are brightly coloured and somewhat off-beat. Food includes mains and a cheap daily special (until 23.00). Most of the 50+ list is Belgian – the house name and Mannekin Pis logo are a clue – but there are several Dutch offerings.

Jopenkerk, Haarlem

Jopenkerk

Gedempte Voldersgracht 2 · **T** 023 533 4114
www.jopen.nl
Daily 10.00–01.00

The Jopen brewpub is an impressive affair, housed in the restored Jacobskerk, with a large terrace on a square to one side. The interior styling is modern, but acknowledges its former ecclesiastical existence, not least the floor-to-ceiling stained-glass windows. Some ceilings are carpeted. Lunches are served in the bar downstairs until 15.00 (snacks until 22.00); more substantive dinners in the mezzanine restaurant above (17.30–22.00, last orders 21.30). Dishes have beer recommendations. The 40-odd beers include at least 10 house brews on tap. Others are available in bottles, and a further 15–20 guest bottles showcase smaller Dutch brewers.

Roemer

Botermarkt 17 · **T** 023 532 5267
www.cafederoemer.nl
Su from 11.00; others from 10.00

On Haarlem's bustling Botermarkt, the Rummer (a bowl once used for drinking toasts) is one of five cafés in a row, each with large terraces. An inner terrace becomes a conservatory in winter. The spacious Art Deco interior includes a striking glass frieze behind the bar. There is a full food menu. The beer list has gone skywards, and we last counted 80+, Jopen, Emelisse, De Molen and Maximus all featuring in the Dutch range, alongside numerous guests.

Studio

Grote Markt 25 · **T** 023 531 0033
www.cafestudio.nl
Sa&Su from 11.00; others from 12.00

One of Haarlem's largest and loudest cafés, with a terrace on the main square. Come during the day to avoid being deafened. The interior shows Art Deco leanings. Lunch means paninis; snacks are available at other times. The list has been waning, and may have slipped below 40, but with half a dozen from Jopen, plus others from De Molen and Maximus, it still scrapes in.

Studio, Haarlem

OTHER **HAARLEM** BEER VENUES:
Koops (Damstraat 4 – **T** 023 532 2760 – www. cafekoops.nl – *daily from 16.00*), with gnarled tables, worn floors, and mustard-coloured walls, is honed from another era. Quirky local boozer **Melkwoud** (Zijlstraat 63 – **T** 023 574 9112 – *Closed Su; others from 16.00*) has décor inspired by Dylan Thomas's Under Milk Wood.

Uiver, Haarlem

And hugely characterful **Uiver** (Riviervisch-markt 13 – **T** 023 532 5399 – www.indenuiver.nl – *Fr&Sa from 14.00; Su 14.00–21.00; others from 16.00*) has a Delft tile and marble bar, an aeronautically themed central room, and a snug with 17th-century leather wallpaper.

BEER TO GO: **Melgers** (Barrevoetestraat 13–15 – **T** 023 531 5884 – www.melgers.nl – *Closed Su; Mo 12.00–18.00, others 09.00–18.00*), just west of Botermarkt, stocks 700+ beers.

HAARLEM (Vijfhuizen)
6km SE of Haarlem

Vijfhuizen (pop. 4,400) is a semi-rural suburb of Haarlem, on the bus 300 route. Reaching its fort requires creative bushwhacking through a housing estate, but is not hard.

Fort
Fortwachter 3 · **T** 023 558 9010
www.fortrestaurant.nl
Sa&Su 10.00–17.00; others 11.00–17.00

You do not get many opportunities to drink in a bunker. This moated citadel was built in the 19th century to protect Amsterdam. Today it is used for exhibitions. Its restaurant is the only outlet for Vijfhuizen beers, made on-site. There is a terrace, and a surprisingly light modern interior with vaulted concrete ceilings. Food runs from snacks and apple pie to full 3-course lunches. The 10 beers are likely to include 3 or 4 of the local brews in bottle, the range dependent on recent activity. The rest are pretty dull.

HEEMSKERK
20km N from Haarlem, off A9 exit 9
Heemskerk or Uitgeest

Modern commuter town (pop. 39,000).

Lokaal
Anthonie Verherenstraat 5a · **T** 0251 249170
www.cafe-lokaal.nl
Closed Mo&Tu (Jul-Aug); Fr&Su from 17.00; Sa from 19.00; others from 20.00

Music café with a stage and regular concerts. Take bus 73 from Uitgeest station to Maerelaan, continuing on to the roundabout, after which it is first on the right. The scruffy, high-ceilinged café is a converted schoolroom. A giant stuffed penguin perching above the bar holds sway. Food is toasties and snacks. The 40 beers are interesting – bottles change following regular tasting sessions held here. Dutch choices have been known to include Maximus and local Noord-Hollands.

HEERHUGOWAARD
8km NE of Alkmaar off N242
Heerhugowaard.

Medium-sized town (pop. 51,000), practically a suburb of Alkmaar.

Geuzen
Middenweg 201 · **T** 072 572 8801
www.bierenproeflokaaldegeuzen.nl
Closed Mo-We; Th&Fr from 17.00; Sa from 18.00; Su 16.00–22.00

Rough-edged basic boozer with a small terrace in a row of shops. White plaster walls and steins give it faux German bierkeller feel. Two beer tanks visible through a glass wall would be more interesting were they not filled with industrial pils. Nibbles only. The 40-odd beer list is strong on Trappists and German Weizen.

ode Steen square, Hoorn

HOORN

🚆 Hoorn

Attractive city (pop. 71,000) that was an important port on the Zuiderzee until a series of dykes closed its route to the sea. Learn about the history of its Golden Age in the West Fries Museum (www.westfriesmuseum.com), a lovely stone gabled building dating from 1632. Central Roode Steen square is one of the prettiest in the Netherlands.

Beiaard 🚲

Kerkplein 3 · **T** 0229 270675
www.beiaardgroep.eu
Closed Mo; Sa&Su from 15.00; others from 16.00

Large café with a terrace beside the Grote Kerk. Inside are three distinct areas, open plan enough to form a single room. Walls are plastered with beer enamels, and adverts for other beverages. Eclectic lighting ranges from Art Deco to crystal chandeliers. Snacks available all day; specials, fish and burgers in the evening. Among the 55 beers are the Beiaard group's Bekeerde Suster range on tap, plus monthly changing guests.

CharlieS

Dubbele Buurt 4 · **T** 0229 217798
www.charlies.nl
Closed Mo&Tu; We&Th from 16.00; Fr&Sa from 15.00; Su 14.00–22.00

Corner café NW of the centre. A front bar has bits of Charlie Chaplin. The back room picks up the cinematic theme and runs with it: posters, projectors, canisters, strips of celluloid, and a painting of Paramount's mountain logo. Snacks only. About one-third of the 65 beers change seasonally. Smaller Dutch brewers regularly feature, including Maallust and Klein Duimpje. There is also a short but interesting whisky list.

IJMUIDEN

12km N of Haarlem, off N208

The two reasons to visit this industrial North Sea port are the Newcastle ferry and the beer shop, each convenient to the other.

BEER TO GO: **Zeewijk** (Zeewijkplein 25 – **T** 0255 540331 – www.zeewijck.nl – *Closed Su; Mo 12.00–18.00; Th 09.00–21.00; Sa 09.00–17.00; others 09.00–18.00*) stocks 300+ well-chosen beers, with a good Dutch range.

KROMMENIE

19km NNW from Amsterdam, off N246
🚆 Krommenie-Assendelft

Small sleeper town (pop. 17,000).

BEER TO GO: **Drinks & Gifts** (Heiligeweg 15a – **T** 075 640 5179 – www.drinks-gifts.nl – *Closed Su; Mo 13.00–18.00; Th 09.00–20.00; Sa 09.00–17.00; others 09.00–18.00*) has 500+ beers, including many better Dutch.

Demmers,
Naarden-Vesting

NAARDEN-VESTING

22km ESE of Amsterdam off A1 exit 6

⇔ Naarden-Bussum

Attractive, moated and fortified medieval town, with narrow cobbled streets. Modern Naarden (pop. 17,000) to the south is less appealing but has the station, 2km from the tourist action.

Demmers

Marktstraat 52 · **T** 06 2551 6408
www.vestinggilde.nl
Mo 16.00–22.00; Sa from 15.00; Su 15.00–22.00; others from 16.00

Atmospheric pub in the old walled area, with a small streetside terrace. In a 17th-century corner house that has been a café since at least 1885. The bar is up steps at the back of the split-level interior, in which wooden floors and beamed ceilings add to a general creakiness. Food is snacks and simple meals. The 40 beers include 4 guest taps. The house Vestinggilde Blond (6.5%) is currently brewed in Belgium, though there are plans to brew it locally.

OUDENDIJK

9km WSW of Hoorn off N243

Rural farming hamlet (pop. 450).

Les Deux Ponts

Slimdijk 2 · **T** 0229 541275 or 541951
www.lesdeuxponts.nl
Closed Tu; others from 11.00

Several cafés could claim to have the nicest setting of any in this guide but the Two Bridges beats most. There are no public transport options that avoid a stiff hike but bus 128 from Hoorn will get you within 1.5km if you get off at Avenhorn, Het Hoog. This is a whitewashed local with a superb canalside terrace over-looking reeds and grebes (and two bridges). The barn-like interior is the hub of village life – step inside and be transported back to the 1970s. Lunches are simple but evening food run to mussels and steak. The 60 beers feature local Lepelaer brews.

OUDESCHILD (on Texel)

The island's commercial fishing port (pop. 1,100), and home to one of the country's largest little breweries.

Texels Proeflokaal

Schilderweg 214 · **T** 0222 313 229
www.speciaalbier.com
Closed Su&Mo (all year), Tu&Th (Nov–Mar) & Fr (mid-Dec–mid-Feb); others 13.00–18.00

Brewery tap to the west of Oudeschild, served by bus 29. The tasting room is around the back – sit on the terrace to be serenaded by sheep. Some interior walls are painted with pastoral and beach scenes, while others are brewery-themed. Snacks only. Most of the house beers are served – four are on draught and the others in bottle. The bar doubles as the shop, and is where you sign up for tours.

Texels Proeflo
Oudeschild (on

*es Deux Ponts,
Oudendijk*

PURMEREND

16km ENE of Amsterdam off N235

🔁 Purmerend

Market town (pop. 79,000) that was originally a fishing port. Koemarkt (Cow Market) is one of the country's largest squares and has a statue of a cow in the middle to recall the days before the cattle auctions moved to more practical premises in 2008.

Aad de Wolf

Koemarkt 15 · **T** 0299 423974
www.aaddewolf.nl
*Closed We; Tu from 09.00, Su from 12.00;
others from 11.30*

Large brown café with a bar area, and more sedate sofa-filled side room. Lunches and dinners are served until 21.00; snacks all day. The 50+ beer list is strong on local ales, with Texel, SNAB, Lepelaer and Dampegheest. After 23.00 at weekends, the Twilight Zone descends – the music goes up, coloured lights flash, and hardboard mounted over the billiards table transforms it into a dancefloor, serviced by perhaps the world's only lace-curtained disco.

Bakker

Koemarkt 44 · **T** 0299 421262
www.proeflokaalbakker.nl
*Closed Mo; Sa from 15.00; Su 15.00–22.00;
others from 16.00*

Bijou, friendly one-room café with a small terrace, the interior has a red-painted wooden-plank ceiling that requires support from two slender central columns. On the walls are photographs of the old cattle markets that took place outside. Snacks only. The are plenty of local North Holland options among the 70+ beers.

Bonte Koe

Koemarkt 24 · **T** 0299 421124
www.biercafedebontekoe.nl
*Closed Mo; Tu 09.00–18.00; We&Th from 16.00;
Fr&Sa from 15.00; Su 14.00–20.00.*

Long-standing ABT member the Spotted Cow is a large and welcoming brown café with a terrace on the square. Sizeable paintings on the walls give it a half-Rembrandt, half-Weinstube feel. Glass cabinets at the rear house a collection of steins and other memorabilia. Snacks only. The 140+ list always features at least one SNAB brew among the 16 taps. The rest of the menu is on a TV screen and usually features US imports from Anchor.

ZAANDAM

15km NNW of Amsterdam off A8 exit 1
🚃 Zaandam

As you leave the station and pass the extraordinary stack of buildings that forms the Inntel Hotel (Google it, you'll understand), this commuter town (pop. 73,000) seems like Disney Holland, with everything orderly and nice. Referred to as Zaanstad by some, the name of the municipality.

HOTEL TIP: **Zaan Inn** ★★★, Grenehout 22 (**T** 075 303 0340 – www.zaaninnhotel.nl) is a modern place beside the station – worth considering as a better-value alternative to staying in Amsterdam.

BEER TO GO: **Vonk** (Tuiniersstraat 8 – www.slijterijvonk.nl – *Closed Su; Mo 13.00–18.00; Th 08.00–21.00; others 08.00–18.00*) is a large drinks shop stocking 400+ beers, including many 75cl bottles.

ZAANDIJK

20km NNW of Amsterdam off A8 exit 2
🚃 Koog-Zaandijk

Small town (pop. 9,000) within the Zaanstad municipality, full of food factories such as the cocoa processing plant, with its unmissable aroma. Across the river is Zaanse Schans, an open air museum, replete with more windmills than Don Quixote could shake a stick at.

Konincksplein

Lagedijk 13 · **T** 075 621 5367
Closed Mo; Tu&We 16.00–21.00; Th&Fr 15.00–01.00; Sa 14.00–01.00; Su 15.00–20.00

This lovely old-world pub is one of those places where time stands still. Its wooden walls are in classic tasting room olive-green. Food is classic Dutch too, with a stoofpot (stew), or whatever else is cooking – there is no menu, so ask. Snacks are also available. The beer range hovers around 50, with 12 taps. There are a few North Holland brews among the mainly Belgian range.

ZANDVOORT

9km W of Haarlem on N201
🚃 Zandvoort aan Zee

Seaside resort (pop. 16,600) with a wide sandy beach backed with tacky cafés, souvenir stalls and hotels. Its proximity to Amsterdam (30 mins by twice-hourly train) and Haarlem (11 minutes) can make it can make a sensible alternative base. This being the North Sea you are more likely to end up in hospital with hypothermia or a sand-blasting injury than through sunburn, but all beachside cafés provide blankets and windshields.

HOTEL TIP: there are dozens in town and hundreds along the coast, with **Zee en Duinzicht**, Marisstraat 11 (**T** 023 571 9650; www.pensionzeeenduinzicht.nl), a pleasant small guesthouse option close to both station and beach.

Bruxelles aan Zee

Strandtent 14 · **T** 023 571 5203
www.bruxellesaanzee.nl
Closed October to February. Others 10.00–24.00

From the promenade, find path number 14 going down to the sand to find this wooden pavilion with a vast decked terrace. Inside, a sofa corner has a wood-burning stove – testament to the realities of the Dutch summer. There is a full food menu, including the same cheap daily deal offered by its sister bar in Haarlem (qv). Only 40 beers but several from 't IJ and Jopen. Without doubt the Netherlands' beeriest beach bar, seeing as currently it has no challengers.

Konincksplein, Zaandijk

Overijssel

Meaning 'beyond the IJssel', the river that forms much of its southwestern border with Gelderland. In essence this is two provinces, divided by Christianity.

The western half is historically Protestant, the eastern bastion of a 'bible belt' that runs southwest from here to Zeeland, featuring small towns like Staphorst, where people would never dream of washing their cars on a Sunday, let alone taking a beer – hence Sunday closing for pubs. Further east, particularly the Twente region near Germany, is more relaxed Catholic in attitude – enjoy life, but confess afterwards.

It used to be the case that you had to head east to find a decent café, though these days western towns like Zwolle and Kampen more than hold their own. Most of the 1.1 million population lives in the cluster of Twente towns comprising Hengelo, Almelo and Enschede. The countryside is agricultural, getting progressively wetter the further north and west you go.

LARGEST CENTRES: **Enschede** (158,000), **Zwolle** (121,000), **Deventer** (98,500), **Hengelo** (81,000), **Almelo** (72,600)

MORE INFORMATION: www.vvv.nl/overijssel; www.beleefoverijssel.nl

BREWERIES: **Berghoeve**, *Den Ham;* **Bombazijn**, *Oldenzaal;* **Grolsch** (SAB Miller), *Enschede;* **Hettinga**, *Zwolle;* **Mommeriete**, *Gramsbergen;* **Ootmarsummer**, *Ootmarsum;* **Pauw**, *Ommen;* **Sallandse**, *Raalte;* & **Twentse**, *Hengelo*

OTHER BEER MAKERS: **DAVO**, *Deventer;* **Eanske**, *Enschede;* **Huttenkloas**, *Hengelo;* **Witte Klavervier**, *Zwolle*

ALBERGEN
8km E of Almelo on N349

Semi-rural Twents village (pop. 3,500).

Morshuis
Ootmarsumseweg 159 · **T** 0546 441238
www.morshuis.nl
Closed We; others 09.00–02.00

Large beer café adjoined to an even bigger party venue, with a terrace on the main road. The latter's centrepiece is a British telephone kiosk – accessible from indoors, but technically 'outside' – this is its all-weather smoking compartment. The café's ceiling is painted with giant sunflowers and the room is filled with various junk, ranging from a cast-iron stove to a petrol pump and a 'keep right' sign. Food is simple lunches and snacks. Of the 100+ beers, only the taps are listed. For the rest, head to the room beside the bar and help yourself from the three chiller cabinets, kept at different temperatures. Local Othmar beers feature amongst the many Dutch choices.

OVERIJSSEL

Drenthe

Kampen

Gramsbergen

Germany

voland

Zwolle

Albergen

Raalte

Almelo   Oldenzaal

Hengelo

Gelderland

E30

Deventer

Enschede

⊢———⊣ 10 km

Morshuis, Albergen

ALMELO

17km NW of Hengelo, off A35 exit 30
🚃 Almelo

Provincial town (pop. 72,600) where one of the major employers is a uranium enrichment plant – the locals are so friendly that they even glow in the dark.

België

Schuttenstraat 2 · **T** 0546 453 365
proeflokaalbelgie.nl
Sa from 12.00; Su from 10.00; others from 13.00

Central corner local with a split-level canalside terrace. Inside, a blue and nicotine-yellow theme is a change from brown – even the billiards table is blue. There is live music some nights, and a monthly pop quiz. Food (16.00–21.30) runs to spare ribs and stews; toasties and snacks at other times. The 80+ beers are mainly Belgian, with one from Ter Dolen on tap.

*OTHER **ALMELO** BEER VENUES:*

The atmospheric old-world **Hookhoes** (9 Grotestraat 126 – **T** 0546 814898 – www. hookhoes.nl – *daily from 16.00*) was a specialist café, but its list has dwindled to 25.

DEVENTER

13km W of Apeldoorn, off A1 exits 23&24
🚃 Deventer

Modern town (pop. 99,000) with a historical heart. Parts of the Proosdij, the oldest stone house in the country, date from 1130. This was once the national centre of carpet making, with five factories at its peak. The only one that remains makes artificial turf for sports fields. Every December sees its Dickens festival (www.dickensfestijn.nl) – when you may encounter people dressed as Mr Macawber or Little Dorrit.

De Heks

De Heks, Deventer

Brink 63 · **T** 0570 613412
www.deheks.nl
Sa from 14.00; others from 15.00

A worth-the-journey ABT stalwart, the Witch is the only pub honoured in miniature in the Madurodam theme park in Den Haag. It has a terrace on the main square, just behind the Waag (or Weighhouse), which now hosts the tourist office and a museum where you can learn about carpets. The pub's single room has witches flying from light fittings. Snacks only, except for a weekly dinner special on Tuesdays (17.00–20.30). The most interesting beers on the 100-strong list are among the 19 taps. The excellent fruity blond Pyromaan (6%), brewed by Rodenburg, is one of the best house beers we have tasted.

ENSCHEDE

🚃 Enschede

Close to the German border, Overijssel's largest city (pop. 158,000) is known in local dialect as Eanske – the name taken by a local brewing concern. On the outskirts is another – the large industrial complex that is home to Grolsch.

Over the years Enschede has been periodically rebuilt and redesigned, following a series of fires that have earned the townsfolk the nickname of Brandstichters (roughly, arsonists). Ironically it last hit the international headlines in 2000 when a fireworks warehouse exploded, destroying an entire neighbourhood.

Today it is better known for FC Twente, the football club where British fans may recall Steve McLaren gained a Dutch accent. *HOTEL TIP:* **Rodenbach**★★★, Parkweg 37 (**T** 053 480 0200; www.rodenbach.nl), a smallish hotel just west of the centre.

Beiaard

Oude Markt 24 · **T** 053 430 6267
www.beiaardgroep.eu
Closed Mo; Sa from 14.00; Su 15.00–22.00; others from 15.00

With a terrace on the main square, the Twente branch of the Beiaard empire. The interior is dominated by its central light fitting – a tangle of twisted metal and wine glasses. Above this is a four-panel ceiling painted with suns and goats – we are guessing representing the seasons. The food menu always has one dish cooked using the beer of the month. The 70 beers feature all the group's Bekeerde Suster range. Bottles are half price on Sunday after 21.00.

België

Oude Markt 20 · **T** 053 574 5616
proeflokaalbelgie.nl
Su from 10.00; others from 11.00

Sister of the like-named café in Almelo, with a terrace on the main square. The large one-room interior has chandeliers dangling from a high ceiling, and a billiards table at the back. Food is snacks, toasties and apple pie. The 70+ beers are almost all Belgian bar a couple from Germany, but 8 of the 10 taps are guests.

ONS

Walstraat 41 · **T** 053 432 3293
www.onsetenendrinken.nl
Daily from 16.30

Central modern and bright split-level café/restaurant with a small terrace close to the St Jacobskerk. Food (until 22.00) is modern Dutch, with dishes going seasonal and organic wherever possible. The beer list is on the up. More than half the 75+ range

were Dutch at the last count, with Emelisse, Maximus and De Molen numbered among them. The wine list isn't bad either.

Vestingbar

Drienerlolaan 5 · **T** 053 489 4530
www.vestingbar.nl
Tu from 20.30; others from 21.00

Out on the UTwente university campus is one of Europe's beeriest student bars. Take bus 1 to UT/Colslaan and you will find it up the steps in the building beyond the sports field – look for the cartoon cow. Run by and for students – although everyone is welcome – this is a typical dive bar, with loud music, a vinyl floor for spillages, and no need for decoration or windows. But there are also 55 well-chosen beers, including De Molen, and several German imports, and even a few decent single malts. Food is from a snack bar dispensing the kind of unhealthy deep-fried fodder the regulars prefer.

Vluchte

Oldenzaalsestraat 153a · **T** 053 433 9159
www.devluchte.nl
Closed Sa&Su; others from 19.00-ish

Another oddity, in a suburban community centre near the Twents Rijksmuseum. Ignore the drab front hall stuffed with locals playing bingo, and make for the drab rear hall: a youth centre with billiards, darts, worn-out carpet, and skittle alleys. No food. And no service, unless you want one of the dull tap beers. To find the beer treasure enter the walk-in cellar beside the bar, a chilled Aladdin's Cave of 130+ Dutch and imported bottles. Help yourself to one, pick up a glass – the button on the floor gets you back out. Your personal opener harvests bottle tops and is used to calculate the bill. Simples.

BEER TO GO: **Hennie Berendsen** (Deurningerstraat 27 – **T** 053 431 5264 – www.hennieberendsen.com – *Closed Su; Mo 13.00-18.00; Th 09.00-21.00; Sa 09.00-17.00; others 09.00-18.00*), a large off-licence north of the station, stocks 350+ beers.

GRAMSBERGEN
45km WNW of Zwolle off N34

🚉 Gramsbergen

A village (pop. 3,100) in the NE of the province. Its nearest town Coevorden is in Drenthe.

Mommeriete

De Oostermaat 66 · **T** 0524 562511
www.mommeriete.nl
Daily from 10.00

Brewery tap in a former lock-keeper's cottage, a lovely building with shuttered windows and flower boxes. The picturesque canalside terrace is beside a wooden drawbridge. Around the back is a beer garden. The bar inside looks unchanged for 100 years, with a large hearth backed with Delftware tiles and a built-in box-bed. Brewing kit occupies a side room. Food is ice cream, rolls and snacks. Five or 6 house brews are available. The house *eau de vie* is made from distilled beer.

HENGELO
8km NW of Enschede, off A35 exit 28

🚉 Hengelo

Provincial town (pop. 81,000) that developed with the arrival of the railways. Accidentally flattened by Allied bombing raids its quick-fix rebuild lacks historical appeal.
HOTEL TIP: **City** ★★★, B.P. Hofstedestraat 50 (**T** 035 677 7217; www.hampshire-hotels.com), a modern place midway between station and centre.

Hengeler

Tuindorpstraat 61 · **T** 074 250 0681
www.hengeler.nl
Sa from 16.00; Su from 15.00; others from 11.00

Twentse brewery tap and restaurant in an industrial building. Heading west from the station, turn left under the tracks, then across the car park. The interior is minimalist chic with ventilation ducts. The brewery is visible through glass. Drinkers gather in a bar-side seating area; elsewhere there are linen

Mommeriete, Gramsbergen

tablecloths. Lunches and dinners are served; snacks all day. The house beer range varies according to what has been brewed.

Pleintje

Burgermeester Jansenplein 25
T 074 291 2425
www.biercafehetpleintje.nl
Sa from 12.00; Su from 14.00; others from 11.00

Central café with a large terrace – the Siamese twin of the adjacent Twee Wezen. They share a kitchen and are conjoined at the back. In theory you can order Pleintje's beers in the latter, though it has no beer menu. The Pleintje is packed to the gills with neon signs and beer enamels. The food menu includes a cheap daily special (12.00–21.00). Its 60+ list leans towards safe. Beer is half price on Mondays after 20.00.

Uurwerk

Langestraat 25 · **T** 074 250 2106
www.cafehetuurwerk.nl
Closed Su&We; Fr from 15.00; Sa from 14.00; others from 16.00

The Clockwork is a friendly local just north of the centre. Dim lighting, low wood ceilings, and wooden walls and floors, giving it the feel of a ship's cabin, or like being in a giant coffin – but with a bar. A lighter, airier space at the back is the preserve of smokers. No food. The 60 beers include a fair choice of 75cl bottles, and sometimes local Twentse.

KAMPEN

15km WNW of Zwolle off N50

⮂ Kampen

Charismatic town (pop. 34,000) with medieval charm, in Overijssel's top-left corner – near the Flevoland no-fly zone for beer lovers.

Stomme van Kampen

Oudestraat 218-220 · **T** 038 337 1721
www.destommevankampen.nl
Fr&Sa from 15.00; Su 16.00-19.00; Th from 17.00; others from 19.00

The Mute of Kampen is a lovely beer café with a small terrace near the IJssel river, just north of the town centre. Two historic premises knocked into one, the bar has uneven floors, panelled walls and a Delftware galleon mural. A younger side area has stucco ceilings and candlelight. A painting on one wall is a copy of a 17th century work by Hendrick Avercamp: De Stomme van Campen. Snacks only, except for burger night on Fridays (18.00-20.00). Most beer taps are embedded in a copper-plate wall – the 60+ range includes the house Belgian white beer, **Anna** (5%), named after the aforementioned artist's unrequited first love.

OLDENZAAL

10km N of Enschede off A1 exit 32&33

⮂ Oldenzaal

Attractive Twente market town (pop. 32,000). Its church is possibly the only one ever dedicated to St Plechelm, an Irish missionary monk who moved here from Lindisfarne in the 8th century.

Engel

Markt 14 · **T** 0541 521903
www.bierlokaaldeengel.nl
Sa&Su from 12.00; others from 14.00

The Angel is a friendly local with a large terrace on the main square. Every inch of wall and most of the wood-beamed ceiling in the spacious sandy-floored interior is covered

de Engel, Oldenzaal

with bric-a-brac. There are several cherubs, but surprisingly few angels. Candlelit tables set the tone. Snacks and toasties only, plus free peanuts – other nibbles are also handed round occasionally. The 60 beers include La Trappe, a few German Weizen, and the house Witte Engel spiced white beer, brewed by Brabandere (formerly Bavik) in Belgium. There is a decent range of whiskies too.

RAALTE

25 km SE of Zwolle off N35

⮂ Raalte

Small market town (pop. 20,000) with a brewery borrowed by half the nation's brewers.

Sallandse

Almelosestraat 2 · **T** 074 259 1311
www.sallandslandbier.nl
We&Sa only 14.00-17.00

Just east of the centre, this brewery tap occupies the basement of the Leeren Lampe events complex. Before the brewery arrived the space was a subterranean miniature golf course. Now it is more like a ski hut for troglodytes, wooden planks covering concrete walls and sporting skis for decoration. No food. Just four taps dispensing the house brews bottles to buy for takehome. If you have paid for a tour, tastings are included. Can be booked for parties.

ZWOLLE
~~ Zwolle

Attractive provincial capital (pop. 121,000), and former Hanseatic city. Although few of the fortifications remain, the centre is still surrounded by a moat. The top attraction is its one remaining city gate, the 1409 Sassenpoort.

HOTEL TIP: **Hanze** ★★★, Rodetorenplein 10-11 (**T** 038 421 8182; www.hanzehotel.com) is small and central.

Abdij 🍺

Gasthuisplein 13 · **T** 038 230 2262
www.deabdij-zwolle.nl
Closed Mo; Tu from 16.00; others from 14.00

Small ABT corner local, with a tiny terrace on a pedestrianised street. Bench seating is at a height to suit standing tables, so expect to dangle. Snacks are available if you ask, though we have never seen a menu. Eleven of the 110+ beers (140 on a good day) are on tap. Around half the bottled range is Dutch, with strength in local beer makers such as Hettinga, Witte Klavervier, and Witte Leeuw. There is also a good range of whiskies.

Bapas

Grote Kerkplein 9 · **T** 038 422 1844
www.bapaszwolle.nl
Closed Su&Mo; Sa 14.00-24.00; others 16.00-24.00

If menu size were everything, this would not get a look in, but we like where they are going. Bapas, short for 'beer tapas', is a small restaurant with a terrace behind the Grote Kerk, with a mock-old interior. Most dishes small or large are original creations rather than poor imitations of Spanish tapas. Bigger ones have beer pairing recommendations. Only 25+ beers, but around half are from Overijssel.

Belgische Keizer

Melkmarkt 58 · **T** 038 421 1011
www.belgischekeizer.nl
Su from 12.00; others from 10.00

The Belgian Emperor is a lovely pub with a terrace on a large square. The high-ceilinged interior has walls that are not quite vertical. An ancient wooden-faced clock forms part of shelving behind the bar and still works – amazingly. Lunches are served until 17.00, dinners from 17.00 and snacks all day. The origins of most of 50+ beer list reflect the pub's name.

Hete Brij

Nieuwe Markt 9 · **T** 038 421 7526
www.cafedehetebrij.nl
Closed Mo; Fr&Sa from 15.30; Su from 15.00; others from 16.00

'Draait om de hete brij' means roughly to skirt around an issue, so the suggested translation is Hot Potato. This friendly café has a small terrace on a quiet square. The interior is a mix of old and new, with carpeted tables and multicoloured cushions. Illustrations on the toilet doors leave little to the imagination – we'll just say 'Adam and Eve', and drop the potato. Snacks only. Plentiful Dutch offerings among the 70+ beers include De Molen, and local Witte Klavervier.

In De Buurt

Luttekestraat 6 · **T** 038 423 5010
www.jebentindebuurt.nl
Closed Mo; others from 14.00

Compact modern bar with a small terrace in the shadow of the Grote Kerk. The blue-ceilinged interior has a deliberately ramshackle feel with crafted peeling plaster and bare brick walls. Occasional live music and DJs at weekends can push the volume levels up at times. Snacks only. The 50+ beers throw up some interesting options, with a healthy showing from 't IJ.

*OTHER **ZWOLLE** BEER VENUES:*

Gezelligheid (Gasthuisplein 11 – **T** 038 331 9140 – www.cafedegezelligheid.nl – *Mo&Tu from 19.00; Sa from 14.00; others from 16.00*), near to the Abdij (above), has 35 beers.

South Holland

A densely populated region (pop. 3.5 million) that, together with the southern part of North Holland and Utrecht, forms the Randstad, a conurbation of 7 million folk. But it is not all apartments. The bulk of the famous bulbfields are in the north of the province. Come in spring to see them in technicolour.

Central South Holland is dominated by the megalopolis encompassing Rotterdam, Den Haag, plus the industrial docklands of the Rotterdam Europoort. Much of what is not built up is covered in greenhouses that produce thousands of tons of good-looking flavourless tomatoes and other fruits. More than 100 sq km of land is covered with glass.

Things are a bit quieter further south, where the Lower Rhine and Maas break up into intertwining channels, creating a network of fertile islands. Near Rotterdam is the sight responsible for more chocolate box lids and jigsaws than anywhere else: the 19 windmills of the Kinderdijk.

The province's beer credentials are secure, with 16 breweries, and three cities – Den Haag, Delft and Rotterdam – worth the journey. At the other end of the scale is its fastest-growing town, Zoetermeer. Forty years ago just 7,000 people lived there. Today 123,000 do, but no one has yet opened a decent beer pub. An opportunity lies waiting.

Endless fields of tulips

SOUTH HOLLAND

10 km

Hillegom

North Holland

Noordwijk

Sassenheim

Uithoorn

Leiden

Scheveningen

Alphen aan den Rijn

Utrecht

Den Haag

Bodegraven

Delft

Gouda

Maasluis

Schiedam

Krimpen aan den Ijssel

Vlaardingen

Rotterdam

Brielle

Gorinchem

Gelderland

Dordrecht

Zeeland

North Brabant

LARGEST CENTRES: **Rotterdam** (617,000),
Den Haag (506,000), **Zoetermeer** (123,000),
Leiden (120,000), **Dordrecht** (119,000), **Delft**
(99,000), **Schiedam** (76,000), **Alphen aan
den Rijn** (73,000), **Spijkenisse** (72,000),
Vlaardingen (71,000), **Gouda** (71,000),
Capelle aan den IJssel (66,000)

MORE INFORMATION: www.vvv.nl/zuid-holland

BREWERIES: **Beijerse**, Oud-Beijerland;
Brouwcafé, Den Haag (Scheveningen);
Dordrecht, Dordrecht; **EleganT**, Leiderdorp;
Fiddler, Den Haag; **Heineken**, Zoeterwoude;
Kaapse, Rotterdam; **Klein Duimpje**, Hillegom;
Koperen Kat, Delft; **Leidsch**, Leiden; **Merciless**,
Bodegraven; **de Molen**, Bodegraven; **Pelgrim**,
Rotterdam (Delfshaven); **Vijfheerenlanden**,
Leerdam; **Vlaardingse**, Vlaardingen

OTHER BEER MAKERS: **Bijdehand**, Tiel;
Kompaan, Den Haag

ALPHEN AAN DEN RIJN
15km E of Leiden off N11
🚉 Alphen aan den Rijn

Largely modern town (pop. 73,000) on the
Oude Rijn. Home of the impressive Avifauna
bird park (www.avifauna.nl), which claims to
have 1,800 species.
HOTEL TIP: **Van Der Valk Avifauna ★★★★**,
Hoorn 65 (**T** 0172 487575 – www.avifauna.nl)
is part of the bird park and also a handy base
for visiting Bodegraven, 9 km SE of here.

Natte
Julianastraat 19 · **T** 0172 426193
Closed Su; others from 16.00

Long, narrow bar with a small terrace on a
shopping street, and an unusually high,
beamed ceiling inside. There is a mezzanine
area above for busy times. Food is snacks
and toasties only – see the cupboard-sized
kitchen beside the bar to understand why.
The 100 beers feature some good local choices,
'local' in this instance including De Molen.

BODEGRAVEN
27km NE of Rotterdam off A12 exit 12/12a
🚉 Bodegraven

Once a sleepy manicured backwater, this
small town (pop. 20,000) is now firmly on
the world beer map. As well as its globally
famous brewery there are now two others.
It also has two excellent beer shops. Despite
this, many residents are unaware of their
town's new incarnation and look on in
bewilderment when their home is invaded
by international beer geeks for the Borefts
festival in September.

HOTEL TIP: Bodegraven's only hotel is
inconveniently out of town. There are better
options in Alphen aan den Rijn and Woerden,
each one train stop away.

De Molen
Overtocht 43 · **T** 0172 610848
www.brouwerijdemolen.nl
Closed Mo; others from 12.00

Brewery tap and restaurant, with a terrace,
in the Arkduif (Ark Dove) windmill. The mill
dates from 1697, but got its name in 1956
following a competition. The ground floor
bar has wooden ceilings and whitewashed
walls, with a canal view out the back.
Lunches and dinners use local ingredients
and come with beer recommendations.
There are around 10 De Molen beers on tap.
If you need more, in theory you can – in
theory at least – order anything stocked in
the adjacent shop, bumping the selection
significantly, but why would you?

BEER TO GO: Besides up to 100 house brews,
including the one-offs, the **De Molen** shop
(Overtocht 43 – **T** 0172 610848 – www.
demolenbeershop.com – shut Mo; others 12.00–
18.30) stocks hundreds more from dozens of
the world's best brewers. You can also order
online for shipping to the most of the EU.
Speciaal Bierwinkel (Overtocht 6 – **T** 06
5736 8883 – www.speciaalbierwinkel.be –
shut Su; Th 08.30–18.00; Fr 08.30–21.00; Sa 08.30–
17.00; other days, call ahead to check) stocks
400+ beers, around 90% of which are from
small Dutch breweries, including the house
Kraan beers.

e mill that changed it all

BRIELLE

26km W of Rotterdam off N218

Picturesque historical town (pop. 16,000), with a charming centre laced with cobbled streets.

Kont van 't Paard

Kaatsbaan 1 · **T** 0181 416161
www.kontvanhetpaard.nl
Daily from 17.00

To find the characterful Horse's Arse, head west from the central square, then turn right at the cast-iron cannon and stocks. There is a terrace outside the old inn, which has undergone several changes in use, including a stint as a slaughterhouse. Dinners are served until 21.30 – the house specials are spare ribs. The 30+ list would not normally warrant a full entry, but guest beers can be interesting, and with such a charming name, how could we not?

OTHER **BRIELLE** *BEER VENUES:*
In the 1788 guardhouse on the picturesque main square, sits **Hoofdwacht** (Markt 7 – **T** 0181 418393 – www.dehoofdwacht-brielle.nl – *daily from 09.00*), which stocks 30 beers.

DELFT

8km SSE of Den Hague off A13 exit 9
Delft & Delft Zuid

If all towns were as beery as Delft (pop. 99,000), this book would need to double in size. However, if arriving by train, your first challenge will be to find the centre, currently hidden beyond major construction work, set to continue until 2017, which will send the railway underground.

Once on the other side you'll find a miniature, more sedate version of Amsterdam: canal-filled streets lined with gabled houses. The precarious 14th-century tower of the Oude Kerk (Heilige Geestkerkhof 25) is notable for its top being two metres out of whack with its base. Those with an interest in history should visit the Prinsenhof museum (www.prinsenhof-delft.nl), where Dutch founding father Willem van Oranje (known as William the Silent) was shot dead in 1584. You can still see the bullet holes in the wall.
HOTEL TIP: **Leeuwenbrug ★★★**, Koornmarkt 16 (**T** 015 214 7741; www.leeuwenbrug.nl) is friendly, canalside, and central.

Bebop

Kromstraat 33 · **T** 015 213 5210
www.jazzcafebebop.nl
Closed Su; Fr from 16.00; Sa from 15.00; others from 19.00

Down a narrow alley, this is a dimly lit laid-back jazz café with a small beer garden at the back. Photos of musicians adorn the walls, and brass instruments dangle from the ceiling, as does a pair of skis. Did these belong to Dizz-ski Gillespie we wonder? Background music sometimes comes from cassettes (if unfamiliar with that term, ask your parents). Peanuts only – hepcats need no food. The best among the 50-odd beers are among the half-dozen guests.

Belvédère

Beestenmarkt 8 · **T** 015 212 3297
www.bbcbelvedere.nl
Sa from 10.00; Su from 12.00; others from 11.00

This popular corner joint is the beeriest option
on lively Beestenmarkt, a square crammed
with terraces in summer. The high-ceilinged
mock-old light brown café has antique bric-
a-brac casually strewn about. Lunches and
dinners are served – the latter coming with beer
recommendations. The 45 beers are entirely
Belgian, but the Trappist range is not bad.

Doerak

Vrouwjuttenland 17 · **T** 06 4569 4928
www.cafedoerak.nl
Sa from 12.00; Su from 15.00; others from 16.00

Airy corner café with big windows looking
onto an adjacent canal, beside which is a
terrace. Empty Westvleteren crates are a
common sight in Benelux beer pubs, but here
they are a statement of intent, used to
decorate the bar. Food stops at snacks, but
170+ beers will feed your soul. Dutch brewers
abound, including De Eem, Emelisse, and
Jopen, and Dupont features among the
Belgians. While the permanent range is excellent, the guests can steal the show – London's
The Kernel was among them on our last visit.

Doerak, Delft

Klomp

Binnenwatersloot 5 · **T** 015 212 3810
www.bierhuisdeklomp.nl
Daily from 16.00

Delft's oldest bar, the Clog, dates from 1652.
We would recommend visiting even if the
beer list was rubbish – which it is not. The
front bar is candlelit and wooden, and the
whole room creaks every time anyone gets up.
A snug behind is smaller and lighter. At the rear
is a Golden Age scullery, with brick floors and
tiled walls, conjuring up images of Vermeer.
Snacks only. The 50 beers include Kompaan,
and Klein Duimpje's historical series brewed for
Bierhistorie Delft. There are also 35 jenevers.

Klooster, Delft

Klooster

Vlamingstraat 2 · **T** 015 212 1013
www.trappistenlokaal.nl
Sa from 14.00; others from 16.00

The Cloister, a lovely street corner local, has a
micro terrace and a macro beer list that is among
the best in the country. Beer memorabilia is
everywhere. No food but dinner in the adjacent
restaurant (Th-Mo only 17.30-22.00) is good. At
the last count the list was at 320+, available in a
newspaper-style menu or scattered around the
room on chalkboards, and reading like a who's who
of international craft brewing, with numerous
Scandinavian, US, British, and other visitors.
Dutch brews comprise a good chunk of the total,
with no fewer than 30 from De Molen alone.
The single malt range is none too shabby either.

Koperen Kat

Schieweg 15-H · **T** 06 4212 3398
www.koperenkat.nl
Closed Mo-Th; others 14.00–20.00

Brewery tap in an old cable factory, a 5-minute walk from Delft Zuid station. There is a terrace in summer, and the large interior is warmed by a wood-burning hearth in winter. Free nibbles become more elaborate on the first Sunday of each month, when there is also live music. Around 5 house beers are served, both on tap and in bottles.

Locus Publicus

Brabantse Turfmarkt 67 · **T** 015 213 4632
www.locuspublicus.nl
Su from 12.00; others from 11.00

This cramped and popular one-room brown café gets narrow at the back, where it is akin to sitting in a train carriage. At busy times it may be elbow to elbow. If you can find space, the terrace out front offers respite. Inside, beer memorabilia adorns every available inch of wall and ceiling. Food is snacks, toasties and rolls. The 170+ beers lean heavily Belgian, with a fair smattering of lambics. Amsterdam's 't IJ and Klein Duimpje's Bierhistorie Delft creations keep the home fires burning.

Proeflokaal

Gasthuislaan 36 · **T** 015 212 4922
www.proeflokaal-delft.nl
Mo-Th from 16.00; Fr-Su from 12.00

Large canalside brown café in a modern brick building - smoke-stained polystyrene ceilings suggest a 1970s origin. Two sitting areas are wrapped around a central bar. The one decked out with football scarves shows live games on TV. Photos and posters of rock bands adorn the other. Snacks include 'English pies'. The list of 100 beers is far shorter than in days of yore, but the selection remains good, with Kompaan and Emelisse among the Dutch, and several UK and US imports there too.

Waag

Markt 11 · **T** 015 213 0393
www.de-waag.nl
Su&Mo 11.00–24.00; others from 10.00

The beautiful stone-façaded 17th-century weigh house has a grand terrace behind the even older town hall. Inside is a brick-floored bar and kitchen surrounded on three sides by mezzanine seating. High above is a blackened oak beam ceiling. A full pub lunch and dinner menu is available. Strictly speaking the 35 beers do not warrant a full entry, but get one because 10+ change on a seasonal basis, and may feature both De Molen and interesting US imports.

Waag, Delft

OTHER DELFT BEER VENUES:

Modern **Huszar** (Hooikade 13 - **T** 015 262 6562 - www.huszar.nl - *daily 10.00–24.00*), in a waterside industrial building south of the centre, stocks 30+ beers with a Dutch focus.

BEER TO GO: **Flink Gegist** (Oosteinde 227 - **T** 015 7851308 - www.flinkgegist.nl - *Closed Mo&Tu; Fr 12.00–21.00; Sa 10.00–18.00; others 12.00–18.00*) stocks 700+ beers from around the world.

DEN HAAG

Den Haag CS & Den Haag HS

Officially known as 's Gravenhage, and to English speakers as The Hague, Den Haag (pop. 506,000) is the nation's centre of government but not its capital city – Amsterdam does that. The royal family maintains a residence here, as do many multinational companies and it is where you will find the countless foreign embassies, being the political hub.

Despite its size, it can seem oddly quiet at times. It is not suffocated with tourists and bicycles like Amsterdam, and nor does it have the metropolis feel of Rotterdam. Indeed it is quite a pleasant place, even if most visitors are here on business and fail to notice.

Two wildly different art galleries are worth your time. For grand Old Masters by Vermeer and Rembrandt, visit the Mauritshuis (www.mauritshuis.nl). Down the road is Escher in het Paleis (www.escherinhetpaleis.nl), filled with the mind-bending graphics of M.C. Escher, whose head-spinning drawings are recommended to be seen before rather than after a session in the pub. Alternatively, if on a short visit just head to Madurodam (www.madurodam.nl), a unique permanent exhibition of virtually every important Dutch building or monument, shrunk to 1:25 scale models.
HOTEL TIP: stay in Delft.

De La Gare

Nieuwe Schoolstraat 13A · **T** 070 744 6255
www.delagare.nl
Closed Mo; others from 15.00

A bar stripped bare, with a terrace on a quiet square two blocks behind the opulent Hotel des Indes. The minimalist interior goes for bare walls, and a ceiling with exposed ventilation ducts and I-beams. Snacks only. The beer menu is the rows of bottles on the back wall. There are 170. Good Dutch range. The whole is greater than the sum of its parts.

The Fiddler, Den Haag

Fiddler

Riviervismarkt 1 · **T** 070 365 1955
www.fiddler.nl
Mo from 17.00; others from 12.00

A large British pub and brewery tap. Wood dominates, including upturned casks used as tables. The brewery is in a side room, and after lying dormant for years was resurrected in 2012 to produce cask-conditioned house ales. Food (until 22.00 Su-Th, 01.00 Fr&Sa) is British pub grub, pre-gastro, with fish&chips and all-day breakfasts. Even without the 5 regular house ales on regulation handpulls, the 180+ list would make it unmissable. The bottled range features numerous UK and US imports, and a small but growing Dutch range.

Huppel the Pub

Oude Molstraat 21 · **T** 070 360 9113
www.dehuppel.nl
Daily from 16.00

Friendly split-level brown café on a narrow shopping street. Food is toasties and snacks. Dutch options among the 45 beers include De Leckere, Jopen, and De Eem. The last also brewed the hoppy house Huppel Blond (6%). The whisky range is outstanding, with 100+ single malts – available by taster plank.

Paas

Dunne Bierkade 16a · **T** 070 360 0019
www.depaas.nl
Daily from 15.00

Just north of HS station, with a canalside terrace, Den Paas is a long-established, light-brown beer café and drinking institution.

Where to find beer · South Holland

...aas, Den Haag

White-tiled walls and marble-topped tables make a change from wood. Food is snacks only. The beer list hovers around 180, with Emelisse, De Molen and Maximus making increasing inroads. There are several German and UK imports too and the usual Belgians, as well as 25 jenevers and 25 single malts.

Rootz

Grote Marktstraat 14 · **T** 070 363 9988
www.rootz.nl
Daily from 10.00

Popular grand café with a modern terrace near Grote Markt. The spacious interior is a former coach house, and retains some 'old chic': brick walls, beamed ceilings, candlelit tables, and chalkboard beer menus. There is a second near-identical dining room above. Food is served 11.00–23.00. The 80 list is mainly Belgian and strong on Trappists and abbey beers. Be warned that things get loud at weekends after 22.00, when it becomes Club Rootz.

OTHER **DEN HAAG** BEER VENUES:
In the former butter market, atmospheric **Boterwaag** (Grote Markt 10 - **T** 070 365 9686 - *daily from 10.00*) has high ceilings, brick floors and around 30 beers.

BEER TO GO: Expat Brit owner Dean Southall holds tastings and brewing demonstrations in his shop, **ABC Beers** (Korte Koediefstraat 5 - **T** 06 3830 4481 - www.abcbeers.nl - *Closed Mo&Tu; Sa 12.00–18.00; Su 14.00–18.00; others 12.00–19.00*), which stocks 200+ well-chosen and mostly Dutch beers.

DEN HAAG (Scheveningen)

The unpronounceable northern and coastal suburb of Den Haag functions almost as a separate town, and is a major beach resort. Take Tram 1 from central Den Haag, or Tram 11 from HS station.

Brouwcafé

Dr. Lelykade 28 · **T** 070 354 0970
www.hetbrouwcafe.nl
Th-Sa from 11.00; others 11.00–23.30

Modern harbourside brewpub with a large terrace. The bar area has the brewery on one side, and a raised seating area on the other. Lunches and full dinners are served 12.00–22.30; snacks all day. The 80+ beers include 12 taps, of which 3 or 4 are from the house. There is always at least one Dutch guest on tap, with Emelisse and De Molen featuring in the bottled range. There are also several 75cl bottles, some of them cellar aged.

Brouwcafé, Den Haag (Scheveningen)

Rootz at the Harbour

Dr. Lelykade 33-37 · **T** 070 355 8800
www.rootzharbour.nl
Daily from 11.00

Sister of the city centre original. Despite the
similarity in address between this and the
previous entry, they are a 10-minute hike
apart, at opposite ends of a massive harbour.
This barn-like place – with a central bar, and a
mezzanine above – occupies part of a refurb-
ished fish auction house. Rear windows and
a long terrace overlook the old dock, which
is now a yachting marina. The food menu
(11.00-23.00) runs from snacks to steaks via
mussels. Standouts among the 80 mainly
Belgian beers are St Bernardus and Het Anker.

DORDRECHT

22km SE of Rotterdam off A16 exit 21
Dordrecht

Large town (pop. 119,000) which has used its
location by a great river to trade around the
globe for centuries. Its central streets and
canals retain an old-world feel. Things nearly
came splashing to a halt in 1421 when a flood
inundated much of the city – a stained-glass
window in the wonky-towered Grote Kerk
commemorates this.

De Tijd

Voorstraat 170 · **T** 078 613 3997
www.detijd.nu
*Closed Tu; Fr 15.00-02.00; Sa 14.00-02.00;
Su 15.00-24.00; others 16.00-24.00*

One-room café with a small terrace, and a rare
example of a Dutch beer institution presided
over by a landlady, the charmingly indomit-
able and knowledgeable Corinne Smeijer.
The building's stepped gable façade dates
from 1603, although it only became a beer
pub in 1988. The pleasingly scruffy interior
features marble-topped tables. Food runs to
snacks, soups, uitsmijters, and occasionally
beer stew. The 150+ beers count Jopen, 't IJ
and La Trappe among a largely Belgian cast.

GORINCHEM

37km ESE of Rotterdam off A15 exit 27
Gorinchem

Attractive old town (pop. 35,000) filled with
narrow cobbled streets.

Keizer

Keizerstraat 14 · **T** 0183 634661
www.cafedekeizer.nl
Daily 16.00-02.00

Contentedly shabby boozer on a side street,
just east of the centre. There are raised
wooden booths down one aide, and
entertainment in the form of a pool table,
dartboards, table football and a piano.
A collection of road and station signs is
littered about, while the giant wall clock
came from Feyenoord's football stadium.
Food is nibbles and toasties, except for
Thursday night's weekly special. The 75
beers are mostly Belgian. There is also
a wide choice of bourbon and whisky.

De Tijd, Dordrecht

De Tijd, Dordrecht

GOUDA

24km NE of Rotterdam off A12 exit 11
🚉 Gouda

Vehicle-unfriendly small city (pop. 71,000) that is home to the nation's best known dairy product. There is a cheese market on the main square every Thursday morning, with men in fancy dress rearranging piles of orange wax-coated wheels for tourists to photograph, we suspect at the behest of an international food group. The giant wedding cake that is the 15th century town hall makes a great backdrop. The cheese is not made in town, but on surrounding farms. What Gouda does make includes clay pipes, candles and syrup waffles, mostly not as photogenic.
HOTEL TIP: **Utrechtsche Dom ★★,** Geuzenstraat 6 (**T** 0182 528833; www. hotelgouda.nl) is central, small, and friendly.

Central

Markt 23 · **T** 0182 512576
www.grandcafecentral.nl
Fr&Sa 09.00–00.30; Su 10.00–23.00; Th 09.00–24.00; others 09.00–23.00

This long-standing café with a terrace on the square first opened in 1916. The rearmost of its three rooms has large murals said to be the missing link between Art Nouveau, Art Deco and De Stijl, and the most intact examples of their kind. They were created in 1924 by Pieter den Besten, who also designed Amsterdam's Tuschinski Theater. A full food menu is available. The 40 Belgian beers are standard, but the list is easily the best in town.
BEER TO GO: **Drankenservice Gouda** (Willem en Marialaan 22 – **T** 0182 580499 – www.drankenservicegouda.nl – *shut Su; others 09.00–18.00*), is a cramped off-licence east of the station, with a decent Dutch selection among its 300+ beers.

HILLEGOM

12km SSW of Haarlem on N208
🚉 Hillegom (2 km NW of town)

Small town (pop. 20,000) among the bulb-fields. From mid-March to mid-May the nearby Keukenhof gardens (www.keukenhof.nl) are home to 7 million tulips, and almost as many tourists.

Klein Duimpje

Hyacintenlaan 2A · **T** 0252 531186
www.kleinduimpje.nl
Closed Mo-Th; Fr&Sa 13.00–20.00; Su 13.00–18.00

Brewery tap in a semi-rural industrial building reached by taking bus 50 from Haarlem or Leiden (or 361 from Schiphol or Noordwijk) to Hillegom Steenfabriek. It is 200 m north from the stop, behind the petrol station. The kit is visible through glass. The bar is modern and functional with little decoration. Bar snacks only, some of which are made with beer. Five or 6 house beers are served on tap, and up to 20 in bottles. There are tasting planks, plus bottles for takehome.

KRIMPEN AAN DEN IJSSEL

9km E of Rotterdam on N210

Sleepy Rotterdam satellite (pop. 29,000), reached by buses 97, 193, 194, 195 or 196 from Capelsebrug Metro station.

Lansingh

van Ostadelaan 4a · **T** 0180 550535
www.eetcafedelansingh.nl
Sa 09.30-18.00; Su 10.00-18.00; Mo 15.00-24.00; others 09.00-24.00

The café of the local swimming baths, 200m SE from the bus station, so do not expect grand. You can access it without a ticket, though the faint whiff of chlorine hangs in the air and an interior window looks out at the pool. Otherwise, this is a faux brown café. Snacks, toasties, pancakes, and some chicken-based mains are available. The 70+ beers orientate towards Belgium, but there are standouts such as Dupont.

LEIDEN

16km NE of Den Haag off A44 exit 8

Leiden

University city (pop. 120,000) with plenty of old streets and canals, with even a few intact city gates. In 1620 it was home to a group of English Puritans who had sought refuge from their immoral homeland. Eventually deciding that the Netherlands was no better, they set sail for a new life, returning to England on the unseaworthy Speedwell, which they switched in Plymouth for the Mayflower and on arrival in New England became known as the Pilgrim Fathers.

It is said that a mere decade later, local physician Franciscus Sylvius became the first person to flavour grain alcohol with juniper and give the world jenever, or gin, a story only spoiled by the fact he was not born for another century and jenever is known to have existed in Flanders two centuries earlier. But that is strong drink for you.

HOTEL TIP: **Mayflower** ★★★, Beestenmarkt 2 (**T** 071 514 2641; www.hotelmayflower.nl) enjoys a prime central spot.

Lemmy's

Morsstraat 24 · **T** 071 512 6402
www.biercafe.nl
Sa&Su from 14.00; others from 17.00

One-room wooden-floored rock and blues bar with photos of music stars on the walls (yes, including that Lemmy). Beyond that it is a rough and ready place with few airs and graces. There are a few tables, but it is mostly standing room only. No food. De Molen, Jopen and local Leidsch are found among 80 mainly Belgian beers, along with a few US and UK imports.

Olivier

Hooigracht 23 · **T** 071 512 2444
www.cafe-olivier.be
Daily from 12.00

Built in 1892 by Franciscan sisters, this was originally a hospital before it became part of a Belgian-themed pub chain. There is a grand wood-panelled bar area at the front, and a

dining room behind. Food (until 22.00) is Belgian, with mussels and Gents waterzooi (braised chicken and potatoes in a creamy broth). No prizes for guessing where the 60 beers originate.

*OTHER **LEIDEN** BEER VENUES:*

The lovely **Bonte Koe** (Hooglandsekerkkoorsteeg 13 – **T** 071 514 1094 – www.cafedebontekoe.net – *Sa from 12.30; Su from 13.30; others from 16.00*) has tiled murals with an Art Nouveau bovine theme, originally intended as a butcher's shop, though it never was. English pub **North End** (Noordeinde 55 – **T** 071 512 1541 – www.north-end.nl – *Mo from 17.00; Tu-We from 16.00; others from 12.00*) has standard beers but 230 single malts.

BEER TO GO: **Bierwinkel** (Hartesteeg 9 – **T** 071 566 5770 – www.bierwinkel-leiden.nl – *Closed Su&Mo; Sa 10.00-18.00; Th 12.00-21.00; others 12.00-18.30*), a cramped central shop with 600+ beers and 200 whiskies. **Special Bierpakket** (Zeemanlaan 22B – **T** 071 240 0285 – www. speciaalbierpakket.nl – *Closed Su; Sa 08.30-17.30; others 09.00-18.00*) stocks 500+ beers with a good Dutch selection and an online store.

MAASSLUIS

17km W of Rotterdam off A20 exit 7

Maassluis

Small waterside town (pop. 32,000), once a fishing and tugboat port, now home to Rotterdam commuters.

Oporto

Govert van Wijnkade 12 · **T** 010 592 8906
www.oporto.nl
Closed Mo (Sep-Apr); Tu from 20.00; We&Th from 17.00; Fr&Sa from 15.00; others 15.00-20.00

Friendly harbourside corner pub with a terrace on one side. The brown interior has a raised seating area along one wall. Music comes courtesy of a vinyl record player. Snacks only, except for an evening main on Fridays – there is a pizzeria next door. This is the unofficial home of Raven Bone Hill, which leads an impressive Dutch contingent among the 70 beers.

BEER TO GO: Suburban off-licence
Zonneveld (Mesdaglaan 231 – **T** 010 591 3232
– www.uwtopslijter.nl – *Closed Su; Mo 13.00–
18.00; Fr 09.00–20.00; Sa 09.00–17.00; others
09.00–18.00*) stocks 300+ beers with a good
Dutch range.

NOORDWIJK

12km NNW of Leiden on N444

Former fishing port, now a seaside resort
(pop. 25,000). Technically the coast is
Noordwijk aan Zee, and inland Noordwijk-
Binnen. The biggest employer outside
tourism is ESTEC: the European Space
Agency's research and technology centre.
If it is European and connected with space
travel, it was probably designed here.

Harbourlights

Koningin Wilhelmina Boulevard 9
T 071 361 7705
www.harbourlights.nl
Su from 12.00; others from 16.00

Modern seaside café, although you cannot
see the water from its terrace as a dune
blocks the view. 'Definitely the best pub in
town' says the sign, and we agree. Large TV
screens give it a sports-bar feel but the
dominant theme is nautical. Food is all day
on Sundays 17.00–22.00 on others, with
fish&chips reflecting its origins as a British
pub. Emelisse, Maximus and Oedipus put up
a good Dutch showing among the 55 beers.
Stocks 25 single malts.

*Boudewijn,
Rotterdam*

ROTTERDAM

Rotterdam CS & Rotterdam Blaak

The Netherlands' second city (pop. 620,000)
is an industrial, commercial and maritime hub.
The Port of Rotterdam, including the city
docks and Europoort, runs west to the North
Sea, is the largest and busiest in Europe,
covering 100 sq km.

The city was badly damaged in World
War II, and post-war policy has been to get
top architects in to build high and build flashy.
This gives it more of a metropolis feel than
anywhere else in the country. Recent high-
rise developments have led to it being dubbed
Manhattan-on-the-Maas. A few areas, most
notably Delfshaven, have escaped unscathed
and have retained their historic nature.

Culturally, the Museum Boijmans Van
Beuningen (www.boijmans.nl) has a collection
of fine art the equal of anything in the
country. For a bird's eye view of the city, go
up the 185m Euromast (www.euromast.nl).

A healthy clutch of decent beer cafés
supports the big city reputation, even if one
former great, Cambrinus, has closed its doors.
HOTEL TIP: **Bazar★★**, Witte de Withstraat 16
(**T** 010 206 5151; www.bazarrotterdam.nl)
is a quirky place with rooms decorated in
global styles.

Boudewijn ①

Nieuwe Binnenweg 53A-B · **T** 010 436 3562
www.bbcboudewijn.nl
Su 12.00–24.00; Mo 16.00–24.00; others from 11.00

Large café with terrace at the front and beer
garden at the back. At the rear it goes split
level with a subterranean seating area and a
mezzanine for diners. Belgian food is served
until 22.00; snacks all day. The best Dutch
branch of the Belgian Beer Café chain, it
dares to go off-piste with its 100+ beer
choices. Experimenters from south of the
border such as Dochter van de Korenaar,
Alvinne and Struise all get a look in, and it
even dares leave Belgium with La Trappe,
and a couple of German and US imports.

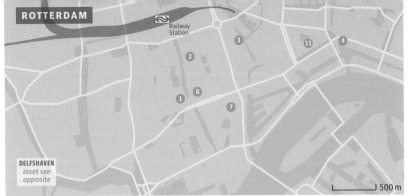
ROTTERDAM

Railway Station

DELFSHAVEN
inset see opposite

500 m

Doelen

Schouwburgplein 52 · **T** 010 414 8688
www.doelencafe.nl
Daily from 11.00

Modern theatre café with a terrace, on a
large square. Music is live jazz on Tuesdays,
often involving the grand piano that lives in
the bar. Food, prepared in an open kitchen is
all-day tapas, bar lunches, or dinner, served in
a restaurant area that occupies half the room.
The 40 beers are kept interesting by the
inclusion of half a dozen from local Pelgrim.

Haagse Bluf

Haagse Veer 90 · **T** 010 433 1405
www.haagsebluf.eu
Su 14.00–20.00; others from 11.00.

An L-shaped café with a canalside terrace at
the rear. The interior's false wood ceiling is
reminiscent of a 1970s bistro. Some tables
have glass tops with jenever bottles
displayed beneath. Food includes a variety of
stamppots – one pot meals containing mashed
potato, vegetables and smoked sausage.
Snacks are available all day. The 40+ beers
are mainly Belgian, with some German.

Locus Publicus

Oostzeedijk 364 · **T** 010 433 1761
www.locus-publicus.com
Daily from 16.00

Open since 1988, this is one of the Netherlands' longest-standing and most respected
beer cafés. The one-room pub is popular and
can get crowded at night. A wood fire is lit in
cooler months. Several tiled wall friezes
depict farming scenes and the growing of
spices – the 1904 building was a grocery and

amazingly made it through the war
undamaged. The only food today is bar
snacks. The 250+ list includes an excellent
range of Belgian, UK, German and US imports,
with the Dutch thus far relatively neglected.

Oude Sluis

Havenstraat 7 · **T** 010 477 3068
www.cafedeoudesluis.nl
Sa&Su from 14.00; others from 12.00

A determinedly scruffy local with a small
terrace, by Delfshaven. Setting the scene are
seldom-swept red concrete floors, marble
tabletops, and scuffed wooden walls dominated by bas reliefs featuring scenes of revelry
in a bygone age. The smoke-blackened ceiling
may once have had something painted on it.
A conservatory at the back, with the best
canalside views in town, is the smoking room.
Lunch is served until 15.00; snacks until 19.00
(not Mo). The landlord likes propping up his
own bar, but you should get served eventually.
While his 40 beers are Belgian and lack
standouts, the pub alone is reason to come.

Oude Sluis, Rotterdam

TTERDAM: Delfshaven

50 m

Reijngoud, Rotterdam

Pelgrim

Aelbrechtskolk 12 · **T** 010 477 1189
www.pelgrimbier.nl
Closed Mo&Tu; others 12.00–24.00

Delfshaven brewery tap beside the Pilgrim Father's church. This building is where the Puritans met up before leaving for America in 1620 – there is a passenger list from the Mayflower on the wall. The brewery is to the left, the café to the right, and there is a terrace out front. The bar has a low wood-beamed ceiling and chiming clocks. Simple lunches and hearty dinners are served until 22.00. Around 6 house tap beers are available. If unsure, go for the tasting plank. You can also buy bottles to take home. This is the nation's only brewery with a wedding licence.

Reijngoud

Schiedamse Vest 148 · **T** 010 414 6050
www.proeflokaalreijngoud.nl
Daily from 10.00

Opened in 2012, this relative new kid is a modern street corner bar with a large terrace, just west of the Maritime Museum. The light and airy interior has high ceilings and minimalist furnishings, with a mezzanine at the rear. Food starts with breakfast and goes on until 22.00; with snacks all day. The 120+ list is arguably the most adventurous in town. Half the 16 taps are guests. Emelisse, De Molen and local brewers feature regularly, as do UK and US imports.

Sijf

Oude Binnenweg 115 · **T** 010 433 2610
www.sijf.nl
Daily from 10.00

Chic corner café with a terrace, on a busy shopping street. A front bar area has high red-painted ceilings and splits into an upstairs-downstairs two-level sitting area at the rear. Food starts with breakfast and ends with various 'unlimited' option dinners that change through the week – spare ribs Tuesday, satay Wednesday and so on – until 22.00 (23.00 Fr&Sa). The 40+ beers include Jopen, and Left Hand from the US.

Vanouds 't Kraantje

Schiedamseweg 2A · **T** 010 477 0153
www.biertapperij.nl
Daily from 12.00

Grand old corner local with a terrace, by Delfshaven. The wooden interior is brightened by Art Deco details in the stained glass windows. Beer and jenever bottles fill windowsills, while a billiards table takes pride of place. We see little evidence of food. The 40 beers feature local Bijdehand on tap, plus Van Eecke and Het Anker from Belgium.

OTHER **ROTTERDAM** BEER VENUES:
Ooievaar 10 (Havenstraat 11 – **T** 010 476 9190 – www.cafedeooievaar.nl – *daily from 10.00*) is a pretty brown café, two doors from the Oude Sluis.

BEER TO GO: Outstanding **Bier en Zo** 🔟 (Hoogstraat 54a – **T** 010 411 2496 – www.bierenzo.nl – *Closed Su&Mo; Sa 10.00–17.00; others 11.00–17.30*) stocks 1,000+ brews, with quality in all areas. They also run a web shop.

SASSENHEIM
10km NNE of Leiden off A44 exit 3
🚉 Sassenheim, 1 km S of town

Small commuter town (pop. 15,000).

Twee Wezen
Oude Haven 2 · **T** none
www.cafede2wezen.nl
Fr&Sa from 13.00; others from 15.00

Lively corner café with a terrace on the small main square. The ceiling is dominated by a large colourful graffiti painting. Boisterous music, and snacks only for food. The 45 beers are predominantly Belgian, led by Trappists, but there are a few Dutch options, and plenty of guests on tap.

SCHIEDAM
5km W of Rotterdam
🚉 Schiedam Centrum

Mid-sized town (pop. 76,000), effectively a suburb of Rotterdam, known for its ridiculously tall windmills. Of the original 20 only six remain, of which one can be visited (www.schiedamsemolens.nl). They were used to grind malt for the city's jenever distilleries, about which more can be learned in the National Jenever Museum (www.jenevermuseum.nl).

Weeshuis
Lange Achterweg 18 · **T** 010 426 1657
www.biertapperij.nl
Su from 14.00; others from 12.00

The Orphanage is a tiny ABT café with a tiny terrace on a tiny square, just off the main shopping drag. Steins and musical instruments dangle for décor but we are not falling for the old €2 coin superglued to the floor routine. No food beyond nuts.

The 60+ beers include Bijdehand's Provenier, first commissioned for the house, but now available elsewhere. The good range of jenevers befits the town's history.

UITHOORN
18km SSW of Amsterdam on N201

Small sleeper town (pop. 28,000).

BEER TO GO: **Schans** (Schans 17–21 – **T** 0297 522106 – www.schansbier.nl – *Closed Su–Tu; Sa 09.00–17.00; others 11.00–18.00*), run by the like-named brewery, stocks 300+ brews, though their own sell out the quickest.

VLAARDINGEN
9km W of Rotterdam off A20 exit 8&9
🚉 Vlaardingen Centrum

Rotterdam commuter suburb (pop. 71,000), once a thriving fishing port. Evidence of its past is the picturesque boat-lined harbour stretching north from the Maas into the heart of town.

Antonius
Hoogstraat 21 · **T** 010 434 8811
www.bierlokaalantonius.nl
Closed Mo; Su 16.00–23.00; others from 16.00

A friendly city centre local with a terrace, on the high street. White walls dotted with beer enamels, white ceilings, and a central brass light fitting add an understated elegance, as does the ancient cash register on the dark stained wooden bar counter. Dishes on the full dinner menu have beer pairings. Belgians dominate the 50+ beer list, among them a couple of specially commissioned Antonius house brews. Also available is local Vlaardingse, hardly a surprise since the brewery is 50m away on the same street, and the brewers drink here.

OTHER VLAARDINGEN BEER VENUES:
Friendly **Oude Stoep** (Smalle Havenstraat 5 – **T** 010 434 7502 – www.oudestoep.nl – *shut Tu; others from 14.00*) has 30 beers, plus plentiful jenevers and single malts.

Utrecht

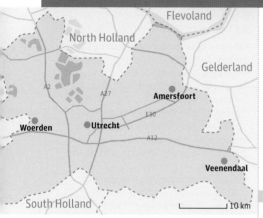

LARGEST CENTRES: **Utrecht** (324,000), **Amersfoort** (150,000), **Veenendaal** (63,000), **Zeist** (62,000), **Nieuwegein** (61,000)

MORE INFORMATION: www.visit-utrecht.com (city); www.utrechtyourway.nl

BREWERIES: **Drie Ringen**, *Amersfoort*; **de Leckere**, *Utrecht (De Meern)*; **Maximus**, *Utrecht (De Meern)*; **Oudaen**, *Utrecht*

OTHER BEER MAKERS: **Duits & Lauret**, *Vleuten*; **Eem**, *Amersfoort*; **Hommeles**, *Houten*; **Rooie Dop**, *Utrecht*

The Netherlands' smallest province is by no means the least beery. Most of the 1,250,000 population live in and around its eponymous main city. The bishopric of Utrecht was founded in 722 AD by Northumbrian monk and missionary Willibrord, patron saint of the Netherlands and Luxembourg, and in the Middle Ages, was among the most powerful city states in Europe.

The east has remained largely forested, as its soil was not good enough to support cultivation. Elsewhere, water dominates. The south is criss-crossed by canals and rivers. The north has manmade lakes formed by peat cutting.

There are no historical breweries – the current longest-running, Drie Ringen, was founded in 1989 – but Utrecht has a growing brewing culture, celebrated each May in the Utrechts Bierfestival, to which only local brewers are invited.

AMERSFOORT
22km ENE of Utrecht off A28 exits 5–8
⇌ Amersfoort

Besides Utrecht, the province's only other major city (pop. 150,000). An important railway hub, the station is 1 km west of the medieval centre. One of the most impressive sights in the latter is the 15th-century Koppelpoort, a combined land and water gate.

Amersfoort's nickname is Keistad (Boulder City), derived from a 9-ton lump of rock found out on the moors. In 1661 a local landowner bet a friend he could persuade the townsfolk to drag it into town. He won by bribing 400 people with beer and pretzels. The stone now sits on a pedestal on Arnhemsestraat as a monument to human folly.
HOTEL TIP: **Tabaksplant ★★★**, Coninckstraat 15 (**T** 033 472 9797; www.tabaksplant.nl) is friendly and central.

Drie Ringen
Kleine Spui 18 · **T** 033 465 6575
www.dedrieringen.nl
Closed Mo-We (all year) & Th (Nov-Mar); Fr-Su 13.00–19.00; others 15.00–21.00

Brewery tap enjoying a scenic canalside location by the imposing Koppelpoort gate. The bright interior is dominated by the copper brewing kettles. Snacks include free boiled eggs – help yourself. Besides 3 house beers among the 8 taps, there are several from Gulpener.

Drie Ringen, Amersfoort, Utrecht

Lobbes

Hof 10a · **T** 033 461 0637
www.cafe-lobbes.nl
Sa from 11.00; Su from 13.00; others from 16.00

Wood-laden one-room brown café with beer enamels on the walls and a terrace on a lively square. The yellowed ceiling betrays decades of smoking. Snacks and toasties are available all day. The 60+ beers are not well publicised though a menu will appear if you ask. Most are Belgian, with a few local surprises such as Maximus.

Markzicht

Lieve Vrouwekerkhof 2a · **T** 033 448 0767
Daily from 12.00

The Market View is the beeriest option on Lieve Vrouwekerkhof, one of the city's nightlife hubs. There is a terrace on the square. Inside there is wood everywhere, broken up by mirrors, beer enamels and party photos. Lunches are served until 17.00; snacks all day. The 50+ beer list is solid, without being extraordinary, and does feature local Drie Ringen.

Zomaar

Appelmarkt 18 · **T** 06 5423 6946
www.cafe-zomaar.nl
Closed Mo; Tu-We 12.00–19.00; Th 12.00–24.00;
Fr 11.00–24.00; Sa 11.00–22.00; Su 14.00–19.00

On a small square with a smaller terrace, this friendly one-room café has a wood-beamed ceiling and a gas-effect fire. Music is provided via vinyl albums – mainly Dutch crooners in our experience, opinions differing on whether that is a good thing. Food includes toasties, sausage rolls and apple pie. The 65 beers include several from local De Eem and De Leckere, and a few in 75cl bottles.

*OTHER **AMERSFOORT** BEER VENUES:*

Lively corner café **Van Zanten** (Bloemendalsestraat 2 – **T** 033 479 0592 – www.cafevanzanten.nl – *daily from 11.00*) has Art Deco leanings, and 35 beers that are one step from a full entry.

UTRECHT

Utrecht CS

The provincial capital and the country's fourth largest city (pop. 324,000) after Rotterdam, Den Haag and Amsterdam. Before the ascendancy of the last of these in the Golden Age the great religious centre of Utrecht was the region's most important settlement.

Due to its strategic central position it remains a major transport hub. Half of all Dutch train lines pass through, and railway buffs should not miss the National Railway Museum (www.spoorwegmuseum.nl).

The most prominent building is the Domtoren, the Netherlands' highest church tower. It is a city icon, and the issue of whether to allow any new skyscraper to surpass its 112m height always sparks arguments. Another unusual landmark is the canal snaking through the centre. The sides of Oudegracht are arranged on two levels, lower wharfside and upper streetside, each filled with café terraces in summer.

Arguably the two most famous Utrechters in history had radically different career paths, though each ended better known under a different name. In 1522, Adriaan Boeyens was elected Pope Adrian VI, the last non-Italian pontiff before John Paul II in 1978. More recently actress Sylvia Kristel made her name starring as Emmanuelle.

An ongoing redevelopment programme means you can expect disruption around the station until 2020.

Hotel tip: the words 'affordable' and 'central' are not comfortable bedfellows here. North of the centre is the more reasonable **Oorsprongpark** ★★, F.C. Dondersstraat 12 (**T** 030 271 6303; www.oorsprongpark.nl).

België

Oudegracht 196 · **T** 030 231 2666
Su&Mo from 13.00; others from 11.00

Long-standing Utrecht institution, just south of the Domtoren, with a couple of benches serving as a terrace. The lack of table service and barren décor give it a student vibe –

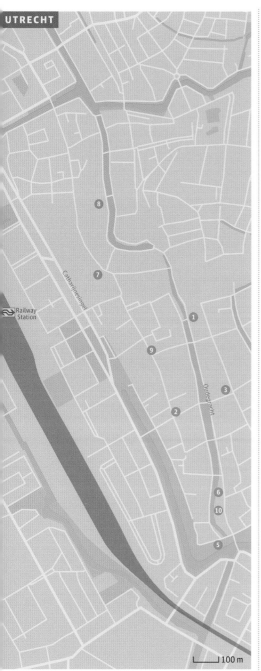

UTRECHT

a shark's head on the wall, a casually reclined full-sized plastic cow, and the equally life-sized Virgin Mary above the bar, adding style of sorts. Otherwise beer menus take pride of wall space. Lunch is served until 16.00; dinner and snacks until 20.30. Despite the name a large chunk of the 200+ beers are not Belgian, but Dutch, American, British or German. The house **Kamikaze IPA** is brewed locally by Maximus.

Derat

Lange Smeestraat 37 · **T** 030 231 9513
www.cafederat.nl
Daily from 14.00

Friendly corner café that is popular with the after-work crowd. Well-worn tables and an upright piano fill the small one-room bar; chamber music fills the air. Rat memorabilia is kept to a tasteful minimum. Snacks only for food. Amazingly, around half the 80+ beers are lambics and including rare imports from De Cam, Cantillon, and Drie Fonteinen. Other unusual offerings appear in 75cl bottles, and the four guest taps can be worth more than a look. The menu is hand-written on paper and pinned behind the bar. There is also a good range of single malt and single cask whiskies, as well as jenevers.

Derat, Utrecht

Drie Dorstige Herten

Lange Nieuwstraat 47 · **T** 030 888 4430
www.dedriedorstigeherten.nl
Closed Mo&Tu; others from 15.00

Opened in 2012 as a serious beer café, the welcoming Three Thirsty Harts is one of the shiniest jewels in the Dutch beer treasure box. One block east of Oudegracht and 200 m south of the Domtoren, this small, tiled-floor bar is filled with basic wooden furniture. Food is homemade cake, tapas, and other snacks. Of the 100+ beers, three-quarters are from small and mainly local Dutch breweries. Maximus always features on tap. The imports are no shirkers either, with some top names from the US and several great European brewing nations. They also stock a fine selection of wines and single malts.

Drie Dorstige Herten, Utrecht

Jan Primus

Jan van Scorelstraat 27–31 · **T** 030 251 4572
Daily from 15.00

Suburban corner café with a tiny terrace on a busy junction. It is a 15-minute walk east of the centre, or bus 4 to Prins Hendriklaan. The interior is comfortably battered, with big picture windows for watching traffic. A 1960s gas heater provides warmth. Besides beer enamels, a lone oar acts as token bric-a-brac. Food is snacks only. A once-great beer list has sadly atrophied, but the remaining 65 are worth checking out.

Jan Primus, Utrec

Ledig Erf

Tolsteegbrug 3 · **T** 030 231 7577
ledigerf.nl
Daily from 10.00

Bright, modern corner café with a terrace, on a small square at the southern end of Oudegracht. Colourful furnishings are a respite from brown, though a massive sepia group photo dominates one wall. Abstract paintings adorn others. Food is toasties, paninis and snacks. The 65 beers are solid, with Trappists to the fore, and feature locals such as De Leckere and De Eem.

Maximus, Utrecht

Lijn 4

Twijnstraat 3 · **T** 030 231 5481
www.cafelijn4.nl
Sa&Su from 14.00; others from 16.00

Trendy brown café on a narrow street just
south of the centre, with leather quilted
booths down one side, and views of the
Oudegracht through the back window.
Mirrors and a collection of black & white
photos fill the walls. Dinners run to spare
ribs and fondues; plus snacks. The 45 beers
throw in occasional pleasant surprises such
as Belgium's De Ranke.

Maximus

Pratumplaats 2A · **T** 06 8345 0013
www.brouwerijmaximus.nl
Closed Mo&Tu; Su 12.00–20.00; others 14.00–22.00

Modern out-of-town brewery tap. Take bus
26 to De Woerd, alight and continue ahead
to find it second on the left. There is a large
terrace in front. The interior has a comforting
unfinished appeal, with concrete floors,
plywood walls, and a packing crate bar fitting
in around the brewing kit. Every second
Wednesday at 18.30 you can reserve a place
at a communal 3-course dinner. Snacks only
on other days. The entire house beer range
is sold, on tap, in bottle and for take away.

Olivier

Achter Clarenburg 6 · **T** 030 236 7876
www.cafe-olivier.be
Su from 12.00; Mo from 11.00; others from 10.00

If you want to admire an impressive organ
whilst supping, this is the place. It is a former
church, with a small terrace on a shopping
street. Some elements of the 1860 interior
have been retained. Ceilings are at church
roof height. A beer-themed slideshow is
projected onto the wall, below a carved
statuette. Other adornments are less
ecclesiastical, including a child's scooter.
Simple lunches give way to a full Belgian
menu in the evening (until 22.00). The 80
beers are also Belgian-dominated, but there
are some from local Maximus.

Olivier, Utrecht

Oudaen

Oudegracht 99 · **T** 030 231 1864
www.oudaen.nl
Daily from 09.00

An unmissable castle-like structure in brick, the late 14th-century Stadskasteel Oudaen is now a well-established brewpub that hides its kit in the basement. Its canalside terrace spreads over two levels. The imposing bar area was a medieval banqueting hall, with high ceilings and windows bedecked with flowing curtains. Bar snacks stretch to lunch and dinner, with a more elegant French restaurant on the first floor. All four permanent brews are sold on tap, plus seasonals.

*OTHER **UTRECHT** BEER VENUES:*

Arthouse cinema **Springhaver** (9) (Springweg 50 – **T** 030 231 3789 – www.springhaver.nl – *daily from 11.30*) has a café serving 30 beers.

BEER TO GO: **Bert's Bierhuis** (10) (Twijnstraat 41 – **T** 030 234 1339 – www.bertsbierhuis.nl – *Closed Su; Mo 13.00–18.00, others 10.00–18.00*) is one of the Netherlands' great beer shops, stocking 800+ beers.

Oudaen, Utrecht

VEENENDAAL

35km E of Utrecht off A12 exit 23

Veenendaal

Conservative modern city (63,000).

Robert's Pub

J.G. Sandbrinkstraat 1a · **T** 0318 508866
www.robertspub.nl
Sa from 13.00; others from 14.00

Popular modern brown-café-cum-English pub, with a large terrace below a brick apartment building. There is a bilingual pub quiz every Wednesday at 20.00, and live music several times a month. Food is largely crisps. The 120 beers err towards safety, especially among the 14 taps, but Maallust and Jopen have been spotted among the bottles.

WOERDEN

22km W of Utrecht off A12 exit 14

Woerden

Provincial commuter town (pop. 35,000). Its moated castle hosts a bock beer festival in October.

Bierhuys

Van Oudheusdenstraat 3a · **T** 0348 418766
www.bierhuys.nl
Closed Mo&Tu; others from 14.00

Friendly one-room corner café with a terrace, on a residential street just west of the centre. The wood-laden interior has a gas hearth for winter nights. There are regular live music events, including open podium acoustic night twice a month. Main meals are served until 21.00; snacks all day. Among the 120 beers are a healthy selection of local and regional Dutch offerings. Two house beers, a blond and a brown are brewed by De Eem. Gevaarlijk gezellig – the sign on the wall – means dangerously convivial. It is not wrong.

Zeeland

There are not many breweries, but one is among the country's best.

LARGEST CENTRES: **Middelburg** (39,600), **Vlissingen** (33,000)

MORE INFORMATION: www.vvvzeeland.nl

BREWERIES: **Emelisse**, *Kamperland*; **Groese Zwaluw**, *Groede*; **Halve Maan**, *Hulst*; **Marckensteijn**, *Groede*

OTHER BEER MAKERS: **Bad Hair Brewing**, *Kapelle*; **La Fontaine**, *Sas van Gent*; **Peelander**, *Kerkwerve*

A relatively deserted province with a population of under 400,000. Nowhere else is the Netherlands' sometimes fraught relationship with the sea more obvious. Once a series of isolated islands in the tangled streams of the Schelde and Maas deltas, the dots have all been joined together – at least by bridges and dykes and in most cases by reclaimed land – though 30% of its potential area remains under water.

The region's vulnerability to the forces of nature was brought into focus in January 1953, when dykes burst during a storm, inundating everywhere and killing 1,800 people. In response, a massive line of sea defences was constructed, another of the modern world's great engineering marvels. For the full story on the Delta Works, visit Deltapark Neeltje Jans (www.neeltjejans.nl), part theme park, part engineering expo, where you can go inside a dam to get a close-up of the tidal flows gushing through the sluices.

The area south of the Schelde, Zeeuws-Vlaanderen, shares its land border with Belgium and used only to be connected to the rest of the Netherands by ferry, until the opening of the 6.6 km Westerschelde Tunnel in 2003.

GROEDE

15km SSW of Middelburg (by crow), 60 km (by road), on N675

Tiny village (pop. 1,100), closer to Bruges than anywhere in the Netherlands, with two breweries, each producing on a microscopic scale. During the Eighty Years War defensive dykes here were broken, and the village lay underwater and abandoned for 30 years.

HOTEL TIP: the **Natte Pi** ★★★ (Slijkstraat 1 – T 06 3041 6175; www.denattepij.nl) is an atmospheric 15-room inn on a historical museum street themed to recreate life in 1900.

Emelisse,
Kamperland

Drie Koningen

Markt 30 · **T** 0117 371511
www.dedriekoningen.com
Summer: daily from 10.00
Winter: Closed Mo&Tu; others from 11.00

The Three Kings is both a lovely café and the Marckensteijn brewery tap, with a terrace on a small square. Although resembling a traditional inn from the outside, the interior is modern, with the brewery on show behind glass at the rear. Breakfasts, lunches, and pancakes (until 17.00); dinners until 21.00; snacks all day. Homemade bread uses spent brewer's grain. At least 3 of Marckensteijn's 5 regular brews should be on tap, with 75cl bottles sometimes available to take away. The other beers are mostly industrial.

KAMPERLAND

20km ENE of Middelburg off N255

Small village (pop. 1,950) with a brewery that has earned a spot at the top table.
B&B TIP: **Pension Kamperland**, Veerweg 25 (**T** 06 5465 2587; bedandbreakfast-kamperland.nl) has four spacious studios.

Emelisse

Nieuweweg 7 · **T** 0113 370262
www.emelisse.nl
Closed Mo&Tu (Sep-Jun) & We&Th (Oct-Mar); others 12.00-24.00

Modern brewpub with a grassy rear terrace. The building is newly constructed to a 19th-century design. At the front is the copper brewing kit and at the back a stylish bar-

restaurant. Snacks, pancakes and full meals available until 21.00. Around 15-20 house beers are served, including 8 on taps that spell out the brewery name. The menu contains all the techie specs of each brew. Bottles are also sold to take away.

MIDDELBURG

Middelburg

Pretty provincial capital (pop. 39,600), dating back to the 9th century and retaining its medieval character. It was originally an island, fortified to protect the mainland against Viking raiders. Both the flamboyant Gothic town hall and the abbey are worth a look. The latter is home to the Zeeuws Museum (www.zeeuwsmuseum.nl). Lange Jan, a 91m church tower can be climbed for a panoramic view.
HOTEL TIP: **Mug** (below) – stay in the region's best café and cut down on travelling.

Mug

Vlasmarkt 54 · **T** 0118 614851
www.demug.nl
Closed Mo; Su 14.00-20.00; others from 14.00

The Midge is one of the Netherlands' longest-running beer cafés, with a small terrace 100 m west of the Markt. It opened in 1973 and forty years on remains a fine hostelry. Formed of two buildings knocked together, one dating from 1665, the other from 1751, it ends up a delightfully wonky warren of light brown wooden rooms filled with candlelit tables. A shop at the back (*13.00-17.30*) sells local produce, and there

Mug, Middelburg

are hotel rooms above. Dinners (17.30–22.30) are served in a rear dining room; all-day snacks are available elsewhere. The 150+ beers feature Schelde's Mug Bitter, originally developed by and brewed exclusively for here. Local Emelisse is also present, as is a small range of cellar-aged 75cl bottles.

OTHER **MIDDELBURG** BEER VENUES:

Beside the Lange Jan tower, music café **Desafinado** (Koorkerkstraat 1 – **T** 0118 640767 – www.desafinado.nl – Closed Mo; others from 11.00) has 30+ beers, plus food (12.00–14.40 & 17.30–21.30).

OOST-SOUBURG

5km SW of Middelburg off A58 exit 40
 Oost-Souburg

Small town (pop. 11,000) joined to Vlissingen.

BEER TO GO: **Souburg (Drank Gigant)** (Paspoortstraat 15–19 – **T** 0118 473833 – www.drankgigant.nl – Closed Su; Mo 12.00–18.00; Th 8.30–20.00; others 8.30–18.00) is a drinks warehouse with 400+ beers and as many whiskies, 500m east of the station.

SLUIS

23km SW of Middelburg by carrier pigeon, off N253

Tiny town (pop. 2,000) on the Belgian border in Zeeuws-Vlaanderen, the westernmost in the Netherlands. The nearest city is Bruges, and most visitors are Belgian. It is a cutesy place with a much-visited windmill and a reputation as a culinary hub.

Molen van Sluis

Nieuwstraat 26 · **T** 0117 461250
www.molenvansluis.nl
Closed Fr (Sep-Jun) & Th (mid-Nov to mid-Apr); others from 10.00

Tearoom built around the base of a 1739 smock mill – you can visit the workings, or sit on the terrace and watch the sails rotate. The mill gift shop opens out into an L-shaped café – the large diesel motor in the middle once provided back-up power. Simple tearoom dishes use bread made from flour milled here. More elaborate lunches are served 12.00–14.00 only. The 50 beers reflect the proximity to Belgium.

Molen van Sluis, Sluis

TERNEUZEN

34km SE from Middelburg via N62 (Westerschelde Tunnel)

Zeeuws-Vlaanderen town (pop. 24,100) on the Westerschelde estuary. The rest of the Netherlands is across 5 km of water, plied by giant ships heading for Antwerp. Its position at the end of the Ghent-Terneuzen Canal has made it the country's third-largest port. Its most famous resident was fictional: Captain Van der Decken cursed God and thus was condemned to sail the oceans aboard the doomed ship the Flying Dutchman, in Frederick Marryat's novel The Phantom Ship.

Vriendschap Terneuzen

Vriendschap

Noordstraat 1 · **T** 0115 612593
Daily 11.00–19.00

The Friendship is a brown café the like of which they make no more: a dilapidated building with peeling paint, now isolated in a sea of characterless modern constructions. It is classic old school with creaking floorboards, solid unyielding chairs, and tabletop carpets to absorb all spillages. It has a vague nautical theme, with model ships and ship's wheels, and some stuffed animals – a squirrel holds sway at the bar. The locals still play cards. Simple lunches until 14.00; snacks at other times. The 75 beers are mainly Belgian. We suspect the two house beers, Vliegende Hollander (Flying Dutchman) in dubbel and tripel – are from Van Steenberge.

*OTHER **TERNEUZEN** BEER VENUES:*
Bée (Noordstraat 85 – **T** 0115 696414 – hours not known) is a quirky joint with such a dense mass of brass and copper pots hanging from the ceiling that it could be transformed into an antiques shop.
BEER TO GO: **Kolijn** (Alvarezlaan 145 – **T** 0115 612450 – www.drankenhandelkolijn.nl – *Closed Su; Fr 08.30–21.00; Sa 09.00–17.00; others 08.30–18.00*) is a large off-licence with 300+ beers.

ZIERIKZEE

42km NE of Middelburg off N59

Characterful port town (pop. 10,500) with medieval charm.

Biet

Nieuwe Haven 141 · **T** 0111 413825
www.cafedebiet.nl
Summer: Th&Fr from 12.00; Sa from 10.00; Su 10.00–21.00;
others from 15.00.
Winter: Sa from 12.00; Su 12.00–21.00; others from 15.00

A local with a harbourside terrace. The 1645 building has been a café since the 19th century. A single bar lollops around both halves of a two-room interior. There is a Wurlitzer jukebox and billiard table, and an odd living room area on one side. A large brass mermaid dangles her assets over punters at the bar. On a rear wall are mural fragments depicting cherubs, thought to have been painted around 1920, protected behind glass. Porcelain beer pumps date from the same period. Lunches (10.00–15.00) include fish & chips. Snacks only after that. Beyond the 50 regular beers is a handful of cellared and over-date bottles to order at your own risk.

*OTHER **ZIERIKZEE** BEER VENUES:*
Modern **Werf** (Vissersdijk 2a – **T** 0111 414244 – www.grandcafedewerf.nl – *Closed Mo (Sep-Jun): others 11.00–21.00*) has a scenic terrace, good food, but a short beer list.

ZOUTELANDE

10km W of Middelburg on N288

Seaside resort village (pop. 1,500) with a wide sandy beach. Big on tourism, mostly German-speaking.

Fiets

Langstraat 15 · **T** 0118 566040
grandcafedefiets.nl
Apr-Oct: daily from 10.00
Nov-Mar: Closed Mo-Th; others from 11.00

The Bicycle is a seaside café with a difference: the view of both beach and water being blocked by a high dyke. The olive-painted one-room bar has a few model penny farthings as a gesture towards the name. The lunch and dinner food menu runs from pancakes to spare ribs. The 95+ beers are numbered for ordering Chinese takeaway style. Most are Belgian, with a handful of Dutch.

Beer tourism

TOURS

Brewery tours

Of the bigger names, Bavaria, Brand, Budels and Gulpener offer tours for groups that must be pre-booked. Grolsch (SAB Miller) runs regular tours that individuals can join, but again you must book ahead.

Of the smaller breweries, Burg, Hemel, 't IJ, Sallandse and Texelse run tours at fixed times that individuals can join without booking. Others require reservation in advance, and usually only accept groups, while some will simply show you around if not busy – but call ahead to make sure someone is there. See the breweries section for details.

Organised tours

We know of no tour companies currently offering dedicated beer tours to the Netherlands from the UK. From the US, www.beertrips.com occasionally dabbles its toes in Dutch culture, although not as often as its regular trips to Belgium, the UK and Germany.

One local enthusiast offers a way to keep fit and drink in the same breath. Dutch-only website www.bierwandeltochten.nl arranges guided walks that begin with some fresh air, then finish with a brewery visit and tasting. Most are 15-20 km.

MUSEUMS

Bierreclamemuseum

Haagweg 375, Breda (North Brabant)
T 076 522 0975
www.bierreclamemuseum.nl
Su only 11.00-23.00

An out-of-hand collector's hobby, this suburban house is stuffed with beer enamels, brewing equipment, neon signs, glasses, labels, ashtrays and beer mats. There are 1,000+ items, most dating from 1900-1960. The upper floor is a recreation of a 1930s café. Downstairs is the real bar. When there's live music it gets packed – come early. Entrance is free.

Bonte Belevenis

Rommelpot 11, Den Hoorn,
Texel (North Holland) · **T** 0222 314180
www.landgoeddebontebelevenis.nl
Closed Su (all year), Fr&Mo (mid Feb-Oct); others 10.00-17.00.

Small countryside farm museum that houses the De Boei brewery and a distillery. Tours of both are included in the ticket price. Sometimes open Sunday (*12.00-17.00*) in high summer.

Brand Brewery tour

De Hemel

Franseplaats 1, Nijmegen (Gelderland)
T 024 360 6167
www.brouwerijdehemel.nl
Closed Mo-We; others 13.00-17.00

Small museum in the Hemel brewery cellars, with brewing equipment, films and displays on the history of the Commanderie building. A tasting of six house beers is included.

Heineken Experience

Stadhouderskade 78, Amsterdam
T 020 523 9222
www.heinekenexperience.com
Fr-Su 11.00-18.30; others 11.00-19.30

Effectively a corporate visitor centre and history museum in what was until 1988 a brewery. You may learn little about how the company makes its products but you will discover how brilliant they are at selling them. The entry fee entitles you to two beers – you'll never guess what those will be.

Lange Gang

Kevelderstraat 15, Groenlo (Overijssel)
T 0544 464860
www.langegang.nl
Closed Mo-We; others from 16.00 (12.00 in Jul&Aug)

The former Klok brewery was the original home of Grolsch, from 1615 to 1876. It is now a restaurant, but there is a small museum in the cellar.

Museumbrouwerij de Roos

St. Sebastiaanstraat 4, Hilvarenbeek (North Brabant) · **T** 013 505 5045
www.museumbrouwerij.nl
Closed Mo&Tu (all year), We-Fr (Sep-Jun in school terms); others 13.00-17.00.

Former village brewery restored and opened as a museum, containing a wealth of information about brewing – we did not know stingray pelts were once used to clarify beer – and records of closed breweries. Audio guides in English are included with the ticket, as is a beer in the bar at the end.

Bierreclamemuseum, Breda

Nationaal Biermuseum De Boom

Houttil 1, Alkmaar (North Holland)
T 072 511 3801
www.biermuseum.nl
Closed Su; others 11.00-17.00 (Apr-Aug), others 13.00-16.00 (Sep-Mar)

Housed in a former brewery, the National Beer Museum is the country's best expo dedicated to all things hops and barley. It has displays of tools and brewing equipment, some 200 years old, including oddities like an ice sled used for transporting barrels. Bottles, glasses, posters and other memorabilia complete the show. Latest admission 30 minutes before closing time. Finish up in the Boom pub below (see North Holland).

Museumbrouwerij de Roos, Hilvarenbeek, North Brabant

Nederlands Openluchtmuseum

Hoeferlaan 4, Arnhem (Gelderland)
T 026 357 6111
www.openairmuseum.nl
*Closed Mo-Fr (Dec-mid Jan); Sa&Su 10.00–18.00
(mid-Jan-Nov); Mo-Fr 10.00–17.00 (Apr-Oct), others
11.00–16.30*

The Netherlands Open Air Museum is home
to a full-scale brewery, in a modern glass
structure that sits rather incongruously amid
a sea of medieval farmhouses. You are free
to wander in and watch the brewers at work,
and there's a historical display to the side.

ve, right and top right)
Nederlands
nluchtmuseum,
Arnhem

Steam Brewery De Keyzer

Wycker Grachtstraat 26, Maastricht
(Limburg) · **T** 043 325 2121
www.brouwerijbosch.nl
Sa only at 14.00 (for groups at other times on request)

Historic brewery, founded in 1758 and closed
in 1970, with its kit intact, some dating from
the late 19th and early 20th centruries.
Tours, which include a tasting, start at the
Tourist Office (VVV), Kleine Staat 1. Buy
tickets there in advance, or reserve online.

Vlaemsche Erfgoed

Slijkstraat 10, Groede (Zeeland)
T 0117 372414
www.het-vlaemsche-erfgoed.nl
*Closed Su (all year) & Mo-Th (Nov-Mar); others
10.00–17.00 (May-Aug), 13.00–16.00 (Nov-Mar),
13.00–17.00 (other months)*

Street museum with shops and other
buildings laid out as they would have looked
in 1900, also home to the Groese Zwaluw
brewery. Buy the beer from the shop. The
brewery is behind glass at the back of this.

Beer festivals and events

The number of Dutch beer festivals is growing relentlessly. Many cafés organise bock beer festivals in October. Space prohibits listing everyone.

There is a disturbing rise in 'Oktoberfest-style' piss-ups – excuses to drink bland pilsener in volume. These are not beer festivals, merely festivals of drinking, thus we ignore them. Real beer lovers are advised to do likewise. They usually advertise with posters featuring young ladies in *dirndls* thrusting out oversized jugs.

JANUARY

3RD WEEKEND: *Su 13.00–19.00*
Winterbierfestival
Wellantcollege, Ronsseweg 555,
Gouda (South Holland)
100+ Dutch seasonals.

MARCH

2ND WEEKEND: *Sa 14.00–23.00*
Noorderlijk Lentebierenfestival
Stadsschouwburg De Harmonie,
Ruiterskwartier 4, Leeuwarden (Friesland)
Fifteen local and regional breweries.

3RD WEEKEND: *Su 13.30–20.00*
Delta Bierfestival
De Goederenloods, Albert Plesmanweg 23,
Goes (Zeeland)
Eight breweries, half local.

APRIL

2ND WEEKEND: *Fr 19.00–23.00; Sa 13.00–17.00 & 19.00–23.00*
Groningen Bierfestival
(www.bierfestivalgroningen.nl)
Martinikerk, Martinikerkhof 3, Groningen
(Groningen)
Several dozen international brewers, with masterclasses. Advance booking advised.

3RD OR 4TH WEEKEND: *Su 13.00–20.00*
Meibockfestival
Posthoornkerk, Haarlemmerstraat 124–126,
Amsterdam (North Holland)
Forty meibocks, most on tap.

MAY

1ST WEEKEND: *Sa 12.00–21.00*
ZeeBra Extreme Beer Festival
Brouwerij Emelisse, Nieuweweg 7,
Kamperland (Zeeland)
100+ extreme and rare beers. Advance booking essential (via website).

1ST WEEKEND: *Su 12.00–17.00*
Nederlands Speciaalbier Festival
Markt, 's-Hertogenbosch (North Brabant)
Outdoor festival with 50 Dutch breweries.

Nederlands Speciaalbier Festi 's-Hertogenbosch North Brabant

2ND WEEKEND: *Sa 12.00–17.30*
Utrechtse Bierbrouwers Festival
Houtzaagmolen de Ster, Molenpark 3,
Utrecht (Utrecht)
By a windmill, with provincial breweries.

Utrechtse Bierbrouwers Festival, Utrecht (Utrecht)

24 Uurs van Maastricht, Maastricht, Limburg

ASCENSION DAY (Hemelvaart): *Th 12.00–20.00*

Bierfestival Oirschot

Oirschots brewery, Koestraat 20, Oirschot (North Brabant)

Around 30 Dutch beers.

Het Week van Het Nederlandse Bier

(Dutch Beer Week – www.weekvanhetnederlandsebier.nl)

11-day celebration of Dutch beer, usually mid to late May. Hundreds of nationwide events in cafés and breweries. Opens with the festival below. The second weekend is Open Brewery Days.

3RD OR 4TH WEEKEND: *Th 18.00–22.00; Fr 16.00–22.00; Sa 14.00–21.00*

Nederlands Bierproeffestival

Spuiplein, Den Haag (South Holland)

Kick-off for Dutch Beer Week, with 30 breweries plus side events.

LAST WEEKEND (or 1st weekend June): *Fr 15.00–24.00; Sa 13.00–24.00*

24 Uurs van Maastricht

Bernardustraat 24A, Maastricht (Limburg)

In and beside the city walls, with 10+ breweries.

WHITSUNDAY: *13.00–19.00*

Nijmeegse Bierfestival

Koningsplein, Nijmegen (Gelderland)

Outdoor festival with 20+ brewers.

JUNE

2ND WEEKEND: *Su 13.00–19.00*

Noord-Holland Bierfestival

Grote Kerk, Koorstraat 2, Alkmaar (North Holland)

Fifteen local brewers, plus workshops.

2ND WEEKEND: *Su 12.00–18.00*

Twents Speciaalbier Festival

Creative Fabriek (Twentse brewery), Tuindorpstraat 61, Hengelo (Overijssel)

Outdoor festival with 10+ regional brewers.

4TH WEEKEND: *Su 12.00–20.00*

Nederlandse Bieren Festival

Vrouwjuttenland, Delft (South Holland)

Outdoor festival with 12+ Dutch brewers.

LAST WEEKEND: *Su 13.30–18.30*

Tilburgs Bierfestival

Heuvel, Tilburg (North Brabant)

Outdoor festival with 20+ brewers.

LAST WEEKEND: *Su 13.00–18.00*

Bierfestival Albergen

Café Morshuis, Ootmarsumseweg 159, Albergen (Overijssel)

Nine breweries, some local.

JULY

1ST WEEKEND: *Su 12.00–18.00*

Biermatinee

Lind Noord, Oisterwijk (North Brabant)

Outdoor festival with 20+ breweries.

AUGUST

1ST WEEKEND: *Sa 12.00–20.00*

Burg Bierfestival

Putterweg 45, Ermelo (Gelderland)

Outdoor festival, with 30+ Dutch brewers.

1ST WEEKEND: *Su 12.30–18.30*

Botermarkt Bierfestival

Botermarkt, Haarlem (North Haarlem)

Twelve mainly regional breweries.

4TH WEEKEND: *Sa 16.00–00.00*

Speciaal Bierfestival

Café de Heks, Waag, Deventer (Overijssel)

Eighty beers from 20 breweries.

LAST WEEKEND: *Su 11.00–19.00*

Delftse Bierfestival

Brabantse Turfmarkt, Delft (South Holland) Outdoor festival with 30 Dutch and other brewers.

Bruisend Apeldoorn, Gelderland

SEPTEMBER

1ST WEEKEND: *Su 12.00-20.00*
Bruisend Apeldoorn
Marktplein, Apeldoorn (Gelderland)
Outdoor festival, with 40+ brewers.

2ND WEEKEND: *Sa 15.00-22.00*
Dalfser Bierfestival
Kerkplein, Dalfsen (Overijssel)
Outdoor festival with 12 local brewers.

2ND WEEKEND: *Sa 10.00-17.00, Su 12.00-17.00*
Delftse Bierhistorisch weekend
Gereedschap Museum Mensert, Drie
Akersstraat 9, Delft (South Holland)
Historical festival with brewing
demonstrations and tastings.

2ND WEEKEND: *Sa 14.00-20.00*
Bierfestival Wormer
Café de Kroon, Markstraat 11, Wormer (North
Holland)
Outdoor festival with 15+ breweries.

2ND WEEKEND: *Su 13.30-18.00*
Historisch Bierfestival
Vrijthof, Hilvarenbeek (North Brabant)
Village green craft festival, with 15 local
brewers.

Historisch Bierfestival, Hilvarenbeek, North Brabant

2ND WEEKEND: *Su 13.00-19.00*
Bierfestival Biereloth
Café Becoloth, Rozemarijnstraat, Boxtel
(North Brabant)
Outdoor festival with 15+ brewers.

3RD WEEKEND: *Sa 14.00-22.00*
Bergs Bierfestival
Provoosthuis, Pottersstraat, Bergen op
Zoom (North Brabant)
Outdoor festival with 15+ breweries.

3RD WEEKEND: *Su 12.00-18.00*
Enschedees Bierfestival
Bij Rozendaal Eten & Drinken, Het Rozendaal
10, Enschede (Overijssel)
Outdoor festival with 10 brewers.

Borefts Beer Fes
Bodegraven, Sou
Holland

LAST WEEKEND: *Fr&Sa 12.00-22.00*
Borefts Beer Festival
Brouwerij de Molen, Doortocht 4,
Bodegraven (South Holland)
Around 20 breweries representing the cream
of European brewing, serving regular brews
and experimental one-offs.

OCTOBER

1ST WEEKEND: *Su 13.00-18.00*
Eindhovens Herfstbierfestival
Hurksestraat 44, Eindhoven (North Brabant)
Outdoor festival with 10 brewers.

2ND WEEKEND: *Fr 16.00-22.00, Sa 14.00-22.00*
Amersfoorts Bockbier Festival
Krankeledenstraat 16-22, Amersfoort (Utrecht)
Around 16 Dutch brewers.

Noorderlijk ntebierenfestival, Leeuwarden

2ND WEEKEND: *Su 15.00–20.00*

Woerdens Bockbierfestival
Het Arsenaal, Groenedaal 26, Woerden
(Utrecht)
Festival in a castle, with 14 Dutch brewers.

2ND WEEKEND: *Su 13.30–19.00*

Bokbiermarkt (Nationale Bokbierdag)
Zutphen (Gelderland)
Citywide festival, with 20 cafés serving bocks.

2ND WEEKEND: *Su 13.00–19.30*

Weerter Bierfestival
Café Dennenoord, Voorhoeveweg 2,
Weert (Limburg)
Around 35 beers from 10 breweries.

LAST WEEKEND: *Fr 17.00–23.00; Sa 12.00–23.00; Su 12.00–19.00*

PINT Bockbierfestival
Beurs van Berlage, Damrak 277, Amsterdam
(North Holland)
Flagship PINT festival, with 80+ bocks on tap.

ockbierfestival, Amsterdam

NOVEMBER

1ST WEEKEND: *Sa 14.00–23.00*

Noorderlijk Speciaalbierfestival
Herenhuis, Spilsluizen 9, Groningen
(Groningen)
Around 10 northern Dutch brewers.

3RD WEEKEND: *Su 13.00–18.00*

Flevo Bierfestival
Poppodium de Meester, Rentmeesterstraat 2,
Almere (Flevoland)
Around 10 Dutch brewers.

DECEMBER

2ND WEEKEND: *Sa 15.00–21.00*

Winterbierfestival Wormer
Sporthal Wormer, Spatterstraat 21,
Wormer (North Holland)
Around 20 Dutch brewers.
Winter and non-seasonal beers.

3RD OR 4TH WEEKEND: *Su 14.00–19.00*

Noorderlijk Kerst- en Winterbieren Festival
Plein, Hoofdstraat Noord, Hoogeveen
(Drenthe)
Outdoor festival with 10+ brewers
and other stalls.

Further research

PUB & BEER GUIDES

National

Around Amsterdam in 80 Beers by Tim Skelton (Cogan & Mater, 2012; ISBN 978-0-9547789-6-5) – 80 venues with 80 different beers – an essential guide for those staying longer in the capital

Good Beer Guide Belgium by Tim Webb & Joe Stange (CAMRA Books, 2014: ISBN 978-1-85249-311-0) – the unique and original in-depth guide to all things beery in Belgium, now in its 7th edition.

LambicLand by Tim Webb, Chris Pollard & Siobhan McGinn (Cogan & Mater, 2010: ISBN 978-0-9547789-7-2) – the only in-depth guide in English to the world of lambic beer.

The Beer Map of the Netherlands/Dé Bierkaart van Nederland (De Bierverbinding, 2013: ISBN 978-90-817344-0-0) — at-a-glance map of beer pubs, shops, festivals and museums.

International

Pocket Beer Book (UK: Octopus-Mitchell Beazley, 2014; ISBN 978-1-84533-916-6) and *Pocket Beer Guide* (US: Sterling Epicure, 2013; ISBN 978-1454906476) by Stephen Beaumont & Tim Webb

The World Atlas of Beer (UK: Octopus-Mitchell Beazley, 2012; ISBN 978-1-84533-633-2 and US: Sterling Epicure, 2013; ISBN 978-1402789618) by Tim Webb & Stephen Beaumont

Dutch Language

Bier! (www.biermagazine.nl) – quarterly beer magazine.

Brouwerijengids van Nederland edited by Fedor Vogel (Birdy Publishing, 2013; ISBN 978-94-91052-03-3) - a directory of all current Dutch brewers.

Nederlandse Bierbrouwerijen by Peter van der Arend (Culinaire Boekerij, 2005; ISBN 978-90-215-8481-6) – the in-depth back story on all 52 breweries that existed in the Netherlands in 2004.

Jonge Bier in Oude Vaten by Annette Wiesman & Tina Westphal (Fontaine Uitgevers, 2010; ISBN 978-90-5956-370-4) – reports on visits to 32 Dutch breweries.

Een Wereld Vol Bier by Alain Schepers (ASCR, 2013; ISBN 978-90-821082-0-0) – 100+ short pieces about the myths, fables and truths surrounding the world of beer.

Minder Trammelant in Bierland by Rick Kempen & Marco Philipsen (Mitra, 2007) – facts and trivia about beer, and in-depth guides to beer styles.

Ontdek de Bieren van Amsterdam by Kees Volkers & Pim van Schaik (Stokerkade, 2013; ISBN 978-9076092164) – a guide to Amsterdam's beer history, including breweries past and present, bars, and pub crawl walking tours.

CONSUMER GROUPS

PINT

Vereniging **P**romotie **IN**formatie **T**raditioneel Bier – www.pint.nl

The Dutch national beer consumer group, founded in 1980 by beer lovers appalled at the state of the local beer scene. PINT played a key role in turning things around, not so much by direct action as by nurturing the folks who made it happen.

Its aims are 'to promote beer culture in the Netherlands, and to inform and promote the interests of Dutch beer consumers'. With nearly 4,000 members it is the nation's largest independent consumers' association. Regional branches organise tastings, brewery visits and festivals in their areas. PINT also organises the national bock beer festival in Amsterdam.

The organisation publishes the bi-monthly PINT Nieuws magazine, and the website has an events agenda. PINT also organises campaigns, most recently in protest against disproportionate tax hikes on beer.

ABT

Alliantie van Bier Tapperijen – alliantie-van-biertapperijen.com

ABT was founded in 1986 as a community of specialist cafés, with the common aim of serving decent, properly kept beer. There is a truism that all ABT members are good beer cafés, but not all good beer cafés are ABT members. There are 42 currently enrolled, all in this guide, but around 70 others have been members at one time or other. They join and leave for a variety reasons. A new operation might use it to gain exposure, while some leave because they do not like to be tied to their Beer of the Month scheme. A few have been loyal since the start. ABT represents members' interests in dealings with the press, breweries, wholesalers, consumer groups and public authorities. From a consumer viewpoint an

ABT café guarantees a wide range of well-kept beers on tap, and at least 40 in bottles. It also means the menu will be clearly presented, the staff will know about what they sell, and there should be no sloppy service.

EBCU

The European Beer Consumers Union – **ebcu.org**

EBCU was formed in 1990 as an umbrella organisation representing 13 national European beer consumer groups. It is non-party political, non-aligned, and designed to co-ordinate the European activities of the various national bodies. It takes steps by lobbying, advertising, publishing or whatever is necessary to campaign for its four Aims and Objectives: the preservation of European beer culture; the promotion of traditional beers; supporting traditional breweries in fending off consolidation; and representing beer drinkers in their campaign for choice, quality and value for money. The current chairperson is Dutch.

KBC

Kleine Brouwerij Collectief –
www.kleinbrouwerijcollectief.nl

The Dutch Brewer's Collective (KBC), founded in 2003, represents the interests of almost 100 small brewers, both with and without their own installations. KBC is run by and for the brewers, and gives them a platform for discussion and exchange of knowledge and experience. It also aims to provide balance in the press to counteract the dominance of the eight major breweries.

Nederlandse Brouwers

www.nederlandsebrouwers.nl

The antithesis of KBC is the trade organisation that represents the interests of the big boys.

BAV

Bier & Verzamelaarsvereniging – **bav.nl**

The Beer and Collectors Association was set up in 1983 as the association of Brewery Items Collectors. It is now a trade organisation for collectors, breweries, beer stores and publicans.

StiBON

Stichting Bieropleidingen Nederland (Dutch Beer Education Foundation) – **www.stibon.nl**

Offers Dutch-language beer sommelier courses for brewers, landlords and others wishing to expand and deepen their tasting and appreciation skills.

BLOGS & WEBSITES

Blogs – English language

dutchbeerpages.com – informed comment on various aspects of the Dutch scene.

barclayperkins.blogspot.nl – beer historian and resident of Amsterdam Ron Pattinson's blog makes occasional forays into Dutch beer.

Blogs – Dutch

dossierhop.nl – the most outspoken and opinionated blog on Dutch (and other) beer.

bier.blog.nl – beer news.

www.bierburo.nl – news and comment.

www.biercolumns.nl – comment and opinion.

www.spoelenmaar.nl – comment and opinion.

lekkerbier.blogspot.nl – comment and opinion.

Other websites

Dutch beer

www.cambrinus.nl – keeps a list of all Dutch breweries, past and present.

www.bierboom.nl – sells books online. Owner Willem Verboom also runs a stall at many Dutch festivals.

www.bierlokaal.nl – bilingual site with Dutch beer bars, beer shops, news and events.

www.debiermeester.nl – aims to bring breweries, cafés and consumers together through tastings and advice.

www.debierverbinding.nl – aims to bring breweries, cafés and consumers together through tastings and advice.

www.europeanbeerguide.net – Ron Pattinson's European beer guide.

www.pinkgron.nl – collector's site with beer labels, and a Dutch brewery map.

www.biernet.nl – industry-sponsored news and information.

International

www.Ratebeer.com

BeerAdvocate.com

UnTappd.com

And...

stiva.nl – STIVA: the Dutch Foundation for Responsible Drinking

General index

Beers index

Below are listed the key words within brand names that should enable you to identify and find any beer we list.

Thank you and acknowledgements

This book would not have been possible without the help of a great many people, some of whom may have provided inspiration without their even knowing it.

Although he won't remember it, I first encountered Tim Webb at a book signing in 2002, during which I protested his description of my adopted home Eindhoven as a 'beer desert'. It may have taken a decade to persuade him otherwise, but the wait was worth it. Thanks first and foremost must therefore go to him, and to Jo Copestick, for caving in to my persistent badgering to get this book made.

Big thanks also go to Dale Tomlinson for his inestimable layout skills, which have made the book look as excellent as it does. And to John Macklin for creating the maps.

A great many of the breweries and cafés in this book came onto my radar as a result of having lived in the Netherlands for 25 years, but there were always going to be some I missed. I am thus grateful to Jan Ausems and the rest of the Cambrinus.nl team for their tireless attempts at keeping up with new breweries as they continue to arrive at a dizzying rate. Likewise, thanks to the Ratebeer community, and to Ron Pattinson's European Beer Pages, both of which were shamelessly plundered for additional café tips.

In the same vein, thank you to all the following for their support and insider's tip-offs about bars, shops and festivals: Peter van der Arend, Paul & Kerry Barclay, Stephen Beaumont, Harry van den Berselaar, everyone at De Bierkoning in Amsterdam, Jeroen Carol-Visser, Des de Moor, Simon Duerden, Theo Flissebalje, Simon Fokkema, Rob Gras, Rick Kempen, Nico Lammers, Bob Molenbroek & Nicole Warners, Michel Orderman & Lydian Zoetman, Graham Povey, Henri Reuchlin, Frans Ruiter, Frans van der Schot, Peter Sherwood, Dean Southall, Joe Stange, Eugene Straver, Mike Thompson, Dave Thornhill, Guy Thornton, Willem & An Verboom, & Derek Walsh.

And to the many brewers, café owners, PINT members and readers of *Around Amsterdam in 80 Beers* who have all showed support and enthusiasm for this project – far too many to name check them all, I'm afraid.

I must give a special extra nod to fellow resident expats Ron Pattinson and Derek Walsh for their technical expertise, to which I doff my cap. Both have surely forgotten more about *Brettanomyces* than I will ever know, and Ron's encyclopaedic grasp of historical brewing is second to none.

A very big thank you to Amanda, for her support, company, proofreading skills, and for agreeing to be designated driver when our research trips to remote locations demanded it.

Finally, an unusual thank you to the Grand Duchy of Luxembourg, without which the book wouldn't exist in this form. It's a long story. Ask me over a beer.